The False Paradigms of Today
and
The Timeless Truth of Tomorrow

The False Paradigms of Today and The Timeless Truth of Tomorrow

Essays on Meaning

JOHN BLISS

Skeptika Press

Atascadero

ISBN: 979-8-9999687-0-8

Book Production by Skeptika Press
Edited by Kay Derochie
Design and Layout by Davor Nikolić
Cover art includes the following paintings:
Giulio Cesare Procaccini (c. 1616/1620). *The Ecstasy of the Magdalen.* Patrons' Permanent Fund. National Gallery of Art, Washington DC.; Tanzio da Varallo (c. 1620/1630). *Saint Sebastian.* Samuel H. Kress Collection. National Gallery of Art, Washington DC.; Orazio Gentileschi (c. 1612/1620). *The Lute Player.* Ailsa Mellon Bruce Fund. National Gallery of Art, Washington DC.; Bernardo Strozzi (c. 1620/1630). *Saint Francis in Prayer.* Gift of Joseph F. McCrindle. National Gallery of Art, Washington DC.

Every effort has been made by the author and publishing house to ensure that the information contained in this book was correct as of press time. The author and publishing house hereby disclaim and do not assume liability for any injury, loss, damage, or disruption caused by errors or omissions, regardless of whether any errors or omissions result from negligence, accident, or any other cause. Readers are encouraged to verify any information contained in this book prior to taking any action on the information.

www.skeptikapress.com

I dedicate this book to three people:

*To William Holton, the Emil Sinclair of our age.
This book is written for you and all young people just like
you, lost in what appears to be a meaningless world.*

*To my wife, Karen, the kindest person ever,
a true blessing from heaven.*

*To Colin Wilson, my inspiration.
I wish we could have met before you passed.*

The Essays on Meaning

PART 2
An Exploration of Truth across Historical, Mystical and Philosophical Dimensions

Author's Introduction

In life, nothing is as simple as we want it to be. Ideally, we could use our powers of logical reasoning to solve our problems, such as:

> A is true, and
> B is true,
> Therefore, C is true.

For example:

> All dogs are animals.
> All animals die.
> Therefore, all dogs die.

But the world is not so simple. It is just not.

Our brains can handle simplicity—simple deductions like the above—but the world is not simple. It is complex. There is a mismatch at play here. If the objective is to understand the world around us, we have the wrong brain for the job. (If our objective is merely to survive and procreate, then our brains will suffice.)

It is very difficult to handle the complexity we encounter in the world. To get around this, we invented Occam's Razor: the idea that, out of all possible solutions, the simplest solution to a problem is likely the most correct one. Is Occam's Razor true? Or is it simply a justification for our inability to comprehend the complexity we find in the world? I think it is merely a justification.

We can never know what is true. What we understand as truths are merely those things that most people can agree on. But we can only agree on those things that everybody can understand, which leaves us with the simple things (such as dogs are animals, life ends, gravity holds the solar system together). Therefore we have Occam's Razor.

In other words, we are simpletons, and we develop justifications that mask our incapacity to comprehend the world. Keep it simple. Cover up the massive complexities with simple theories and equations. That is all our simple mind circuitry can do.

Why am I even going here? This is supposed to be an introduction to a book. Well, the main topic we are to discuss is complex. I can present the pieces simply, and I do. But the whole, it is not a simple theory or equation. It is complex.

What I am suggesting is that simple logic cannot bring you to the understanding that I propose to lead you to. Instead, we have to approach this differently, like a jigsaw puzzle. I will place pieces on the table, and many pieces will connect with each other. Eventually, a big picture will come into view. That is how this book works.

If you are looking for a "logical" sequential argument, you are in the wrong place. The topic cannot be handled in that manner. It just cannot. Think of the message of Jesus, or of the Buddha—can those messages be conveyed with simple logic? They cannot. They require an unconscious understanding. Pieces of a puzzle. Put them together and a picture emerges. The prophets' lives and words are the pieces. Just as mine are. (Don't worry, I am not comparing myself to those men. I am just a seeker like yourself.)

So I am asking you to be patient. I will supply you with the pieces, and as you proceed through the essays, they will connect together in some unconscious way, and you will develop a more complete picture. Do I present the entire picture of reality in this book? No. I am a human.

Humans cannot do these types of things. But I have pieced together a good alternative framework, a good partial picture. And I believe it is way more accurate than the framework that generations have used before me.

I am hoping you will be able to fill in more pieces of the puzzle on your own, and some of you, I hope, will write an even more complete book on this topic, and bring humanity another step closer to wherever it is we are headed.

PART 1

Your Understanding of Reality is More Fabricated Than You Think

The first seven of these Essays on Meaning delve into different topics; but really they all converge onto the same thing, which you can figure out for yourself.

Hopefully the essays will leave you with the unsettling realization that what you thought was true really isn't, and never was. I am hoping that in some unconscious way the essays will persuade you to drop any sense of assuredness you may have about your conception of the world. (Sorry, you are just wrong, but don't worry, I know that I am wrong too—it is just part of being human.)

Then will come Part 2, where we seek to rip and claw less and actually construct something that can work.

But back to Part 1, as that is where we are now. Here we will explore the various circumstances, forces and thought systems that are shaping my reality and your reality. As much as you think that you think for yourself, you are really constrained.

We will look at biology, sociology, science, mysticism, religion and history and question commonly held assumptions that distort our perceptions of reality. A lot of what we assume to be true is not. And if our assumptions are wrong, then our logic isn't worth a damn.

By delving into these topics, I am hoping to lay bare a set of untruths. I am sure that I will piss off every reader somewhere in these pages, but if you encounter that feeling of pissed-offedness then that only means I hit a nerve—which is a great thing. It doesn't mean the author is trash, or the book is trash. And it doesn't mean that you are wrong. It only means you should probably think about why this point, whatever it is, excites so much emotion in you. Why are you so tied to the belief under discussion? Always remember, as Eckhart Tolle says, "you are not your mind." The book is not attacking you.

I hope you have some fun with these essays.

Essay 1
The Illusion of Progress
in Modern Times

Pessimism becomes a self-fulfilling prophecy; it
reproduces itself by crippling our willingness to act.
—HOWARD ZINN

An Era of Rapid Change – the First False Paradigm

We like to think of our era as one of accelerated change, and this is true in that the pace of technological change has accelerated in what seems a geometric manner. These changes have dramatically affected our lives, usually for the better. In Caesar's time, news was carried by horseback, and it remained that way for another 1,900 years. In the last hundred years, humankind has progressed from horseback to telegraph to radio to television to internet and satellite. In 1980, most people were not aware of the internet; but now, it has become a central operating system of our lives. We use it for shopping, research, news, entertainment and even for finding love.

But the past holds other eras of rapid change. In those eras, sometimes the driving forces of change were political upheavals or intellectual revolutions rather than technological advancements. Although the forms of change are distinct, they are not aways independent and can impact each other. Massive change in one will affect the others, but not necessarily in a revolutionary manner. For example, our era of massive technological change has not resulted in new forms of government in the United States. With a few tweaks here and there, the United States government remains the same. And thought has not changed much since the end of World War I. I contend we remain in roughly the same era of intellectual pessimism that we arrived at with the coming of World War I, even though the United States was catapulted from being a minor country before the war to the global superpower it remains today.

Typically in history, massive change does not develop in fits and spurts, as our technology of today is developing. Massive change is a gradual process that ends in a sudden cataclysmic destruction of old systems and the implementation of new ones.

Think of it like boiling water. You put steady heat on a pot of water. The water slowly gets hotter, like tension building in society. Bubbles form at the bottom, like small problems appearing. The surface of the water is no longer calm, but it is agitated, and it becomes increasingly chaotic. When the water reaches boiling point, things change fast. The water boils and transforms into steam. Most of this steam won't return to the pot. Scientists call this a phase change (from water to steam).

Using that metaphor, old proven institutions can no longer serve the changing needs of the people. The old social calm is gone, while people get progressively more frustrated. Unrest grows and then suddenly there is a massive chaotic shift, an irreversible change in state. Historians call this a revolution.

Fall of the Roman Republic

Consider the roughly one-hundred-year period from 134 BCE to 44 BCE, a very tumultuous period in Rome, which we call the Fall of the Roman Republic. During that era Rome lost its traditional governing institutions as it was transformed into a dictatorship. As with everything in history, many factors contributed to the political turmoil in Rome, but much of it could be attributed to the great success of Rome in conquering neighboring states and expanding its territories. With victories came wealth and slaves. And with that, a growing disparity in wealth between the rich and the poor. The massive influx of slaves allowed wealthy landholders to accumulate large landholdings and farm them with slave labor, displacing the small landholders.

A related problem was that only landowners could serve in the Roman army. With the growing need for Roman legions and the shrinking landholder class, Rome's army gradually became insufficient in numbers to secure its growing borders. The systems and rules that had sustained Rome could not maintain the growing empire. Something had to be changed for the good of the state; but the wealthy interests continually opposed change, as they were benefitting from the status quo.

Because the senatorial class, the wealthy, made the laws and dominated the government, nothing happened. Instead, tension mounted as the rest of the people wanted change. Then along came Tiberius Gracchus, a tribune, a representative of the people. He broke precedent and used the legal powers of his office, boldly bypassing the Senate, to pass a law that would break up the large landholdings. Then the poor could own land and thus serve in the legions. This action solved many of the problems the state faced. But it did not go over well with those who had something to lose. Tiberius was killed by a mob of Senators in 133 BCE. Ten years later, his brother, Gaius Sempronius Gracchus, also as tribune, passed even bolder laws aimed at land reform. He sought to make Italian allies into Roman citizens. He, too, was murdered by the rich interests, just twelve years after his brother. Then came Lucius Apuleius Saturninus, another tribune reformer, imprisoned by the Senate and murdered twenty-one years later. And then Marcus Livius Drusus, another reformer, murdered nine years after that. Each of these men was making bolder attempts at reform than the last.[1]

---

[1] Then there was a great general who favored the poor, Gaius Marius, who, in 87 BC had to flee Italy to Africa, as he was pursued by assassins. Later, Lucius Sergius Catilina, when

Can you imagine the rage and fury that the lower classes would have had, having four of their champions murdered in a period of forty-two years?

During this time, Roman citizenry was given to all free Italians, providing ample soldiers for the Roman legions. The poor of Rome were given a dole. The senate, purged of its strongest and most capable men, was left intact but powerless. Factional strife was ended with government in the hands of a sole dictator.

The fall of the Roman Republic is complicated, well-documented and absolutely fascinating. I cannot do it justice in one essay and even less so in a few paragraphs. My point here is that in 91 BCE, Rome had a political system of consuls, senators and tribunes that 106 years later was completely transformed into a dictatorship. (Have you noticed that all successful populist revolutions seem to end with a dictator?)

If we compare the Roman revolution, a time of great political change, to the United States in the period from 1918 to present, much more political change happened in Rome than has happened in the U.S. in the last slightly more than 100 years. The Roman pot boiled over and resulted in a change of state, while today we are only witnessing more heat being applied to aging systems. So when we talk of rapid change, maybe we should qualify that statement some. We have witnessed a rapid change in technology and its effect on how we work and entertain ourselves. We have not experienced rapid intellectual or political changes. But their time will come, as it does for every society. It is clear that bubbles appear to be forming on the bottom of the pot.

Kaczynski's Principles of History

The fall of the Roman Empire fits right into Theodore Kaczynski's theory of history. Kaczynski (1942–2023) was also known as the Unabomber, the infamous domestic terrorist in the U.S., who specialized

---

running for Consul, was unfairly maligned by Cicero and killed by the Senate in 62 BC; and, finally, Gaius Julius Caesar, the last in the line of defenders of the poor in that era, was killed by the Senate in 44 BC.

in sending mail bombs to people who were advancing technology. He killed three and injured twenty-three others before he was captured.

As a child, Kaczynski was a prodigy in mathematics. In fifth grade his IQ was measured at 167. He entered Harvard at sixteen and received his Ph.D. in mathematics at twenty-five. He lasted two years as assistant professor at University of California Berkeley before he quit to live in the woods of Montana without running water or electricity. His bombing campaign stretched from 1978 until 1995, when he sent a letter to *The New York Times*, promising to stop sending letter bombs if *The New York Times* or *The Washington Post* would publish his manifesto, which they did. The publication of his work eventually led to his capture. He died in 2023, having committed suicide while still in prison.

Kaczynski's theory of history states that history has its own arc that cannot be pre-defined. Nobody knows where it is headed, nobody can accurately guide its direction. Reform is a temporary aberration in the general arc of history. Kaczynski wrote,

> *Generally speaking an attempt at social reform either acts in the direction in which the society is developing anyway (so that it merely accelerates a change that would have occurred in any case) or else it only has a transitory effect, so that the society soon slips back into its old groove. To make a lasting change in the direction of development of any important aspect of a society, reform is insufficient and revolution is required. (A revolution does not necessarily involve an armed uprising or the overthrow of a government.)...A revolution never changes only one aspect of a society; and...changes occur that were never expected or desired by the revolutionaries...(And finally,) when revolutionaries or utopians set up a new kind of society, it never works out as planned.*[2]

In short, no one is a prophet. Revolutions always go awry, as nobody knows how things will play out. Would Tiberius Gracchus have initiated

---

[2] Theordore Kaczynski, "Industrial Society and Its Future," #108.

his reforms had he known that he was sowing seeds that would lead to dictatorship in Rome? Probably not. Had he studied Kaczynski's theory of history, he might have proceeded differently. Do you think the early makers of the middle-class French and Russian revolutions would have continued on their course had they known that their movements would devolve into dictatorships? Would Martin Luther have taken his dramatic anti-Catholic steps had he known that a century of wars would result?

One of Kaczynski's five principles of history states that,

> *A new kind of society cannot be designed on paper. That is, you cannot plan out a new form of society in advance, then set it up and expect it to function as it was designed to.*[3]

He is right. It is as if history were just one big example of the Law of Unintended Consequences. We are all actors on the world stage, and we will never know how our story ends.

The German New Age of Total Responsibility

Revolutionary change need not only be political. Sometimes it can be intellectual, where a new way of thinking totally reorients a people's understanding of their place in the world.[4] The self-imposed limits that once constrained them are lifted. For example, the Germans in the beginning of the nineteenth century moved from mental serfdom to self-empowerment.

The Holy Roman Empire at the turn of the nineteenth century was on its last legs. Begun in 800 CE with the crowning of Charlemagne, the Empire was by 1800 a poorly organized grouping of about 250 "states," most with their own laws, taxes, religions, customs, dress and coinage. Some of these states spoke dialects incomprehensible in other parts of

---

[3] Kaczynski, #104.

[4] These changes take a lot of time, of course. The students and intellectuals embrace the ideas first, and eventually they filter down to the others.

the German world, even though they shared the same written language.[5] Each principality was ruled by a leader who exercised varying degrees of authority.

By 1800, the Holy Roman Empire's government had become largely ineffective. The Empire had devolved into a complex patchwork of territories including kingdoms, duchies, principalities, and free cities, each with varying degrees of autonomy. While these states nominally recognized the authority of the Holy Roman Emperor, in practice, his power was limited and the Empire struggled to function as a unified political entity. As the states gained in power, the central authority weakened.

In 1788, only fourteen out of a hundred eligible princes answered a summons to appear at an Imperial Diet (that would be their congress of sorts) and only eight out of fifty eligible town chieftains. This made decision-making for the empire impossible. The level of commitment to the empire had worn thin. The princes were more concerned about their own internal affairs. This inability to come together for their common defense eventually contributed to Napoleon's victories at Austerlitz and Jena. In 1806, after Napoleon had annexed the states of Western Germany as a protectorate,[6] the Holy Roman Empire was finished for good.

At the same time, the early 1800s was a time of great intellectual ferment in Germany and rapid intellectual change. The water was beginning to boil. The old medieval ideas were losing their hold on the people and were being replaced with new visions of hope and change. The new mental orientations of the Enlightenment and the French Revolution were seeping into the Western Germanic states.

Religious institutions in the German states were losing their hold on the young. They were increasingly being seen to be existing only to persecute

---

[5] Will Durant and Ariel Durant, *The Age of Napoleon* (Simon & Schuster, 1975), 587.

[6] Durant and Durant, 588–590.

any unorthodox challengers and protect their own privileges, rather than in providing any sort of useful framework on which to base a life.

Just as the old governmental and religious institutions were failing, so the universities were struggling as well. Many German university students of the time were thrilled when the revolutionary French defeated the anti-revolutionist German armies. The universities, like other institutions in the German principalities, were frozen in traditional forms that just didn't work anymore. The university that the philosopher Hegel attended in Tubingen saw its mission as passing on orthodox correct Christian beliefs to the students. It was primarily a Protestant seminary. Teaching focused on the memorization of established Christian dogma and the reproduction of theological arguments. While England and France were exploring science to understand reality, in German universities, reality could be determined only through divine revelation, the authority of texts, or rational deduction. For many, the German universities were considered outdated institutions, steeped in medieval scholasticism, failing to generate new knowledge and fostering a corrupt, anti-intellectual student culture of duels and drunkenness. [7]

Student enrollment at universities was dropping precipitously. Graduates had few prospects for employment. Many called for the shuttering of the outmoded universities and replacing them with science-based institutions. As a result, during the Napoleonic era, twenty-two German universities ceased to exist.

Even before Napoleon's victories, a great change had begun—a revolution in thought. In 1781, a Prussian philosopher Immanuel Kant (1724–1804) in his *Critique of Pure Reason* claimed that we cannot know true reality. Whatever is out there in the universe is filtered and thereby tainted by our senses and by the limitations of our intellect. Despite what we may think, we have no firm grip on the reality of the world. Even the laws of nature, though based on something in the world, are still crafted by our minds and senses. We are the center of our

---

[7] Terry Pinkard, *Hegel, A Biography* (Cambridge University, 2000), 19–20.

worlds. The world as we understand it, then, conforms to us, rather than us having to conform to the world. This was a groundbreaking change in thought. Kant left behind the Christian foundation of holy texts and divine messages to argue that our minds shaped how we experience the world.

Johann Gottlieb Fichte (1762–1814), another German philosopher, took it a step further and taught that the basic reality for each of us is our individual self and not our surroundings. Therefore, nothing external to us has any real meaning, only the meaning we ascribe to it.

You might ask, why do these ideas matter?

Well, it did matter to the German students, intellectuals and artists of the time. People were really excited about these ideas because they formed the basis of a revolution in thinking. If Kant and Fichte were right, then we get to sit in judgement on every tradition, law, prohibition and creed and determine whether they should be obeyed.[8] Applying these revolutionary ideas to the useless, oppressive German political, religious and social institutions and seeing that French people across the Rhine were actually eliminating and replacing their medieval institutions, why couldn't the Germans remake society too? This was the beginning of both the German Idealist Movement and the early German Romantic Movement. The center of this explosion in thought was the University of Jena in Saxony in the 1790s. The university underwent a massive transformation away from the old medieval ways. The famous German writer Johann Wolfgang von Goethe (1749–1832) served as an administrator of the university at that time; and its many famous professors, including Reinhold, Fichte, Hegel, Schelling and Schlegel, attracted hundreds of young idealists.

---

[8] Durant and Durant, 628.

Freedom and Punishing Dissent

Fichte, an especially popular professor of philosophy, formulated a new set of ideas stressing personal responsibility. He proclaimed,

> *The dark ages are over. . .when you were told in God's name that you were herds of cattle set on earth to fetch and carry, to serve a dozen mortals in high place, and to be their possessions. You are not their property, not even God's property, but your own.*[9]

As religious institutions and the monarchy lost their authority over the human mind, individuals began to embrace their own reasoning. It became clear that humans were free to choose how to live for themselves. Indeed, humans were responsible to live according to their own beliefs, rather than the beliefs dictated to them by the authorities. Fichte's call for students to liberate themselves by assuming moral responsibility for their own lives filled the void left by the outdated religious and social institutions. He said that the duty of the scholar, a "priest of truth," was to educate mankind, for only the scholar could understand the truth that was necessary for all people to achieve their proper humanity. And, the students were called on to further a cause beyond themselves, to advance both themselves and society around them.

Fichte gave intellectuals hope, something to strive for. For a time, Fichte was a rockstar of a professor. Students came from all over to study under him.[10] The irony of Fichte and all his talk of freedom is that he was fired from the University for his unconventional thinking. He had audaciously scheduled lectures on Sundays. That had not been done before. He had written that God was the active moral order of the universe, not some old man in heaven who responds to our requests for a more pleasant life. He wrote that believing that God is someone to ask

---

[9] Johann Gottlieb Fichte, *Restoration of Freedom of Thought by the Princes of Europe, in Durant and Durant,* 637.

[10] These lectures have been since published as *The Vocation of a Scholar (*in German, *Einige Vorlesungen* über *die Bestimmung des Gelehrten).* Despite Fichte later being run out of town as an atheist, he helped create a powerful new movement of German thought.

favors of is to believe in myths and is tantamount to atheism. Unlike in earlier times, when the authorities might have killed or exiled him, he was merely fired.

Fichte was right, I suppose. We are free, but that doesn't free us from the often-unfortunate consequences of what we do. Fichte's dismissal is proof of that.

Never before in human history had individuals been so free to choose their occupations, their mates, their religion or moral code."[11] Throughout much of human history, people had not been allowed the true freedom to think and do as they wanted. It took centuries to bring Western Civilization to the freedom of expression that Jena was experiencing in the early 1800s.

As we, that is, you and I, were born into this era of total freedom, we will never be able to understand how restricted people's lives really were and how truly liberating this shift in thinking was. But we must acknowledge it—we in the West share a long history of intellectual slavery. For centuries we were told what to believe. A great example of this is demonstrated in Homer's *The Iliad*. When the warriors of Greece had gathered to discuss the war with Troy, Thersites spoke as an individual. He questioned whether it was wise for them to follow King Agamemnon. Why risk your own life, when there is little to gain because the King gets all the spoils?

Your shelters are filled with bronze, there are plenty of the choicest
women for you within your shelter...
Or is it still more gold you will be wanting...
My good fools...of Achaia,
let us go back home in our ships, and leave this man here
by himself in Troy to mull his prizes of honor...

[In response, King Odysseus thrashed Thersites with his scepter, and Thersites]

---

[11] Durant and Durant, 629.

doubled over, and a round tear dropped from him,
and a bloody welt stood up between his shoulders under
the golden scepter's stroke, and he sat down again, frightened,
in pain, and looking helplessly about wiped off the tear-drops.
Sorry though the men were, they laughed over him happily...

[and said among themselves,]

this is far the best thing he ever has accomplished
among the Argives, to keep this thrower of words, this braggart
out of assembly. Never again will his proud heart stir him
up, to wrangle with the princes in words of revilement.
So the multitude spoke.[12]

This passage has always bothered me. In the forty years since I first read it, I've never forgotten Thersites. People who think for themselves, at least in our age, we often see as heroes. Jesus Christ, Socrates, Mohandas Gandhi, John Snow, and the Batman are people such as these.[13] But in Homer's pre-classical Greece, the freethinker was seen as an animal, and he was punished accordingly. Thus it has been throughout the ages, until very recently in human history. People who dared to think and write original thoughts questioning the orthodoxy were silenced, exiled, or killed, whether by civic assemblies, corporations, nations, political parties or religions.

Catholic Persecution of Heresy—Straying from Its Beginnings

The Church has been the great enslaver of the minds of countless generations, but it wasn't always that way. People generally join emerging religions of their own free will until the government gets involved. Certainly, early Christianity was composed of eager volunteers. Jesus was such a remarkable being that people devoted their lives to Him. They were willing to endure poverty, beatings, tortures and execution

---

[12] Homer, *The Iliad*, trans. Richard Lattimore (Phoenix Books, Cambridge University, 1925), 82–83, lines 225–278.

[13] Kaczynski was another free thinker, but he lives in the opposite camp from heroes.

for His sake. Jesus was life-changing for these people. Christianity was in many ways a breath of fresh air in pagan times.

Unlike the pagan religions of Europe and the Middle East, Christianity welcomed all classes and races of peoples, even slaves. Everyone was equal in the eyes of God. Through its tight-knit communities of believers, early Christianity offered a sense of belonging that was missing in most pagan cults. Christianity stressed service, love, charity and forgiveness. It called on people to take care of each other, to be better versions of themselves. Rather than pray to the gods asking for good fortune, the religion stressed serving and loving your fellow man. Those were entirely new concepts to build a religious system on.

Christianity offered hope and vindication and retribution in the afterlife. The common people may suffer in the present, but a clearly defined eternal life in heaven was certain to come, while the elite oppressors would pay for their sins and endure the worst suffering imaginable in hell for the rest of time. That message was attractive to the victims of the time. Most pagan religions didn't provide this consolation.

Some freedom of thought existed in the early Christian period. Prior to the conversion of the Roman Emperor Constantine to Catholicism in 312 CE, many strains of Christianity existed in the Roman Empire. Each of Jesus's disciples, along with Paul, understood Jesus differently, and their communities of followers had distinctly different beliefs. And from those initial communities of faith, as is natural in human nature, sprang offshoots with even more different strains of belief and, of course, the accompanying controversy.

But when Christianity became the official religion of the Roman Empire, that is when the trouble started. Once a government becomes associated with a religion, it often uses policies and violence to punish or convert unbelievers. Yes, the religion may grow, but usually at the price of its soul. It is a dangerous combination—the ideological inflexibility of religions combined with the state's monopoly on coercion and violence.

Religion can then become a tool to maintain power over the thoughts and behavior of the people. And it did in the Roman Empire.

After his conversion, Constantine aligned the Church and the Roman state. He supported the Church with state resources. He built churches. He involved the Church in governmental affairs. And, in response to all the high church leaders bickering about theology, he convened the infamous Council of Nicaea in 325 CE. At the time, officially recognized church leaders felt it was important to standardize beliefs across the growing church. They could then establish a true orthodoxy in which they could decide what was acceptable and unacceptable to think and do.

In the Council of Nicaea, Church elders determined what was and was not acceptable faith. They formulated the Nicene Creed, each statement of which at the time was the subject of much controversy. A version of it is still used in the Catholic Mass today. The Council declared Arian teachings heretical and exiled Arius and his supporters to the Balkans. Even two of the bishops who attended the Council were deposed and exiled. That was just the beginning for the Roman state.

Fifty-five years later, in 380 CE, Theodosius I's "Edict of Thessalonica" declared Nicene Christianity the sole official religion of the Roman Empire. It mandated that all subjects adhere to the Christian doctrine as defined by the bishops of Rome and Alexandria. The edict outlawed other forms of worship and adopted the term "heresy" for state use, formalizing the punishment of heretics to enforce the State's version of Christianity.[14] Thereafter, those who did not believe in the "true" doctrine were punished, often with exile and sometimes with death, and their books were burned.[15] Many of the gospels of the first and second

---

[14] Theodosius I ruled Rome from 379–395 CE. He was the last Roman emperor to rule the united empire, which was afterwards split into the East and West.

[15] But something similar had already happened elsewhere. In the kingdoms of Armenia (~301 CE), Georgia (~326 CE), and Ethiopia (~330 CE), the kings proclaimed Christianity the state religion well before what came next in Rome—the Edict of Thessalonica in 380 CE, where Christianity became the state religion of Rome. The difference though is that there are no records of punishing heretics or forcing religion on the common people as

centuries have been lost forever as a result. The first Christian heretic to be executed by the Roman state was Priscillian, the Bishop of Ávila, in 385 CE. Nobody today knows exactly what Priscillian believed. (Killing heretics and burning their books is often an effective way to erase and rewrite history.) According to Edward Gibbon[16], many more believers in Christ were killed by the Roman Catholic Church for wrong beliefs than were killed by the Roman pagan governments. Much like the consolidation and purging that occurred after the French and Russian Revolutions, the Catholic Roman state purged those whose beliefs were not quite right, and many of their beliefs and ideas were lost forever.[17]

Throughout the centuries that followed, perhaps up to the invention of the printing press in the fifteenth century, the Church expanded its control over the lives and minds of the people. But even after the breaking up of the Church in the Protestant Reformation of the sixteenth century, people were not allowed freedom of belief. Whatever religion the lord of the realm believed was the religion that the people were forced to believe, at least outwardly, with severe consequences for the unorthodox.

As late as 1765, when Jean Jacques Rousseau was living in the Swiss canton of Neuchâtel, he was pelted with stones by the townsfolk when he went for walks after being denounced as an Anti-Christ by his minister. He had been banished from the Canton of Bern twice for his ideas. Only seventy years earlier, the infamous Salem witch trials were conducted

---

was done in Rome.

[16] Edward Gibbon wrote *The History of the Decline and Fall of the Roman Empire*, (Encyclopedia Britannica, 1923) Ch 16, 233. "It must still be acknowledged that the Christians, in the course of their intestine dissensions, have inflicted far greater severities on each other than they had experienced from the zeal of the infidels."

[17] There are some exceptions, of course. In 1948, a farmer found the remains of fifty-two mostly Gnostic texts, along with a partial translation of Plato's Republic, buried in a sealed jar. These texts included many of the gospels that were banned by the Council of Nicaea. Some believe that the texts may have belonged to a nearby monastery and were buried after Saint Athanasius condemned the use of non-canonical books in 367 CE. For more information, see *The Gnostic Gospels by Elaine Pagels*.

in Massachusetts, in which nineteen people were hung and five others died in prison. The witch trials were a case of mass hysteria, but the Spanish Inquisition lasted about 350 years, too long a period to be considered hysteria. Although only a few thousand were executed by the inquisitors, it is estimated that 150,000 people were charged with crimes. The Spanish Inquisition lost much of its power during the reign of Joseph Bonaparte in the early 1800s but was not formally terminated until 1834. During those centuries, hundreds of thousands of people were forced to either convert to Christianity or conform to the Church's teachings.

And this did not just happen in Europe. Many conquered peoples were required to become Christians as a condition of peace. One only need think of the peoples of Mexico and Central and South America and how they were forced into Christianity "for their own good." Their native shrines, temples and religious idols were destroyed. Backsliders were killed, tortured or otherwise punished.

The pattern wasn't exclusive to Catholicism. During the sixteenth century, the English King Henry VIII (1491–1547) forced his subjects to proclaim loyalty to his new Church of England, rather than to the Catholic Church. The pressure of the state worked. Most of the people converted to the Church of England. However, it is estimated that thousands of people, including clergy, nobles, and commoners refused to take the oath and were subsequently persecuted or executed for their dissent.

In 1620 the Pilgrims fled Europe to avoid religious persecution by the English government under King James I and the Church of England. Then, once in the New World, the Pilgrims repeated the pattern excluding and persecuting those not towing the Puritan line. The oppressed became the oppressors.

And it is not just Christianity that would do such a thing. Islam also has had its share of state-sponsored violence and murder in the name of religion, including the 1840s massacre of Babi men, women and children because the Babis rejected many of the traditional Islamic practices and beliefs, including prayer, fasting, pilgrimage and the authority of the traditional religious leaders.

Modern Repression of Thought

In the Western world, over the centuries since the creation of the printing press, we have slowly won the freedom to think and speak for ourselves. Of course, there have been short-term setbacks, such as the totalitarian societies of the Soviet Bloc and the repressive American laws and practices during World War I and the Cold War. But the overall long-term trend has been towards freedom to express our thoughts and live as we choose.

When I was twenty, a bearded ragamuffin, I spent the fall of 1983 travelling through Western Europe. This was the time of Reagan, Thatcher and Andropov. The arms race was in full force. East-West tensions were high. The Soviet Eastern Bloc was still intact. Berlin was still divided. The West Germans were convinced that an imminent World War III was to be a nuclear exchange on German soil. Needless to say, they were not very happy with the idea of Americans fighting an American war on their soil. The nuclear freeze movement was very popular at the time.

I remember visiting East Berlin for a day. It was hard to miss the stark difference between the two sides of the city. The buildings in East Berlin still had bullet holes in them from World War II, almost forty years before. The people were poor. The markets were mostly empty by Western standards. I remember that gray afternoon well. (I think all afternoons were gray in East Berlin.)

I sat at a counter in a diner and ordered something to eat. A man, who turned out to be a geology professor, was sitting a couple of seats away. We started speaking in German. We made the ordinary polite talk that curious strangers make, constrained, of course, by my elementary German. He asked all the normal questions: Where are you from? How do you like Germany? And I answered them. I asked him questions about what he did. But being the odd duck that I was, I started explaining to him that nobody in the United States wanted a war with the Soviet Union, that we were not enemies, that this wall between East and West Berlin was dumb, and that we are all just people trying to get on with our lives. And before I had finished blathering all over him, the professor became frightened. He quit talking and ignored me as he hurriedly finished his meal. I cluelessly continued to talk, but he acted as if I had not said anything. He really did ignore me. It was awkward. Then he quickly left without saying goodbye.

Back in West Berlin, my German friends explained that he was scared that we might have been overheard by informants for the Stasi, the German secret police. One of the Stasi's main tasks was spying on the population through a network of up to 500,000 informants, which amounted to about one in thirty-two people in East Germany. There were also about 100,000 Stasi agents, which came to about one in 166 people, whereas the Soviet Union had only one in about 6,000. East Germany had more spies than any recent totalitarian government. The Stasi had agents in every apartment building, in every large factory. They had doctors, lawyers, writers, actors, sports stars, even waiters and hotel employees.[18]

The Stasi kept records on millions of East Germans. But why would the Stasi collect all this information? The Stasi wanted to know what people were *thinking*. Rather than wait for people to act against the regime, the Stasi wanted to know in advance what people were thinking and planning. Those who voiced unacceptable opinions were imprisoned and ruined. Over 250,000 East Germans were imprisoned on suspicion of thinking wrong thoughts. Many were murdered. East Germans knew that they were surrounded by informers, and this created mistrust and widespread fear, which are the most important tools to oppress people in any dictatorship.[19] People had to keep their thoughts to themselves.

---

[18] John Koehler, *Stasi: The Untold Story of the German Secret Police* (Westview, 1999), 9.

[19] Hubertus Knabe, "The dark secrets of a surveillance state," TED Salon, Berlin, 2014, https://youtu.be/IWjzT2l5C34?si=FnvnAEykx50djJM9.

In *The Gulag Archipelago*, Aleksandr Solzhenitsyn (1918–2008) wrote about the Soviet Union's forced labor camps, collectively known as the Gulag, which were established by law in 1919 and lasted until the 1960s. It is estimated that the Soviet Gulag held five million or more prisoners at a time from 1936 to 1953, the population continually being replenished with more prisoners to replace the dead. Most of the inhabitants of the Gulag were political prisoners who had thought, said, or done the wrong things or in many cases had just been put there because quotas needed filling. Estimates of people who died in the Gulag vary from 1.6 million to over 10 million.

Solzhenitsyn also tells of an unbelievably comic and tragic example of fear in the Soviet Union of the 1920s.

A district party conference was underway in Moscow Province, led by a new secretary of the District Party Committee, who had replaced one who was arrested by the Soviet secret police. At the end of the conference, a tribute to Comrade Stalin was proposed. The attendees all stood up, applauding fervently as they had done each time Stalin's name was mentioned during the event. The applause escalated into an ovation and lasted for minutes on end—three, four, five minutes—until the people's hands were sore and their arms ached. Even the most devoted were weary.

No one dared to end the applause first. The new secretary of the District Party Committee, who had initiated it, could have ended the applause, but he was too afraid to stop. He was a newcomer and the previous secretary had been arrested. He didn't want to follow him to the Gulag. And to make it worse, there were secret police in the room, watching to see who would quit first. The applause dragged on for six, seven, eight minutes, becoming absurd even to Stalin's admirers. Everyone was trapped, fearing the consequences of stopping first.

With make-believe enthusiasm on their faces, looking at each other with faint hope, the district leaders were just going to go on and on applauding until they fell where they stood, until they were carried out of the hall on stretchers! And, even then, those who were left would not falter.

Among those on the platform was the director of the local paper factory, a man known for his independence and strength of character. He understood the farce but continued clapping for nine, ten minutes, watching the secretary for any sign of stopping.

After eleven minutes, in a moment of decision, the factory director finally sat down, assuming a businesslike demeanor. Miraculously, the applause ceased immediately as everyone else also sat down, relieved. However, this act of independence marked him. That very night, he was arrested and later imprisoned for 10 years for an unrelated offense. His interrogator made it clear why he was really there: "Don't ever be the first to stop applauding!"

This was how they discovered who the independent thinkers were, and this was how they went about eliminating them.[20]

Fortunately, the Soviet Union is dead, the repressive governments of the Soviet Bloc are dead. But repression continues in many non-Western countries, where people are murdered or jailed for their beliefs. Freedom of thought is a Western tradition. Western people will not stand for government repression.[21]

Freedom Limited by Conformity

Today, more than a century after the German-led intellectual revolution moved us toward acceptance of divergent thought, we mostly share the belief that we are truly free to speak our minds. However, even if the state is not monitoring and repressing our speech, and even in this age

---

[20] Aleksandr Solzhenitsyn, *The Gulag Archipelago*, vol. 1–2 (Harper & Row, 1974), 69.

[21] Unfortunately, this is changing. We are now seeing increasing levels of social pressure on people to speak, write and think "correctly" by the progressives in Western countries. In Europe people are being jailed for posting wrong thinking online. But there has been pushback recently. We will see what happens.

of "free speech," other forces limit how we think, speak and act—forces many of us are not aware of.

Perhaps the most powerful force that limits our thinking and expression is the need to fit in with everyone else. We don't want to be shunned. We need to be accepted and loved. In the early 1950s, psychologist Ruth Berenda carried out an interesting experiment with teenagers. The experiment was designed to show how people handled group pressure. Groups of ten adolescents were brought into a room for a simple test. The teenagers were instructed to raise their hands when the teacher pointed to the longest line on three separate charts. I cannot think of an easier test. Nine of the people in the room were confederates, previously instructed to point to the second longest line. Only one of the students was really being tested. The experiment began, of course, with the nine confederates voting for the wrong line.

> *The stooge would typically glance around, frown in confusion, and slip his hand up with the group. The instructions were repeated and the next card was raised. Time after time, the self-conscious stooge would sit there saying a short line is longer than a long line, simply because he lacked the courage to challenge the group. This remarkable conformity occurred in about 75% of the cases, and was true of small children and high-school students as well.*[22]

This truth is sad to me. But it is in our nature. We are herd animals. Attend a college or professional football game, and you will see it: the fans of a team wearing the same colors, often the same clothes even, all belonging to the same herd.

As in the line-length experiment, we often do not feel free to think or say things that contradict the prevailing social schemas. In the scientific world, to dare to consider telepathy as possible or to doubt the theory of evolution would invite ridicule and probably endanger one's career or funding. By publicly expressing opinions contrary to these "known"

---

[22] Charles R. Swindoll, *Living Above the Level of Mediocrity (Thomas Nelson, 1989), 225.*

theories, one risks being considered "not substantial," a crank, foolish and, in the end, unwanted. Is this outcome any different from medieval times when the Church held such sway over our thoughts? I suppose the only difference between then and now is that our social institutions no longer torture, jail and kill us for having a different viewpoint. But we still have the lesser, although substantial, fear of being shamed and scorned, our reputations damaged and careers limited, so we don't speak out.

A second force limiting freedom of thought and speech is our belief in what we have been taught by those around us. Many of those beliefs are based on assumptions that are just not true, but most of us have not really examined our societal assumptions. In every age and in every group, individuals are constrained by the thinking of the group. Often the rules for acceptable thought, speech, and behavior are unspoken; but we all understand them without being consciously aware that the rules even exist. We obey the will of the group without even knowing it. We will delve into this more in an essay to come.

We all know that our governing institutions in the United States have been failing the people for quite some time. Our leaders often make decisions for self-serving political reasons, not for the good of the people. Yet despite all of this, most of us are firm believers in our political system.

Imagine if a leading politician published a piece explaining that the solution to the United States's political and social issues was a monarchy—a benevolent ruler who had the people's best interests at heart would indeed be the most effective ruler. This ruler could choose the best experts to craft plans to remedy any social or physical challenges we had. They could effectively remake society for the good of all of us. This ruler would not need to waste energy placating the opposition and dealing with endless regulations. Decisions would not be made for political reasons. The benevolent ruler would instead do what they thought was best, spending their energy making positive change. Some people would still oppose their policies; but without our messy political system, they would be powerless to block progress.

The father of sociology, Auguste Comte (1798–1857), pushed for this, but how many of us Americans have seriously considered this idea? Regardless as to whether it be a good or bad idea, has it been entertained by many in the United States? I would say no, because we unconsciously believe that government is elected by the people in order to serve the people. To Americans, that is the nature of government. This is a fundamental tenet that exists here and now in the United States; but it does not exist everywhere, nor is it a fundamental law. It is one of those postulates that we Americans base our schema on, and to question it is un-American. Imagine the criticism a political leader, sports superstar or actor would receive after suggesting the United States should be a monarchy!

Much of our thinking that limits our own freedom is based on such postulates, statements we take to be true, but that cannot be proven true and, therefore, are not necessarily so. Based on these postulates, we create a worldview, a schema.

We do this individually as well. "I am not good enough," "Nobody will ever love me," etc. In life, many of us create our own hells on earth that we must endure. It is the same for societies. Societies can embrace a schema that makes them miserable, weak or even suicidal. Just as we can free ourselves from our own personal self-limiting thoughts, societies can rid themselves of self-limiting postulates that hold them back.

One of the objectives of this series of essays is to identify some of the postulates that most of us share in the Western World and identify them as either erroneous or limiting.

Martin Luther (1483–1546) opened a Pandora's Box when he rejected the Church's authority over the Western World and said anyone can interpret the Word of God. That was a revolution in thought. And then there were the French and Russian revolutions, claiming that people could rule themselves without kings. Those were radical revolutions. Perhaps just as radical as Fichte's proclamation that we are responsible for our own beliefs and, therefore, "each of us may sit in judgement upon every tradition, prohibition, law, or creed and bid it show why it should be obeyed."[23]

The Reformation led to a hundred years of war and, with it, killing, pillaging and destruction. It led to the propagation of hundreds of Christian denominations, each proclaiming they are the only true faith and that those following other faiths were hell-bound. The French and Russian revolutions gave free rein to the evil that abides in our dark unconsciousness with widespread killing, theft, anarchy, and suffering. It took a dictator to reestablish order. Changes on such a fundamental level are messy and typically carry with them suffering and death on a massive scale. And, once the horrible transition is over, the new order may or may not make the terrible ordeal worth it.

I believe the United States went through a similar process in the 1960s, where the Baby Boomers challenged and overthrew many traditional American beliefs and customs. Such revolutionary thought doesn't always end well, as noted. The 1960s brought us broken families, drug addiction and rampant political activism, which led to over-regulation and stagnation.

I am not suggesting that we look upon our laws and traditions and decide for ourselves whether we want to heed them or not. If we did that, nobody would pay taxes or obey the speed limits. That would be disastrous. Instead, we should understand what constitutes the building blocks of our common beliefs and question them. Once we see that some of these beliefs are flawed, we can reshape our individual and collective mindsets with more accurate and liberating foundational beliefs.

So, why don't we? The problem is that we may not be conscious of many of these fundamental postulates that we base our worldview on. And worse than that, if we have some inkling that they may be wrong, most of us dare not oppose the prevailing social sentiments, as wrong as they may be. The punishment may not be worth it.

---

[23] Durant and Durant, 628.

But it can be done. Tony Robbins does this with thousands of his seminar attendees each year. He leads the participants to discover their root beliefs and tendencies, from which the rest of their worldview, or schema, is developed. Then, based on what they want to achieve in their lives, they change their root beliefs to reconstruct their worldview. As Robbins says, "We need to realize that the direction of our lives is controlled by the magnetic pull of our values. They are the force in front of us, consistently leading us to make decisions that create the direction and ultimate destination of our lives."[24] Change someone's schema, and you will change their life. Change an organization's or a nation's schema and you change its trajectory in history.

1918 to 2017: An Era of Relative Stagnation

In the beginning of the essay, I spoke about the common conception of change and how the echo chamber of society repeats over and over that the rate of change is accelerating faster than ever. I hope I have shown you that when people speak this way, they are referring to technological change and how that affects our standards of living, how we work and how we entertain ourselves. But in terms of intellectual or political change, we have been in a stagnant period. Very little has happened relative to other periods in history, such as the fall of the Roman Republic or the swift transition from medieval thinking to German idealism. The question that occurs to me is, why has there been so little change in political or ideological systems in this time?

Every generation is different from the last and each has its own schema. But on a very broad scale, one can see that during the period of the sixteenth century up to the twentieth century, Western Civilization was incrementally freeing itself from the intellectual, social and political constraints imposed on it by the Church and feudal rule. At the same time, science was unlocking the mysteries of the world. Over those few centuries, a revitalized Western Civilization emerged, embracing

---

[24] Tony Robbins, *Awaken the Giant Within* (Simon & Schuster, 2007), 344.

newfound liberty, using science to unveil new truths and experimenting with new systems of organization. The overarching ideals were of the progress and promise of humanity. For the most part, as a race, we were hopeful and working towards a better future. We were finally free to manifest our lives and our societies as we wanted.

In the eighteenth century, the Romantics believed in the human spirit. They believed in the infinite possibility of man, and they built buildings and created art and literature to that effect. Buildings were made to last. The beautiful Gothic revival architecture of Europe was inspired by Romanticism. Visual arts were meaningful then. Painting and sculpture spoke to us of human possibility, beauty and hope. Art of the past spoke through the symbolic language that is common to all men. Art spoke directly to our unconscious minds of the great human ideals of love, devotion, duty, honor, justice, mastery and beauty.

The Great War, World War I, marked the end of our time in the sun. That war was billed as "the war to end all wars," and our forefathers believed it. They still had hope in progress. But the realities of that devastating war changed all of that. The war made clear that humanity was not developing as had been hoped. The new era of promise had not come, and the world was plunged into senseless killing and destruction. Rather than just professional armies and mercenaries fighting and dying, entire nations participated in the mass murder of 20 million people. The great hope that was science had been transformed into a killing machine with airplanes, tanks, machine guns, poison gas and flame throwers. This was followed, only twenty years later, by 200 million more people murdered in World War II. Neither the old Christianity or its disgraced replacement, science, had any answers for the suicidal insanity of the Great Wars. It was hard to accept the bewildering explanation "God works in mysterious ways." Christianity was no longer credible for most of us.

The result was a dismal existentialism, the leading philosophy of the twentieth century. Existentialism proclaims that there is no meaning in life. Rather, meaning is whatever you choose to fool yourself into believing. The existentialists called reality "nausea," a feeling of emptiness, meaninglessness and isolation.

We no longer had our old spiritual realm to comfort us because we had rejected it. We only had the inhospitable world we saw around us, and we had to make our way as best we could.

Along with that dismal philosophy came the degradation of art. Beauty no longer had a place. Marcel Duchamp pioneered the idea that true art is conceptual, a mental construct. It should be pleasing to the intellect. No need any more for talent with a brush or pencil. He denigrated art that appealed to the eye, calling it "retinal art." "That kind of painter who just puts down what he sees is stupid."[25] Since the latter part of the twentieth century, beauty in art has been rejected as sexist. Good art could be made from assembled items purchased at the local store, such as Duchamp's famous stool with a bicycle wheel protruding from it. The curators and other influencers in the art world agreed with Duchamp, and the art world has never been the same. Art lost its connection with the eye and with our unconscious minds and has become so intellectual that people have to be taught what makes "art" worthwhile and meaningful; whereas before true art would touch every soul though the symbolism and imagery that we naturally respond to. Andres Serrano, a famous conceptual artist, wrote on his website, "I learned everything I know about art from Marcel Duchamp, who taught me that anything, including a photograph, could be a work of art."[26] In the 1980s, this man, Serrano, became famous and infamous when he exhibited a plastic crucifix in a jar of his own urine. That work is the epitome of conceptual art—art for a lost age.

Literature of the twentieth century was mostly the literature of despair and meaninglessness. The protagonist in Jean-Paul Sartre's novel Nausea feels this haunting sense of meaninglessness. Sartre believed that to see life in any other way was to deceive oneself. A person in Franz

---

[25] Calvin Tomkins, *The World of Marcel Duchamp, 1887* (Time Life Books, 1966), 9.

[26] Andre Serrano, andresserrano.org/biography, accessed January 1, 2025.

Kafka's novel *Metamorphosis* wakes up to find that he is a hideous and unbearable insect. The world described by these authors is meaningless. Life becomes absurd, insignificant, cruel and empty. Kafka and Sartre were not alone. Hundreds of novels were published presenting our lives in this way, with us just cogs in the wheel of a machine. In the twentieth century we called that "literature."

The result, of course, is that we are living in postmodern society, based on the existentialist cleansing of humanity's place in the spiritual world. Since life has no intrinsic meaning, it is our responsibility to give our lives meaning. This poses a problem, because it is more convenient and easier to distract ourselves in empty and unsustainable materialism than give our lives meaning. So it is in things, acquisition, and entertainment that we look for spiritual sustenance. It is easier to purchase a car than to earnestly confront reality and our place in it. I know, I bought one last year. We can be excited for a few months about a new car; but ultimately, we find only emptiness. We are still here.

How is it that this has come to pass? We have progressed from idealism, romanticism and a belief in unlimited possibilities to the negativity, despair, materialism and meaninglessness of the postmodern world. Can we change our perspectives and the course of our lives and our societies? I hope so. As noted before, the point of this essay is not to trace the decay of Western Civilization. Rather, it and the essays that follow are my humble attempt to nudge Western society toward a positive and hopeful new direction.

Unfortunately, the old spiritual systems of the traditional Western religions cannot provide the needed direction. Those bridges have been burned. Through centuries of abuse, humanity has been betrayed by Christianity. And after over 100 years of exposure, the truths of Eastern religions still have not caught the imagination of most of the Western world. The Eastern way cannot appeal to the mainstream Western mind. It is too different. What we need is a new way of understanding that can account for our place in the world; explain our sad and tragic history; and serve, rather than hinder, humanity. We have been stuck for a century plus in negativity and despair. Contrary to what everyone is saying, this is not an era of rapid change at all. Except for the impact of advancing technology, which may only intensify our hopelessness and alienation, this has been a stagnant, pessimistic age. And this needs to, and will, change. The world will enter into another positive era. The question is whether we will be alive to see it.

Wrapping It Up

It should be clear to you by now what I am trying to accomplish in writing these essays is not a clear-cut logical progression of ideas like a geometric proof. It is more like a jigsaw puzzle. Several pieces must be filled in before you can begin to perceive what the image actually is.

As I see it, it is important to assault the reader in many places, weakening lots of firmly held beliefs simultaneously. Then, perhaps, the reader's entire schema can crumble. That would be a valuable read.

I know, some will say, *why be so damn abstract? Just tell us the point and don't waste our time.* In my opinion, the points I am writing about deserve a thorough, rather than concise, treatment. The points I write about can be more profound and lasting for you if you figure them out yourself, rather than my just giving you a short direct treatment of the topics. Elevator pitches sound trite to me. Can you imagine how life changing an elevator pitch from Jesus or Buddha might be? If you ask me, not at all. You have to immerse yourself in their writings, and then their work as a whole can make a statement with some weight.

Still, I am providing a summary of each essay. These summaries may provide contours that reveal where each piece in these essays fits into the whole. But don't skip to the summaries. The essays are the good part, much more illuminating and, I dare say, interesting than the summaries.

Here are the main points:

- We are in an era of rapid technological change, but we are not in an era of rapid political or intellectual change.

- Progress is not just about technology. It is the changing minds of the multitudes that is the real story. We went from acceptance of intellectual and physical slavery to submission to kings and the Church to demanding representative governments that we choose for ourselves. Whereas we were not allowed to think for ourselves in ancient and medieval times, we now have that freedom (although we often choose not to use it). That is real change.

- The idea of freedom to decide for yourself is relatively new.

- Aberrations in this pattern of liberation have occurred. Nations have been lost for decades in totalitarian rule, where there was no freedom; but then they were released. Overall, the pattern toward freedom of thought holds.

- But even now in the "free" Western World, our freedom is limited by our need to conform and our unconscious assimilation of values from those around us.

- Many of our individual outlooks on life are based on unproven, unproveable assumptions that we are not even aware of. These bedrocks of internal thought empower and limit us in ways we are not aware of.

- In the same way, our societies have unique outlooks that are also based on unproven, unproveable assumptions that also empower and limit them.

- If you can change an individual's or a society's outlook (schema), you can change the trajectory of their future. The postulates that hold us back should be identified and replaced with growth-oriented, actualizing postulates.

❧ As a result of the Enlightenment and the Romantic era, Western civilization had evolved into one of idealism, romanticism and the belief in unlimited possibilities for the human spirit. People believed in the progress of science.

❧ But we sank into an era of pessimism after World War I. Our schema transitioned from one of hope and change to one of resignation and bitterness. The degradation of our music and art is a sign of this, as they veered from Chopin, Renoir and Tolstoy to John Cage, Marcel Duchamp, Jackson Pollack and Jean-Paul Sartre.

❧ As our religions have been discredited by their horrible histories, we have been left with the existentialist idea that there is no meaning in life, which means that it is our own responsibility to give life meaning (because we must have a reason). So we turn to inconsequential hobbies, an unsatiable need for possessions, identification with our favorite sports teams and political ideologies, or anything really, since everything is equally unimportant.

❧ Western society has been trapped in a period of negativity and despair, but it won't go on forever. A new schema will form, and this change will require the dropping of some of the hidden postulates that we all unconsciously hold dear.

Essay 2
We are Blind to the Tyranny
in Our Own Minds

Why look for conspiracy when stupidity
can explain so much?
— GOETHE

Skewed Understanding

When we examine ourselves or humanity in general, we necessarily nearly always do it from our own perspective. From our own point of view, we don't look so bad. But let's try for a moment to view humanity from a more advanced outsider's perspective. It could be from the perspective of some greater beings such as extra-terrestrials, God, angels, demons, or spirits. It doesn't matter if they exist or not. What matters is that they are outside of us, have a non-human perspective and can view all of human society dispassionately.

From this hypothetical higher perspective, I don't think we humans look so sharp. Within each society, conflicting forces often work at cross purposes, wasting tremendous amounts of human energy. One group builds while the other group destroys. It appears this is always going on. But when it is all added together, some preponderance moves in some direction and that determines the general direction in which society moves.

It is the same with individuals. When I was young, I wanted to be rich, but I hated rich people. I had two different conceptions that were working at cross-purposes. In my case, I experienced little to no movement towards wealth because the side of me that wanted to be rich was undermined by the side that despised the rich. I am not alone. It is common to sabotage ourselves with these conflicting interests, both individually and as societies. Because both individuals and societies often pursue contradicting trajectories, a lot of vital energy is wasted and progress towards any goal is slow. In this way, most individuals and societies are self-defeating by nature.

People tend to put a lot of faith in their intelligence. Just because we appear to be the most intelligent creature on the planet does not mean that our intelligence is worth a damn. We get by, but we don't necessarily understand. Imagine a farm with pigs, dogs, ducks, goats and cows. The pigs may be the most intelligent creature on the farm, but that distinction does not mean a pig can create a spaceship or a suspension bridge. Similarly, just because we are smarter than other animals does not mean we have the capacity to accurately perceive and understand the world around us. Still, it seems the more intelligent someone is, the more they rely on their intellect to comprehend things that might be beyond human understanding. I consider this to be a form of arrogance.

The reality is that we cannot understand many things. Our inability to understand is inherent in the way we think. We are limited by our mental wiring. We fool ourselves into believing that we can understand ourselves, the world and our place in it. The basis of this shortcoming is in the nature of how we see ourselves. We cling too tightly to our world-view, our schema, our belief system—and our schemas are most often not right at all. Once we recognize that our identities have been shaped by misconceptions, we might be open to embracing more beneficial truths. But first, let's explore our schema and the inherent flaws in our perception of the world.

Defining Schema

A schema is a belief system that we use to determine which actions are acceptable for us and others. It is our worldview, a lens through which we filter and interpret all of our observations. A schema is the framework on which we base our lives. It is the story we tell ourselves. Even though we may think we are seeing the world accurately, we are not. All of our schemas are flawed, as we shall see.

Individual Schemas

Our personal belief systems, also known as our personal schema, shape our perceptions and actions. These schemas often lead to misunderstandings and conflicts, especially when they clash with the schemas of others. Let's delve into a real-life example to illustrate this.

Conflicting Personal Schemas: Rich and Poor

One day when I was walking to work, I saw two cars pull up right next to me and stop very quickly right there in the road. Just that in itself was very unusual. These were fast stops with screeching tires just like in the movies. Two men very quickly got out of their cars and began cursing at each other. One of the men was in a rusty contractor's truck with toolboxes in the back and the other in an expensive looking black Lincoln Continental. The contractor was in his thirties wearing typical work clothes, jeans and a tee shirt, while the other man was in his sixties, wearing slacks, a nice dress shirt, coat and tie. He might have been a successful lawyer. The contractor yelled "You rich pig! You think you own the road." The lawyer yelled back, "You good for nothing piece of crap..." (Well, he didn't use those words exactly.) Then they proceeded to fight. Right there, in front of me. I stood frozen, mouth agape. I just watched. I had never seen anything like that before. Who knows what caused the incident, probably one of them cut in front of the other. But what I found most interesting was how clear it was that different stories were playing in each of their heads. These stories likely had nothing to do with what happened. Based on the limited dialog, I imagined that the contractor saw the rich man as entitled and felt that wealthy people were the reason behind his own struggles, disappointments and failures. It is easy for the working class to blame the rich. As he likely saw it, the rich get rich by screwing over the rest of us and they need to be knocked down a notch. I imagined that the rich man saw the working man as a nonentity who should know his place and stay out of the way. Each of these men viewed this everyday traffic incident through his own filter, and they inflated the incident to become greater and more significant than it really was. It had become a class struggle.

I suppose my imagination could have added more meaning to this event than was really there. (That is what journalists, authors and historians do all the time.) But their dialog definitely supported the fact that the two men were telling themselves totally different stories that had little to do with a traffic altercation.

This fight is just one example of how a single event can spark wildly different interpretations, none fully capturing what actually happened. The truth is probably that one man's driving irritated the other man. Both men were probably agitated to begin with. They needed to release their anger at something, and so they fought. It was like being at the zoo and watching animals engage in authentic behavior. All I could do was stare, my mouth agape, utterly transfixed.

How Information Processing Supports Schema

We all take two steps as we monitor the world around us. First, we determine what stimuli to register and which to ignore. There is just too much to take it all in. We automatically and unconsciously ignore most stimuli with only a small amount making it into our consciousness.

Many years ago, psychologists performed an experiment with a cat.

A wire was connected to the nerve between the cat's ear and its brain, and the other end of the wire was connected to a dial for measuring electrical impulses. When a loud noise sounded near the cat's ear, the needle of the dial swung over violently. Then a cage of mice was placed in front of the cat. It watched them intently. The same loud noise was sounded close to its ear. But the needle did not stir. The cat was so intent on the mice that it ignored the sound—somehow it had "switched off" the connection between the ear and the brain. It unconsciously chose to focus on something else.[27]

Humans, like cats, have this power to focus on what interests them and to shut off everything else. This filtering process is not objective at all. We humans often take in content that is linked to our emotions. For example, how many times when walking in nature have we seen a twig up ahead in the path and instantly mistaken it for a snake. I do it a lot. At that moment, our focus narrows in on the twig, as it is potentially life-threatening, and we fail to notice the flowers and birds nearby. We notice the twig. We focus on the twig because it induces fear, an emotion. It is the same with anything that is associated with strong emotion. We notice it and filter out the rest.

The second step in processing information is that we automatically ascribe meaning to whatever information we do take in, and this meaning usually is defined based on our schemas. Almost always, we then use the assigned meaning to confirm that we are correct in our view of the world. Thus, we are continuously reinforcing our schemas with our perceptions and labeling of the world around us. In this sense, schema is self-sustaining. Both of those characters in my road rage story probably left the encounter feeling even more entrenched in their classist schemas. If we view ourselves as being "kept down by The Man," we will look for confirming evidence everywhere—and that evidence will confirm that, indeed, we are right.

---

[27] Colin Wilson, *The Occult* (Hodder and Stoughton, 1971), 49.

Cognitive Dissonance and Defense Mechanisms

Cognitive dissonance is the term applied when people become painfully aware that their actions do not correspond to their beliefs or that they hold two contradictory beliefs. The usual reaction to this situation is to "save the schema" at the expense of gathering a better understanding of the world and making adjustments to our schema. We do this using many different types of defense mechanisms: denial, repression, suppression, etc.[28] Many of us will find ways to deny the offending information or somehow invalidate it: "The news station is biased. I don't believe anything that guy says." Or, some of us know deep inside that our worldview is wrong but we will not admit it to ourselves; and instead, we repress this realization, hoping it never comes up to haunt us (as a mental breakdown or an illness).

When we encounter someone who speaks slowly, with a limited vocabulary and only in short sentences with pauses between them, we naturally think this person may not be very intelligent. George Bush the Younger spoke this way, and he was considered stupid by the Left, while his supporters brushed this off—both reactions due to previously-held schemas. If someone scores high on the SAT, we generally assume that person is smart. George Bush actually scored a 1306 out of 1600 on his SAT scores, which was actually pretty good considering 980 was average in 1963, the year he took the test.[29]

I often heard the "save the schema" Democratic response to this fact, "Well, he is from a rich family and probably took classes to increase his test scores." Whether he took classes or not—I do not know—SAT prep classes have been available and generally affordable to the middle class for years. Anyone else could have taken them as well. Regardless, it does not invalidate the fact that he scored well and, therefore, may not be stupid after all. But, in the minds of some progressives, their erroneous

---

[28] James F. Welles, *Understanding Stupidity* (Mount Pleasant, 1986), 54.

[29] Apparently, there is some controversy on his SAT tests. Some say he took it in 1964, and he got a 1204 score, which is still a very good score.

view of reality was justified by their judgement of his speech patterns. To them, he remained stupid. For progressive people to contend that George W. Bush was smart might cause problems with their peers and with their own schema. Rather than face cognitive dissonance, it is far easier to rationalize the incongruent information away. And very smart people did, and do, just that.

Large Changes to Schema

It is tough to admit that we've been wrong about the world all our lives and have acted foolishly, harming ourselves or others based on our misconceptions. If we were to recognize this, we would have to make large-scale changes to our worldviews.[30] But large-scale changes can be emotionally devastating. They are threatening. Why? Because we think we are our schemas. Changing our schema means changing ourselves.[31] It also means that people will respond differently to us. We may no longer fit into the groups we presently belong to. In fact, we may need to cut ties with the people we associate with, so that they do not drag us back into our old way of living. Rather than make such wholesale changes in our lives that a change of schemas could set off, we usually revert to defense mechanisms first. After all, a wholesale change in schema would mean we had been wrong all these years. And who likes to be wrong.

"Me? Wrong? Never!"

If our defense mechanisms fail and we still suffer from painful cognitive dissonance, we may be forced to change our beliefs. But how often does that happen? Think about it. How many times have you done it? A sudden conversion to a religion is a good example of this. Near death experiences or other very traumatic experiences can also lead to these massive changes in schema. But generally, large, all-at-once changes in schema do not happen very often.

---

30 Welles, *Understanding Stupidity*, 9.

31 Welles, *Understanding Stupidity*, 77.

More often, rather than altering our perceptions to fit our schema, we make small changes to our belief systems. This occurs when we encounter facts that do not fit with our schemas. We do it all the time with little emotion, even unconsciously. We call this learning, refining our knowledge of the world. Sometimes large schematic changes can be made incrementally through many small changes in succession.

On the other hand, it is amazing what people will do to match what they think of themselves. In an experiment conducted by Jonathan Freeman and Scott Fraser, homeowners in Palo Alto were asked to place large six-foot by three-foot Drive Carefully signs in their front yards. The researchers knew that most people would not want these unsightly signs on their lawns. The results bore that out. Only 17% of homeowners agreed to have the signs placed in their yards. But Freeman and Fraser tricked a different group of Palo Alto homeowners into a 76% compliance rate. They got 400% more homeowners to choose to display the ugly signs. For this group, researchers had asked the homeowners two weeks earlier if they would place small signs in their windows that said, "Be a Safe Driver." A different group then returned two weeks later asking to place the larger signs in their lawns. Freeman and Fraser concluded that by placing the small signs in their windows, the residents came to see themselves as concerned citizens. This became part of their schema. They then were more likely to have the large sign placed in their yard because they were motivated to act in accordance with their new self-perception as concerned citizens (their new schema).[32] Political campaigns are now using this technique, asking for small donations, knowing that once you have given a little, you see yourself as a supporter and will be willing to comply with further requests in order to maintain your perception of yourself. Robert Cialdini, the famous social researcher on social influence, will not sign petitions for

---

[32] J. L Freedman and S. C. Fraser, "Compliance without pressure: The Foot-in-the-Door Technique," *Journal of Personality and Social Psychology* (1966), vol. 4, 195-202, in Robert B. Cialdini, *Influence: The Psychology of Persuasion*, (Collins, 2007).

this reason because he fears that he may find himself later unconsciously donating to causes he really does not care that much about.

Twisting Reality to Maintain Our Schema

The great majority of us have this need to be right and approve of ourselves—this makes life so much more comfortable. We convince ourselves that our schema must be right. We will bend reality and often go to ridiculous extremes in order to make it appear right to us. It is not just something that the majority of us do; this is fundamental to being human—this self-deceiving flaw is in our makeup. Data from the real world that opposes our flattering self-image is blocked or reinterpreted to reinforce our cherished beliefs. This allows us to continue to feel good about ourselves, even when we are doing evil or stupid things. To this end, much of the negative feedback we receive gets twisted:[33]

"Susie says I am greedy, but she is just envious that I have such nice things. I am sure she would trade places with me in a second."

Maybe Susie is spot on, and I am greedy. But as long as I entertain this defensive point of view, I can never take her criticism seriously.

"The stock market has dropped 20%, but that is because institutional investors are getting people to sell so they can scoop up bargains. There is no way it is going to drop farther. Now is the time to buy."

I thought that once and lost a lot of money in the crash of 2000. They call that catching a falling knife. I refused to see reality—that stocks had grown too fast, were overvalued and were due for a massive correction. Instead, I believed what I wanted to believe, which is that the market cannot drop any further than this. I was being stupid, ignoring the feedback right in front of me.

---

[33] If you really think about it, we never know if or when we are twisting reality because we never really know all the facts. We never really know why people do what they do. They often do not even know why. Every explanation we have for anything, really is, to some degree, a distorting of the truth, since we cannot know the truth anyway.

Much of our negative feedback will never even penetrate our minds. We tell ourselves,

"I don't listen to anything Susie says; she is just envious."

"I don't care about the daily ups and downs of the stock price. It is certain to be a winner in the long term."

This propensity causes us to make big mistakes because we don't see negative feedback. We all have this blind spot to different degrees. The less self-aware people and groups are, the less they can handle negative criticism and the less they are able to self-correct.[34] Some just do not want to know the truth, because they fear it will be upsetting.[35] These are typically the people and groups that blame others for their failings.

Ideology Blinds

In 2013, Yale law professor Dan Kahan and his team conducted a study showing how people distort facts to align with their existing beliefs, blinding them to reality.[36] Kahan and his colleagues assessed 1,000 Americans, determining their political views and their math skills. Part of the test involved a brain teaser about skin creme. In the hypothetical story, a number of people were given the skin creme, some got better, and some got worse. Others were not given the skin creme and some got better and some got worse. The skin creme results are shown in the table below:

---

[34] Welles, *Understanding Stupidity*, 75.

[35] Welles, *Understanding Stupidity*, 76.

[36] Daniel Kahan, "How Politics Makes Us Stupid," *Vox*, April 26, 2014, https://tinyurl. com/pwedrno. Most of the discussion that follows on Kahan's study is from this article.

	Rash Got Better	Rash Got Worse
Patients Who Used the New Skin Creme	225	75
Patients Who Did Not Use the New Skin Creme	107	21

From looking at the results, most people concluded that the skin creme was more effective at treating rashes than not using the skin creme. They came to this conclusion due to the larger number, 225, of those who improved. That is a wrong assessment. Not using the skin creme was more effective in curing the rash. By considering percentages and not number of cases, it is clear that not using the skin creme was the better solution. The rash got better for about 75% of those using the skin creme, while it got better for about 84% of those who did not use the skin creme. Better not to use it. The people who were better at math and critical thinking were able to figure this out. Let's call them the "smarter" people for this argument here. (I am not claiming they are "smarter," we just need a name for this group.)

The researchers gave the same table of results (the same numbers) to the same surveyed population, but this time the question was about a politicized issue, the carrying of concealed weapons. In some cases, the 2x2 table of results showed that the ban on carrying concealed weapons cut crime; and in some cases, the table of results showed that the ban increased crime.

The study showed that "smarter" subjects actually interpreted the results based on ideology, not on the facts that were presented to them in the table. "Smart" liberals, who opposed legal concealed carry policies, were very good at interpreting the table of results when it demonstrated that they were correct in their beliefs on gun control. But when presented with a table of results that showed that concealed carry policies actually reduced crime, a result opposite to their beliefs, the math skills of the "smart" liberals often failed. So, they were able to continue to believe that they were correct in their belief that gun control would reduce crime. "Smart" conservatives exhibited the same pattern, only in reverse. For both groups, ideology drove the answers.

Kahan concluded that being better at math actually made partisans less likely to solve the problem correctly when it meant betraying their political beliefs. Kahan has done other tests as well that demonstrated that the smarter people are, the more likely they are to disregard factual evidence and search harder for evidence to support their beliefs. Smarter people reason harder to get the answer they want.

Schema as Identity

The reason for this dismal test performance is that people cling so tightly to their schemas. It is irrational. As Eckhert Tolle (1948–) has stressed repeatedly, we are so identified with our mind that we don't even know we are its slaves.[37] We take pride in our mind, beliefs and thoughts; and most of us hold onto them proudly and will defend them against all rational argument. Our schemas supply the answers to questions like: What is important? What is right? Who am I? Who are we? What is the purpose of living? In fact, when asked who we are, many of us will describe our minds, which, is another word, really, for our schemas. We are proud of our minds, our schemas, which we have worked so hard to develop. Not only are we proud of our minds, many of us we believe we are our minds.

People are often so wedded to their beliefs, their schemas, they will fight for them to the grave. It is all about survival of the perceived self. If we believe we are our schemas, then we *have to* defend them. Many writers refer to it as being on par with defending one's life. People need to know that they are right. That is why after an event has occurred, which objectively can be seen as a failure, there will be some who will explain that it was indeed a success or, if not a success, the failure was caused by obstructionists.

---

[37] Eckhart Tolle, *The Power of Now* (New World Library, 1999), 13.

The global warming/climate change debate has been controversial recently. At some point, ample evidence will show that one side in the debate is wrong. But the triumph will be frustrating to the side whose views are proven closer to the truth, because the side that was wrong will never admit it. It is likely that no matter what the objective truth is regarding climate change, some people on both sides of the debate will never change their minds and will die still believing that the events that they have witnessed have justified their cherished beliefs. We need to believe we are right and good.

Twisting Reality Inhibits Self-Improvement

As I hope I have demonstrated, we can never objectively take in information. We are too biased. To help us conform to our schema, our minds keep us ignorant. We ignore or alter our perceptions so that we feel more self-assured of our schemas. But by filtering and altering, we are also inhibiting self-improvement. We prefer to remain oblivious to the differences between our schema and reality because changing our schema may lead to us being rejected from the group. And to feel a sense of belonging is paramount. And even more threatening is that without our schema, we lose our sense of self. So, our schemas, which function to help us get along in the world comfortably, serve at the same time to inhibit us from improving ourselves. We often do not see that we are in the wrong; we do not see that we could have done things better.

Wrapping It Up

- We tend to evaluate ourselves and humanity from our personal perspective, which can lead to a skewed understanding of reality. An external perspective (albeit imagined) can be inciteful.

- Individuals have conflicting beliefs which work at cross purposes, inhibiting any real progress. Goals and values often conflict, and we base our schemas on these. This internal conflict results in our wasting our lives and energies—and we never achieve our goals.

- Societies usually have the same problem. Different sectors working against each other, not in alignment, leads to stagnation.

- Because we are the most intelligent species on the planet, we fool ourselves into believing that we can understand ourselves, the world and our place in it. This is arrogance, the kind you see in Greek tragedies.

- A schema is a belief system that shapes our worldview and influences our decision-making and actions.

- Our inability to develop an accurate understanding of the world is based in our tight connection to our flawed schemas. We filter and interpret information to reinforce our schemas. Ideology makes us dumb.

- The need to maintain our schemas inhibits personal growth, as we tend to ignore or alter perceptions to avoid confronting the uncomfortable truth that we don't know as much as we thought we did, or even worse, that we may be wrong.

Essay 3
The New Religion of Science Falls Short

There are two types of theories, those that have been falsified and those that have yet to be falsified.
— Richard Feynman

The Promise of Science

During the Scientific Revolution of the seventeenth and eighteenth centuries, it was commonly thought that the application of the scientific method and rational thinking fostered the progress of humanity. What a breath of fresh air that was, as compared to the previous centuries where Christian dogma stifled human thought.

As science has developed and delivered, we continue to look today to our rational minds and our science to pave the way forward for the salvation of mankind. Rather than treat our lives as waiting stations for the salvation of the afterlife, we have come to believe that science can bring heaven to our daily lives. And to a degree, that has been true.

According to Auguste Comte, a French philosopher, mankind had in his time mastered the sciences one by one, progressing from the easiest to the more difficult: mathematics first, then astronomy, physics, chemistry, biology. And only one more was left to be mastered, the most difficult, and that was the science of social phenomena, which he termed "social physics" and which today we call sociology. Comte felt that social physics was to be the queen of all sciences.

It is said that Comte was among the first to develop theories of social evolution. He claimed that humanity was on an evolutionary path, progressing from theology, where everything was attributed to the gods and later to monotheism and then to metaphysics, where ideals were held to be most high (such as *liberté, égalité, fraternité).* But there was no scientific proof that ideals such as liberty or equality were worth striving for. The metaphysics stage was an advancement though, because at least people were questioning and thinking. In Comte's system, the last step was the scientific stage, where man's institutions and shared beliefs would be based on known facts. It was this stage that Comte sought to usher into the world. And it did come to pass. We now believe that reality is based on known facts; except, as our discussion of schema demonstrated, beliefs don't often square with facts.

The Great Progress of Science

Entering Comte's scientific stage has clearly brought us great benefits. If you could imagine what life was like only a few hundred years ago and then compare it to what is like today, for us, the changes are incredible.

Even in this present age of negativity, a few have been shining a light on the progress that humanity has experienced. Steven Pinker demonstrated the great progress of humanity in his book of graphs, entitled *Enlightenment Now: The Case for Reason, Science, Humanism and Progress.*[38] The visionary Peter Diamandis writes along similar lines, highlighting

____

[38] Steven Pinker, *Enlightenment Now: The Case for Reason, Science, Humanism and Progress* (Penguin, 2018).

humanity's progress and how we should be excited for the future.[39] Our lives are exponentially easier than they were 200 years ago, and much of this is due to applications of scientific knowledge.

Take a look: Over the past 200 years, the world GDP has shot up 100 times. This means, we are all on average 100 times richer than we were 200 years ago. The graph below depicts the world's output per person over the past 2,000 years (not accounting for wars, famine and disease).[40]

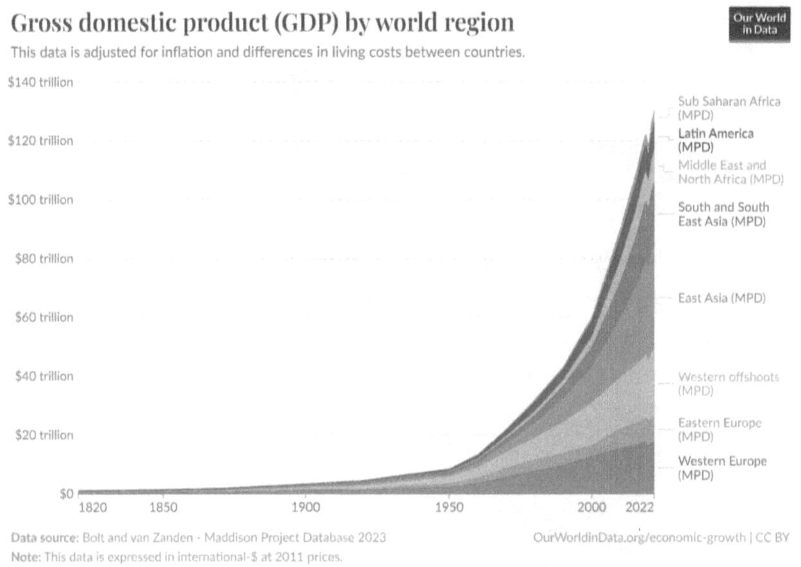

The world's average life expectancy has skyrocketed over the past 300 years. 200 years ago, average life expectancy in the UK was about forty; while in 2017, it hovered around eighty. In India and South Korea the change is even more dramatic.[41]

---

[39] Peter H. Diamandis, "The World Is (Still) Better Than You Think," Oct. 10, 2017, diamandis.com/blog/the-world-is-still-better-than-you-think, accessed June 2024. Diamandis's graphs came from the extraordinary website, ourworldindata.org, also accessed in June 2024. The site continues to update the graphs as new data comes in.

[40] Ourworldindata.org/grapher/gdp-world-regions-stacked-area, accessed April 2025.

[41] Ourworldindata.org/life-expectancy, accessed April 2025.

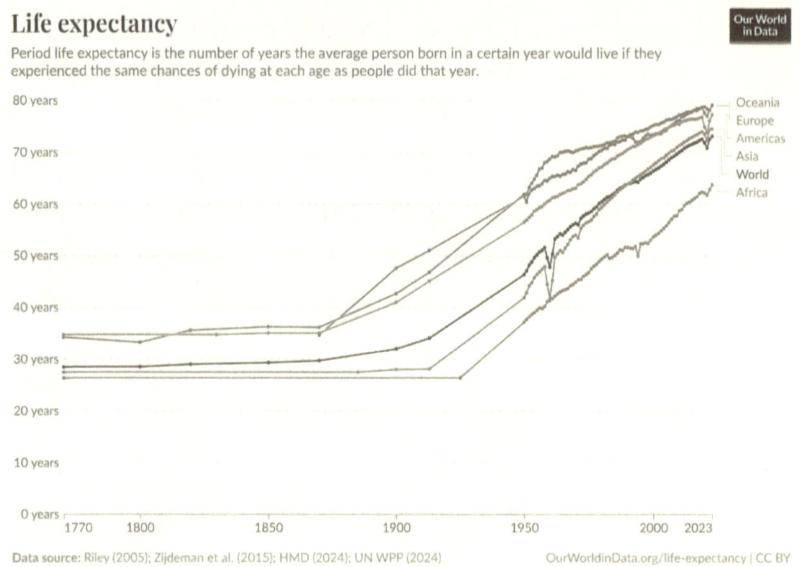

The homicide rate of Western Europe has dropped dramatically throughout the centuries. (The United States homicide rate is higher than Western Europe, but even the U.S. homicide rate has dropped recently.)[42]

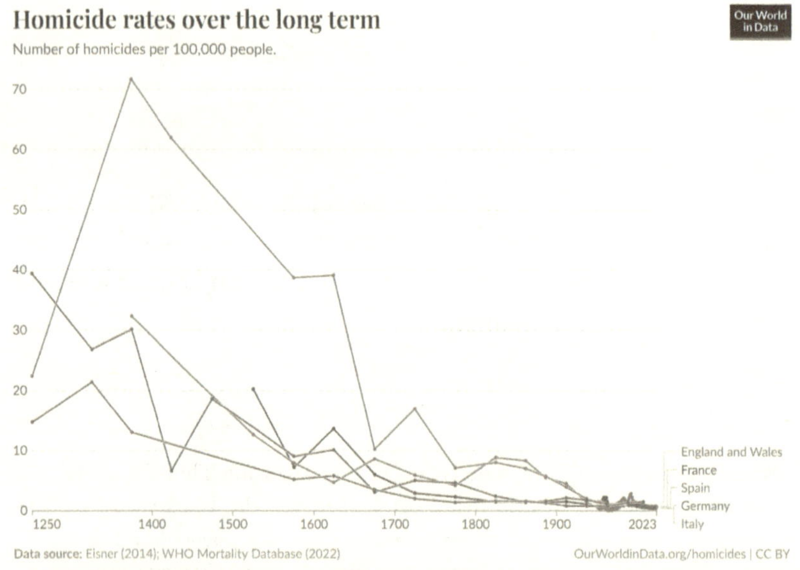

---

[42] Graph is available here, accessed April 2025: https://ourworldindata.org/grapher/homicide-rates-across-western-europe.

The global death rate from natural disasters, including famine, has also plummeted, most likely due to better building standards to protect from earthquakes; better agricultural methods, refrigeration, international cooperation and transportation of food to protect from famine; and early warning systems to protect from flooding. All of this is due to the application of scientific advancements.[43]

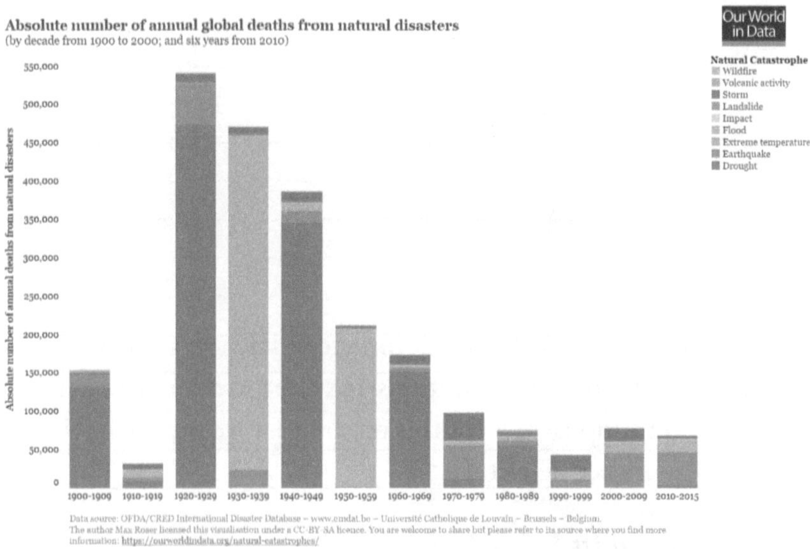

Fewer and fewer of us are now subjected to starvation due to better agricultural methods, transportation and refrigeration, and international cooperation.[44]

---

[43] The graph format has changed in the past few years. I like the older one better, which is presented here. This version was accessible in April 2025 at diamandis.com/blog/the-world-is-still-better-than-you-think. The new version was available in April 2025 at ourworldindata.org/grapher/natural-disaster-death-rates.

[44] Diamandis.com/blog/the-world-is-still-better-than-you-think, accessed April 2025.

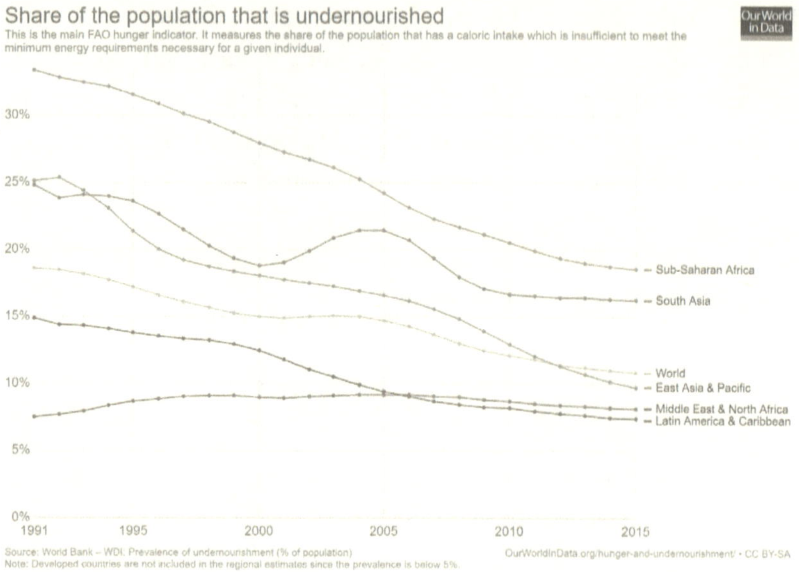

Nobody can deny that the development of science, along with the maturing of our political institutions, has enhanced our lives tremendously. And I suppose it is for this reason that we put such faith in science; it has indeed delivered.

Scientism and Its Priesthood

Centuries before the birth of Comte, the Medieval Church dominated the minds of the West. Today science dominates. Never before has a belief system had the success that science has, not just in materially enriching mankind but also in implanting itself as the dominant belief system of all of humanity. The Church was never as successful as science has become in forming the basis of our understanding of the world.[45] The Church never was dominant in parts of Asia and Africa. Today Scientism is the chief religion of the entire world, with scientists as our priests—to the extent that even many of the religious have greater faith in science than in religion. This is what Francis Bacon (1561–1626) hoped for in his *New Atlantis*, where a scientific priesthood would make

---

[45] Rupert Sheldrake, *The Science Delusion (Coronet, 2013), 23.*

decisions for the good of the state. He envisioned a scientific priesthood linked to the state, like an established church of science.[46] Comte had a similar dream, except Comte's leaders would be experts in social physics.

We have something like that now. The state and corporations fund most scientific research today. It is no longer done by unaffiliated individuals like Newton or Leibniz. George Sarton (1884–1956), a historian of science, wrote:

> *Truth can be determined only by the judgement of experts . . .everything is decided by a small group of men. . .The people have nothing to say but simply to accept the decisions handed out to them. Scientific activities are controlled by universities, academies and scientific societies, but such control is as far removed from popular control as it possibly could be.*[47]

This situation reminds me of the old days of the Church. We have replaced the high priests of the Church with the high priests of science. In the medieval period, only the clergy could read the Bible. The rest were illiterate. Only the clergy knew what was in the Bible. Only the clergy decided what God wanted to tell the people. The people were told what to believe, and the great majority complied, many out of fear of punishment, physical or spiritual.

Today, modern scientific knowledge is deeply specialized, with scientists within each field understanding complex truths, while the rest of us have simplified and often distorted understandings. Today, only quantum physicists have a deep understanding of string theory and only epidemiologists understand how diseases mutate and spread. Some scientists write books in simple language for the people, so we can learn about the universe. They tell us what to believe, and we are just as gullible now as we were 1,000 years ago. It appears nothing has

---

[46] Sheldrake, *The Science Delusion*, 14–15.

[47] Tom Chivers, "Neuroscience, Free Will and Determinism: I'm Just a Machine," *Daily Telegraph*, Oct 12, 2010, in Sheldrake, *The Science Delusion*, 16.

changed really. The "truth" is still known by just a few, and we rely on the priests to enlighten us.

We Rely on Science to Determine What is True

A very common unstated and unnoticed postulate most of us share is that if science cannot validate our beliefs, then our beliefs must not be true. For most of us, this is part of our schema. Comte took it further saying if something was not verifiable through science, then there was no point even thinking about it. This matches one unwritten postulate of science—if science cannot prove it, it is not true. "God doesn't exist, because you cannot prove it." "There is no such thing as ghosts" because we cannot prove their existence using experiments.

Some people who are open to such controversial ideas as telepathy, the existence of the soul or even God will often attempt to justify their beliefs using scientific evidence. The fact that they require science to prove supernatural phenomena to themselves demonstrates how fundamental science is to their belief systems. If you can rationalize it using science—only then is it okay to believe.

Here is an example: in 1907 Duncan MacDougall, a physician, published a paper about his experiment where he weighed bodies before and after death to test his hypothesis that souls have weight. One of the six bodies he measured[48] lost twenty-one grams at death. He concluded that the human soul does weigh something. Many of us have incorporated this study into our schema. If a scientific study showed that bodies weigh less after death than before death, then the soul must be physical and real. In our minds, science has proved it so. And, therefore, it is okay then to believe that souls exist.

Science has become most people's justification to believe whatever they want to believe. What they are not recognizing is that they are assuming that "science" is the only valuable method of determining what is true

---

[48] MacDougall wrote in his research report that he based his conclusion on "one of the six" bodies he tested losing weight, not on every one of the six as one might expect.

and what is false. If scientists say there is a soul, then people believe that it must be true. Do you see the assumption they are making there? The postulate? They are assuming that science is the great and only determiner of truth.

People are generally not aware of the implicit assumptions they are making when they "reason" something out. By unconsciously accepting science as the great determiner of what is true, people are tricked into believing that the world is mechanical and predictable—whereas the world is vaster than that. It has many elements that we cannot perceive or comprehend. Some things are just unpredictable. For example, can we predict how the flame of a fire will look in any one moment? I don't think so. The world is just what it is. Nevertheless, we try to neatly package the world around us with our overly simplistic science-based schemas, even though there is so much that science just cannot address.

Science and Its Theories

At its root, a theory is a conceptual device we use to unify a large number of observations into a convenient, understandable package that our minds can grasp. Theories usually go beyond what is observed in order to bring together a coherent, elegant description of reality. Theories are really powerful explainers of our world; but theory construction is based on not only a collection of facts, data and observations, but some imagination as well.

In the same way that our minds are a tool that we can use to understand or manipulate our world, science is a tool that humankind can use for the same purposes—to understand and manipulate our world. Science is based on observation and from these observations come theories and laws. And it is from these theories and laws that we form our collective view of the world, our collective schema.

We unconsciously take these scientific theories as statements of fact, when, in fact, they are not. They are theories. Theories are not statements of truth; but we unthinkingly assume that they are. We do not know that the Big Bang Theory is true. We do not know that the Theory of Evolution is true. We do not know that global warming is created by mankind. These are all theories that have a lot of data to back them up. But that doesn't make them true. This is important, because a large part of the Western World's collective schema today is based on scientific theories—just as our schema used to be based on theological beliefs, what Comte would call superstition.

Scientific Fallibility

H. L. Mencken (1880–1956), the infamous American columnist of the depression era, respected chemists but had no admiration for mathematicians or physicists. According to Mencken, if the chemistry community could not explain something, they would keep experimenting until they found a solution. On the other hand, mathematicians and physicists, when confronted with an unsolvable riddle, would instead devise far-fetched theories that could neither be proven or disproven by physical experiment. We then take that for science, and we consider their theories as authoritative truth. Without thinking too much about it, we adopt their unprovable theories as part of our schema.

Wait! That contradicts what Comte said: if you cannot prove it, don't bother with it. But no, our modern way is: if you don't understand something, then make up a theory.

The Big Bang Theory

The Big Bang Theory is considered truth by most people in the West. It has been defended as unquestionable truth by the vast majority of cosmological theorists for decades. Leading scientists, no, nearly all known scientists, believe it. Devised in 1931, the Big Bang Theory tells us that the entire universe was once a single point and 14 billion years ago it exploded for some reason and matter is still shooting outward from that massive explosion. This explains why our scientific instruments detected a red shift when viewing astronomical bodies far away.

The problem with the Big Bang Theory is that it is not certain truth. It is a theory. It cannot be proven nor disproven by observation or experiment. We cannot reproduce the big bang. But if the theory is true, then certain observations should follow. And many have. But other observations have contradicted the theory's predictions, and scientists have had to patch up the theory. This isn't true science but rather attempts to salvage long-held speculative ideas. Eventually, these conjectures collapse, only to be replaced by new, equally unprovable notions.

Logically, most theories are just as valid as a belief in God, aliens or reincarnation. We can use the existence of God, aliens or reincarnation to explain various things we have experienced in the world. But just like the Big Bang Theory, we have been unable to prove their existence using observation and experiment. Just because something is a good explanation does not mean that it is truth. Yet, we have been taught by society that it *is* truth; and we passively believed it, as we do all scientific pronouncements.

Falsification of Data

Think back to your physics labs in high school. I am sure you remember how frustrating it was that the results of your experiments never worked as neatly as the physics equations said they should. I am sure all of us were tempted at some point to change our experimental results. I was. If we didn't outright change the data, we might have been tempted to discard some results and conduct more tests to get an outcome that more closely aligned with the equations. At the time we were only trying to achieve good grades or do what was expected of us.

Professional scientists have a much bigger stake. Their reputations, their funding and their livelihoods depend on their results. So what happens if their experiments are giving answers that are contrary to "known" theories? What does that mean about them as researchers? Are they sloppy in their work? Why should anyone fund them or employ them if they cannot do experiments right? So, what do they do with this questionable data? Do they throw out the results from the worst test runs and keep doing tests until they get data that seems right? Do they make a few changes to the data? Nobody would know.

So, the problem with science is that it is conducted by humans who are not gods but are fallible and weak like the rest of us. It is difficult for scientists to get funding, to get published, to achieve prestige. Success involves fitting into a discipline's scientific community and avoiding appearing stupid in front of colleagues. Research that does not fit accepted beliefs may not be published, may meet increased scrutiny and ridicule and may deem one unfit for further grants. Scientists publish only a small percentage of their experimental data. According to Rupert Sheldrake (1942–), a British scientist himself, it may be as little as 5% to 10%.

> *Scientists are more likely to publish their 'best' results, rather than negative or inconclusive findings...In addition, scientific journals are often unwilling to publish negative results.*[49]

This means that scientists are not always sharing the whole truth of their work, but often a prettified set of data that fits known conventional thinking or desired results. Just like we did in high school physics class.

The Speed of Light has Varied

Science isn't always clear-cut and convenient. Often the data is a jumbled mess. Early measurements of the speed of light varied to a large degree; but by 1927, the scientific community had agreed on the speed of light at 299,796 kilometers per second. A leading authority at the time concluded, "The present value [of the speed of light] is entirely satisfactory, and can be considered more or less permanently established." Between 1928 and 1945, experiments in laboratories around of the world were showing that the speed of light had dropped by 20 kilometers per second, with experimental data by the most respected researchers coming in very close to each other. And then in the late 1940s, experiments were showing that the speed of light increased by

---

[49] Sheldrake, *The Science Delusion*, 308.

20 kilometers per second, and a new consensus was derived around this higher value. Two possibilities arise from this story. Either the speed of light varies and is not a fixed constant or human experimenters were willing to discard questionable data and adjust data to agree with the data from the more reputable experimenters. Isn't that reminiscent of the study participants faced with gun control facts that didn't support their mindsets. How else could consensus be reached like this? In 1976, to avoid further embarrassment, the authorities fixed the speed of light by definition.[50]

The takeaway: scientists are human and, as a result, fallible, which means science is itself fallible. Humans are the weakest link. Science would be more effective if it were produced by gods, not men and women.

Scientific Realism vs. Scientific Instrumentalism

For the lay person, our simplistic approach to science has been: if it works, it must be true. If our scientific experiments and our engineering successes are based on a theory and we have yet to see an exception to the theory, then it must be true. I believe this is how most people view science. Some astrophysicists have witnessed light bending around galaxies; therefore, Einstein's space time curvature of space must be true.[51] Even though we couldn't get our high school physics experiments to work, we know Newtonian physics works because we were able to land a man on the moon. That should be proof enough. This school of thought I have just described is called Scientific Realism.

On the other hand, the Scientific Instrumentalists claim that theories are really nice tools we use to organize our experiences and make predictions about future experiences, but they are not literal claims about what is true or false. The famous philosopher, Bishop George Berkeley (1685–1753)

---

[50] Sheldrake, *The Science Delusion*, *92, 298.*

[51] I am not questioning the theory per se. Other observations also conform to the theory, such as deviations in Mercury's orbit from Newtonian physics, gravitational waves that are ripples in space time and other phenomena.

claimed that the function of scientific theorizing was not to explain the world but to organize our experiences in convenient packages.[52]

Most scientists recognize that scientific theories are hypothetical and may be proven false. The theories may happen to be true, but we really cannot know whether they are true or not.[53]

The Bankruptcy of Science Arguments

If you take the long view of things, it is likely that most of what we believe today will seem like nonsense 500 years from now. We are always changing what we choose to believe. Theories come and go, and other theories and beliefs replace them. So, what makes us think we finally have a hold on the truth now? This churning of theories doesn't stop. For as long as mankind continues to breathe, every generation will create a new set of theories and beliefs, discarding those of their parents. That is just how it is. If you can take this long view, then maybe you can see how silly it is to have a strong confidence in what has been "accepted" as true by the scientific community.

I just recently learned that my objection to unquestioning acceptance of scientific theories is not new. This controversy was raging around the turn of the twentieth century in Paris. In 1893, the famous Russian novelist Leo Tolstoy wrote:

> *Does not each year produce its new scientific discoveries, which after astonishing the boobies of the whole world and bringing fame and fortune to the inventors, are eventually admitted to be ridiculous mistakes even by those who promulgated them?...Unless then our century forms an exception (which is a supposition we have no right to make), it needs no great boldness to conclude by analogy that among the kinds of knowledge occupying the attention of our learned men*

---

[52] Yuri Balashov and Alex Rosenberg, *Philosophy of Science, Contemporary Readings* (Routledge, 2002), 194.

[53] "Scientific Progress," Stanford Encyclopedia of Philosophy, plato.stanford.edu/entries/ scientific-progress/#ProVsDev, accessed January 1, 2023.

and called science, there must necessarily be some which will be regarded by our descendants much as we now regard the rhetoric of the ancients and the scholasticism of the Middle Ages.[54]

In 1900, the brilliant French polymath Henri Poincare defined the problem at the International Congress of Physics in Paris.

> *The people of world are struck to see how ephemeral scientific theories are. After some years of prosperity, they see them successively abandoned; they see ruins accumulated on ruins; they predict that the theories in fashion today will quickly succumb in their turn, and they conclude that they are absolutely futile. This is what they call the bankruptcy of science.*[55]

So I wonder, if scientific theories are just hypothetical and temporary, why do we base our beliefs on them? Why have we made scientific theories the central tenant of our worldview and why do we use them to define who we are? It has become just this for a great many of us. We do not realize to what extent science has replaced the Catholic Church in providing much of the foundation of our collective understanding of the world. In the past, people would be aghast if you stated that Christ was not God but was instead a divinely inspired man. You would be shunned, tortured or perhaps executed as a heretic if you spread those blasphemous thoughts. It is similar today with regards to science. In much of Western society, if someone professed that evolution is a fanciful theory and is not true or, even better, that the Earth does not rotate around the sun, you would be considered an idiot and would likely be shunned as ignorant or crazy.

This comparison of religion yesterday and science today is not new. Tolstoy wrote,

---

[54] Leo Tolstoy, "Non-Acting," *Essays and Letters* (Grant Richards, 1903), 105.

[55] "Realism and Theory Change in Science," *Stanford Encyclopedia of Philosophy*, trans. from the French, stanford.edu/entries/realism-theory-change, accessed January 1, 2022.

> *The greater part of what is called religion is simply the superstition of past ages; the greater part of what is called science is nothing but the superstition of today. And I suppose that the proportion of error and of truth is much about the same in the one as in the other.*[56]

We forget, or perhaps, we never even considered that these scientific theories are just theories. Some are good theories, as we haven't been able to disprove them. But they are not statements of fact.

Galileo's Great Leap of Faith

Let's consider Galileo Galilei (1564–1642) for a moment. The popular story is that Galileo was persecuted by the Church for introducing his heliocentric theory. His theory really did require a huge leap of faith for people of that time. The existing Ptolemaic model seemed to work just fine for understanding and forecasting the planets' behavior, as far as most people were concerned. But Galileo's theory was simpler to use. It was more elegant. Still the big problem with it was that he said that the Earth moved around the Sun. Nobody had witnessed the Earth move, but all had seen the Sun and planets "move." So why would anyone want to believe Galileo's theory? Any person with common sense could see it was utter rubbish. This new idea flew in the face of everything people had observed and believed throughout history. Galileo's theory required people to abandon what was obviously true in favor of an abstract and absurd theory. The Church asked Galileo to state that his theory was not the truth, per se, but rather a useful characterization that allows for easier prediction of the motions of the planets. If he said that, they would leave him alone; but Galileo refused to accept this Instrumentalist view of his theory and suffered house arrest for the remainder of his life.[57] He said his theory was true, but it was not true. It was a theory, and we may still decide it is no longer valid at some point.

---

[56] Tolstoy, 107.

[57] Balashov and Rosenberg, 194.

String Theory and M-Theory

Even some ardent atheists will occasionally take this Instrumentalist view of scientific theories. Stephen Hawking in his and Leonard Mlodinow's 2010 book, *The Grand Design*, describes some of the more fanciful (albeit commonly accepted) theories of physics, String Theory and M Theory, about which he is quoted saying,

> *Each theory may have its own version of reality, but. . .that is acceptable so long as the theories agree in their predictions whenever they overlap, that is, whenever they can both be applied.*[58]

This is what the Church was telling Galileo, after all. As long as his theories overlapped with the accepted Catholic teachings, his theories were acceptable. Hawking's reasoning is consistent with the old Church's view that we routinely disparage.

String theories and M-theories are currently untestable, so their accuracy can be determined only by comparing them to other models. This is what our greatest minds are busying themselves with?

According to Hawking,

> *M-theory has solutions that allow for different universes with different apparent laws, depending on how the internal space is curled. M-theory has solutions that allow for many different internal spaces, perhaps as many as 10^{500}, which means it allows for 10^{500} different universes, each with its own laws.*[59]

Just for those of us who are reading quickly, let me tell you, 10^{500} means a 10 with 500 zeros after it.[60] It's quite a lot.

---

[58] Stephen Hawking and Leonard Mlodinow, *The Grand Design* (Bantam Books, 2010), 117, in Sheldrake, *The Science Delusion*, 10–11.

[59] Hawking and Mlodinow, 119, in Sheldrake, *The Science Delusion*, 11.

[60] To gauge this number, 10^{50} seconds would be 3.17×10^{42} years. The universe is estimated to be 13.8×10^{9} years.

I don't know how many of my friends throughout the years have tried to convince me to read books on String Theory and other speculative physics, thinking that somehow this would get me closer to the truth that I was seeking. I would never read those books. I am not a fan of scientific speculation. I would rather read science fiction.[61]

Because string theory and M-theory are untestable, they can never be invalidated. Innately, some of us, like H. L. Mencken and Tolstoy, have always known that the theories are all fanciful intellectual foolishness, consisting of nothing but intensely misguided intellectualization by some of the most intelligent people on the planet.

Pursuing such dead ends is nothing new, by the way. For centuries, the most intelligent minds of Western Europe, including Isaac Newton, Tyco Brahe and Robert Boyle, spent countless hours on alchemy, trying to convert baser metals into gold. Although many alchemists have claimed to have successfully achieved this, today it is commonly believed they were con men. James Price (1752–1783), an English alchemist and member of the Royal Society, claimed to have converted mercury into gold. He performed the process seven times in front of witnesses and even presented the resulting gold to King George III. The Royal Society remained skeptical and asked him to perform the process before them. Months passed as Price prepared the materials for the process. Only three members of the Royal Society appeared for the demonstration. After welcoming them, Price drank a flask of poison he had prepared and collapsed onstage and died.[62]

At least many of the fraudulent alchemists knew they were frauds. That is not to say the physicists who expound on String and M theories are frauds; they are merely misguided. To be wrong or possibly wrong is a

---

[61] As I see it, science fiction is much preferable. Upfront about its speculative nature, it often delves into thought-provoking social commentary and it sometimes even anticipates real-world scientific advancements.

[62] This doesn't prove that all alchemists were frauds, or even that Mr. Price was. But most secrets see the light of day and become common knowledge. You would think the secret of producing gold, if real, would have been divulged by now.

right we all share. What these speculative physicists and the alchemists do have in common is that in both cases we have the most brilliant among us wasting their talents and years of their lives on efforts that will lead nowhere. The churchmen of the Early Middle Ages did the same thing, contriving arcane theological theories and justifications for these theories, none of which could be proven and many of which were later abandoned. Nothing is new under the sun.

Countering the Bankruptcy of Scientific Argument

To this point, I have been poking at scientific theories because they are not necessarily true but are accepted as true by most of us. We live our lives assuming we know things, when for the most part, we are mostly mistaken. We just don't know.

On the other hand, some have a more nuanced approach to theories. They admit that scientific theories are approximations but contend that they are generally good ones. They understand that theories are not truth. Typically, scientific theories are replaced after centuries when new experiments or observations reveal their limitations. But from this refined viewpoint of theories being to some degree correct, their eventual obsolescence is not a problem; because despite their unprovability, newer theories move us closer to the truth. We will never hit the truth; but that doesn't matter because we are always zeroing in on it. It is almost like Zeno's Dichotomy Paradox. Suppose you are trying to go somewhere. You go halfway and rest. Then you go half the remaining distance and rest, and this process continues. You will never get there because there is always a halfway point to rest at before you arrive at your destination. This is like science, I suppose, with each new theory we get a little closer, but never quite there. That's how some see it.

I guess you can call this perspective about science a theory, the Theory of Scientific Progress. If you try to look it up, you won't find it, as it hasn't been put forth as a theory. Academics might call it a philosophic outlook. But it is a theory and it is believed by many, just not named. Still, as Richard Feynman said, "It doesn't matter how beautiful your theory is, it doesn't matter how smart you are. If it doesn't agree with experiment, it's wrong."[63] If I believe Feynman is right, then I have to conclude that this Theory of Scientific Progress is wrong.

Why? because it is true sometimes new scientific theories really do lead us astray. A case in point may be String Theory. String theorists believe that the fundamental units in the universe are strings, not particles. And these strings are not just smaller facsimiles of that white stuff that cats play with. No. A string is a metaphorical representation of the fundamental unit. A string has an elongated one-dimensional nature and vibrates at different frequencies, which gives rise to various properties like gravity, mass or charge. But that is as far as I go; it is getting too dense for me. I don't know string theory. I am not convinced you should either, and I am going to stop describing it before I make a fool of myself.

Let's assume for a moment that string theory is a fantasy. If so, where did it get us? What did it replace? Well, before string theory, the Standard Model viewed matter as fundamental particles like quarks and leptons. If string theory is finally rejected in the future, we will then go back to the idea of fundamental units being particles. So then, if proven false, the string theory will have been a diversion, because we will be back where we started. The theory will not have gotten us any closer to the truth, but instead led us astray and actually wasted our best minds for decades.

But, even that is not so simple. Nothing ever is. String theory is only a theory and there are competing theoretical frameworks in modern theoretical physics. It is not as if all the theoretical physicists are string theory believers, just many of the most vocal ones. What I am trying to get across is that every commonly accepted theory is not necessarily truer than the one it replaced.

---

[63] Richard Feynman, *The Character of Physical Law* (Massachusetts Institute of Technology, 1965), 156.

Lamarckian vs. Mendelian

Here is an example of a theory that not only led us astray but people's adherence to it led to catastrophe.

First some background. Like in other sciences, the theories of genetic evolution evolved from one theory to the next. Lamarckian theory was introduced in the late eighteenth century and was popular into the early nineteenth century. The Mendelian theory became popular in the mid-nineteenth century, for the most part replacing Lamarckism, and it remains popular today.

Both theories held that living organisms pass on traits from generation to generation. The earlier theory, the Lamarckian theory, held that individuals develop new traits in one lifespan can pass these acquired traits onto succeeding generations. For example, if a dog was trained to catch frisbees by his owner and the dog became a grand champion frisbee catcher, the dog's offspring would inherit this new frisbee catching skill. Conversely, traits that were not used could be lost in succeeding generations.

The later theory, the Mendelian theory, held that acquired traits have no effect on succeeding generations. The amount of use or underuse of a trait has no effect on later generations. Instead, organisms pass only genetic traits from generation to generation. And, of course, mutations and natural selection play a role. This is the same stuff you were taught in school. The champion frisbee-catching dog's offspring wouldn't be any better at frisbee catching than those of any other dog except to the extent the offspring might have inherited physiology from the parent that helps with catching frisbees.

After World War II, even though the Mendelian theory was the predominant paradigm of genetics, the Soviets re-embraced a form of Lamarckism. Trofim Lysenko (1898–1976), a Soviet agronomist, managed to successfully promote his version of Lamarckism, and his theories were supported by Stalin. Mendelism was rejected because it was considered a bourgeoisie science. About 3,000 Mendelians were dismissed from their positions and many were imprisoned for refusing to denounce any works that contradicted Lysenko's theories. Some geneticists were even executed.

Lysenko did not believe in genes. He believed that plants of the same class do not compete against each other. Instead, the plants work together to guarantee a good harvest of seeds for the next generation. Some plants, if necessary, are willing to die, so that the stronger plants can flourish (just like good socialists). For this reason, he suggested that seeds be planted very close to each other.

In 1928, Stalin began consolidating all of the farms of the nation into collective farms, forcing the peasants who lost their land to work on the collective farms. The results were not good. Many experienced farmers were forcibly relocated, marginalized and generally demoralized. Poor planning led to soil degradation and loss of viable farmland. Productivity decreased, causing food shortages and famine. Stalin then adopted Lysenko's methods, which exacerbated the problems. Some of his methods included tightly packing seeds together, pretreating seeds with cold, scraping seeds with sandpaper, preventing the use of pesticides and fertilizers.

It is believed that Lysenko's theories resulted in the Soviet famines that killed millions. The Chinese, under Mao, accepted Lysenko's theories, which apparently resulted in the Chinese famines of 1959 and 1962, which killed between fifteen and fifty-five million.

After Stalin's death in 1953, Lysenkoism slowly lost prestige in the Soviet Union until 1964, when it was finally condemned by the Soviet and international scientific communities. The Soviets then went back to Mendelism.

Science is Human

Science does not always close in on the truth, as previously noted. Science is human, and with humans you get interference from politics and money. Robert F. Kennedy, Jr. (1953–) made his career bringing lawsuits against large corporations primarily for polluting the environment. During an interview he said:

> *But scientists are corruptible. And the way that I can tell you that is that I've brought over 500...[lawsuits] and almost all of them involve scientific controversies. And there are scientists on both sides in every one. And when we sued Monsanto, on the Monsanto side, there was a Yale scientist, a Stanford scientist, and a Harvard scientist. And on our side, there was a Yale, Stanford and Harvard scientist. And they were saying exactly opposite things. In fact, there's a word for those kind [sic] of scientists who take money for their opinion, and the word is biostitutes. And they are very, very common. And I've been dealing them with them my whole career.[64]*

Kennedy experienced the impact of money on science. Pay the scientist and they will tell you what you want to hear. Isn't that what we see on both sides of the climate change debate? There are thousands of scientists on both sides of the controversy. Are they all speaking the truth?

Science has also become corporate. In the past, science was mostly supported through private patronage, or individual scientists paid for their research themselves. Galileo's work, for example, was funded mostly by wealthy patrons, including the Pope. Scientific discoveries today require more costly equipment and facilities. Science has become expensive. Today, for the most part, it is funded by corporations, government agencies, institutions and foundations. Scientists may be employees of corporations or may work for an institute and compete for grant funding. This unfortunate fusion of money and science leads to bias. If you are paid by your employer to prove that a new drug is safe and effective and you have a track record of proving new drugs are not safe or effective, soon you may be looking for a new position. If you are paid by the oil industry to disprove climate change, you better deliver or look

---

[64] "Robert F. Kennedy Jr., "CIA, Power, Corruption, War, Freedom, and Meaning," *Lex Fridman Podcast #388*, lexfridman.com/robert-f-kennedy-jr-transcript.

for another job. In a perfect world, with each new discovery, scientific theories would become more applicable to the world and science would lead us closer to the truth. But because science is tainted with money, we have less reason to believe its findings or put faith in it.

Political influence is even worse than financial influence. Lysenkoism was political. Either believe or suffer the consequences. Can you think of any scientific controversies that are clouded by politics today? Are there any science-based statements you think are untrue; but in the current political environment, you know it is best to keep silent?

This is much like what living under the Church was like in the fifth century. Speak out and be a martyr or keep silent and maintain your position, your possessions and your life. Do you think those high church officials who attended those church councils were all in earnest. Certainly, they must have included weak or wily ones who maintained their status by assenting to whatever was required of them. Is there one God or three Gods in One? Is climate change caused by humans or is it not? Does the COVID-19 vaccine prevent contracting the virus or does it not?

A Mechanistic Understanding of the Universe

The Enlightenment was a revolutionary era, mostly centered in eighteenth century France, where leading thinkers pushed the then-novel idea that people could think for themselves. After the great scientific discoveries of the previous century, Enlightenment thinkers felt emboldened to question the foundation of the existing order. People didn't need kings or the Church dictating what they could do and believe. Using reason, rather than tradition or the Bible as their basis of thought, famous thinkers such as Diderot, Voltaire, Kant, Rousseau, Adam Smith, Helvetius and others questioned and ridiculed the prevailing social order and beliefs. They promoted ideals such as reason, liberty, progress, individualism, religious tolerance, constitutional government and separation of church and state.

Their teachings were initially spread among the nobility and the growing middle classes in France, and eventually they were percolated throughout the rest of Western society. Their bold questioning built up the pressure on existing political and religious systems until they could no longer withstand it (remember the boiling water example). The old systems collapsed during the French and American Revolutions. The monarchy in France was overthrown, the Americans formed their republic, and the power of the Church was significantly diminished. These revolutions were a great step towards freedom. Thought indeed can be powerful. It just takes a while for lasting revolutionary change to occur.

Until the Enlightenment, people in the West used to believe that the universe was alive. It was animated by the Spirit of God. Based on the writings of Aristotle and, later, St. Thomas Aquinas, the universities and theologians taught that all plants and animals had souls and that the planets, the sun, and the stars were living beings.

The Enlightenment built on the discoveries of the previous century's Scientific Revolution. During the Scientific Revolution, the solar system came to be seen as a machine created by God, running on the Laws of Nature, which could be accurately described using mathematics. Galileo wrote,

> *When God produces the world, he produces a thoroughly mathematical structure that obeys the laws of number, geometrical figure and quantitative function. Nature is embodied in mathematical systems.*[65]

René Descartes (1596–1650) claimed that animals were machines that obeyed mathematical and physical laws. Much of the biological sciences and the medical establishment have latched onto this idea. In this mechanistic view, not only are animals machines, but people are too. Our decisions and actions are based on chemical reactions and neurological impulses in our brain. Francis Crick (1916–2004), who

---

[65] Francis Crick in Sheldrake, *The Science Delusion*, 31.

won a Nobel Prize for the discovery of the structure of DNA, in his book *Of Molecules and Men* explained that "the ultimate aim of the modern movement in biology is in fact to explain all biology in terms of physics and chemistry."[66]

According to adherents of this mechanistic view of the world, the soul doesn't even exist anymore. It never did. They assert the only reality is material reality, and material reality obeys the laws of physics and chemistry. Many people today see the world this way.

Love is Chemistry, Not Magic

Just about all of us have unthinkingly accepted a materialistic world-view. We were born into it. We see animals and plants, the world, the stars and planets as purely mechanical and chemical entities. Many of us today believe humans are machines, our behavior determined by chemical reactions and micro-biological processes. People have made science the fundamental tenant of our current Western schema, robbing life of its beauty.

I remember a plane ride sitting next to a physicist who was a very enthusiastic proponent of the mechanistic basis of everything. He was so kind, upbeat and cheerful that I had a hard time telling him that I believed that life was magical, which I define as "not being verifiable or testable by science." I told him materialists like himself were missing out on the magic of life. Everyone should read the Romantics (just don't ask how they died). We should all get lost in beautiful paintings or dance performances. He hated that word "magic." I asked him about love, "Mr. Science, how do you explain love?" He proceeded to explain that love is merely a chemical reaction.

Unbeknownst to me at the time, plenty of research backs this up. A researcher studied small mammals that mate for life and found that if you inject the female with oxytocin, she will bond with the nearest male available. For males, he found that vasopressin provides the same

---

[66] Crick in Sheldrake, *The Science Delusion*, 45.

effect.[67] Apparently, this research applies to humans as well. That is not what I wanted to read.

A Swedish researcher found that there is an AVPR1A gene in some human males that restricts the effect of vasopressin in men, and these males are less likely to be married, more likely to have problems in their marriages when they are married, and are less loving than other men.[68] One can conclude from this that our actions may be predetermined by chemistry.

Questioning the Mechanistic View

What does this mean? That our actions are predestined based on our genes and chemical processes within us? That the me inside me has no say in my fate or decisions? That there is no magic in our lives? No magic in love? Just like Mr. Science, you can use this mechanical understanding of the world to derive other soulless conclusions, such as human history and even human evolution itself are random and are not progressing towards any positive end. According to mechanistic adherents, *life has no meaning at all*. And they are content to view the world this way.

But we are not machines. Nor are animals or plants machines. Machines are created by others. Machines do not grow from eggs or spores. Machines do not reproduce. Machines do not regrow injured parts.

---

[67] Z. R. Donaldson and L. J. Young, "Oxytocin, vasopressin, and the neurogenetics of sociality," *Science,* Nov. 7, 2008, pubmed.ncbi.nlm.nih.gov/18988842.

[68] Hasse Walum, et al, "Genetic variation in the vasopressin receptor 1a gene (AVPR1A) associates with pair-bonding behavior in humans," *PNAS,* Sept. 16, 2008, pnas.org/content/pnas/105/37/14153.full.pdf, and "Love is a Chemical Reaction, Scientists Say," *PBS News,* Feb. 13, 2009, pbs.org/newshour/science/science-jan-june09-love_02-13.

Wrapping It Up

- In centuries past, Western thinking and societies were rooted in Christian theology. The way we think now is relatively new. We can thank the Scientific Revolution of the seventeenth century for freeing us from the chains of the Church.

- Science has delivered indeed. Our standards of living, our life expectancies, the number of murders per capital, everything has improved dramatically in the past few centuries, thanks to science.

- Our modern belief system is based on science now, based on "facts" rather than theology. The priests from medieval times have been replaced with the priests of science today.

- The general public relies on science as the ultimate determiner of truth.

- Scientific theories are not true. They are approximations that after a few hundred years or so will be replaced with other theories. Theories are stories we tell ourselves that seem to work until they don't.

- "Better" theories that replace outmoded theories are not always better. The path of science does not always point to better understanding.

- Science is corrupted by money and politics, which leads to biased findings. Scientists often prioritize the funders' agendas over truth. Only a small portion of actual results are ever published. Most are discarded as they do not match the objective of the funder. This interference of money and politics undermines science's ability to approach truth.

❦ The problem we have is that, since science has become the fountain of truth in Western society, we assume that whatever scientists tell us is true. We base our worldviews in part on scientific theories, which are, by definition, not true.[69]

❦ Anyone who questions the status quo scientific beliefs is considered mentally challenged and not a "serious person" by the smug adherents of science.

❦ It is easier to blindly accept the "truths" our scientific priesthood tells us than it is to challenge them. Most of us don't have the time or the intellectual chops to do so. And the opprobrium we would experience would be terrible. . .so we accept, at least outwardly.

❦ Finally, many or most scientists seem to be wed to the mechanistic view of the universe—everything can be explained by physics, chemistry and mathematics. This viewpoint strips the wonder from life. The universe and the living and the non-living things in it cannot be understood solely through the mechanistic view.

---

[69] Some people have issues with my claim that scientific theories are not "true." It comes down to what do they mean by "true." Apparently, the scientific puritans define true as "our best approximation of what is true backed by all sorts of evidence"; whereas, I define "true" as "that which really is true." I call that weak defense cognitive dissonance. What is true is what is true, not what we think is true. They bend words so that "true" no longer means "true."

Essay 4
The Illusion of Scientific Certainty

*We are here and it is now. Further than that, all human
knowledge is moonshine.*
— H. L. MENCKEN

Why Believe Science?

Although science is open to new measurable discoveries, not all
phenomena are measurable with the instruments we have at this
time. One hundred years ago, we did not know what we now know about
the universe, mostly due to the limitations of our tools and methods.
We know more now; but again, one hundred years from now, many of
our theories of astronomy and most other sciences will be discarded or
amended as we discover new information. So then, science can only
provide an incomplete understanding of the world around us. It is the
best we can do right now. Recognizing this, believers in science should
not be mocking those who think differently.

Here is an example. The discovery of radium in 1898 revealed gaps in
scientists' previous understanding of matter. As a result of this discovery,
scientific estimates of the age of the Earth had to be reformulated.
Up to that point, they had estimated the Earth's age based on the

conduction of heat. This heat method assumed that matter was completely understood and did not account for the fact that radium generates heat itself. Nobody knew at that time. Before the discovery of radium, any criticism of the estimated age of the earth based on the grounds that we do not understand all the properties of matter would have been mocked.[70]

Then there is the problem that we do not even understand wholly what we are studying. When Charles Hamilton Sorley delivered a set of Gifford Lectures in Scotland in 1914 and 1915, we knew much less about the structure of matter than we do now.

> *In physical science we pass from masses to particles, from particles to molecules, from molecule to atoms, from atoms to electrons. There we may be content to rest for the present—but only for the present. Atoms served for many centuries as the ultimate units...After only twenty years' familiarity with electrons, it is too soon to say that they are the ultimate units.[71]*

As Sorley predicted, science's understanding of the elemental particle continues to change, which means that, according to scientific belief itself, it has never been right. Up until 1910, the existence of atoms was still controversial, as they had not yet been observed. Even as late as the 1980s, the Standard Model of elemental particles, which had been formalized in the 1970s, was amended based on new discoveries like the W/Z bosons. So when can we say we have reached the ultimate elementary particle? It is entirely possible that there is no ultimate elementary particle. Who came up with the rule that there should be? If our greatest minds of science have been wrong for centuries, why would we think they should be right now? Or that they would ever be right?

---

[70] Charles Hamilton Sorley, *Moral Values and the Idea of God*, (Cambridge University, 1919), 244.

[71] Sorley, 245. In addition to the quotation, much of the thoughts in the following paragraphs are taken from this source.

Looking at science this way, how is it that so many people who have rooted their schemas in science are convinced that they understand the world because "the science is settled?" Basing our schemas on science is naïve, and there is so much more we are missing as a result.

Who Said We Should Be Able to Understand the World?

Over the centuries we have learned much about physics and chemistry and have improved our lives immensely as a result. Our knowledge has taken us far. But does it follow that we should be able to understand the world and our place in it? Many of us believe that the world should be explainable and understandable by science, if only we were given enough centuries to discover all of the laws of nature. Every year, we may get closer to the whole truth, but it doesn't follow logically that we should ever be able to understand the world correctly.

I know I have made this argument before, but I am going to make it again. I think I is important. It may be that the chimpanzee is the most intelligent animal in the zoo. Chimpanzees have excellent memory. They can use tools, and they have developed language skills. But just because the chimpanzee is the most intelligent, does it follow that the chimpanzee can build spaceships? If they are really smart, why would they live in the zoo and not in luxury hotels? They have not even created a printing press, they don't read books, and they are broke. I suppose, then, we can conclude that the smartest animal in the zoo maybe isn't so smart after all.

Aren't we, humankind, the smartest animal on the planet? We like to think so. The planet is just a bigger zoo. And just like the chimps, we are merely the smartest in the collection of species, but that does not mean, by default, that we can understand everything. Nonetheless, that is a conscious or unconscious postulate in most people's thinking. We are the smartest, therefore, we can understand the world given enough time for science to figure it out. This postulate is based on what? It is extrapolation of the worst kind.

We are just not wired right in our minds to understand the complexity of the world and our place in it. But who said we should be? We insist on there being a beginning and an ending to everything. We cannot comprehend something that just goes on forever and never ends and never started. It is unfathomable to us. How much is a half of infinity? Isn't that the same as infinity? How does that work? We just do not have the mental capacity to understand many things. It is in our mental wiring.

This is not a new idea, David Hume said this in the middle of the eighteenth century,

> *Everyone agrees—and the plainest observation and experience makes it obvious—that the capacity of the mind is limited, and can never attain a full and adequate conception of infinity.*[72]

As noted in a prior essay, it appears to me that the most intelligent among us place the most faith in our capacity to understand everything. To me, this seems not only foolish, but arrogant. Still, throughout the ages, our most brilliant minds have tried to solve the puzzle of existence.

Philosophy, the Precursor to Science

Initially, the effort to understand existence was attempted through philosophy, but then science became predominant and left philosophers rubbing their beards wondering why nobody listens to them anymore.

Philosophy, "the queen of the sciences," dates back as far as the written record. At least as long as people could write, they have been speculating, seeking to understand the universe and their place in it. Early philosophy contained what today we call philosophy but also rudimentary science, as well, because philosophy was, after all "the search for the truth." Before the rise of the scientific method and systematic experimentation, the physical world was understood based on observation and theoretical reasoning, not experimentation.

---

[72] David Hume, *A Treatise of Human Nature (1739)*, Book 1, part 2, section 2.

As scientific knowledge accumulated in the seventeenth century, different branches of the sciences broke off from philosophy, in the order in which they developed. First came mathematics, then astronomy, then physics, then anatomy, and the rest followed.

But first, let's take a quick look at philosophy.

Why is it that philosophy textbooks, or even the works of prodigious philosophers, often spend enormous amounts of time on the subject "what is philosophy?" Why do philosophers have to always be discussing the same things over and over, but with completely different views? For centuries philosophers were concerned about the simple question of whether we can perceive reality at all. As a child, I am sure you heard the question "What if our entire world is but an atom inside the fingernail of a giant monster?" I suppose it is possible. We can never know. We are limited in what we can know by the limitations of our senses and our minds.

So, philosophy can get frustrating if you look at it historically, since nobody seems to come up with a final answer. With so much disagreement, at first it seems impossible to believe that any advance in philosophy has occurred at any time throughout the centuries. Plato, who wrote 2,400 years ago, appears to have covered the important topics. How do you top that? Thinkers have attempted to, and many believe that Plato's thoughts had shortcomings, which have been to some degree addressed by subsequent philosophers.

One great difference between science and philosophy is that although scientists do disagree, scientists tend to build on the works of others. They take as proven the works of scientists who have come before them and take that knowledge further. Philosophers, on the other hand, often will ignore all the philosophical knowledge that has come before them and start afresh with a new perspective on the world. When new philosophers arrive on the scene, they often will develop a completely new system of thought, replacing all the others, starting from the beginning with rudimentary questions such as "What is knowledge?" or "What can we know?"

Many of the great philosophers believed that with their own system, a new era in thinking had begun and that they had found the final truth. Immanuel Kant wrote in the preface to his greatest work that from then on philosophy would be able to work as well as science had. But of course, that never happened. And just as scientists have many times in the past thought that they had discovered all there was to discover, only to be proven wrong, so have philosophers thought that they had resolved the problems of existence, only to be refuted by others that followed.

Root Problems with Science

Okay, so philosophy has its shortcomings. No surprise there. But let's get back to science. There are some inherent problems with science, and the problem is us.

Our Senses Are Limited

How can we claim to understand the world around us when we cannot even perceive what is out there? Bumblebees and butterflies can see ultraviolet. We cannot. Dogs and vultures can smell objects miles away. We cannot. The reality is that what animals experience is different from what we can perceive. We are missing a lot of what is out there. We have gaps in our senses, just as we have gaps between our fingers. Our limited perception means we are missing vast swaths of reality that other creatures routinely experience. This incomplete sensory picture severely constrains our understanding of the world around us.

What is worse is that we may not even be getting an accurate representation of what we do perceive. Science tells us that sounds are perceived by our senses as wave vibrations in the air around us, while colors are perceived from electromagnetic waves of light, and heat is perceived through temperature changes detected by our skin. Let's consider light. We register vibrations of 400 nanometers as blue; and 700 nanometers, as red. But no guarantee exists that just because something is radiating 400 nanometers it is actually blue in reality, beyond the veil of our senses. Maybe it just appears as blue to us. There may actually be no color in the universe, just different objects radiating different wavelengths. But we cannot know that.

And what we imagine as blue in our minds, may be completely different from what other people imagine as blue in theirs. We cannot see into their minds to know if our eyes are translating the vibrations in the same way as theirs—we just call them the same colors because we have been told that that thing there is blue. But I may be perceiving blue, while you may be perceiving what I would call green. It makes you think twice about art and how we seem to agree that some paintings are great and we disagree about others. Could part of this disagreement on art be that our senses are registering the colors in the paintings differently? Perhaps our vision is not as uniform or accurate as we assume.

Our mind also affects what we perceive through our eyes. When Isaac Newton was in his twenties, he was conducting experiments on light and color. As an experiment, he stared at the sun without looking away for three hours. (Now that's a serious scientist!) Well, actually, he was in a darkened room, so that his pupils would be fully dilated. He then, with one eye, stared in a mirror which was pointed at the sun. And he did it for three hours. After he stopped staring at the sun, when he looked at a dark wall with that one eye, he saw circles of color, which decayed in time and then vanished. Newton found that by actually trying to see the circles again,

> *intending my fancy upon them. . .I found, to my amazement, that they began to return, and by little and little to become as lively and vivid as when I had newly looked upon the sun. But when I ceased to intend my fancy upon them, they vanished again. After this, I found, that as often as I went into the dark and intended my mind upon them. . .I could make the phantasm return without looking any more upon the sun; and the oftener I made it return, the more easily I could make it return again. . .and, which is still*

> *stranger, though I looked upon the sun with my right eye only, and not with my left, yet my fancy began to make an impression upon my left eye, as well us upon my right. For if I shut my right eye, or looked upon a book, or the clouds, with my left eye, I could see the spectrum of the sun almost as plain as with my right eye.*[73]

Many years later, he was still able to bring back this phantasm of sight.

> *But now I have been very well for many years, though I am apt to think, if I durst venture my eyes, I could still make the phantasm return by the power of my fancy.*[74]

What does this mean? That his vision was partly fantasy? That he was able to conjure visions that were not there?

Many of us have unconsciously (not willfully, like Newton) seen things that were not there. Have you ever driven long hours late into the night? You know you need a break when your head nods, your eyes close momentarily, and you start seeing things that are not there. I have seen monsters, like the swamp thing, just appear on the side of road, lunging at the car. I don't believe these monsters exist. Instead, I know that when I am too tired, my eyes will probably trick me, just like Newton's eyes tricked him. Many people on LSD have reported seeing skeletons or animals staring back at them in the mirror. Some have had the horrible experience of watching themselves in the mirror age decades in mere seconds. The mind can play tricks on us, leading us to believe we are seeing things that are not in front of us.

Our perceptions then, may not reflect reality. According to science, our eyes detect light waves, which our brains interpret as objects, but these interpretations often differ from what really exists. Like grand theories such as the Big Bang, our sensory models are approximations—they are limited and fallible. We have no real understanding about the true

---

[73] "Letter from Isaac Newton to John Locke, June 30, 1691," *The Correspondence of Isaac Newton, 1688-1694,* ed. H.W. Turnbull (Cambridge University, 1961), 152–154.
[74] Newton in Turnbull.

nature of the world. Earlier philosophers recognized this problem and maintained that there was a veil between us and the world around us.[75]

Plato's famous Allegory of the Cave presents the problem very simply. Imagine that a group of men were imprisoned in a cave, anchored in place, facing a wall. Let's call this wall a projection screen. They were immobilized in such a way that they could only focus on the images cast upon the screen before them. Behind the men was a wall, and behind it there was a large fire which projected light onto the screen in front of the men. Between the fire and the wall people raised puppets that resembled men or other things. The shadows projected from the puppets were visible to the imprisoned men on the screen, but they could not see the shadows of the puppeteers themselves. The speaking and sounds of the puppeteers echoed off the cave walls, so that the imprisoned men thought the sounds were coming from the shadows on the projection screen. To these imprisoned men, the projections on the screen were the only reality they knew, as they had never seen anything else. They did not know that the images were only shadows of real objects. This allegory represents our inability to know the true world around us, bound as we are in our bodies and prevented from perceiving reality by the limitations of our senses.

René Descartes was a first-order seventeenth century mathematician, scientific thinker, and philosopher. His famous "I think therefore I am" essay from the early seventeenth century was treating just this subject. His basic question was how can we know anything about the world. And he ended up with "well, at least I know I exist."

Bishop Berkeley, in the early eighteenth century, wrote that things only exist if they are perceived by a mind. It takes a mind (and senses) to give those incoming vibrations some sort of representation as an object. If these vibrations are not perceived by a mind, then the object is not put

---

[75] Well, mystics throughout history have claimed the ability to perceive reality directly, transcending the limitations of the senses and brain. Rather than sense, evaluate and form images or ideas, mystics would just feel reality. We will go into mysticism in later essays. For now, we will stay in the material plane.

into a mental image anywhere, and so it does not exist. You have heard the question: "If a tree falls in a forest and nobody hears it, did it make a sound?" Sounds are only produced in our heads, so perhaps the answer is no. This whole distinction between "things in themselves" versus "things as they appear" has troubled philosophers for ages. The point is, we cannot really sense what is out there.

Enough about our senses. What about our minds?

Our Minds Are Limited

Descartes rightly realized that our minds are limited in what they can grasp.

> *For since we are finite, it would be absurd for us to determine anything concerning the infinite; for this would be to attempt to limit it and grasp it. So we shall not bother to reply to those who ask if half an infinite line would itself be infinite or whether an infinite number is odd or even, and so on. It seems that nobody has any business to think about such matters unless he regards his own mind as infinite.*[76]

The philosopher Immanuel Kant continued this line of thought in the late eighteenth century. He wrote that not only are we limited in our perception of reality due to the limitations of our senses, but we are also limited by the structure of our minds. Kant asserted that the very nature of our minds requires that what we perceive be fitted into space and time, even though space and time may or may not exist. How can we know if they do?

It is not just the senses then. It is the mind itself that is questionable. Our minds are limited. They process only in a certain way, and our minds' limitations affect us in ways we are often not aware of. Have you ever wondered why popular magazines have those articles whose titles always

---

[76] René Descartes, "Principles of Philosophy," *Philosophical Writings, I,* 201, in James Gleick, *Isaac Newton,* (Vintage Books, 2003), 40.

have a number? 104 great tips, techniques, and tools, 55 holiday gifts to share, 12 hot sex tips. It is because marketers understand how the mind thinks. We are attracted to lists because they provide an already-made structure for information. They make the potentially complex appear more manageable. The appeal of lists is that they organize information in a way that's easy for our brains to process.

Another sales technique that has been used on all of us is called anchoring. You see it all the time on TV ads. If you see an ad for some gadget on a TV commercial, they will always say that it "usually sells for" and mention a high number. This high number is the anchor. Now any number that is lower than the original high number is considered low, because you are comparing the actual price to that high number that they originally threw at you. If they say they usually sell for $100 but during this special they will sell them to you for $20, then you think it is a steal, and you want it. If instead they said they usually sell for $25 and will sell them at $20, you are not as likely to want them. Same knives, but not so appealing now.[77] Marketers and salespeople use these tricks on you because they know how the mind works.

The human brain is hardwired to think in certain ways that are not logical. The skilled marketers and salespeople know this and take advantage of people. Social scientist, Robert Cialdini, who wrote the bestseller *Influence*,[78] has made a living investigating and teaching others these tricks. The mind is limited, flawed and predictable. It is not a perfect instrument for perceiving reality, as Descartes, Kant and other

---

[77] Anchoring is not limited just to the price of the item for sale. Any high number will do. Let's assume you are hawking the same knife set at a county fair. If you mention a high number, such as, "I just had to pay my tax bill; it was $1,000. It was so awful! I am still trying to recover." That is anchoring. If the knives are selling at $100, the $100 price tag seems low compared to the original number thrown out there even though it had nothing to do with the price of the knives.

[78] Robert Cialdini is not a fan of unscrupulous sales techniques at all. He admonishes the reader not to use his findings to take advantage of people. Cialdini's *Influence* is a must-read for someone who prefers not to be manipulated.

philosophers have pointed out, and many marketers take advantage of its limitations.

Cause and Effect Is a Myth

Many of the truths that form the foundation of our schemas are rooted in the fundamental belief of causality—the idea that one event leads to another. We accept as fact that sunbathing too long results in a sunburn, for instance. This cause-and-effect relationship seems intuitive and forms the basis of much of our understanding of the world. However, the philosopher David Hume challenged this notion, demonstrating that causality itself cannot be proven. In fact, Hume argued that we cannot prove anything based solely on experience or experimentation.

Despite this philosophical conundrum, most of science operates on the assumption that if one event or condition has consistently followed another in the past, this pattern will persist in the future. This belief stems from the idea that the first event causes the second; and, therefore, this pairing will continue to occur. Yet, this assumption, while practical, remains philosophically unproven. It may not be true.

Our minds are so structured that we need to make these types of generalizations in order to understand and operate in our world. But it doesn't mean is the assumptions are true.

David Hume gave science a black eye when he demonstrated that just because something occurs over and over does not mean that it will happen the next time. As the famous story about the philosopher chicken goes, the chicken had learned (or in philosophical terms, induced from empirical experience) that every time the tall human with red hair came by, there would be a great feast. For her entire lifetime, the chicken experienced this very same event and made a scientific law: the red-haired human brings banquets and good fortune. This is causality—the idea that one thing leads to another. But in the case of the philosopher chicken, one day, the red-haired human came with an axe and cut off the philosopher chicken's head.

So once again, the limitations of our minds can lead to potentially erroneous thoughts and thinking patterns. This too contributes to the problem that we are not able to perceive reality clearly.

Is Logic the Answer?

If we cannot be certain of anything we witness through our senses and if we cannot be certain that the way things have happened in the past has any correlation to how things will happen in the future, then by using logic, we can conclude that all of our beliefs must be illogical and baseless. Hume used this logical argument to undermine the idea that logical thinking leads to a greater understanding of the world.[79] In other words, he used logical thinking to prove that logic cannot help us to understand the world.

As it turns out, the great appeal of reason and logic is not that it leads to the truth, but that it can be used by anyone to support any cause whatsoever.[80] Philosophers, politicians and salespeople know that nobody is convinced of anything by using reason. This is not to stop us from proudly believing we make our decisions rationally. But really we don't, and to believe so is presumptuous. We are like speculators on the stock market, proclaiming the market has hit a high or a low, but we never know. The market does as it will. We cannot guess its course, though many will claim to. The point is we should humbly recognize our incapacity to make good decisions. We do the best we can, and sometimes we blunder to our personal benefit.

I hope to this point I have demonstrated that the mind and senses are limited in their capacity for perceiving and understanding the world and that people who are both thoughtful and humble have known this for centuries.

---

[79] Welles, *Understanding Stupidity*, 184.

[80] Welles, *Understanding Stupidity*, 106.

Mathematics Does Not Necessarily Describe Reality

Hume claimed that mathematics is the only field in which logic can lead to a certain outcome. But this is only because of the way that mathematical concepts are defined with its set of arbitrary rules and symbols. Mathematics is like a fixed game where the winner is known before the game is even played. By definition, the outcome has been already determined. Math offers no surprises. Nothing is messy. Mathematics is a logical system of thinking.

But just because we have developed mathematical systems that work perfectly in themselves, it does not necessarily follow that mathematics accurately describes reality. In the simple case of adding one orange and two oranges, mathematics is a great tool. Mathematics can describe simple systems, such as the trajectory of a cannon ball. But mathematics requires that these simple systems be perfect—no friction, no wind, all surfaces smooth, etc. As phenomena get more complex, mathematics can only approximate reality.

Scientists use data, create models that have equations and then call these equations relationships or physical laws. Then we are taught these equations as if they were true, when in reality, physics equations are only representations or generalizations.

Remember my physics example from the prior essay. Our classroom experimental data never worked as neatly as the physics equations. I remember my physics teacher always said, "Physics doesn't work." Until I accepted his quip as true, I always attributed the scatter in the data to my own shortcomings. I believed and was taught that the equations were true. So I assumed my inadequacies were the problem. Well, I may have been inadequate, but the equations may not have been true either, or they may have been true only under special circumstances that we could not recreate in our lab.

In school, physical laws are depicted as perfect lines or curves on graphs, often omitting the scattered data points that shaped these relationships. This polished presentation can lead you to assume these laws are precisely defined by mathematical functions. When scatter is present, then you realize that either these laws are not perfect, that some element is still missing from the equation, that our measurement techniques are not yet perfect or that our mathematical models are not perfectly describing the phenomenon. This was a shock to me to recognize this.

Mathematics can explain some things well, some things not so well, and some things not at all. Why is it that we all just assumed that everything is reducible into mathematics? Who came up with that idea? And why have we all accepted it without questioning it?

Humanity has made a serious logical error in assuming mathematics describes reality. Just because it describes some things well does not mean that it can describe all things. This is the fallacy of unwarranted extrapolation, and extrapolating is almost always wrong. A clear analogy of this erroneous thinking might be to say just because my bicycle can transport me from my house to the store, it can take me anywhere, even to the moon.

When physicists use mathematics to "prove" theories that can never be proven by experiment, why should we believe them? After all, they are basing their proof on an incorrect root postulate that mathematics can prove their theory. Some have based their life's work on this postulate, only to fool themselves and anyone who believes them.

So, I want you to recognize that science, which in many people's minds represents the truth and is the basis of their understanding of the world, is nothing like truth. Scientific "truths" are merely tools we use to represent reality; they are not necessarily right.

Just Live – The Pragmatists

A later school of philosophers, the Pragmatists, viewed thought and words as mere tools for prediction, problem solving and action, nothing more. To them, thought and words are not meant to accurately define reality, as we can never know whether they can or not. Reality is untestable because we cannot directly observe it. Instead of fooling ourselves into thinking we can understand reality, we should just value thought, meaning, belief and science in terms of their usefulness—not in terms of how well they describe reality.[81]

The pragmatists would say that nature is a collection of "interacting, unreasoning influences or forces" and is not necessarily logical. When we try to understand nature, we generalize and apply logic, but generalizations and logic can only approximate nature, just like mathematic models can only approximate your high school physics lab results.

So, what we have are a collection of generalizations, which taken together, form our schema. Even though these generalizations may not be accurate, they seem to work well enough. They always have. We manage to get by assuming that what we see really does exist and that in the future things will happen just like they did in the past. So really, all this philosophy, although interesting, may be just a waste of time. We still have lives to live.

We have already established that we are as clueless about the world as Plato's men in the cave. But we choose to believe we are in control and that we know what is really going on. We do this because we need some type of bedrock upon which to base our understanding—something that is constant and never changes and is always true. How can we live in a world where nothing is stable, tragedies occur without reason, and our own perceptions deceive us?

Somehow we do and we have persevered for centuries.

It would be reassuring to know that some things are constant. The ocean will always be there. The sun will always return after a storm. God is always present and watching over us. Natural laws never change. I understand we have a need for this type of security in this ever-changing world. But we have no reason to believe that anything is a constant, especially when not even we are constant. We are all going to die and

---

[81] So then, as pragmatists, we can agree with the Church, which tried to silence Galileo. "Nothing is true, Galileo, not even your theory, but it is a good, useful model." That is what they said.

be no more. So why would anything else persevere if we can't even do it? We won't be around to find out. In this context, why would any relationship that physicists and chemists study last forever? Why would we believe that they would? Maybe we do because we have this deep need to believe in stability and security. And as our brains are wired to simplify things, these constants are a comforting illusion we use to paper over our uncertain existence.

Who Wrote the Laws of Nature?

Constants, such as the speed of light, are laws of nature, right? Light always travels at the same speed. Remember the speed of light as we discussed it in the last essay, that it was supposed to be a constant, but it kept changing until they artificially defined it as unchangeable? The gravitational constant, G, has had the same issues. G is hard to pin down over time; it keeps changing. Still, we choose to see constants as constant, whether they are or not.

Rupert Sheldrake in *Morphic Resonance* questions this whole idea of "laws of nature." Laws are rules that are imposed by external authorities. Did God set these "laws"? What happens if Nature breaks these laws? Does it get punished? Sheldrake asks, do these "laws" that appear to apply now, will always apply? Did they always apply? Maybe they should not be called laws, because they are not. As discussed, according to the Big Bang Theory, there was once a single point, from which the entire universe later came. Did Newtons laws apply then? Every force is met with an equal and opposite force. There were no forces back then, there was a point. What about the axioms of geometry? Did they apply? Two points define a line. No, there was only one point before the Big Bang, no lines, no triangles, either. So maybe these "laws" apply sometimes, but not other times. Much like human laws apply sometimes and not other times.[82]

Much of science is debatable, at its very core.

---

[82] Rupert Sheldrake, *Morphic Resonance* (Park Street, 2009), xiii.

Parts and the Whole

We discussed the mechanistic approach to the world in the last essay. But we did not address a very integral part of the mechanistic approach—reductionism, the belief that we can understand things by reducing them into their constituent parts. A flaw in this approach is that by doing so, not only do we end up missing the point of whatever it is we are studying, we often end up destroying the object of our study.

Living organisms are complete, integrated systems. When we attempt to understand them by breaking them down into their chemical components through dissection and analysis, we actually destroy the very essence of what makes them living organisms in the first place.[83] Many molecular biologists focus on biomolecules and their interactions, aiming to understand the human body, but they miss the bigger picture, the body itself.

Consider Aristotle studying the pieces of a mechanical clock from the future. He could study the composition of those pieces and make generalizations regarding their shapes, their content, their properties; but he would never be able to guess from looking at the pieces that in a particular combination that they would be able to keep track of time. Never.

We may be able to understand different parts of an object, but we often cannot understand the relation of the parts to each other. No matter how great one's mastery of mathematics and the chemical properties of oxygen and hydrogen, nobody could have guessed that combining these two gases in a particular way would give water.

According to Wilhelm Wundt's (1832–1920) principle of creative resultants, one cannot determine the properties of the whole from a study of the parts, analysis will not disclose them. One can only learn the properties of the whole from the observation of the whole's behavior.[84]

---

[83] Sheldrake, *Morphic Resonance*, 46.

[84] William R. Sorley, *Moral Values and the Idea of God* (Cambridge University, 1919), 246.

Missing Parts?

Another question that arises: do we even know all the constituent parts of whatever we are studying? We don't. We only know about the parts that we have identified, which are usually those we can see. But who is to say we have identified all of the parts? Could some parts be invisible to us? If they are undetectable, how would we know they are present?

Sir Isaac Newton understood that some qualities of things we study are not material. The soul or spirit of the thing matters, too.

> *But so long as wee are ignorant of the nature of both soule & body wee cannot clearly distinguish how far an act of sensation proceeds from the soule & how far from the body.*[85]

Just because Newton wrote it, does not mean it is true. But if he is right, and I believe he is, then there must be some unseen qualities of things that contribute to making up a thing's essence. If that is true, then we are missing something. Does some criterion exist from which we can conclusively state that we have identified all of the parts? There isn't. Or that we understand everything about an object? No, there is not.

The gap in understanding points to a deeper issue. We cannot grasp even the most fundamental essence of anything really, not even an object. We can talk about an object's physical qualities, such as weight, composition, mass, density, but "there is no knowledge, no matter how abstract, which does not point to some *it*."[86] This *it* represents whatever it is we have not been able to classify. This *it* is the indefinable essence we point to when we say an individual in a group is unique. "Unique" is a term that represents that quality that we cannot mentally apprehend. It is indescribable.[87] *It* is whatever makes that dog alive, rather than dead. *It* is whatever makes that one horse open gates and escape, while

---

[85] Isaac Newton, *Quaestiones quaedam Philosophiae* (Certain Philosophical Questions), Section 101v, https://tinyurl.com/28ha9jua, accessed January 1, 2025.

[86] M. R. Cohen, *The Meaning of Human History*, 2nd ed. (Open Court, 1961), 42, in Arnold J. Toynbee, A Study of History, vol. 12 (Reconsiderations), (Oxford University, 1961), 10.

[87] Toynbee, *A Study of History*, vol. 12, 11.

other horses are well-behaved. How are you going to identify, measure, quantify or study that?

Where Does Consciousness Reside?

This topic of parts versus the whole is most interesting when we consider living beings. "Life" and "consciousness" are properties that belong to a whole creature, such as a horse, but do the cells that make up a horse have "life" or "consciousness"? What about the atoms or the electrons? Where does consciousness begin and end? Or does it end? Should it end? Let's assume consciousness exists in atoms, then is there a difference between the carbon atom of a rock and the carbon atom of a person? If one is conscious, shouldn't they both be conscious? But, we are deviating too far from the point of this essay, so we will let these questions go. They do, however, illustrate the endless number of questions that will arise around anything we study.

Back to the main point: much or all of our science is primarily concerned with studying parts, but this does not lead to an understanding of the whole. Goethe, too, criticized this method of analysis:

> *To understand the living whole*
> *They start by driving out the soul;*
> *They count the parts, and when all's done,*
> *Alas! the spirit-bond is gone.*[88]

This spirit-bond cannot be measured by our mechanistic science, we cannot capture it.

Where Do the Boundaries End?

Even after accepting the fact that whatever it is we are studying may have some intrinsic features that we cannot measure, we must also accept that environment is also a part of whatever it is we are studying. Blood in a test tube is not the same thing as blood in the veins or blood in a frying

---

[88] Sorley, 248.

pan, because blood behaves differently depending on its environment. In the same way, the meaning of a word may change depending on the sentence in which it is used. When trying to understand something, we must understand how it interacts with its environment.

Humans do not stop at the skin, as is commonly perceived. The human boundary includes the environment. Here is an example: Cut the heart out of a human and the human will die. Drain the blood from a human and the human will die. Take air away from a human and the human will die. So then, what makes air, an element of the human's environment, any different from a heart or blood, which reside within the human body? They are all vital components for human life. As we'll see in a later essay, human beings cannot survive alone. We are group animals. We need the company of other humans to survive. If the heart, blood and air are part of human life, does that mean that other people are part of a human as well?

Perhaps, as Alan Watts (1915–1973) claimed,

> *The soul is not in the body, but the body is in the soul, and the soul is the entire network of relationships and processes which make up your environment.*[89]

Think of it like this: just as the essence of a clock (a time telling device) is more than just the sum of its parts, like gears and springs, the essence or soul of an individual is more than just the sum of its parts, like gall bladder and bones. It's the whole that matters, the essence or spirit of the thing—something we just cannot put our finger on.

Humanity is the Greater Whole

We should take this further. When we focus on our individual lives, we make the same mistake. We overlook the essence of humanity as a whole, which is the greater thing. When we view the world from our own

---

[89] Alan Watts, *The Book on the Taboo Against Knowing Who You Are* (Vintage Books, 1989), 68–69.

individual viewpoint, we experience triviality, mundanity, and life can appear limited, repetitive and unfulfilling. Most of us don't understand or even try to understand the larger picture. We do not feel the connection with the mass of humankind nor claim oneness with the rest of humanity living our common history. This must be another innate limitation of the human mind.[90] It is easier to see things from our own limited view. But in doing so, we often miss the greater truth. Humanity is an entity in itself, and it is doing something. And we are a part of it.

The Holistic Approach

Jan Smuts was a South African military leader, statesman and philosopher. In 1926, in the introduction to his book *Holism and Evolution*, he wrote, "The old concepts and formulas are no longer adequate to express our modern outlook. The old bottles will no longer hold the new wine." He went on to introduce to the world not only to the term "holism" but also introduced a new rival schema to the mechanistic model, the holistic approach. Smuts held that all nature is alive—molecules, atoms, even crystals are alive. Everywhere we look in nature, we find wholes that are made up of parts, which are themselves wholes. Every whole has its own intrinsic character, which is greater than the sum of its parts, with properties that cannot be predicted by analyzing the individual parts.

> *The machine metaphor, the idea that we are soulless machines, has long outlived its usefulness, and holds back scientific thinking in physics, biology and medicine. Our growing, evolving universe is much more like an organism, and so is the earth, and so are oak trees, and so are dogs, and so are you.*[91]

According to Smuts, the mechanistic phase of human understanding was a necessary step. Similarly, the mechanical view of the universe is

---

[90] There are other limitations of the human mind that Kant raised. We will address them in a later essay.

[91] Sheldrake, *Morphic Resonance*, 53.

just one stage in humanity's evolution towards a more holistic and integrated worldview.[92]

In *The Book: On the Taboo Against Knowing Who You Are*, Alan Watts attempts to reveal to us the unity of everything as one whole and us as part of that whole. As I quoted earlier, "The soul is not in us, we are in the soul." But let's take it one step at a time. The one step I am asking you to take is more than enough. It is a huge step. We recognize that we are individual people with individual schemas and priorities. But consider all of us together as a group. Together as one unit we take on a different character that is awe-inspiring, powerful and potentially dangerous. The proper combination of hydrogen and oxygen is water, something completely different than its component parts. The entire collection of billions of people, many already dead, some still alive, combined their efforts to put a man on the moon. It wasn't the product of a collection of engineers at NASA. It was a product of all of humanity, those living in 1969 and those who had died previously, including Sir Isaac Newton. It took centuries for the accumulation of knowledge and organizational mastery to reach such an accomplishment. Putting a man on the moon is an awe-inspiring feat. Imagine how we would regard chimpanzees if they had done such a thing as that.

Wrapping It Up

- There is no reason to think humanity will ever fully understand the world. People conflate the idea of being the most intelligent species with having the capacity to understand everything given enough time to figure it out. This is not a logical argument.

- It is naïve to believe that the scientific outlook is accurate.

- Our senses are limited in what they can perceive. We are missing all sorts of sensory clues about the world, clues that animals receive. Our individual understandings of color and sound may

---

[92] Jan Smuts, *Holism and Evolution*, (Sierra Sunrise, 1999), 194.

be different from those of other people, certainly color-blind, partially blind and deaf people.

⸱ Our capacity to think is defective in how it analyzes and categorizes data. For example, we cannot comprehend infinity. We think with emotions, not logic, despite what we tell ourselves.

⸱ Cause and effect is the foundation of scientific observation. Hume (and the life of the philosopher chicken) proved that repeated occurrences do not guarantee future outcomes. If cause and effect is not necessarily true, then why should we believe that any scientific truths are true?

⸱ If sensory perceptions (our premises) and cause-and-effect relationships (our conclusions) are uncertain, then relying on logic (premises and cause-and-effect reasoning) may lead to flawed conclusions. Hume used logic to argue that logic does not necessarily lead to a true understanding of the world.

⸱ Mathematics is a useful tool, but it does not necessarily accurately describe reality. Math can only approximate complex phenomena. Mathematical models are generalizations, rather than absolute truths.

⸱ Our senses, our brains, science, math and logic are flawed. Perhaps the best attitude is to recognize that we can never understand the world with these tools, but that they are useful and can help us navigate the world.

⸱ Much of scientific study is based on breaking a thing into component parts and studying them. Understanding the parts does not correlate to understanding the whole. Once you break up a whole into parts, you have destroyed the *it,* the spirit of the whole.

⸱ Humanity should be viewed as a whole, rather than as a collection of individuals.

⸱ Whether you recognize it or not, humanity is busy doing something.

Essay 5
Groups: Living Organisms in Pursuit of Immortality

*A social organism is like an individual organism in
these essential traits: that it grows; that while growing
it becomes more complex; that while becoming more
complex, its parts acquire increasing mutual dependence;
that its life is immense in length compared with the lives
of its component units.*
— OSWALD SPENGLER

Groups Are Organisms

Before we move on in the next essay to how groups can perversely affect our sensibilities, it is important to examine the nature of groups themselves. Just as a person is considered an individual entity, a group can be as well. Groups have different organs that perform different tasks, just like our bodies do. Groups need a goal or they founder, just like people do. Groups are composed of individuals who come and go, just like we are composed of cells that are created, then die and then are disposed of while the group and our bodies live on. Groups will do whatever it takes to survive, just like we will. Groups with poor leadership or poor leadership structures falter and die just as humans with compromised or deceived minds often falter and die due to poor decision-making.

Group Maintenance Becomes the Sole Purpose of Groups

If you really think about it, there are two overarching purposes for a group: first, to obtain some goal and, second, to maintain the group's existence. Over time, this second purpose, group maintenance, grows in importance. Sometime just preserving the group becomes the sole purpose of the group.[93] Once groups reach a certain stage, they reach a sort of self-consciousness, and they don't want to die. They will fight to live forever and to pass on their "genetic material" to future generations of members. In the fight to survive, they will violate any of their stated fundamental standards. This is a law of groups.

Government Exists for Itself

The most extreme example of a group that exists to perpetuate itself is government. Governments are created often for the good of the people, at least in name. Government entities keep us safe from criminals and from other countries that might try to enslave and kill us. They provide infrastructure, regulations and education to enhance our productivity, and ultimately this makes most of us wealthier and happier. They maintain the forests and parks. They provide us with protections, so that our employers don't enslave us and industry does not poison us with unsafe foods, medicines or pollution. They take care of us when everything falls apart. Government can be our best friend, until it is not. If we decide we want to replace our form of government, then government will ruin or kill everyone who threatens it. We see it over and over again in any attempted revolution. Personal freedoms are taken away. Agitators disappear, often never to be seen again. Soldiers shoot into crowds of protestors. The government then reveals its dark side,

---

[93] Welles, *Understanding Stupidity,* 12.

having no respect at all for the lives of the governed. This is the most extreme, yet historically very commonplace, example of a group. Once it becomes conscious, the group exists primarily for itself. When the group is threatened, it forgets its original reason for existence and will do whatever it takes to survive.

One can argue that putting down anti-government agitators is all in the interest of promoting stability so that economic activity can continue and the majority (who are not agitators) can flourish. But, on the other hand, when the anti-government forces become the majority, this argument can no longer be made. If the government really cared about stability and economic activity, then the government would willingly concede when the majority of people demanded it. It happened in Eastern Europe in the 1990s with the fall of the communist governments, but that was after decades of oppression. A government voluntarily giving up power rarely happens. Usually when feeling threatened, a government will turn guns on the people to save itself.

What Happens When a Group Achieves Its Goals

Groups rarely achieve their goals. In the U.S., the Democratic Party may elect a president, but having achieved that goal, the party does not disband. Another election will take place in four years. The party's goal, and likely that of the Republicans, may be to rule the country forever. (Hopefully, this goal will never be achieved for either party.)

Religions can never meet their goal, unless the ultimate supernatural event, such as the Rapture, occurs. Religions can increase membership, spread the faith to more and more people, but they will always be seeking out others wandering in the darkness who should be brought to the light. Religions will always have work to do. The Boy Scouts, the Freemasons and other fraternal organizations will never meet their goals either. They may provide fellowship and education for their members, but their work is never ceasing, as there will always be young ones who need guidance.

On the other hand, some groups achieve their goals or utterly fail to meet them or perhaps the chance to accomplish their goals may slip away. But once the goals have been achieved or the window of opportunity has passed, these organizations often find some excuse to continue existing. Groups are like creatures, and few creatures willingly accept death. They will struggle to survive, no matter what the cost. They will change their missions, their natures, whatever it takes. Countless organizations, having faced existential crisis, have devolved to the point where the original reason for the existence of the organization has become much less important than continuing to maintain membership, receive funding and ensure the careers of its officers and employees. The discussions that follow present how a handful of groups responded to the uncomfortable situation of accomplishing their stated goals.

NATO

With the fall of the Soviet Union in 1991, the North Atlantic Treaty Organization (NATO) had met its goal. Why is it still here? NATO was established in 1949 as a collective security organization characterized by agreements among Western European countries, the United States and Canada to defend member nations from any incursions by the Soviet Union. They were successful. The Soviets did not invade. Instead, the Soviet Union collapsed. As there was no longer a Soviet Union to defend against, there was no reason to continue NATO, right?

Wrong. NATO became a group in search of a problem to solve. A 1999 Brookings Institution Report stated that NATO's mission was unclear. That was eight years after the Soviet dissolution. At that time, NATO was seen as the "'go-to' organization in cases where the threat or use of force was deemed appropriate in and around Europe."[94] Since the breakup of the Soviet Union, NATO has admitted sixteen nations[95] from Eastern Europe, most of which were former communist states.

---

[94] Ivo H. Daalder, "NATO in the 21st Century: What Purpose? What Missions?" *Brookings*, April 1, 1999, https://tinyurl.com/ywznpter.
[95] As of December 2024. The number keeps changing.

NATO was involved in bringing the Bosnian Crisis to an end and was involved in the Iraqi Wars and the American effort in Afghanistan.

NATO has changed its mission statement more than once. Today, its "essential and enduring purpose is to safeguard the freedom and security of all its members. It does this through political and military means, ensuring the collective defence of all Allies, against all threats, from all directions."[96] NATO appears to have successfully changed its purpose and will continue to do so for some time into the future. Survival is everything to groups.

Congress of Racial Equality

The Congress of Racial Equality (CORE) was founded in 1942 and became one of the leading civil rights organizations during the early 1960s. The organizations founding principles were: (1) that it involves the people themselves rather than experts, (2) that it rejects segregation, and (3) that it does so through nonviolent direct action.

As we shall see, CORE met its goal of desegregation. But as it turned out, the goal was not so satisfactory to its members after all, so they adopted the opposite goal—segregation—and reoriented the organization the other way. Eventually, this goal too was dropped for a pro-business conservative orientation, another radical change of direction. Then the organization limped on for decades.

CORE was multi-racial (33% black, 66% white) during its first two decades. Their method of activism was based on the non-violent methods of protest made popular by Mahatma Gandhi. In the late 1940s, using sit-ins and other non-violent methods, CORE was successful in pushing racial integration of restaurants and businesses in Chicago. Martin Luther King worked with CORE in the 1950s and early 1960s.

---

[96] When I originally wrote this essay in late 2018, the mission statement was different, and it is quite possible it will change from what I write today. The current mission statement at any time is posted on the NATO website (currently at https://tinyurl.com/yjewq4gd). If it changes, you *cannot* look up the link on the internet archive, which holds records of all (well, apparently not all) websites throughout the decades.

CORE led the Freedom Rides, which sought to desegregate interstate transportation facilities and supported the Freedom Summer voter registration project and the 1963 March on Washington, at which Martin Luther King spoke.

CORE's original objective was to end racial segregation. Unlike the end of slavery, which became the law of the country all at once, ending segregation took a long time to achieve. In 1955, the Federal ruling, Brown v. Board of Education, called on schools to integrate with "all deliberate speed." For many states, that meant slower than a snail's pace. They just did not comply. The southern universities desegregated in the 1950s and early 1960s. The Civil Rights Act of 1964 prohibited segregation in public facilities, but resistance by some school boards lasted into the 1970s. However, by 1966, with Brown v. Board of Education, the Civil Rights Act, and the desegregation of the universities, one could say CORE's goal of integration to a large extent had been met. Those hold-out school districts that were resisting integration were being defeated one by one.

In 1966, fourteen years after its founding, CORE's goal had been largely met. So how did CORE respond to meeting their stated goal of desegregation? They changed their mission.

Even with integration in place, the group realized that racism was a problem that was not going to go away. If racism was going to always be with us, then perhaps segregation would be better after all. This ideological divide sparked an internal conflict in 1966, resulting in James Farmer, a founding member, a pacifist, and an integration advocate being replaced as national director by Floyd McKissick, who was committed to black separatism. Farmer then left the group as it no longer corresponded to his ideals, and CORE became a primarily black organization promoting black power and black nationalism, pressing for political and economic justice. White activists were allegedly purged from the group. McKissick led the organization for just two years, but the organization continued to remain committed to the Black Power movement.

Roy Innis took the helm in 1968, initially maintaining the black nationalist position, but later he transformed the organization into a black conservative organization. Its major project under Innis involved supporting the use of DDT to prevent malaria in Africa. CORE collaborated with conservative think tanks, and according to Mother Jones, took money from Monsanto and Exxon to promote their agendas.

Innis led the organization for forty-nine years until his death in 2017. Niger Innis, the son of Ron Innis, is now the National Spokesperson for CORE. Their website appears to be frozen in time. In May 2025, the latest event listed was twenty years prior. The page on the leadership of the group still has Ron Innis listed as the National Chairman even though he died eight years ago.

According to an interview with Farmer in 1993, "CORE has no functioning chapters; it holds no conventions, no elections, no meetings, sets no policies, has no social programs and does no fundraising. In my opinion, CORE is fraudulent."[97] Most histories on CORE become silent after 1968. Farmer, who has also passed, appeared to be right. CORE's initial goals were met when the country was desegregated in the 1960s, but the group continued on, radically switching its goals more than once, and apparently it has withered away, but it is not dead as of May 2025.

American Colonization Society

The American Colonization Society (ACS) was established in 1816 to promote the colonization of freed American black slaves outside of the country. The number of freed slaves had been growing in the United States, from 60,000 in 1790 to 300,000 in 1830. Slaveowners were concerned that free Blacks might encourage those still enslaved to revolt or escape. Others, including Abraham Lincoln for much of his life, believed that Blacks and Whites could never coexist peaceably, that

---

[97] African American Registry, "The Congress of Racial Equality is Founded," aaregistry. org/story/c-o-r-e-effective-against-racism/, accessed January 1, 2025.

integration was impossible. Based on those premises, the ACS would work to transport freed slaves elsewhere, to Panama, Haiti and an area of Africa later named Liberia. Only volunteers were transported.

The ACS had three goals: (1) provide a place outside of the United States for freed slaves to live, where they would not be subject to racism; (2) the colony would have what it needed to succeed; and (3) suppression of the Atlantic slave trade. The organization received funding from Congress and did manage to move 20,000 freed slaves to what would later become Liberia. Long after the American Civil War, the group continued to send emigrants to Liberia and to promote the growth of the colony. The project was for the most part a failure for multiple reasons: many of the freed slaves died of disease and most freed slaves felt that they belonged in the United States and did not volunteer to leave. Frederick Douglas opposed the concept of repatriation to Africa:

> *Our minds are made up to live here if we can, or die here if we must. . .Shame upon the guilty wretches that dare propose, and all that countenance such a proposition. We live here—have lived here—have a right to live here, and mean to live here.* [98]

Abolitionists were hostile to the organization and abolitionist thought became mainstream in the North by the time of the Civil War. Another impediment to the process was the cost of transporting people all the way to Africa. So, the project was not completely successful in that they were hoping to transport a much larger population than they did. Still, it can be argued that ACS met all three goals outlined above. But what is most amazing is that the group didn't dissolve until 1964, almost 100 years after the Civil War!

---

[98] Frederick Douglass, *The North Star*, January 26, 1849. In "DBQ: Extent of influence the American Colonization Society had at reducing sectional tensions concerning slavery in the United States," doc. 6, digital.library.sc.edu/blogs/academy/2019/06/10/dbq-extent-of-influence-the-american-colonization-society-had-at-reducing-sectional-tensions-concerning-slavery-in-the-united-states, accessed January 1, 2025.

Summary of Groups that Met Goals

It took me some hard thinking to come up with organizations that had met their goals. Of the three I write about here,[99] all of them tried to survive and most of them did for quite some time after their original goal had been met. It's just what groups do. Once they reach a certain stage of development and organization, like any living entity, they will do whatever they can to survive. If there is no objective, rational reason for their existence, they will find a new reason, like NATO, CORE and the ACU did. Certainly many groups out there were once notable, but are now a shell of themselves, barely hanging onto life.

Changing Society and Declining Organizations

As society evolves from generation to generation, its needs change and groups that were once-essential are just not needed anymore. Membership falls off. And, as noted with NATO, CORE and the ACS, leadership will do whatever it can do to keep the group relevant. We have seen how in order to survive, the organization might resort to changing original principles.

In other cases, when faced with declining membership, leadership will lower admissions standards in an attempt to increase membership. But lowering standards is a surefire way to ruin an organization. What is the point in admitting so many new people if it is at the cost of its original values being diluted to the point that nobody remembers what the group originally stood for? This is the sad story of many organizations struggling to survive. They pay for those compromises by losing what made them special in the first place. A case in point in are the mainline Protestant denominations.

---

[99] There are two more groups that I wrote about, but I deleted them from this essay. (It was getting too long.) If you are inclined, look into the Women's Christian Temperance Union (WTCU), and the American Anti-Slavery Society.

Mainline Protestant Churches

The Lutherans, Episcopalians, Presbyterians, Methodists and other mainline Protestant denominations have been losing members for decades., It is estimated that in 1948, 69% of the U.S. population considered itself Protestant; whereas by 2019, the Protestant population had dropped to 35%. From 1993 to 2010, in a period of just seventeen years, the Presbyterians lost 30% of their membership.[100] It took the Methodists forty-two years to lose 30% (from 1967 to 2009), and the Episcopal Church lost 43% from their highest membership level in just forty-four years, from 1966 to 2010. Meanwhile, in the same period, the Mormons grew their membership over 300% and those who respond "no denomination" in surveys (these are the evangelicals) have grown over 600%.[101] So why have the evangelical and Mormon churches grown, while many of the mainline Protestant denominations have shrunk?

It has something to do with how these churches responded to a changing society that is no longer so firmly based in Christian beliefs. As society has changed and become laxer in standards of conduct, the declining mainline denominations have met society half-way, relaxing their rules of decorum, while the evangelicals and Mormons have for the most part stood pat on their teachings.

The Association of Religious Data Archives has collected fascinating information about the various denominations. When Mormons and Evangelicals were asked whether their denomination should preserve traditional beliefs and practices, they responded 73% and 61% affirmative, respectively, while the Episcopalians, Presbyterians and Methodists answered yes 25%, 33% and 39% affirmative. The majorities in these

---

[100] I don't write about the Baptists, which are the largest mainline denomination because there are three different main Baptist sects, which makes it difficult to track. I don't write about Lutherans either. There are fourteen denominations of Lutherans. Their numbers have dropped significantly though.

[101] Association of Religion Data Archives, thearda.com/Denoms/D_1117.asp, accessed January 1, 2025.

mainline Protestant churches just don't care about their traditions anymore.

The decline of mainline Protestantism started with the second generation of Puritans in the 1660s, when the Puritan-controlled Congregational churches of colonial New England adopted the Half-Way Covenant as a way to relax standards so that their less fervent children could be members of the church.

Through the generations, the mainline Protestant churches have continued to retreat from their strict beginnings. They set aside prohibitions on colorful dress, dancing and alcohol. They relaxed expectations for Sabbath observance and softened standards of daily conduct to the point that in 2003, the Episcopalians even ordained an openly gay bishop. Presbyterians redefined marriage in 2014 to include any two people. This is a complete about-face from their seventeenth century fire-and-brimstone roots.[102]

It is understandable that they changed. Society has changed, and the mainline Protestant churches evolved along with it to remain relevant. But the cost was high—their purpose has grown indistinct. As most restrictions have been removed, almost anything goes now, just like in the outside world. Because people can get elsewhere what the churches are offering, the churches do not seem very important anymore.[103] Few can say with certainty what their church believes. Those who cherished the original teachings drifted away, and newcomers found little distinctive to draw them in.

On the other hand, groups like the Mormons and evangelicals held steady. They are newer groups; but they maintain firm doctrines, offer a clear path to redemption and their membership continues to rise. Toeing the line in the Mormon and evangelical churches requires a

---

[102] Dean M. Kelly, *Why Conservative Churches are Growing* (Harper & Rowe, 1977). Nearly all of the ideas in this section are covered in this book.

[103] Benton Johnson, Dean R. Hoge and Donald A. Luidens, *Mainline Churches: The Real Reason for Decline*, March 1993, leaderu.com/ftissues/ft9303/articles/johnson.html.

commitment to strict standards. And it is this commitment to the strict standards that keeps people engaged.

So who was behind the relaxing of standards in the Protestant mainline churches? It appears that the membership chose the course the churches have taken. This erosion of the old standards has been popular among the grass roots, and the leadership did little or nothing to stop the process.[104] Lax leaders bear much of the responsibility for the decline of their churches.

Society is changing; and by responding to society's changing inclinations, these failing mainline Protestant organizations have focused on offering what society seems to want: social activities and social activism. The problem with this approach is that they have overlooked the main commodities that only churches can offer: comfort in knowing that there is a meaning to all the sadness in life and, for many, salvation—the knowledge that by following the strict rules of the church, members are almost certain to make it to heaven.[105]

If any group does not police itself, it may drift like the mainline Protestant churches did, with the result that members lose passion for the organization. To survive, a group needs to stand for something. The churches did not, and now congregants do not invite their friends to events. Their children do not attend church activities anymore. The denomination becomes watered down to the point that there perhaps is no point in belonging at all. In trying to appeal to more people, the original appeal is lost. Members no longer get what they need, and these churches struggle with the dying process.

---

[104] Johnson, Hoge and Luidens.

[105] Dean Kelly, 92. On this point, Kelly is describing George LeNoue's arguments, whose work was not published.

The Resilience of Strict Groups

Society does change and with time fewer people may want to be in a particular group. But that does not mean a group has to die. Groups ebb and flow. Some groups may shrink but remain vital for decades as they still provide whatever it is that they were intended to provide for their members. Zoroastrianism has been around since 1000 BCE. It was strong until the Arabs conquered the Persian Empire in the eighth century. The religion has been on the verge of extinction for over 1,200 years, but there are still about 200,000 members. Some groups just won't die. Zoroastrians have tried to maintain purity. They will not accept converts or interfaith marriages, and they have survived.

A hostile society was not a problem for early Christians in the pagan Roman world. It has not been a problem for the strong churches Dean Kelly wrote about: the Black Muslims, Jehovah's Witnesses, Evangelicals, Orthodox Jews, Churches of Christ, Mormons, Seventh Day Adventists and a few others. As I've noted, these organizations share something in common—strong organizations are strict.

> *The strong religious organization makes very high demands upon its members. They must give it absolute and unswerving allegiance; be able to work, suffer, and die for it; abandon all competing activities, allegiances, and responsibilities in its favor; tell its Good News tirelessly and unselfconsciously to strangers; wear its stigmata of humiliation on their bodies [uniforms]; submit to its strictures, conformities and disciplines; go where they are sent and do what they are told.* [106]

It is tough to be in these groups.

And for this reason, most members stay.

These lessons are not limited to religious organizations. They apply to other types of organizations as well. The Freemasons, the Elks, the Odd Fellows and many other fraternal lodges are experiencing the same

---

[106] Dean Kelly, 99–100.

problem of dilution. The Boy Scouts is another example, which you probably know now includes girls and has changed its name Scouts USA, removing the word "Boy" to be more inclusive.

Groups Require Uniformity of Thought

Strong groups must have some uniformity of thought and action. This is part of group maintenance. It is very important for groups to maintain order and eliminate any threats from within. To remain in good standing in a strong group, individuals must conform. To belong to a strong group, individuals must buy into the group's schema and, to an extent, allow their thinking and actions to be shaped in order to fit in. Intellectual integrity with oneself is a threat to the group. And, for the group to maintain this type of coherence, it must police its members.

Troublemaker Roger Williams

It is likely that group cohesiveness was especially important in the English colonies as they were establishing themselves. In order to survive, the settlers had to work together as a group. They could not afford to be at odds over theological or political differences.

Of the twenty thousand people who migrated to New England in the 1630s, most were Puritans, an unwanted and persecuted group of religious dissenters in England. In the New England settlements, Plymouth, Salem and Boston, the early leadership was Puritan. Those who were allowed to vote for leadership only included freemen who had been determined to have correct religious views and who were members of the local Puritan churches. The leadership was intolerant towards other religious views. They left one intolerant society only to set up their own! Wait, that is what Roger Williams said.

One of the colonists, Roger Williams, a well-known Puritan preacher from England, arrived in 1630. Williams wrote and opined based on his own thinking, rather than complying with the group. Williams questioned whether the King had the right to grant the land to the colony, as it belonged to the native peoples who were already there when the English arrived. Williams also had an issue with Church leadership acting as political leadership. This was exactly the problem they were escaping in England. When churchmen lead the government, dissenters are punished—just as the Puritans were in the Old World. To remedy this, Williams championed the "separation of church and state" and was punished for it. For these and other controversial opinions, Williams was banished from the colony in 1635. He proceeded to found Providence Plantations (in today's Rhode Island), which was a colony of dissenters, Quakers, Jews and other outsiders. For decades, Puritan leaders viewed Providence as a hotbed of political and religious radicalism. Of course, this colony of dissenters had their own rules and standards as well, from which some dissented and were punished. It is the nature of human organizations to gravitate toward homogeny.

For the good of the group, dissent must be kept within bounds. Dissent can lead to division; sometimes chaos; or, in times of crisis, collapse. It can weaken the group, to the detriment of all. If you remember Thersites, discussed in a previous essay, who dared question King Agamemnon's decision to begin the Trojan War—he too was punished. An army must have one mind. There is no room for soldiers to question battle plans, just as there is limited room for dissent in any group. Am I making excuses for oppressive groups? No. But as an individual, you must be mindful of the nature of groups. Dissent must be kept within bounds. It is just in the nature of groups.

James Damore – Not a Team Player

If you are accused of being "not a team player," that is a good sign you are not adequately conforming to group norms. It is also a sign that the group does not want you as a member anymore. I suppose James Damore, who was expelled from Google for wrong-thinking, was not a team player.

Damore, along with other Google employees, published a critical memo in July 2017 and another memo in August 2017 on an internal Google message board. In August, it was leaked and went viral around the world. The memo critiques Google's gender and race quota systems and its dismissal and derision of unpopular conservative political viewpoints. In the memo, Damore suggested that the gender disparity in programming and engineering might be partly the result of biological differences between men and women. He pointed out that studies indicate that men are more interested in technology-related fields, while women are more interested in people-related fields. His memo also discussed the differences in political ideologies between liberals and conservatives. He suggested that neither left nor right had a lock on truth but that a balance between the two would be best for society and Google.[107]

He wrote,

> *I hope it's clear that I'm not saying that diversity is bad, that Google or society is 100% fair, that we shouldn't try to correct for existing biases or that minorities have the same experience of those in the majority. My larger point is that we have an intolerance for ideas and evidence that don't fit a certain ideology. I'm also not saying that we should restrict people to certain gender roles; I'm advocating for quite the opposite: treat people as individuals, not as just another member of their group (tribalism).*[108]

In an internal mass email, management characterized the memo as "repulsive and intellectually dishonest." Employees began sending threatening and insulting emails to Damore. One director posted, "Yes, this is 'silencing.' I intend to silence these views; they are violently offensive. Take your false equivalence and fake symmetry and shove them hard up where the sun doesn't shine."[109] One manager compared

---

[107] James Damore and David Gudeman v Google, LLC, scribd.com/document/368692388/James-Damore-Lawsuit, accessed January 1, 2003.

[108] Damore's memo, Appendix A, Damore lawsuit.

[109] All quotes are from Damore lawsuit.

Damore's memo to one that "slave owners would have written for their slaves to help them understand how to interact with their masters."[110]

Damore was fired a few days later for "perpetuating gender stereotypes." Google then gave bonuses to employees who vigorously defended the Google schema, arguing against Damore's "un-Googley" viewpoints.[111]

Damore and a few others sued Google. The lawsuit states that "Google employees have witnessed multiple instances in which hundreds of 'progressive' Googlers would target a single co-worker for harassment, and even potential violence, over a politicized matter, humiliating the person and sabotaging his career."[112] For this reason the other parties to the lawsuit chose not to divulge their identities.

Damore did not fit in the Google culture; and unlike others who just kept silent, he spoke up and "got what was coming to him." They tossed him out.

Groups can be your friend until they are not. They require compliance. I am not suggesting that you keep your mouth shut and unquestionably conform to the group's desires. No. You should just know the nature of groups. They can nourish you and protect you, but they can also destroy you.

---

[110] Damore lawsuit.

[111] The tangle between Google and James Damore presents the age-old question: should we safeguard opportunity for individuals simply because they are individuals or limit individual opportunity in order to pursue the advancement of certain groups? It's a question as old as liberal democracy itself. Max Diamond addresses this question in "The Philosophical Question Underlying the Google-Damore Dispute," *The Weekly Standard*, Feb. 6, 2018, https://tinyurl.com/2xmkgzqy.

[112] Damore lawsuit.

Wrapping it Up

- Like humans, groups are creatures, but of a different kind. They consist of members who come and go, yet the group persists.

- The primary objectives of any group are to achieve specific goals and to maintain its existence. Once a group reaches a certain stage of membership and organization, it reaches a sort of consciousness, and it doesn't want to die. It will fight to live forever and to pass on its "genetic material" to future generations of members. In a fight for survival, the group will violate any of its stated values or standards.

- Governments are examples of groups that will prioritize self-preservation over their original purpose of serving and protecting their citizens. When threatened, a government may resort to oppressive measures against dissenters to maintain control, such as killing the very citizens it was established to protect.

- Groups rarely disband after achieving their goals, as they often find new purposes to justify their continued existence. As survival of the group is paramount, groups will find new missions. NATO is an example of this.

- In response to changing social standards, mainline Protestant denominations like Lutherans, Episcopalians, and Methodists have relaxed their standards, with the result that they have diluted their original values and lost their distinctiveness—their original identity really.

- Groups like Mormons, Evangelicals and Seventh Day Adventists not only survive but have been growing despite these same societal shifts. They have done this by enforcing strict standards, demanding strong allegiance, and preserving core beliefs.

- Successful groups require a degree of uniformity in thought and action among their members. This can lead to the suppression of dissenting views, as maintaining order and cohesion is essential for the group's survival.

- Both Roger Williams and James Damore were expelled from their groups (Puritan New England and Google) for expressing controversial views. While groups can provide support and protection, they can also enforce compliance and punish those who challenge prevailing ideologies.

- To belong to a strong group and to fit in, individuals must buy into the group's schema and, to an extent, allow their own thinking and actions to be shaped by the group. Intellectual integrity to oneself is a threat to the group.

Essay 6
How Collective Delusions
Shape and Distort Our Reality

*I love and treasure individuals as I meet them, I loathe
and despise the groups they identify with and belong to.*
— GEORGE CARLIN

Clueless

I hope you recognize by this point that our understandings of the
world are all flawed. We base our beliefs on uncertain information
that we take to be true, but which may not be. Due to our mental hard
wiring, we are incapable of perceiving reality correctly. Nobody does
now and nobody ever will. Another big reason that we will never see
reality clearly is our strong identification with groups, which by their
nature constrain and distort our perceptions. We need groups to help
us identify who we are and to guide us through life, but membership
in groups takes a toll on our understanding of the world.

Born without a Clue

We were born without a clue. Our minds were initially pliable and took years to solidify into what they become in adulthood. But now that our minds are developed, we still do not have an innate knowledge of what we are supposed to be living for. Unlike the newborn's instinctive urge to suckle, we have no hardwired understanding of life's purpose. Instead, we have to look outside ourselves to society to give us clues. Like moths drawn to a flame, we are drawn towards respected individuals or groups, hoping their light will illuminate our path.

Some of us recognize that we have no idea what we are supposed to accomplish in this life. Others know of their cluelessness only unconsciously and haven't really thought about it. Some vague empty feeling may taunt them from time to time. But we all know to some degree that we are lost in this life without a guidebook—even those people who are convinced they have the truth, like the "well-adjusted," "normal" people. Secretly inside, part of them is terrified that they might be wrong. And it is this terror that makes them so closed-minded and incapable of listening to any dissenting opinions.

Some are relentless in their search for Truth. We will address them in a later essay. They are a minority of the population anyway. But what about the rest of us? Most people are not consciously looking for Truth. Occasionally, inner questioning voices may haunt us, but most find life's daily struggles demanding enough without having to confront these issues. We are busy. Our obligations demand nearly all of our attention. We have money to earn, rent to pay, bosses to appease. The kids are fighting. We have to do our taxes. Most of us do not have time to really confront these mysteries of life; and if we did, we are too darned tired. We just need to relax so we can survive another day in this stressful world. So we numb our minds with distractions like television, sports, social media, alcohol, you name it. But that doesn't make the problem go away.

We still all crave a source of guidance in our lives. Navigating through our lives becomes easier when we believe we are moving toward a meaningful destination. This guidance doesn't necessarily have to be spiritual; it can take many forms. Whether it's from a supportive community like a church, the wisdom of a mentor or insights found in a self-help book, we seek examples to illuminate our journey. Ultimately, we yearn for something—or someone—to help us find our way.

Endgame Unknown

Life is a difficult game. Fortune is a fickle mistress. You think you are winning, and then you lose. You can never know that what you are doing will turn out for the best. And all too often, when you finally achieved your hard-won dreams, you end up worse off than where you began.

An extreme example is lottery winners. Most people dream of winning a lottery and never having to work again. They can travel anywhere they want. They can launch any business venture they desire. They can help their family and friends. They can give to charities. But unfortunately, a large number of winners end up wishing they had never won in the first place. The onslaught of greedy relatives and friends who want more, the business opportunities offered by naïve friends and con men and the avalanche of charities asking for handouts. I know of a family that after winning it big went into hiding. They have armed guards now that accompany them everywhere. Some lottery winners end up dead, often killed by avaricious relatives.[113] Many find themselves penniless, with less money than they had before they struck it rich.

The same is true for everyday life. Whenever you take a job, you do not know what types of problems the job will lead to. You could end up being overstressed and turn to drugs and alcohol. The culture at the office could transform you into a hopeless gambler or an aficionado of strip clubs and prostitutes. You might get tangled up in the crimes your boss commits. You might transform into the type of person you hate.

---

[113] Kathy Benjamin, "Lottery Winners Who Were Murdered," *Grunge*, June 5, 2023, grunge.com/1301397/lottery-winners-murdered, accessed August 2024. This article details the stories of ten lottery winners who were murdered.

You could even die on the job. It is the same with choosing a spouse, or even a date. The one-night stand sometimes ends up a mugging, a kidnapping or a murder. Countless marriages end up miserable. Nothing is for certain.

Group Protection and Guidance

So if Fortune is so unpredictable, how do we make the best decisions? None of us knows the future. That is why we rely on leaders and groups. Leaders and groups give us guidance. Group culture will keep us focused on what is "important" and will keep us out of trouble. We can look at a leader and the group and think *yes, if I am like them, it will turn out well; I want to be one of them.*

Countless people are looking to be led. If you are a leader and start a group, plenty of individuals will want to join. Most people want to be led by someone or some group that appears to know more than they do. We followers want to be safe knowing that the big questions have been answered for us. We don't have to deal with Sartre's nausea, unsure of what we are supposed to be doing—remaining keenly aware that our time is slipping away, our death is approaching and we are getting nowhere. Our leader has it all figured out for us. We get meaning and validation through taking on the values of the group, by being a member of the best group (as opposed to those other groups). Everything is all figured out for us. It is the path of least resistance. Let the other guys show us the way. That is what we humans do. We take this easy road. These groups could be anything—fan clubs, political or charitable organizations, church communities, even militias.

Who to Follow?

One of the problems with this approach is how do we know we are picking the right leader or group to follow. You would think Willie Brown would be a good judge of people. Willie Brown (1934–) was a very successful leader of the California Democratic Party in the 1990s. He was the Speaker of the California Assembly for fifteen years and two-term mayor of San Francisco. To get that far, you have to have superior people skills. And Willie Brown did.

In 1976, as he introduced a charismatic leader at an event, Willie Brown gushed that this man was "what you should see every day when you look in the mirror in the early morning hours. . .a combination of Martin Luther King, Jr., Angela Davis, Albert Einstein. . .Chairman Mao."[114] That charismatic leader that Brown so admired, Jim Jones (1931–1978), two years later compelled 913 of his People's Temple followers to drink cyanide-laced purple Kool-Aid in one of the greatest mass suicides in history. "Death is a million times preferable to ten more days of this life," Jones told his group, "If you knew what was ahead of you, you'd be glad to be stepping over tonight." Well, almost all of them did step over. If Willie Brown can be fooled, then I suppose most of the rest of us can be as well.

History is filled with countless instances where people followed a leader to their own demise. To me the most interesting ones are where the group initially met with success, until they met with catastrophe in the same generation. Among these are Hitler's Germany, the Paris Commune or really, any successful revolt or nation that is finally toppled. The reckoning can be terrible, often ending in the violent death of almost everyone involved.

The Slave Revolt

In 72 BCE, in Capua, an ancient Roman city sixteen miles north of Naples, a miracle happened. Two hundred slaves and condemned criminals from a gladiator school tried to escape and seventy-eight actually succeeded.

Many of these slaves were Goths and Germans, the despised blond-haired, blue-eyed barbarians. They armed themselves and raided nearby towns for food. They chose a Thracian to lead them. This Thracian had served in the Roman army and knew how to organize and lead soldiers.

---

[114] Deborah Layton, *Seductive Poison (Anchor, 1999), 105.*

He issued a call for all slaves in Italy to revolt, and soon he had 70,000 men hungry for liberty and revenge against their Roman masters. He taught them to make their own weapons and how to fight with such discipline that for years they defeated more than ten Roman legions sent against them. The rebels overran most of southern Italy. These victories filled the slaves with hope, to the effect that the army's numbers swelled to 120,000 men. The Thracian marched his army to the Alps, so that after crossing, each man could go back to his own home. On the way north, they looted the towns of Northern Italy and left two Roman armies dead in the field. But the slave army, having gained so much confidence, decided to continue ravaging Italy. So they turned south and headed towards Rome. Hearing the news of the victories of the slave army, half of the slaves of Italy were on the verge of insurrection. No Roman felt safe in their own home. The Romans who had enjoyed every luxury that slavery could produce, trembled at the thought of losing their property, their freedom and their lives. They were terrified.

Fortunately for the Romans the Thracian knew that he could not conquer the Roman Empire. And even if he could, he could never hold it. He remained true to his goal—freedom for his people. He bypassed Rome and headed south hoping to transport his men to Sicily. But the Cilician pirates, hired to ferry his men, betrayed him, taking his payment and abandoning the plan. As the legions of Crassus and Pompey were pressing on them, and the slave leader was forced into battle, what turned out to be one last time. The legions destroyed the slave army once and for all. The Thracian leader, himself, was cut to pieces so that his body could not be identified. The great majority of his followers were slaughtered with him. Others fled and were captured by the Romans. Six thousand captives were crucified on the Appian Way from Capua to Rome. Their rotting bodies were left to hang for months, "so that all masters might take comfort, and all slaves take heed."[115] Thus ended Spartacus' slave revolt.

---

[115] Will Durant, *Caesar and Christ* (Simon & Schuster, 1944), 137–138.

Imagine living the life of an escaped slave in Spartacus' army. Years and years of impossible victories over your past masters. Your team has destroyed ten Roman armies. You have been unstoppable. And now your invincible army is heading to the Alps and from there you can all go home to freedom. Complete victory is in sight. But you just never know. Fortune is a fickle mistress. It is always best not to tempt her too often. The dream of returning home appears just within reach as you approach the Alps. And then it all goes wrong. Before you know it, all of your friends are killed before your eyes. They lie there dead on the field. You try to escape but you know it is hopeless. Nowhere to hide. You are captured, beaten, starved, humiliated, and finally they nail you to a cross. They aren't even nice about it. It hurts and nobody cares. Instead they spit on you and laugh. You wait for hours for death to relieve you of your suffering. You picked a losing team.

This pattern repeats over and over in history. One group's dreams appear to be coming true and then they are shattered by sudden catastrophe, leaving most to lose everything, including their lives. We can never know if we have picked the right group until, perhaps, the day we die. And even then, we still may not know. If catastrophe has not struck during your lifetime, then perhaps the group was the right choice. Based on this reasoning, a slave fighter in Spartacus's army who died of natural causes during the first two years might have died in a euphoric state, being part of the great liberation. The group was the right choice for him. For the slave fighter of Spartacus' army who was crucified on the Appian Way, joining the slave revolt was perhaps a bad choice. Had he remained obedient and enslaved, he would have lived many more years and died under far less painful circumstances. Being a member of the slave revolt could have been wonderful or terrible, depending on timing—on luck really.

Nobody knew then, just like nobody knows now, how things will end up for them. So how do we pick a good group to guide us? There's no way to know; remember, we have no guidebook.

The Franciscans

Less than fifty years after St. Francis (1181–1226) started the Franciscan Order based on the virtues of poverty and love, the Order was conducting the Holy Inquisition for the Pope. They used torture to extract confessions of heretics. I suppose you can torture heretics with a happy heart because you love them, but that was hardly the type of love that St. Francis espoused. Those brothers who tried to live by Saint Francis' original vow of poverty were later suppressed as heretics, and four of his most loyal supporters were burned at the stake in 1318 by the Inquisition.[116] Again, what could have been the right group at one time, can later morph into a nightmare.

So I have to ask once more, how do you pick a good group to join?

I don't have an answer here. I just want to point out that it is not so clear that a group will bring you good or bad fortune. It is guesswork, or perhaps fate.

Social Indoctrination

More than anything, if we want to belong to or thrive in any group, we must fit in and comply with the tendency of the group. If you break spoken or unspoken rules, you can be shunned, shamed, hated, ostracized, attacked or even killed. Comfort, and even survival, demand that we conform. That is all there is to it.

We are all constantly bombarded with social forces that are wielded in order to shape our behavior. As infants, we were first rewarded for looking cute and later were punished when we misbehaved. And we learned from infancy on that we had to conform to the group (the family) in order to get what we wanted: love, attention, food and whatever else it might have been. As we progressed in years, our parents, siblings and playmates continued to give us the clues we needed to fit in.

---

[116] Will Durant, *The Age of Faith (Simon & Schuster 1950),* 802.

We were indoctrinated in school with "proper" thought and action. We learned from our religious institutions, the clubs we belonged to and our sports teams. All of them were working to shape our personalities to fit within their respective groups.

So we constrained our behavior to conform, driven by the need for the belonging and acceptance that these groups promised. By that very process of curbing our thoughts and actions, our personalities were shaped by the groups we belonged to. Our minds were formed by others. Our schemas, formed by others. And we let this happen, not realizing what was taking place. So. . .we are not as individual as we think we are.

Such indoctrination is like hypnosis. Osho (1931–1990) described it:

> *You go on suggesting to the child, "You are a Hindu, you are a Hindu," you take him to the temple, you lead him through. . .religious rituals. . .and. . .he becomes conditioned to the idea that he is a Hindu, that all that is Hindu is right and all that is non-Hindu is wrong.*[117]

Meanwhile half-way around the world, another child is being told, "You are a Christian, you are a Christian," and he becomes conditioned to the idea that he is a Christian and that all that is Christian is right and all that is non-Christian is wrong.

It is the same all over the world. This same process is repeated in every society. Additionally, once we start believing something, we will find all kinds of supports for it, all kinds of arguments to help it.[118]

And it is all done for the sake of the larger group, society.

> *Society is very interested in giving you conclusions, society is not interested in giving you consciousness so that you can conclude on your own. Before you become conscious, before any inquiry*

---

[117] Osho, *The Secret of Secrets* (Rajneesh Foundation International, 1982), 216.
[118] Osho, *The Secret of Secrets*, 217.

starts, society stuffs you with all kinds of conclusions to STOP the inquiry.[119]

Inquirers are dangerous to society; whereas, non-inquirers are obedient. They simply take orders and follow them. They are conformists, they are conventional. Once the group has stuffed our minds with a belief, it has drugged us. Belief is a drug. We start believing and eventually we start thinking that our belief is our experience.

According to Osho, belief can stunt us. We believe things without even knowing we do. We were indoctrinated unknowingly by unknowing indoctrinators, who themselves were indoctrinated by the unknowing, and so it goes on in perpetuity. "The man who believes is a closed man." Belief "is good for the society, but very hazardous for the health of the individual."[120]

American Self-Reliance

Different groups attempt to implant different schemas in our heads. But overall, there are some common values that influence us and that cross over most groups. Those common values are what make up a nation. There is a reason that people from other countries think Americans are confident, arrogant, outspoken and pushy. It is because we are confident, arrogant, outspoken and pushy; at least compared to people of many other nations. What does this stem from?

We Americans have an ethos of self-reliance. When asked if "success in life is pretty much determined by forces outside our control," Americans disagreed far more than citizens of other advanced economies. I hate double negatives, so let me restate. We Americans, more than other peoples, think that we are the masters of our destinies, rather than just having our destinies predetermined by class, race and our parents' backgrounds. The American Dream is the shared schema we all ascribe

---

[119] Osho, *The Secret of Secrets,* 217.

[120] Osho, The Secret of Secrets, 111–112.

to with varying intensities. And, the American promise of freedom is as permanent a feature of Americana as apple pie and baseball.[121]

We get this individualism from prior generations' idealization of the frontiersman. You make it by your own wits and hard work. It is commonly believed in the United States that to become successful, you must work harder and smarter than the next person. The majority in our country believes that anyone can succeed. In the abstract, that may be true. But in reality, it is harder for some people than others. Take, for example, a poor, black girl from Mississippi, raised by a single mother, serial raped at age nine, and pregnant at fourteen. Any one of these things would hinder most of us in achieving our goals: poor, black, girl, Mississippi, single mother, serial-raped, pregnant at fourteen. These impediments can affect your psychology and hold you back forever. If you believe the world is not fair, it won't be. If you believe success is not for people like yourself, you will not be successful. That is all there is to it. Even if you have a success mindset, it is harder to succeed when you come from a "different" background, like this girl did. You have to work a lot harder than the next person. This girl did. She went on to become the wealthiest woman in the United States, Oprah Winfrey. We like to believe success stories like this only happen in America. In the American schema, the successful do not rely on others. They do it themselves. The way is open for you if you work hard, and you work smart.

Americans value an individual's hard work, determination, and grit. Other countries do not have this same drive, at least not as intensely as we do. According to the International Labour Organization, Americans work 137 more hours per year than Japanese workers, 260 more hours per year than British workers and 499 more hours per year than French workers.[122] Much of this overtime is voluntary. We pride ourselves in our hard work.

---

[121] Jared Keller, "What Makes Americans So Optimistic?" *The Atlantic*, March 25, 2015, https://www.theatlantic.com/politics/archive/2015/03/the-american-ethic-and-the-spirit-of-optimism/388538.

[122] G. E. Miller, "The U.S. Is the Most Overworked Developed Nation in the World,"

Many people with inherited wealth in the United States pretend to be "self-made." Part of the reason may be that they are not given anywhere near the respect that a self-made individual commands. While there are old-money families who disdain new-monied individuals; on the other side of the issue, rank-and-file Americans often scorn those who have unearned wealth. This work-hard, do-it-yourself schema may also account for many wealthy heirs, often wracked with guilt, burning through their wealth.[123] It is said that wealth in America usually only lasts an average of three generations before it is squandered. "70% of wealthy families lose their wealth by the second generation, and a stunning 90% by the third."[124]

Dr. Edward C. Chang, a clinical psychologist who runs the Perfectionism and Optimism-Pessimism Lab at the University of Michigan said,

> *American culture…centers entirely on the independent self and the happiness of the self…It's ingrained in the culture as an explicit, essential value — we're hit over the head with American freedom and liberty and rugged individualism so much so that explicit pessimism isn't actually tolerated that much in our society. It's treated as a mental illness, a sign of depression.*[125]

20Something Finance, updated Jan 13, 2020, https://tinyurl.com/jhuyv9c.

[123] Grant E. Donnally and Michael Norton, "Even for the Very Rich, More Money Brings Happiness," *The Wall Street Journal*, Dec 7, 2017, wsj.com/articles/even-for-the-very-rich-more-money-brings-happiness-1512662638. This article by Harvard Business School researchers demonstrated that "those who earned their wealth reported significantly greater happiness than those who primarily inherited or married into it. Of course, there are likely other differences between people who earned versus inherited their wealth that may contribute to these different levels of happiness."

[124] Chris Taylor, "70% of Rich Families Lose Their Wealth by the Second Generation," *Money*, June 17, 2015, money.com/rich-families-lose-wealth.

[125] Jared Keller.

American Equality

Americans, by and large, are strong believers in equality and individualism. In our minds, nobody should have power over us. And nobody should have privileges we cannot obtain for ourselves through intelligence and hard work. We have a completely different legacy than European countries, which have centuries of feudalism ingrained into the population's psyche. Europe's aristocrats had different rules and privileges than the majority of the population. In contrast, in theory at least, America has been an equal opportunity country from the start.[126] Today we believe that none of us is more important than anyone else. Nobody has a right to be above the law in America. These are uniquely American beliefs. That is why we get so angry when we read about people being discriminated against, harassed or killed because of the group they belong to. These horrible incidents contradict what we believe America to be, because fundamental to all of our beliefs is one: that "all men are created equal."[127] As a result, we value our own opinion as important, and it makes us appear to foreigners as confident, arrogant, outspoken and pushy. However, as independent as we may appear to others, we are still conforming. We just conform to the American way of thinking, the American schema.

Collective Schemas

Every group, including nations and regions within nations, behave and think differently. They do this because each has a different collective schema that has been formed by generations of shared history in a unique physical environment. Shared tragedies, victories and defeats are never forgotten, and they shape the collective schema.

---

[126] There are plenty of legitimate arguments to the contrary: the treatment of African slaves, of indigenous people, of Italians, Irish, Slavs, women, etc. But the majority of the nation has been indoctrinated with the idea of equal opportunity, and the idea has taken hold as the way it *should* be.

[127] Thomas Jefferson, Declaration of Independence, 1776.

Just as a fish cannot perceive water, most of us cannot perceive our own collective schema. We are swimming in it. We are blind to it. We don't even know the basic postulates that our worldview is based on. We just assume that our truths are universal, that they are true for all people. But they are not. They may not be even true for us.

How to Not Lose at Parties

I have been to a fair number of parties and, later, trade shows, which are similar, except the players are more mature. In both cases, you have individuals milling around often with an objective in mind. Find a mate for the night, find a prospect for a sale. Same thing really. One thing is true in both circumstances: nobody wants to stand alone in a crowded room where everyone is appearing to have a great time talking to each other. You end up wondering if something is wrong with you. Why will nobody speak with me? For the most part, that was my college party history.

It took me several years, but finally I did realize a few things. People at social events stand in groups, mostly because they are scared to stand alone. They do not want to feel what my friends and I felt when we were young. Unwanted. Shunned. Undesirable. Anything but that!

When you see a large group of, say, seven people, only two or three are talking. A few may be listening intently and at least two are just standing there, feeling bored and awkward. They don't want to leave the group and risk standing alone like a loser. Or, you might see someone standing in a group, absolutely not interested in what the group is saying, searching around the room for someone else to speak to. When they see a potential target, if that person appears to be in a receptive state, they will leave the group and join the other person. Again, they are safe. Safety is felt in a group, but not alone. In a group we are free of the demeaning inner dialogs. But, perhaps more central, we also seem to have this hardwired need to not be alone in a crowd—that is the worst place to feel alone. It is deep and powerful, probably instinctive.

So when I am at a party or a trade show, I will look for those people standing alone and approach them and start talking. Usually they are very receptive, as I have just saved them from feeling unwanted. I also approach people who are in a group but are clearly uninterested in the group and are just standing there to feel safe. These people can easily be led away from the group and will eagerly join me in conversation. My actions communicated to them that they are worthy, that they are important. Most everyone likes that.

Most people attend parties having never clearly identified their objectives. If you have a mission, you can set out to achieve it. Rather than just standing there and responding to the situation around you, you can be the situation and let the party respond to you. I came to realize that the typical reason I was at a party was to connect with people, and hopefully one of these connections would result in a beneficial friendship. (When I was young, I was often just looking for my next girlfriend.)

When I began viewing the event as a challenge, I could set an objective for the gathering and I could focus on that, rather than on my feelings of inadequacy. Now I had something to do. My goal became to stay at the party until I had had ten good five-minute conversations with people. I would converse with people as long as we both found it interesting. Some of these conversations would last for 30 minutes or more, as they were fun. All of a sudden, I was the one having fun. I didn't care about the rest of the group and what they were doing. We became the only group that mattered to me.[128]

This party story is very similar to our lives in general. We need to belong. To be alone is uncomfortable, and sometimes deadly to social animals. Life, you can say, is a party. We are here now. People show up at different

---

[128] The cell phone has added a complication to my party behavior. Now people who stand alone will be looking at their phones, which could or could not mean that they are open to conversation. They don't feel that fear and rejection as much, because they have diverted their attention away from the uncomfortable situation. When you approach them, you may be welcomed or you may be interrupting a pleasant diversion. The cell phone has hurt my game tremendously.

times. They leave at different times, alone or in groups. Some enjoy themselves, some do not. Some don't care what anyone else thinks of them. Most care too much about what everyone else thinks. Some become intoxicated and foolish. Others are critical of everyone else. But most of all, we need a group to be in. We need to belong or we become very uncomfortable.

Groups Warp and Restrain Individual Thought

Some groups we are in, we didn't choose. These are the involuntary groups. Most notably racial groups, ethnic groups, nationalities and the families we are born into; these are involuntary groups. On the other hand, we get to choose our voluntary groups. And these latter groups are usually a collection of individuals who share the same schema—the same values, the same norms, the same beliefs.[129] These groups validate us and define us. In a group, we become important, needed, valuable. But in order to belong to a group, we lose some of our individuality.[130] That's the rub.

The thing is, the group needs us too. The price of admission, though, is always conformity. Conformity is defined by the American Psychological Association as the adjustment of a person's opinions or thoughts so that they fall closer in line to those of other people or closer to their group's opinions and thoughts. Conformity includes temporary compliance, as well as more enduring private acceptance of, or conversion to, group schema.[131]

The Asch Experiment

In a previous essay, I wrote of an experiment by Ruth Berenda, in which children and high school students were asked to pick the longest lines from a group of three lines. Due to peer pressure, they would usually

---

[129] James F. Welles, *The Story of Stupidity: A History of Western Idiocy from the Days of Greece to the Moment You Saw This Book* (Pleasant Mountain, 1986), 55.

[130] Welles, *Story of Stupidity*, 55.

[131] *APA Dictionary of Psychology*, s.v. "conformity," dictionary.apa.org/conformity.

pick the wrong line. Solomon Asch was studying the same thing as Berenda, at the same time, the early 1950s.

Asch had fifty students from Swarthmore College participate in a "vision test." Each of the fifty test subjects was put in a room with seven actors who were instructed to give the same incorrect answers to an obvious question: which line on the right is the same length as the line on the left?

Each actor would state the same wrong answer, and the test subject was always asked last. Asch found that on average 32% of the test subjects went along with the actors, that is, conformed all the time. About 75% selected the wrong answer at least once, that is, 75% conformed sometimes. Only 25% never conformed and selected what they thought was the best answer. In order to make sure that the test subjects were not choosing the wrong lines due to poor vision, Asch also had a control group, in which there were no actors, only the test subject. This control group had only a 1% error rate.

After the test, the subjects were interviewed and most of them admitted that they did not really believe their wrong answers. Instead, they had gone along with the group out of fear of being ridiculed or thought "peculiar." A few even said they believed the groups' answers were right. Apparently, then, people conform because they want to fit in or because they trust the group's perceptions more than their own.[132]

Group Identity

Certainly, we are individuals. We see ourselves as unique. Most of us believe ourselves to be better than most other people. Alan Watts explained that in the very act of describing ourselves to others, we are comparing ourselves to other people. If I tell you I am honest, what I am saying is that I am more honest than other people and they are not honest. If I believed all people were honest, what would be the point

---

[132] Saul McLeod, "Solomen Asch Conformity Line Experiment," *Simply Psychology,* simplypsychology.org/asch-conformity.html, accessed January 1, 2023.

of saying that I am honest? Groups do the same thing. Groups see themselves as having certain qualities that make them uniquely different than other groups. Followers of an Indian guru likely see themselves as "seekers of Truth" and are willing to look for Truth outside mainstream thought, unlike those other groups of political partisans, gardeners or Dallas Cowboy fans, who prioritize other things.

The clothes we wear are like badges that identify which groups we belong to. This explains why most of us dress like everyone else in our group. When I was in college, the male professors wore tweed sportscoats and button up plain dull-colored shirts. To be a member of a group, you need to be identifiable as one of them. Nobody wants to be rejected by their group. When someone is different from the rest, it can get uncomfortable.

Underneath our clothes, most of us look pretty much the same. If we all walked around naked, bald and without jewelry, tattoos, makeup or any identifying marks, we probably would not be able to tell who was rich or poor; who was successful or not; who was a Democrat, a Republican or an independent; who was a Catholic, Jew, Protestant, Muslim or atheist or who loved or hated the New England Patriots.

Clothes, jewelry and tattoos are costumes, whether we realize it or not, and are a signal to others of which group we belong to. Once people figure that out, then they know how to treat us. We wear a costume to communicate to others the image of how we want to be seen. If you want to be a successful lawyer, you probably should dress like one. If lawyers dressed like crack dealers, they probably wouldn't have many clients, as few would trust them. Similarly, if crack dealers dressed like lawyers, they also would have a problem finding customers who would trust *them*. Imagine getting pulled over by a cop dressed like an '80s, big-haired hard rock superstar. If you dress wrong, people won't take you for what you want to be taken for. It is a game we all have to play. Those who understand the game can use the costume to good effect, furthering their own goals. Those who opt out of the game claim to wear clothes because they are "comfortable." As a result, they look like slobs to the rest of us. We would not hire them as a lawyer, pick them for our prophet or idolize them as a rock star. We might not even purchase crack from them.

Evolution, Cave Men and Conformity

So why do we feel this need to fit in and not stick out?

Humans are group animals. Our need for acceptance emerged as a survival mechanism. Solitary human beings could not have survived during the six million years of human evolution while we were living on the African savannah.[133] We evolved to live in cooperative societies; and for most of our history, we lived in groups for survival. Resources were scarce and everything was dangerous. Humans who bonded with others and could rely on one another survived. Together we could build shelters, keep warm, kill dangerous animals and protect ourselves from enemies. It was important to know who was in your tribe and who was not, as tribemates would help you and outsiders might rob or kill you.

We have since developed civilizations, formed cities and now carry cell phones, but we still have primitive brains. We continue to look for members of our tribe, which are the people who dress like us, have the same skin color or hair style as us or who root for the same team we do. After all these thousands of years of evolution, if you look different, you are usually not treated as well as you would be if you looked like the rest of the group. Ask any black person in America trying to rent a home or get a taxi in some white neighborhoods.

Submit to the Schema and You Belong

As I wrote earlier, many reasons exist for why the individual needs to belong to a group. But to belong, we have to submit to group pressure and make the group schema our own; or, like Roger Williams or James Damore, we may be kicked out of the group.

---

[133] Kristin Weir, "The Pain of Social Rejection," *Monitor on Psychology*, April 2012 (American Psychological Association), 50.

We are happy to do what it takes to belong. To maintain our connection to the groups we value, we adopt their core values and views. Without realizing it, we resist facts that threaten the group's defining values.[134] In essence, we allow ourselves to be selectively blinded in order to fit into our groups. The Asch experiment is a case in point.

We see this every day, especially in today's polarized political environment in the United States. Dan Kahan noted in his study that

> *nothing any ordinary member of the public personally believes about the existence, causes or likely consequences of global warming will affect the risk that climate change poses to her, or to anyone or anything she cares about.*[135]

This is absolutely true. If it is going to lead to catastrophe, it will. If it is not going to, then it won't. It doesn't matter what you believe about it.

> *However, if she forms the wrong position on climate change relative to the one that people with whom she has a close affinity—and on whose high regard and support she depends on in myriad ways in her daily life—she could suffer extremely unpleasant consequence, from shunning to the loss of employment.*[136]

In short, it is important your beliefs fit in with those around you or you will encounter problems. A case in point: regardless of the thousands of documented cases of ghosts, if you speak of them in a professional setting, you will lose all credibility among your colleagues.

Collective Delusion

Our instinct to align with the group leads to the dismissal or denial of facts that contradict the group's beliefs. This process narrows the group's perspective. We call this "groupthink." Individuals inside the

---

[134] Perhaps this is common knowledge, but I know James F. Welles wrote about it in his *History of Stupidity.*

[135] Kahan.

[136] Kahan.

group are unaware of how their thinking has been limited, but outsiders are often aware of defects in the way the group sees reality. In essence, groups, by their nature, have blinders on--even the "good" groups that you and I belong to. This blindness caused by group cohesion can lead to the group doing silly, ineffective or evil things.[137]

How can we know that our group is lacking a complete perspective?

We should just assume it is, because it is. That is the nature of groups. As for determining our own groups' blind spots, it is difficult, if not impossible, to objectively judge our group from our non-objective viewpoint of being inside the group. If we are members, then we have either consciously or unconsciously bought into the group's schema. By conforming to any group, we compromise our own unique capacity to understand the world around us.

If we are outside of a particular group, we, as individuals, cannot judge a group objectively either, because we belong to other groups which have a bias towards the group being evaluated. Members of the College Republicans may view ROTC members positively, perceiving them as having values similar to those they have internalized from their group. This perceived similarity creates a positive bias. I assume their internal thought process may be something like "they are like me and must therefore be good, because I am good." But what about those Goths who hang out at malls and cemeteries, wearing black clothes, black lipstick, combat boots and outrageous hair? The College Republicans may steer clear of the Goths, viewing them as irresponsible, lazy and weird. The Goths may see the College Republicans as heartless, money-grubbing sell-outs, who have no passionate, artistic or imaginative bone in their bodies. Although there may be some truth in both opposing viewpoints, neither viewpoint is an accurate reflection of the other group. Their opposing group schemas prevent them from seeing each other clearly. We are not capable of understanding people from other groups for what they are; or, at least, we do not allow ourselves to understand them.

---

[137] Welles, *Understanding Stupidity*, 80.

The philosopher Friedrich Nietzsche (1844–1900) wrote that madness in groups is the norm and that madness in the individual is the exception. Madness in groups stems from the collective denial of reality that does not fit its schema. We see this all the time. Madness in individuals comes when they are shut off from the group and they are left to create their own schema. Lone individuals become either madmen or geniuses, depending on who makes the determination.[138]

Hiding Our Dissent

We all have secret thoughts that we believe, but dare not express, because if we did voice them, we fear that others might reject us. Instead, we parrot, or at least do not question, the socially acceptable maxims so we can belong. We just "go along to get along." If we told the truth, the fallout we would receive from those around us might not be worth it. Examples may include working for a corrupt company while hiding our disgust, continuing to attend church services even though we question the faith's tenets, or secretly voting for the "evil" opposition candidate while not admitting it to anyone. Bucking the prevailing schema of the group can make your life uncomfortable and can lead to the worst consequences imaginable. After all, we get to exist only because the group allows us to. Once we have been singled out as different or detestable, we can lose our friends, our possessions, our freedom, even our lives. People get destroyed all the time.

Some Important Conclusions about Groups

Just because everyone around you believes something does not mean it is right. This is a very inconvenient truth.

The world as you understand it to be is not there, and never was. We are living a lie. Our beliefs are the lies we tell ourselves to simplify our lives and make them easy, until the lies cease to work. Then we become lost

---

[138] Welles, *Understanding Stupidity*, 84.

for a spell until we grab onto another simplification we can live with. And we go on merrily living the new lie.

Just because we are clueless and feel we need to rely on someone else to guide us, doesn't mean that groups of us are any more astute than we are alone. As respectable as they may appear, groups are clueless too. We are all living in a world of misconceptions and lies. We always have been and always will be. Nobody and no group has it right.

Groups may or may not be good for us. Much like the victorious slave soldiers of Spartacus' army, we can never know how things will turn out with the group. We might die on top of the world, having accomplished the impossible or we might die humiliated on a cross.

On the other hand, when we manage to break free of the group, it is liberating to be able to discount their shared schema. Once you recognize that the group is even more compromised than you are, you can open your life up to all sorts of possibilities. You can be free of the constraints of the group.

Wrapping It Up

- When we were born, we were not given a rulebook for how to live. We were born clueless. We look to individuals and groups to give structure, direction and meaning to our lives. Examples of groups include religious communities, sports teams, political organizations and business or success groups.

- Life is unpredictable. We may think we are on a winning track and then meet catastrophe, or we may think we are losing and end up with success.

- People rely on leaders and groups for guidance, believing that aligning with them will lead to positive outcomes. History shows that following the wrong leader can lead to disaster. We may think we are on the right track until we realize too late that we are not. Examples include the followers of Spartacus and Jim Jones.

- Groups need uniformity of thought to survive. If individuals want to be in a group, they must conform their thinking and actions with those of the group. We usually don't even notice when we are conforming.

- From infancy, individuals are shaped by group expectations, leading to conformity. "Well-adjusted" individuals are those who have been successfully indoctrinated by the groups they belong to. Society teaches us to conform, not to think or question social norms. Certainly not to listen to our own inner promptings.

- Groups have distinct collective schemas shaped by shared history. These schemas influence group expectations, perceptions and behavior. Groups are unaware of their own biases and individuals within the group are usually unaware of the biases they have taken on.

- Just as individuals will distort or deny facts to fit into their schemas, groups will do the same thing. Groupthink causes groups to make irrational and harmful decisions.

- Just as individuals do not have a clue about the nature and meaning of the world, groups don't either. Why would we think groups can comprehend clearly? Especially when there are so many groups that obviously have it wrong. None of them are right.

- Groups may appear respectable and to have it all figured out, but they don't. They are just as lost as we individuals are.

Essay 7
Exploring Morality – Group Psychology, Historical Shifts and Species Survival

Morality is just a fiction used by the herd of inferior human beings to hold back the few superior men.
— FRIEDRICH NIETZSCHE

Value Systems Compromised

In the last essay, I hope I conveyed to you how by belonging to groups we further compromise our understanding of reality. We never could clearly perceive the world in the first place, and our group identification only distorts our understanding more. Groups have no better grip on reality than individuals do.

I suppose no better example exists than the political divide the United States experiences every presidential election season. Adherents of the two opposing groups, the Democrats and Republicans, are spoon fed wild exaggerations by their favorite media sources. Partisans of both sides only want to hear news and opinions that reinforce their views. It is uncomfortable to pay attention to the other team's media, so people avoid it. Both sides are convinced they are in the right. Can they both be 100% right when their views appear to be 100% in opposition? Obviously not. Both sides are lying to their followers, but nobody wants to admit their party's own arguments are based on a selective portrayal of facts, embellishments and illogical reasoning. The grip on reality of everyone connected to a party is compromised by their party identifications.

As we have seen, to fit into our groups, Democrat, Goth, Mormon or whatever, we must abide by the groups' standards. We must voice the party line and suppress any contradictory points of view we may have. Adherence to the groups' dogmas colors our perceptions and impairs our logic, not necessarily in a more correct direction. We become less true to our own suppressed inner voices, deep inside. This is the tradeoff we make to belong and earn the regard of others in the group.[139] The group allows only limited dissent with a line you do not cross. The group is moving in a particular direction, and we can either join in or face the consequences. The result is often that we may be swayed into believing and doing things that we might otherwise never have believed or done.

Unethical Pro-organizational Behavior

If we were asked to name the worst groups in Western history, most people would probably name the German Nazi party or the Russian Communists as the worst. And that would be reasonable. Repressive regimes can be soul-killing (and murderous) organizations. But corporations can also destroy members' souls and outsiders' lives.

We have all heard countless stories of evil corporate behavior. Having worked for a corporation, I was often shocked at how unscrupulous individuals in corporations can be. Millions of people suspend their sense of ethics and cheat or lie for the sake of the company, even though they would never do it for personal gain. These people are

---

[139] Welles, *Understanding Stupidity,* 80.

more common than you think. I like to pride myself on spotting them a mile away.

For years, immoral individual behavior in corporations has been a topic of academic study. Social psychology scholars have differentiated unethical behavior in organizations into two classes. One type of unethical behavior is done for the good of the individual. An easy example would be the stereotypical used car salesman who knowingly lies and confuses you in order to sell you a piece of junk. The salesman then receives a hefty commission on the sale. The other type is when employees take part in unethical behavior for the sake of the company, not for themselves. They may benefit indirectly if the company succeeds, but essentially the main motivation appears to be the good of the company. This type of behavior appears to be common in some companies, but not in others.

This "unethical pro-organizational behavior" (UPB) can be defined as "actions that are intended to promote the effective functioning of the organization or its members (e.g., leaders) and violate core societal values, norms, laws or standards of proper conduct." An example is a tendency to "exaggerate the truth about one's company's products or services to customers and clients to benefit one's company."[140]

UPB happens all the time. And in many instances, it is a group effort. I have been in a room full of salespeople and executives, all of them lying to the prospect in order to make the sale—the peer pressure to maintain the lie was intense. Employees of many startups will lie (they call it "embellishing the truth") in order to obtain funding or to gain their first large client. These same people would not lie when selling their used car to someone in their church. No, they would not. Academics call it *pro-organizational* behavior for a reason. Liars will do it for the team. In my case, I was called into my supervisor's office and warned

---

[140] E. E. Umphress, J. B. Bingham, M. S. Mitchell, "Unethical behavior in the name of the company: the moderating effect of organizational identification and positive reciprocity beliefs on unethical pro-organizational behavior," *Journal of Applied Psychology*, 2010, vol. 95(4), 769–780, doi.org/10.1037/a0019214, accessed January 1, 2023.

that I needed to discard my "misguided conception of ethics" and help the company make a two-million-dollar sale.

I would never sacrifice my integrity for any group. That must be what my supervisor was talking about when he referenced my "misguided conception of ethics." I don't know how he knew that about me. Maybe he could smell it. Snakes smell, you know. So, there we were in the room with the prospects, two Texas bubbas, Buck and Cletus, who were entirely unsophisticated, easy to fool and had the authority to spend millions. I showed them my software. It was vaporware at the time—it didn't really exist. The client asked a boneheaded question: "Will it do such and such?" The entire room, my colleagues, all nodded their heads and said, "Of course it will" or something to that effect. One of the prospects pointed at me and said, "I want to hear what he says." I told him the truth. I told him that the software could never do what he wanted it to do. I told him that only good engineers can do what he wanted, not software. It was a powerful moment for me (and possibly disastrous for my company). In that moment, I glimpsed the truth and saw my colleagues for what they were, otherwise good people who would lie for the sake of the company. Needless to say, we lost the sale, and I instantly became a pariah. It was really uncomfortable. For days, my colleagues wouldn't even look at me—they would look away or leave a room when I entered. To their great pleasure, I soon thereafter left the company. I reiterate: these were mostly good people in that room, but these good people were willing to lie in order to fleece a prospect for the good of the team. It was easy to rationalize, I suppose. It wasn't Buck and Cletus' money, after all. It was their company's money, a publicly traded company. Nobody actually owned the money, so we can take it. We needed it. I had never seen anything like that before—honest people doing really bad things for the group. Unfortunately, I wasn't like the others. I had crossed the line and let my personal beliefs get in the way of group success.

What I witnessed was a medium-size lie. If you really think about it, almost all employees will tolerate the "little" lies from the marketing department. "We have the best. . .We are the best. . .We care about our customers. . .We care about sustainability." Individuals in the company may not lie, but they will tolerate lies from their marketing department. At what point is a lie personally untenable? The threshold is different for different people.

I think the pressure is highest to engage in unethical behavior when the company is a startup. Established businesses have proven that they can survive on their own without outside investors. But startups experience tremendous pressure to gain sales and to become profitable before the investors lose hope and shut down the company.

Startups are full of people working eighty-plus-hour weeks—they are committed to succeeding. The mantra is clear: "We're in this as a team and our hard work will pay off big." We have all worked so hard for our success. No way will we let the team down. In these conditions, it is easy to let your moral standards slip when there is so much focus on sales and profits. Why worry about a small lie when you've all sacrificed so much for the company? One little fib to guarantee the company's success—it's a trivial point when compared to the huge payoff.

Usually, if UPB is widespread, it starts at the top. According to social identity theory, leaders help individuals establish standards of "right" behavior in the organization. When leaders engage in UPB, individuals think they should as well and even convince themselves that such behavior is ethical. Often, they feel that the risks associated with lying, cheating or stealing are less when they see leaders engage in these acts.[141] Leaders' UPB can and does affect the individual's view of what is right and wrong.

If what society at large considers unethical (such as lying or falsifying records) appears to help the organization, then it is not entirely clear

---

[141] Yun Zhang, Bin He, Xu Sun, "The Contagion of Unethical Pro-organizational Behavior: From Leaders to Followers," *Frontiers in Psychology*, vol. 9 (2018), in National Library of Medicine, ncbi.nlm.nih.gov/pmc/articles/PMC6038011/, accessed January 1, 2025.

to individuals in the organization whether this behavior is unethical or not. It is, after all, good for the company. "When the categorization of a particular behavior is not clear, people tend to classify the behavior in a positive way in order to avoid negatively updating their moral self-image."[142] So when a leader's UPB is observed, individuals may change their moral judgement about this type of behavior and consider it appropriate behavior in the context. "Accordingly, individuals will convince themselves that UPB is appropriate and be willing to follow suit."[143]

Experimental studies have shown just that: when people are surrounded by the unethical behavior of their peers, they are likely to imitate the behavior of those peers, because such behaviors demonstrate apparently appropriate organizational norms.[144] "Therefore, when observing [leadership's UPB], subordinates will likely consider such behavior to be what the organization expects of them and they may then follow and engage in UPB themselves."[145]

Wells Fargo

In the year 2016, news got out that Wells Fargo Bank had been secretly enrolling their existing banking clients into over two million additional checking and credit card accounts without their clients' knowledge, complete with phony signatures, email addresses and PIN numbers. These unsuspecting clients were then hit with new monthly fees without understanding what they were for. Almost all of them paid the new fees. The policy of maximizing the number of accounts per client started at the top and employees felt the pressure to conform. The bankers (aka

---

[142] M. E. Schweitzer and C. K. Hsee, "Stretching the Truth: Elastic Justification and Motivated Communication of Uncertain Information," *Journal of Risk and Uncertainty*, vol. 25 (2002), 185–201, in Yun Zhang, Bin He, and Xu Sun.

[143] F. Gino, S. Ayal, D. Ariely, "Self-serving altruism? The lure of unethical actions that benefit others," *Journal of Economic Behavior and Organization*, vol. 93 (2013), 285–292, in Yun Zhang, Bin He, and Xu Sun.

[144] F. Gino, S. Ayal, D. Ariely.

[145] Yun Zhang, Bin He, and Xu Sun.

salespeople) and their managers received commissions on their sales both real and forged. Bankers were expected to sell up to twenty new accounts daily.[146] Employees who missed sales quotas were penalized with having to work nights and weekends. According to The Week,[147] Wells Fargo earned tens of billions of dollars using these dishonest sales tactics. After being caught, the bank fired about 5,300 employees, but only one top executive was punished.

This was not the only recent scandal. Wells Fargo has been punished for several other crimes previously and since with fines totaling over $10 billion. Still, Wells Fargo employed about 269,000 employees in 2016 and 258,000 employees in 2018. Here is the real question that comes to mind: why would employees continue to work for such a dishonest company? Especially in 2019 and early 2020. Unemployment was at its lowest level in history and it would have been easy to find another job, but these people stayed. Why would anyone work for a criminally dishonest employer?

California Energy Crisis

I am sure there are thousands of examples of UPB, good people doing bad things for the "good" of the group, and you can probably think of many. Another ugly example that stands out is the California power crisis of 2000—I know, before some of you were born.

In 2000, California partially-deregulated its electricity markets and as a result experienced massive electricity shortages and spikes in prices. The problem was that the three investor-owned utilities (IOUs) in California—Pacific Gas and Electric (PG&E), Southern California Edison (SCE) and San Diego Gas & Electric (SDG&E)—by law had an upper limit, a cap, on electricity prices they could charge consumers, but they also had to purchase electricity on the open market at variable

---

[146] Chris Arnold, "Former Wells Fargo Employees Describe Toxic Sales Culture, Even at HQ," *NPR* online edition, October 4, 2016, https://tinyurl.com/28jja68y.

[147] "Wells Fargo Phony-Account Scandal Explained," The Week, online edition, September 16, 2016, https://tinyurl.com/2bwfkgho

prices. Deregulation required that their generating assets be sold off, and they were. The cap on retail prices should not have been a problem. California at the time had a generating capacity of 45 GW and a demand of only 28 GW, more than enough generating capacity—it just wasn't in the hands of the investor-owned utilities anymore. The new deregulated system was poorly designed and invited market manipulation by companies such as Enron, Dynegy, Duke Energy and Reliant Energy and many others who owned the electricity plants and gas pipelines.[148] These companies were then able to game the wholesale electricity markets by closing generation plants, shutting down gas pipelines, and other shenanigans to create artificial shortages of electricity. Using these tactics, these out-of-state companies were able to sell electricity to the IOUs at a rate up to 800% higher than before deregulation started. As a result, rolling blackouts occurred and California rate payers paid $11 billion more for electricity in the summer of 2000 than the prior summer. PG&E and SCE racked up $20 billion in debt. PG&E declared bankruptcy, and SCE almost did. Finally, the governor signed long-term electricity contracts that locked individual and business ratepayers into overpriced contracts for the next decade. It was a disaster for ratepayers.[149]

This went on for a long time. Enron employees even contrived names such as the Death Star, Ricochet and the Black Widow for the strategies they used to defraud California ratepayers. In the Death Star strategy, Enron would be paid money by the State of California, as recorded in an internal document, "to relieve congestion [in the distribution system] without actually moving any energy or relieving any congestion."[150] In the Ricochet strategy, Enron would move power generated in California

---

[148] Over 40% of electricity production in California in 2000 was from natural gas power plants.

[149] Federal Energy Regulatory Commission (FERC), "Final Report on Price Manipulation in Western Markets," March 2003, https://tinyurl.com/29qxhghz.

[150] Kathryn Kranhold, Bryan Lee, and Mitchel Benson, "New Documents Show Enron Traders Manipulated California Energy Costs," *The Wall Street Journal,* online edition, May 7, 2002, wsj.com/articles/SB1020718637382274400. Quote comes from an internal Enron document.

to neighboring states and then sell it back into California at a high price, avoiding the price cap on California-generated electricity.[151] If Enron lost money in a transaction, they would intentionally introduce errors into the transaction to neutralize the losses—this was called the Black Widow strategy.[152]

California authorities had not planned on electricity providers gaming the market like that—but it happened. A lawsuit was filed, of course. In 2005 Enron reached a $1.52 billion settlement with California, but having already declared bankruptcy in 2001, it paid only a small fraction of the total. In 2004, through the Freedom of Information Act, tapes of Enron employee conversations were released by the Federal Government. What follows is from a taped conversation about the settlements.

> *"They're f------g taking all the money back from you guys?" complains an Enron employee on the tapes. "All the money you guys stole from those poor grandmothers in California?"*
>
> *"Yeah, grandma Millie, man."*
>
> *"Yeah, now she wants her f------g money back for all the power you've charged right up, jammed right up her a------ for f------g $250 a megawatt hour."[153]*

Corporate Sociopathy

It has been often remarked that if corporations were people, they would be considered sociopaths. So how do you define sociopathic? Sociopaths use charm, cleverness, deceit, and violence to manipulate others to get what they want. You can spot a sociopath by the following symptoms: lack of conscience or sense of guilt, lack of empathy, egocentricity, pathological lying, repeated violations of social norms, disregard for the law, shallow emotions and a history of victimizing others. Countless

---

[151] Kranhold, Lee, and Benson.

[152] Kranhold, Lee, and Benson.

[153] Joel Roberts, "Enron Traders Caught on Tape," CBS News, June 1, 2004. cbsnews.com/news/enron-traders-caught-on-tape.

corporations routinely destroy people's lives, lie, break laws, cover up their wrongdoings, and feel justified doing it. They demonstrate no empathy for their victims. When the corporations are caught doing harm, corporate lawyers usually clean it all up by blaming others, bribing relevant officials or trying to sweep it under the carpet. So then, I guess it is not that far a stretch to claim that some businesses are indeed sociopathic.

It isn't that business itself is evil. It is not. Businesses provide us with the wealth we have in the Western World. It is the entrepreneurial capitalist spirit that has brought us the food revolutions that allow us to feed the planet. It has brought us most of the technological innovations that have made our lives more comfortable and prosperous: computers, airplanes, automobiles and, yes, electricity, you name it.

Successful companies exist in order to profit. Profit, in itself, is not good or bad. It just seems to work, keeping the economy moving for everyone. The profit motive of companies owned by an individual or a family is often tempered by a set of personal values. The company owned by an individual is an extension of the individual. The owner has control and is ultimately responsible for everything that the company does. If a private company does bad things, ultimately only one person is responsible. True, there are some individual business owners who will lie, cheat and steal to make a profit. But their businesses usually don't make it, as they will build up a bad reputation and will be shunned. Most small businesses that thrive have integrity, enjoy good reputations, happy customers and happy employees.

Public corporations, on the other hand, are not associated with an owner's set of values like a small business is. They are controlled by a group, a board of directors or high-level management. In corporations, often there is no accountability for evil doing. Individuals may be fired, but the corporation lives on with the same lack of accountability. Usually the same management, systems and motivations remain in place. And, most wrongdoers are left intact and continue to be bad actors.

Corporations are often fined, as was Wells Fargo. But individuals usually get off. Did the traders who stole from Grandma Millie go to jail? No. In the Enron scandal, only seventeen people were punished by the law. Did the thousands of Wells Fargo bankers who falsified documents go to jail? No. Nobody from Wells Fargo was jailed. Instead, thousands were fired for falsifying documents. If a person off the street forged documents like those, they would be charged and arrested. For the most part, nobody is accountable for the wrongdoings of the corporate world.

Add to this, corporations, by law, are bound to the interests of the share-holders, who invest in order to make a profit. In public corporations, profit is the overriding goal. Corporate officers are legally bound to put profit before everything else, including the public good. This is their job. If a CEO accepts an annual loss for the company in order to do some public good, such as cleaning up the environment, prices of the company's stock can drop. The Board of Directors and the major stockholders will lose massive amounts of money as stock prices decline. The stockholders will revolt, demanding the CEO's head. And the CEO will be fired. This is by design the nature of public corporations.

In order to increase profits, compensation for CEOs and for many managers is often based on profits. More profits translate to more pay. These incentives motivate management to make profitable decisions, and ultimately this benefits the shareholders. But incentives can also lead management and workers to make morally questionable calls in order to safeguard their jobs, move up the organizational ladder and gain more pay. Recall the Wells Fargo scandal I mentioned. The workers had to meet quotas for new accounts or be punished. The traders at Enron earned commissions from their dishonest dealings. Jeff Skilling, the CEO at Enron, owned stock and received bonuses based on the company's performance.

Because the drive for profit overrides ethical considerations, the inherent design of public corporations tends to promote unethical conduct. Managing a public corporation is a game, and the game is set up so that sociopaths can prosper. The combination of the lack of personal accountability, the requirement that corporations provide profits to shareholders regardless of the cost and the linking of compensation to profit, together form the structural evil we often see in corporations. This is not to say that all public corporations are inherently bad or that they cannot do good. When corporations contribute positively to society, it is something to celebrate, especially given that their very structure does not promote that sort of thing. Still, it's important to recognize that the tendency for public corporations to perform evil acts is built into the corporate structure. It is in their nature.

When led by less scrupulous individuals, corporations can easily become groups of the worst kind. And when you add in the individual's need to belong to and contribute to the group and people's tendency to filter and distort reality to match the schema of the group, then you get an Enron or a Wells Fargo.

The Worst Group Ever

It can get worse, of course, like in Nazi Germany, where ordinary good people cooperated to do terrible things. What probably comes to mind first as the most egregious case of unethical pro-organizational behavior are the actions of security guards in the Nazi concentration camps. Yet worse, perhaps, were the German soldiers who were working to liberate Slavic territories for the German people in World War II.

Lebensraum (living space), a German concept that predated Hitler, was similar to the American Manifest Destiny idea. (Hitler actually studied Manifest Destiny developing his Lebensraum ideas.) According to Manifest Destiny, God had given to the American nation an empty continent to expand into. Americans need only claim, cultivate, and exploit it—and replace the "inferior" indigenous people who happened to be there. Taking the land, repopulating and developing it was seen as progress.

In a similar fashion, the German people needed land to expand into. The land to the East had great reserves of timber, minerals and fertile farmland, which could support the German people. The only problem was that the targeted land (in Poland and parts of Czechoslovakia, the Baltic States and the western USSR) was already populated by Slavs, Jews and Gypsies (Romani), whom the Germans considered inferior peoples. Taking that land, repopulating and developing it, would be considered progress. Hitler's plan was to clear the land for the German people by the killing, starvation or removal of the thirty million people already living there. Generalplan Ost stated that "many tens of millions of people in this territory will become superfluous and will have to die or migrate to Siberia."[154]

Implementation of Generalplan Ost began in 1939 after the annexation of parts of Czechoslovakia and the invasion of Poland. In 1941, with 3 million soldiers, Hitler launched Operation Barbarossa, the invasion of the Soviet Union. The army was not charged with killing civilians; instead, the Einsatzgruppen was assigned this task. Having already killed 65,000 civilians, mostly composed of leaders, teachers, Jews, Romani and the mentally ill, in Poland in the two years before Barbarossa, the Einsatzgruppen was tasked with cleaning up captured Soviet lands in Barbarossa. Their targets were Jews, Soviet Commissars, Romani, Slavs and the mentally ill.

It is likely that most German civilians did not know of the Einsatzgruppen and its massacres of civilians. This is just like Americans today don't know what our special forces are doing now all over the world. The Nazis tightly controlled Germany's media, flooding newspapers and radios with messages glorifying the Reich and vilifying Jews.[155] Many Germans probably knew that the Jews were sent away and their possessions taken. That would be hard to miss in German cities.

---

[154] Although this quote is from a translation of Generalplan Ost, it was found in the *Holocaust Encyclopedia* article on Lebensraum, https://encyclopedia.ushmm.org/content/en/article/lebensraum.

[155] William Shirer's *Berlin Diary* (Alfred A. Knopf, 1941) documents his time in Germany during the 1930s and early 1940s. He wrote about the media lies and how those people who were sharp enough to disbelieve the media still had no clue what was actually taking place.

But the Americans knew the same thing during World War II about the Japanese living in the United States—people taken away, lands appropriated and sold. The press instructed both populations about the evil of these minority populations. Neither the Germans nor the Americans knew what was really going on with these minorities. And, if some did hear stories about what was really occurring, as we have discussed in earlier essays, when people receive unwelcome information, it is so easy to dismiss. "After all, it isn't in any of the newspapers, so why should I believe this far-fetched story?"

So why did members of the Einsatzgruppen commit massacres? As children, they were indoctrinated with Nazi ideology, and then they grew up. I believe it is as simple as that. Nazi ideology became their reality; and even if they questioned it, they went along to avoid standing out. The Nazi youth groups started as early as 1922 and by 1933 had grown to 2.3 million youth. These groups trained boys, ages fourteen to eighteen, to become part of the Nazi war machine. During their formative years, they were groomed and indoctrinated. They learned Nazi ideology, hatred of Jews and basic military operations. The groups gave them an identity, a community and a purpose. Upon reaching adulthood, they did as they were trained to do, and many became part of the Einsatzgruppen. Being patriotic Germans, they were happy to play a part in the great struggle to bring about the inevitable domination of the Aryan race.

The point is that good people in bad groups can do terrible things. Those people who were in the Einsatzgruppen were humans, after all. They did horrendous deeds. But before they did, maybe many years before, they were good people, just like the people we don't even notice every day on the streets. They had mothers who loved them. Many probably had lovers or wives back home. Probably, like the rest of us, most of them wanted the same things we want, a home, a happy family, a sense of importance and security.

These examples reveal the raw strength of groups, twisting minds and lives beyond recognition. In fact, groups bend history. Groups are the force, the prime mover, of human history. As I have written elsewhere, I don't trust groups. They can crush any individual for the good of the group, and they often do. It need not be just. The rights, even the lives, of individual members or of members of competing groups are of little to no importance to the larger group. It is all about group maintenance.

Kaczynski and Groups versus the Individual

Theodore Kaczynski starts *Industrial Society and Its Future* with a detailed description of American "leftism." He presents his theory as to why people are leftists. Mostly, he is writing about people from the majority group in the United States—straight, white, able-bodied people.

> *Many leftists have an intense identification with the problems of groups that have an image of being weak (women), defeated (American Indians), repellent (homosexuals), or otherwise inferior.*[156]

They are overly sensitive to any terms they might interpret as derogatory to these groups.

> *The leftists themselves feel that these groups are inferior. They would never admit it to themselves that they have such feelings, but it is precisely because they do see these groups as inferior that they identify with their problems. (We do not suggest that women, Indians, etc., ARE inferior; we are only making a point about leftist psychology).*[157]

Kaczynski's theory is that leftists hate anything strong, good or successful: the military, the United States, the police, large corporations, rich people, strong men, winning sports teams, white males and especially rich white males. This hatred comes from an inherent feeling of inferiority, which

---

[156] Kaczynski, #13.

[157] Kaczynski, #13.

he defines as "low self-esteem, feelings of powerlessness, depressive tendencies, defeatism, guilt, self-hatred, etc."[158]

> *Words like "self-confidence," "self-reliance," "initiative," "enterprise," "optimism," etc. play little role in the liberal and leftist vocabulary. The leftist is anti-individualistic, pro-collectivist. He wants society to solve everyone's needs for them, take care of them. He is not the sort of person who has an inner sense of confidence in his own ability to solve his own problems and satisfy his own needs. The leftist is antagonistic to the concept of competition because, deep inside, he feels like a loser.*[159]

In my own case, he was right on. He accurately described my mindset as a youth. I was a hard-core leftist and full of hatred of the strong. And why was I so hateful? It was because deep inside I was convinced that I was weak and worthless. I heard this too much as a child and I believed what I was told. I really was physically weak, skinny and sickly. That didn't help matters. The strong were the winners, and I was a loser. Of course I hated the strong.

In general, conservatives do not have this feeling of being oppressed by the strong. In general, they feel empowered and able to define their own destinies. They like to stand alone and be left alone to do whatever they want to do in the world. Conversely liberals, feeling weak inside and oppressed by the strong man, bind themselves together into movements (aka groups) in order to defeat the oppressors, who dare to stand alone.

The leftists are onto something. Groups are powerful. In most cases, they are so much stronger than an individual. Groups kill individuals. Individuals do not kill groups.[160] What happens when a praying mantis falls in an anthill? The mantis is about 100 times larger than an ant. It can easily dispatch ants left and right. It is so much more powerful

---

[158] Kaczynski, #10.

[159] Kaczynski, #16.

[160] Individuals within a group can kill it. Usually this is done by bad leadership. But outsiders generally cannot take on and kill a group.

than any ant, but it will find itself no match to an unrelenting swarm of ants—the nonstop attack, climbing, riding, biting. The mantis, despite its size advantage, eventually will succumb to the collective assault. In the end, the ants will dismember and consume the fallen giant, demonstrating the power of their collective strength against what seems to be a superior foe.

In groups we can be powerful. In groups, we become a force to be reckoned with.

Groups are not evil by nature. They just are what they are. Wherever people are cooperating, there are groups. Even fish and cows form groups. We need to belong to groups to survive and to define who we are. Yet by joining, we give groups the power to distort our minds and lead us into doing evil. Groups can destroy our souls. It is important to remain mindful that our groups can push us towards good or evil and that they have a deep influence on our lives. Some groups either consciously, like Nazi Germany, or unconsciously, like corporate cultures, define the morality of their members.

Crafting Morality for the Masses

So what about morality? Throughout the ages, people have thought hard about it, where it comes from and how to instill it in people for a healthy society. People are by nature greedy, jealous, combative and promiscuous, but there must be a way to make them behave and get along. Perhaps a set of rules would do it. In some mysterious manner most of us have been imprinted with a set of rules. I think we call these rules morality.

Plato and His Plan to Instill Morality

In his *Republic*, Plato came up with a good solution for instilling morality, that is, a plan to keep people in check and working towards the greater good. He suggested that there should be a god-centered religion that can moderate man's baser instincts. The religion should include a belief in the afterlife so that we can more easily face death.

According to Plato, even though this proposed religion may be totally contrived, it would do society great good to adhere to it. Sound familiar?

What is truly amazing to me is that the medieval Catholic Church appears to have come straight from Plato. The ideas of heaven, purgatory and hell, at least in their medieval form, can be traced to Plato's *Republic*.[161] The conception of three classes of society, the workers, the soldiers and the learned (clergy) are in *The Republic*. The clergy, although small in number, "monopolized the instruments and opportunities of culture." They were the only ones who could read and write. The clergy ruled with almost unlimited authority half of the most powerful continent on the globe.[162] They were free from the distraction of raising families, just as described by Plato. As the historian Will Durant (1885–1981) wrote:

> *With this body of doctrine [Catholicism], the people of Europe were ruled with hardly any resort to force; and they accepted this rule so readily that for a thousand years they contributed plentiful material support to their rulers and asked no voice in the government...merchants and soldiers, feudal chieftains and civil powers all bent the knee to Rome.*[163]

So I guess you can say that our moral system springs from Plato's *Republic*, and the rudiments of the system it described were put into place by the Emperor Constantine 700 years after Plato wrote it. But did the early Church fathers use *The Republic* as a guidebook? It is not likely.[164] Platonism was popular at about that time, but Plato's Republic was not well-known and did not become popular until the Renaissance.

---

[161] Will Durant, *The Story of Philosophy* (Simon & Schuster, 1926), 27.

[162] Will Durant, *The Story of Philosophy*, 41.

[163] Will Durant, *The Story of Philosophy*, 41.

[164] It sure would be a good conspiracy theory, though, to claim that the powers that be set up the Church to establish their own power and to keep the population docile. Conspiracy or not, it worked. And, it sounds much like conspiracy theories today about the New World Order and the World Economic Council, etc., and their plans to guarantee both their power and a docile world society.

The Medieval Church

In medieval times when the Church dominated the lives of most Europeans, these subject people complied with the Christian ethic. Certainly, there were some outliers, including some Church leaders who were the era's most notorious wrongdoers. But there was a common code that was known by all, and society was structured around the religion and its code. The Church determined what actions were morally correct, justified their pronouncements with painstakingly contrived theologies, enforced it all with heinous punishments and the unlettered people accepted it. People needed to believe in something—we still need to believe—and the Church leaders gave them a working theology.

Morality in the Modern Era

With the fall of the CatholicChurch from predominance in our modern lives, we have no fundamental basis for morality anymore. This may be the first age in history in which a large percentage of people have no common and authoritative belief to base their lives on. Until Martin Luther's time, one could point to the Church's teachings and claim they were definitively true. The Church was put in place by God to shepherd His people to heaven. The Church's interpretation of the gospels was authoritative. But that sense of unquestionable authority was destroyed by Martin Luther, a formerly good Catholic, when he claimed that individuals could interpret the gospel however they wanted. And to make this possible, Luther translated the entire Bible into German, so that the German-speaking people could see what was actually in these books. Before that, for centuries, the Bible had been available only in Latin or Greek, languages that only the clerics could understand.[165]

---

[165] It is actually a little more complicated that. There were several earlier translations of the Bible into German, all of them in the fifteenth century. These other translations were often only parts of the Bible, and/or were translated into more archaic hard-to-read German. Luther's book was written in easy-to-understand language. His translation, and not the others, was widely published. Hundreds of thousands of copies were printed.

Now that people could read the Bible for themselves, the mysteries disappeared. People could, for the first time "see behind the curtain," like when the Dorothy saw that the Great and Powerful Oz was just a bumbling old man. The gospels were now available for anyone to interpret as they saw fit. Imagine the effect that had on the Church. No longer were priests needed to hear the word of God. The Church was not needed. You could learn God's Will on your own. Martin Luther did later realize that he had taken it too far, as the idea of individual interpretation resulted in Anabaptist, Quaker and other "blasphemous" devils preaching all sorts of "dangerous" heresies. In response to this religious anarchy, Lutheranism became systematized into a creed. Individual belief was no longer tolerated by Martin Luther nor the authorities, who hastened to kill, burn and wipe out these unsanctioned heretics.

A long time has passed since that break from the Catholic Church. The Church has never recovered the near-complete control it once had over more than fifty generations in the West. Science has since further undermined the Church's teachings. Few people believe anymore that the world was actually created in seven days, that Eve came from Adam's rib and that there is a small number of the elect who make it to heaven while the rest of us burn in hell or languish in purgatory. When we read about the Tower of Babel, few really believe it occurred; and instead, we consider this, along with the rest of the Bible's supernatural stories, to be some kind of literary device to impart knowledge of God to simple, unlettered, ancient peoples.

Today, while many profess to believe in God, it might be difficult to pin them down to a particular creed. Despite hundreds of Christian creeds to choose from, we can no longer point authoritatively to the one church and dogma that God has sent to guide us, so we must decide for ourselves. But decide based on what evidence? As we can no longer believe what the Bible says literally, we are left to use our own minds to try to make sense of it. In medieval times, using your own judgment meant you were a heretic, and the punishment was severe. Today, most of us use a shopping cart approach to Christianity. We pick and choose what to think. This is the first era in which Western people are free to live as they choose, without having to suffer shame, isolation or violence for having their own unique beliefs about God.

So how do we handle morality in this era? We have been living in an experimental era for a few centuries now. The Church no longer sets our code of conduct. Society seems to work for the most part. Violence and other forms of heartlessness towards other people are down, so maybe we don't need the Church anymore to keep us in line. According to Phil Zuckerman's book, *Society without God*, Denmark and Sweden, among the least religious countries in the history of the world, have the lowest violent crime rates and lowest levels of corruption. Apparently, they don't need the Church to have secure and civil societies. Zukerman explains though that while we may not need the Church now, the Church did establish the moral systems we have today in the Western world. Before Christianity arrived in Scandinavia, the inhabitants were violent, murderous peoples, whose morality was based on power, fighting prowess and domination.

Theories of Morality

Conscience, Morality, Moral Laws and Ethics—they all mean the same to most of us. To moral philosophers, there is a difference; but I don't think there is much to be gained by a painstaking parsing of these concepts. All that really matters is whether the points I try to impart are actually meaningful to you. So, let's begin.

Morality, or whatever term you may want to use, is a set of behavioral standards or codes of conduct that are considered proper, good or right. These standards are instilled in us by society at large. When you violate the code, you feel remorse, guilt, fear and, I am sure, other awful things. But who gets to define what is moral?

People have devised many modern theories to explain where our sense of morality comes from. Most of them are based on the group; and that makes sense, as I have defined morality to be something that society imposes on us. Systems of morality are of primary importance for a group to maintain itself. Without a clear-cut moral code, no society could survive. It would be plagued by continuous fighting over resources and power, as every individual would be concerned only about their own security, wealth and power. Killing others and stealing their things in order to meet one's needs would be the order of the day.

C.S. Lewis and Michael Ruse

One theory, expounded by C.S. Lewis (1898–1963), is that we all ascribe to the same moral principles regardless of which culture or group we belong to.

> *Human beings, all over the earth, have this curious idea that they ought to behave in a certain way, and cannot really get rid of it.*[166]

In *Mere Christianity*, Lewis argued that different cultures and times have had only slightly different moralities, that they have been mostly the same. For example,

> *Think of a country where people were admired for running away in battle, or where a man felt proud of double-crossing all the people who had been kindest to him.*[167]

People may differ about how outsiders should be treated, but they have always agreed that one should never put one's own self first.

We are all subject to these moral laws, but we are not bound to them. We can all break them, and we do all the time. And then we feel terrible. Why is it that drivers would rather hit the brakes than run over a rabbit? And if we kill the rabbit, why do we feel bad about it? Where did that come from? The Bible does not address it. Not needlessly killing animals would be considered a common moral law that nearly all humans share. Why is it that stealing from someone in your group is considered wrong in every culture? Prohibitions against stealing are another moral law.

---

[166] C.S. Lewis, *Mere Christianity* (Harper Collins, 2001), 95.
[167] C.S. Lewis, 95.

These moral laws are common concepts consistent across times and cultures. According to C.S. Lewis, that implies that moral laws are derived from some supernatural force, perhaps God, Himself.

I have a difficult time believing C.S. Lewis's theory. One need only think of the barbarous nations in the past in which killing was valued more than loving. I do not believe the Vikings, the Huns, the Comanches or the Mongols felt morally compromised about killing men, raping women and enslaving survivors in the villages they assaulted. It was who they were. It was part of their self-definition. They were valiant conquerors, mighty heroes and the champions of their region.

Others have argued, as C.S. Lewis suggested, that morality is ingrained in our minds but that it appeared as a byproduct of natural selection, not from a divine being. Animals and societies that are more cooperative are more effective at dominating the environment. Our morality is useful to the species to survive and reproduce. Societies that advocate immoral behavior such as theft or murder within the group would kill themselves off, reducing the capability of the human race to endure. These immoral societies would be reduced to a Mad Max type of dystopian world. According to Michael Ruse (1940–), a contemporary Canadian philosopher, "morality is an illusion put in place by your genes to make you a social cooperator."[168] We are humans with our gene-based psychology working flat out to make us think we should be moral.[169]

> *Morality. . .is not something handed down to Moses on Mount Sinai. It is something forged in the struggle for existence and reproduction, something fashioned by natural selection. It is as much a natural human adaptation as our ears or noses or teeth.*[170]

So while C.S. Lewis, the Christian apologist, contends that morality stems from God, Michael Ruse, the atheist, contends that morality

---

[168] Michael Ruse, "God is Dead, Long Live Morality," *The Guardian*, March 15, 2010, theguardian.com/commentisfree/belief/2010/mar/15/morality-evolution-philosophy.
[169] Michael Ruse.
[170] Michael Ruse.

was bred into us through natural selection and is now hardwired in us. Either way, their theories suggest morality is associated with all of humanity, the entire species.

That is a long way away from Plato's suggestion and the medieval experience that we need a God and His Church to infuse society with morality. In Plato's world, morality was cultural. Provide the people with a different God and a different Church, and you get a different morality.

But perhaps neither of these views is really true. I don't think they are. Sociopaths feel no moral compunction at all for harming others. They do not appear to have the common morality, or any morality at all. We have no consistent estimates on the relative number of sociopaths in our world. Dr. Martha Stout, a Harvard University psychologist, claims 4% of Americans are sociopaths. That is one in twenty-five. Some say 10% of the people in the financial industry are sociopaths and prison populations are at 20% to 25% sociopathic.[171] At any rate, the moral law argument cannot explain sociopaths. Sociopaths are an exception to the rule.

The natural selection argument might call sociopaths mutations which are ill-suited for society and are rooted out, jailed, exiled and executed and in the end do not contribute much to the gene pool. On the other hand, sociopathy can prove beneficial to political leaders, who can then

---

[171] But you should not take these numbers as fact. The variation has to do with the population being studied and the definition of "sociopath" being used. Very few human qualities have clear differentiation. Instead, human qualities are largely on a spectrum, probably shaped like a bell curve. Some people are more sociopathic or more empathetic, and the majority of us are in the middle part of the curve. When we try to estimate the percentage of sociopaths, some sort of cutoff line in the spectrum must be applied, where we can definitively declare that someone does not merely display sociopathic tendencies, but actually is a sociopath. But just where is that line? That is where the definitions come into play. Different definitions of sociopathy, that is, different demarcation points in the spectrum lead to different percentages of the population being considered sociopathic. So you have to recognize that these percentages are subjective guesses based on some criterion that looks official.

make decisions without having to suffer sadness or guilt for the suffering their decisions have brought about. Some sociopaths contribute to the gene pool and do make it to supreme leader status, determining the destiny of an entire nation.

Putting the existence of sociopaths aside, there are other arguments why these two theories of morality, innate or evolutionary, don't work. Cruelty to animals and running over rabbits is something that is considered repugnant to Western European societies, but according to Theodore Roosevelt, animal cruelty among some of the Native American tribes was commonplace.

> *Any one (sic) who has ever been in an encampment of wild Indians, and has had the misfortune to witness the delight the children take in torturing little animals, will admit that the Indian's love of cruelty for cruelty's sake cannot possibly be exaggerated. The young are so trained that when old they shall find their keenest pleasure in inflicting pain in its most appalling form. Among the most brutal white borderers [sic] a man would be instantly lynched if he practised [sic] on any creature the fiendish torture which in an Indian camp either attracts no notice at all, or else excites merely laughter.*[172]

The Romans were infamous for their cruelty in the arena. During the Roman era, it is said that so many animals were killed in the Roman arenas that some animals came close to extinction. According to Lucius Cassius Dio, in one day, Commodus, the Roman Emperor, son of Marcus Aurelias, "killed a hundred bears all by himself, shooting down at them from the railing of the balustrade."[173]

Could another theory better account for sociopathy and cruelty?

---

[172] Theodore Roosevelt, *The Winning of the West, Part 1* (G.P. Putnum and Sons, 1900), 115.

[173] Earnest Cary, Ph.D., *Dio's Roman History with an English Translation*, vol. 9 (Harvard University, 1955), 107.

Swedenborgian Morality

Emanuel Swedenborg (1688–1772), a Swedish polymath, wrote that we live in the midst of an endless cosmic war between benevolent and malevolent spirits or, as some call them, angels and demons. After death, our souls remain here on Earth as bodyless spirits for a long time before moving on to heaven or hell. But it is only during this life in a human body that our souls can make substantial spiritual progress, not in the afterlife. And progressing spiritually, reaching towards God—that is the entire point of our existence.

Swedenborg wrote that a vast realm of spirits surrounds us. We cannot see them, but they are always there. They do their best to influence us to do either good or evil. The angels try to guide us closer to God, while the demons try to lead us astray.

The nature of these spirits is as varied as the nature of living human beings. That only follows, right? Upon death, the soul in a nasty person is released from the body to become a nasty spirit, who then torments the living and corrupts them. The spirits of unruly teenagers delight in getting humans to do stupid things that ruin their lives on Earth and impede their spiritual progress. It is fun to them.

On the other hand, the spirits from good people are loving, compassionate and nurturing. Some of us call them angels. For many of these benevolent spirits, their mission in the afterlife is to guide us living humans into making spiritually beneficial decisions. They lead us towards God. Their guidance is often experienced as subtle promptings in the direction of the right action or "truth." Sometimes they even nudge us to make small decisions that save us from physical harm or even physical death. From these angels, according to Swedenborg, we get what we call our morality. By listening to the spiritual guidance of the angels (many call it intuition), we can live virtuous lives.

The evil spirits also try to influence our thoughts and actions. According to Swedenborg, their guidance is experienced as louder, more emotional impulses, often drowning out the gentle whispers from the benevolent spirits. Acts of anger or selfishness are often the result of the promptings from these evil spirits. Every idea, inclination or impulse that we have is the result of guidance from spirits, good or ill. Our ideas do not originate with us; they come from beyond the veil. We, the living, just receive ideas and impulses and choose among them. We are just not aware of the process. We think it all originates in us. These spirits are in a non-ending war for our souls. This view of morality explains evil and sociopathy. Some people tend to take the advice of the evil spirits that surround us.

Morality, then, in this Swedenborgian view, is absolute. It comes from the spiritual plane, through the angels and ultimately from God, and reflects the moral law of the universe. There is a right and a wrong that transcends cultures. According to Swedenborg then, just like C.S. Lewis and Michael Ruse, morality is species-wide, not associated with any particular group's teachings.

If one single morality should cover all cultures, why is it then that some tribes practice incest and wife stealing, both of which are taboo in other cultures? Can a whole tribe through many generations listen to evil spirits? According to Swedenborgians, yes. Although many members may be aware of the subtle promptings of the benevolent spirits, communicating that perhaps they should not partake in these rituals, the social force to do so is stronger, and the individual is compelled to comply with the group's schema. In a tribe in the Amazon or in Borneo, if you refuse to comply with tribal customs, you might be shunned or exiled. And how are you going to survive without a tribe?

One could say that morality in this Swedenborgian sense also benefits the group, although this time the group is the species and includes both the living and the dead. Angels are tasked with steering individuals towards good behavior and spiritual evolution. But do the angels benefit in any way from helping the living? I asked the Swedenborg Foundation, and they responded:

Think of it like the overall health of the human body. When one part of the body gets healthier, the whole body feels better and happier, because there is greater well-being for all. . . Angels experience this as the joy of welcoming more [of us] into the heavenly mindset. . .and the joy of greater sharing love and healing and insights with more minds and hearts, which brings them great delight, because they can feel how much joy that brings to God.[174]

So moral living then, according to the Swedenborg's teachings, benefits the species—including both the living and the dead.

We've been looking at theories of moral laws that apply to all cultures and times, a fixed moral law. If it true that morality is universal, then it follows that some cultures are just immoral. It is as simple as that.

Morality Defined by the Group

On the other hand, perhaps morality is based on whatever the group thinks. Let's take a look at that theory next.

Whereas Michael Ruse claimed that morality was bred into us by evolution, perhaps instead our society teaches us morality. This is the good, old nature-versus-nurture argument. We recognize that our schema, of which morality is a part, is shaped by a variety of forces, mostly social. We are taught by our families and our society most of the values and beliefs that form our schema. That common schema serves as a unifying force for the society in which we live.

People praise actions advantageous to the group (compassion, patience, tolerance, leadership, etc.) and call them virtues, while condemning those activities injurious to the group (selfishness, debauchery, drunkenness, etc.). In the 1750s, Claude Adrien Helvetius, an influential French Enlightenment thinker, claimed that there is no innate moral sense, rather one's moral sense is derived from the groups one is a member of, one's family, one's community, one's government and one's

---

[174] Email to author from Karin at Swedenborg Foundation, November 7, 2020.

church. Morality is "the science of the means invented by men to live together in the happiest manner."[175] Our morality arises from the group. We are a social animal. We work best in groups; but, for the group to survive, we must conform; so we are programmed with morality.

This might explain why different civilizations have conflicting ideas of how to live an ideal life. Different groups, due to their histories, climates, religions and types of knowledge, have different moralities. If we are to believe this, then morality is not associated with humanity itself, as the other theories suggested. Nurture beats Nature!

The Nietzschean View of Morality

Nietzsche saw it completely differently. He described two very different social schemas and associated moralities: that of classical antiquity, especially the Roman world versus that of the modern world. He terms them the *Herren-Moral*, the morality of masters (the Roman morality), and the Herden-Moral, the morality of herds (modern Western morality).

For the Romans, even for common Romans, virtue was represented by courage, strength, manhood, enterprise and bravery. In the ancient world, generally, armies would sack a town, kill the men, rape the women, take their belongings and enslave any survivors. Respect came from prowess in fighting. Countless stories abound of Roman statesmen, generals and tax collectors, who without any pangs of conscience would kill, enslave and loot nations—and feel noble in doing so. That is how they earned their glory and wealth. This was their rightful privilege, being Romans. Theirs was the morality of masters. Since that time, Christianity has rejected the old pagan attitudes of pride, contempt for the weak, thirst for conquest, and the celebration of passion, revenge, anger, sensuality and adventure.[176] According to Nietzsche, all of those qualities are noble, but Christianity has taught us that they are contemptible. Christianity

---

[175] Claude Adrien Helvetius, *Treatise on Man* (B. Frankin, 1969), V, iii.

[176] Bertrand Russell, *History of Western Philosophy* (Simon & Schuster, 1945), 765.

aims at "destroying the strong. . .breaking their spirit. . .exploiting their moments of weariness and debility. . .converting their proud assurance into anxiety and conscience-trouble."

Christianity

> *knows how to poison the noblest instincts and to infect them with disease, until their strength, their will to power, turns inwards, against themselves—until the strong perish through their excessive self-contempt and self-immolation.* [177]

Today, from our Herden-Moral perspective, we would describe the ancients as unfeeling, selfish and cruel animals. Yet, this morality of masters prevailed widely in ancient times and later in tribes yet untamed by the Christian ethics.

The morality of herds was introduced into Europe by the Jews of Asia, who experienced crushing political subjection over and over again. Their once fiercely independent spirit was crushed by disastrous wars, enslavements, and forced migrations, developing into a morality of compassion. Nietzche adds more on this:

> *Subjection breeds humility, helplessness breeds altruism, which is an appeal for help. Under this herd morality, love of danger and power give way to love of security and peace. . . the pride of honor [gives way to] the whip of conscience. Honor is pagan, Roman, feudal, aristocratic; conscience is Jewish, Christian, bourgeois, democratic. . .The 'world' and 'flesh' became synonyms with evil, and poverty a proof of virtue.* [178]

And now you have Christianity.

No great man of antiquity has ever resembled the Christian ideal. On the other hand, the teachings of Jesus were the epitome of the Herden-Moral. With Christianity every man was of equal value and deserved

---

[177] Russell, 765.

[178] Will Durant, *The Story of Philosophy*, 420.

equal rights. Progress was now defined in these Herden-Moral terms of social, political and economic equality. From these new ideals emerged democracy, utilitarianism and socialism. [179] This Judeo-Christian herd morality is the basis of contemporary Western thought. We profess love for our fellow man. All people are created equal. We have rule by the weak in democracies rather than rule by the strong in tyrannies and monarchies.

From the Herren-Moral point of view, this democratization of society eroded the intellectual, cultural and more standards once upheld by the elite. In arriving at the collective standard, society dismissed outliers of inferiority and excellence, leading to a culture of mediocrity. This shift towards equality, while elevating the masses, at the same time diminished the pursuit of individual excellence.[180]

Nietzsche saw our current morality of herds as decay, the final stage of which, was "the exaltation of pity and self-sacrifice, the sentimental comforting of criminals, the 'inability of a society to excrete.'"[181]

So when did the basic moral tenant of the Western world change? It came about slowly starting with the ascension of Christianity as the Roman religion. New values such as humility and compassion were esteemed, and martial values declined in importance. The character of the people changed. Hundreds of thousands retreated from the world to live in monasteries and nunneries starting in the third century CE. After decades of Christian ascension, as people were praised for selfless acts rather than of dominance, mastery, theft and oppression, the character of the people changed. Historian Edward Gibbon (1734–1794) describes this change with at least some apparent contempt.

> *The clergy successfully preached the doctrines of patience and pusil-lanimity; the active virtues of society were discouraged; and the last remains of military spirit were buried in the cloister: a large*

---

179 Will Durant, 420.

180 Will Durant, 420.

181 Will Durant, 420.

portion of public and private wealth was consecrated to the specious demands of charity and devotion; and the soldiers' pay was lavished on the useless multitudes of both sexes who could only plead the merits of abstinence and chastity...The sacred indolence of the monks was devoutly embraced by a servile and effeminate age...but the pure and genuine influence of Christianity may be traced in its beneficial, though imperfect, effects on the barbarian proselytes of the North. If the decline of the Roman empire was hastened by the conversion of Constantine, his victorious religion broke the violence of the fall, and mollified the ferocious temper of the conquerors.[182]

To be a killer in ancient times was to be virtuous. To be virtuous today in Western societies is to respect all life.

The Morality of the Hive

As far as I know, nobody has ever claimed that bees should be subject to Christian ethics, but if morality is associated with community survival, then what better species to study than bees, one of the most social groups that exist. The code of the bee appears to be one of cooperation for the good of the whole. But even bees will kill their own when it benefits the group.

Whenever we look at a colony of bees, we think of the castes that make up the colony. The roles of the different types of bees—the queen bee, the drones and the worker bees—are distinctly different. Within the worker bee caste, subgroups can be separated out by their occupations. Some worker bees defend the hive, some worker bees attend to the queen, some nurse the young, some make honeycomb. The drones' primary purpose is reproduction. They don't work. Their bodies are not suited for it. Once they have mated with the queen bee, they die shortly afterwards. Each colony has only one queen bee, and she can perform her duties for only a few years. When she gets weak, the workers will

---

[182] Edward Gibbon, *The History of the Decline and Fall of the Roman Empire*, vol. 1 (Everyman's Library, 1993), 475.

raise a second queen. Sometimes the two queens will then fight to the death. Other times, the new queen will leave the colony with a portion of the bees to start a colony elsewhere.

Each caste has its own roles, responsibilities and morality. A queen will kill another queen. But a worker will never kill another worker. A drone will not kill another drone either. But the workers will kill the "lazy" drones in the fall, rather than feed them throughout the long winter.

It makes you wonder, are there separate moralities for the different levels of human society? I think yes, we are just like the bees in that respect. Leadership has one set of morals, while the lower orders have their own.

The Morality of the State

I attended a Jesuit high school in the late 1970s, where I absorbed most of the Catholic values that they taught me, even chastity, and that was awkward. They taught us that it was a sin to be wealthy while there were poor in the world. We had a textbook entitled, *Rich Christians in an Age of Hunger*. It was our moral duty to do something about poverty and inequality in the world; and if we did not try, we were not sufficiently devoted to Christ. From this perspective, it became easy to be aligned with the socialistic revolutionary theology movement in Latin America at the time, where it was Christian duty to struggle violently against oppressive regimes. But none of us at my school were devout enough to pick up the gun. I wanted to. In college, I applied to study abroad in the Dominican Republic. I was planning, once there, on joining the guerilla struggle, which the priests were leading against American corporations at that time. It was real revolutionary stuff, but my college sensed that something was amiss and rejected my application. I have no idea how they figured out that I was planning to spend my year abroad as a guerilla fighter.

I remember being excited about the socialist revolution in Nicaragua in 1980 and 1981. The priests at my high school taught us about the murderous Somoza regime in Nicaragua and how the Church, the small business community and the people all joined together to overthrow the corrupt and violent oppressor. It is said that the dictator, Somoza, owned 20% of the land in the country and that he and his friends controlled the major corporations in the country. After the successful revolution, the Sandinistas redistributed over 250,000 acres of land to poor farmers. Rather than leave the land in the hands of large corporations and the rich growing crops for export, now the land was in the hands of small farmers growing food to feed the country. They taught the farmers how to read, reducing the 50% illiteracy rate to 12%. It appeared to be a government for the people, rather than a government for the rich few. But the American government was opposed to this people's revolution. United States foreign policy was to fight communism wherever it appeared. Ronald Reagan's administration funded the Contras, a military resistance group, to overthrow the Sandinista government, which resulted in nearly a decade of organized murder in a country the size of the state of Mississippi.[183]

A similar struggle was going on in El Salvador, except the revolutionaries never won there. In high school we saw a documentary showing young idealistic people like ourselves being murdered by death squads in El Salvador. Thirteen wealthy families controlled El Salvador and repressed the people with terror. People who protested the inequity were murdered, including nuns and priests. Like the Contras, the Salvadorian oppressors were working in conjunction with the United States government. Anyone in El Salvador who agitated for fairness or representative government, usually in the guise of socialism, was the enemy of the United States.

The U.S. has had a history of raining death upon any organized groups that opposed its commercial interests in a region. To a young Catholic infused with Jesuit values of equality, fairness and love, U. S. foreign policy could not have been any worse if the devil himself had run it.

---

[183] The great shame about the Nicaraguan revolution is that Daniel Ortega, the leader of the Sandinista revolution, replaced Somoza in many ways—his wealth, his control, his repression of dissent. It is hard not to be cynical about people's revolutions after watching Nicaragua.

Repression and murder of innocent people was all being done for profits for American companies. I felt rage to the very core of my being.

How naïve I was. Back then I expected that countries and political leaders should abide by the same set of moral rules as an individual. It had never occurred to me that morality for individuals and political leaders is not the same. Once I realized that political leaders follow one ethical code, and the rest of us another, I couldn't be angry anymore. I had to just accept it.

Perhaps we could argue about political ends and political means, but we should never try to apply our set of individual moral values to a nation or its leaders. It is a silly line of reasoning. Statesmen have a different set of ethics to live up to. I don't like it, but this is a natural law. (I know you are not convinced yet, just read on.)

If a political leader were concerned about displaying Christian values, being fair and honest to everyone and turning the other cheek, they would be manipulated and taken advantage of by other more realistic, less "virtuous" leaders. Perhaps this difference is clear when comparing British Prime Minister Neville Chamberlain and German Chancellor Adolf Hitler. In 1938 Hitler gave Chamberlain the ultimatum between allowing Germany to annex the western part of Czechoslovakia, where more than three million German speakers resided, or go to war. Hitler repeatedly exclaimed his desire for peace; but as the German leader, he also repeatedly proclaimed his need to unite his people, and that came first. He had already annexed Austria just six months earlier. Hitler claimed that the western part of Czechoslovakia would be his last territorial claim in Europe and Europe needed to choose between war or peacefully allowing the German people to be reunited. Europe still had not recovered from World War I and did not want another war.

Chamberlain agreed to Hitler's terms and excitedly reported his agreement to the English:

> *The settlement of the Czechoslovak problem, which has now been achieved, is, in my view, only the prelude to a larger settlement*

> *in which all Europe may find peace. . .We regard the agreement*
> *signed last night and the Anglo-German Naval Agreement as*
> *symbolic of the desire of our two peoples never to go to war with one*
> *another again.*[184]

Once Hitler got what he wanted from Chamberlain, the Germans then invaded the rest of Czechoslovakia. In less than a year, England declared war on Germany. Hitler lied like a stateman, while Chamberlain acted like a gentleman. And Chamberlain has been slandered by historians ever since.

This idea of different moralities for individuals and heads of governments is not new. Frederick the Great, the eighteenth-century King of Prussia, wrote in his memoirs,

> *The word of an individual involves the misfortune of only one*
> *man; that of a sovereign may bring a general calamity to whole*
> *nations. . .Is it better that the people should perish than that the*
> *prince should violate a treaty? What imbecile would hesitate to*
> *decide this question?*[185]

This concept has been around for centuries. Why else would "the entire history of ancient and modern states [be] merely a series of revolting crimes?"[186]

> *[Why would] kings and ministers, past and present, of all times and*
> *all countries—statesmen, diplomats, bureaucrats, and warriors—if*
> *judged from the standpoint of simple morality and human justice,*
> *have a hundred, a thousand times over earned their sentence to*
> *hard labour or to the gallows?*[187]

Here I am quoting from the famous nineteenth century Russian revolutionary anarchist, Mikhail Alexandrovich Bakunin (1814–1876).

---

[184] Neville Chamberlain's famous "Peace in Our Time" speech, September 20, 1938.

[185] Frederick the Great, *Histoire de mon temps, in Will Durant's Age of Rousseau, 458.*

[186] Mikhail Bakunin, "Rousseau's Theory of the State," www.marxists.org.

[187] Bakunin.

His thoughts are dangerous to the order and stability of nations. He detested statesmen and nation states. Bakunin asserted

> *There are a good many laws which govern [society] without its being aware of them, but these are natural laws, inherent in the body social, just as physical laws are inherent in material bodies. Most of these laws remain unknown to this day; nevertheless, they have governed human society ever since its birth, independent of the thinking and the will of the men composing the society.*[188]

Many of these laws of power were noted by Niccolo Machiavelli when he wrote his infamous work, *The Prince*, in the early sixteenth century. Machiavelli has since been acclaimed to be the father of political science. He explained that private and public moralities were two different things. According to Machiavelli, "the ends justify the means." Bakunin noted that Machiavelli was

> *the first to understand that great and powerful states could be founded and maintained by crime alone—by many great crimes—and by a radical contempt for all that goes under the name of honesty.*[189]

And only in the presence of order can there be peace and prosperity. If you think of the ugly things politicians do, perhaps it all makes sense in this light.

Bakunin saw the State for what it really was. Despite any reassurances of its friendly intentions, the State is an inexorable creature that exists solely for its own sake, with not one bit of compassion for any who oppose it. Here Bakunin explains the difference in morality between statesmen and individuals.

> *From [the] point of view. . .of the statesmen, the strong men of all times and of all countries. . .whatever conduces to the preservation, the grandeur and the power of the State, no matter how sacrilegious*

---

[188] Bakunin.

[189] Bakunin

or morally revolting it may seem, that is the good. And conversely, whatever opposes the State's interests, no matter how holy or just otherwise, that is evil. Such is the secular morality and practice of every State.[190]

While the State does protect its own citizens and recognize their rights,

since it recognizes no rights outside itself, it logically arrogates to itself the right to exercise the most ferocious inhumanity toward all foreign populations, which it can plunder, exterminate, or enslave at will.[191]

If a king conquers a neighboring country, kills and enslaves the people of the defeated country and plunders it, bringing back wealth for his own country, his country becomes strong militarily. It becomes wealthy enough to foster the arts and sciences. It becomes a great place to live with order and security within its boundaries. Would this be a good king? Or would this king be immoral and bad? Why is it that Americans are so set on thinking that their president should be of good character? Leaders need not have the morality of workers.[192]

Perhaps accepting these dual moral standards can help explain the pairing of the grandeur of ancient Athens with the harsh political realities of the Athenian nation-state. During its Golden Age, Athens produced Herodotus, Thucydides, Plato, Socrates, Hippocrates, Aeschylus, Sophocles and Euripides. Athens of the Golden Age was a land of intelligence, democracy, and luxury. However, in order to nurture and maintain such brilliance, Athens had to dominate, despoil and kill neighboring peoples. For example, Melos, a small island, neutral in the war with Sparta, was offered a chance to join the Athenians or be

---

[190] Bakunin.

[191] Bakunin.

[192] In our presidential elections we have all heard that this candidate may be a crook and that candidate, of bad character. These things may or may not be true. Even if they were, would that interfere with them defending the country, promoting prosperity and maintaining our freedoms? I don't think so.

conquered. They resisted and the Athenians then put all Melian men to death and sold all Melian women and children into slavery.[193] Many of the Athenian allies had to pay burdensome tribute to Athens. For all of the good things one hears about Athens, they did many terrible things to people in other city-states in order to maintain their prosperity. They treated their own allies and enemies poorly, certainly not like a gentleman would.

States need not always treat conquered people poorly. The United States was lenient and helped to rebuild Japan after WWII. Only two people were executed for war crimes in Japan after the war. When a state acts with leniency, it is usually a political act for political means. The United States did not want Japan to go Communist. As a result of the unusual American occupation of Japan, the Japanese admired and emulated the Americans. Leniency towards the conquered in situations like this, as Bakunin explains, "is never done from a sense of duty, for the State has an absolute right to dispose of a conquered people at will."194

Am I suggesting that Hitler was correct or more correct than Chamberlain? Was he more moral? Absolutely not. Instead, I am suggesting that leaders play by a different set of rules than we civilians. Chamberlain apparently did not understand this. Or perhaps he was so desirous of peace that he was willing to ignore the signs of impending betrayal. Do you know of any U.S. president who did not lie? Maybe Jimmy Carter had a truthful career, but he is considered one of the most ineffective presidents in history. He is beloved as a great human being, as he should be, but not as an effective president. Presidents lie. Politicians lie. Just as soldiers kill. Can you imagine a great soldier who would not kill to protect his nation? Different moralities exist for the different roles in society.

---

[193] You may be confused here, I was...People from Melos were called Melians, not Melossians, like I once imagined.
[194] Bakunin.

All about the Group

Let's get back to the honeybees. I have always understood a bee colony as a collection of tens of thousands of individual bees working as a community, towards one common end, which is to survive. They harvest in spring, summer and fall; and in the winter, they remain in the hive huddled close together vibrating their wing muscles, generating heat to keep the hive warm.

But there is a better way to conceptualize the honeybee colony. The colony can be viewed as a creature in itself. As a human is composed of trillions of cells, so is a honeybee colony composed of tens of thousands of bees. The cells in the human body perform different functions, just as the bees in the hive perform different functions. The cells work in harmony to enable the human to survive. The different classes of bees work in harmony for the survival of the hive. Cells live for a while, age and are replaced with new ones. Bees live for a while, age and are then replaced.

We discussed in an earlier essay how we humans, when we try to understand something, tend to break things into pieces. Studying bees as individual creatures is exactly that type of thinking. Instead, the bee colony itself is the entity worthy of study, irrespective of the individual bee. All of the bees share a unified will to sustain the colony.

Human groups, societies and nations can be thought of in the same way as bee colonies. Humans are like individual bees, each with separate roles, responsibilities and moralities, but all of them together make up the creature we call a group, a society, a nation and, ultimately, humanity itself. Groups are the entities that really matter.

Of course, the corollary is that individuals do not matter. The group itself is everything. For example, the University of California at Berkeley has existed for decades, but its component parts last only briefly. The students, administrators, professors and grounds crew come and go. The buildings come and go, the courses come, change and then go. Nothing is constant, only the group, the University, which has processes and a reputation, both of which also change with time. The same can be said of any group, any company, any nation or of humanity itself. In the long run, the individuals that make up the group do not matter; it is only the group that survives. And it is only the group that matters.

Any individual in a group, just like any cell in your body, can be replaced. Sadly, we are interchangeable, and frankly, forgettable. This may be hard for us to accept, as we have heard the contrary all our lives. We who have been raised in the United States believe in the primacy of the individual, not the collective. We believe that the group exists to support us individuals. "It's all about me." But it is not true, and it never has been. Even particular leaders are not needed. Others are always waiting to assume the leadership position when a leader is removed.

The group does not need us, instead, we need the group. The group defines who we are, teaches us how to live and provides us with community. We belong to the group, until we die, and then the group continues on without us.

The Universal Will

Perhaps it is silly to think that rules for bees may apply to humans, but I don't think so. Animals and humans share a lot in common. Humans probably have a more advanced intellect than the other animals, but we still share fundamental qualities with them. When we see monkeys at the zoo, we see ourselves. What about fish, seals and birds? We usually don't recognize the kinship, but it is there. We suffer pain. We want to survive. We recognize our own species. We can learn about our fundamental nature from understanding the behaviors and instincts (and moral codes) of animals.

Salmon are the only fish that can survive in both fresh water and salt water. Salmon live in the ocean for about seven years before they return to mate in the freshwater stream where they were born. This journey to the mouth of their stream will take some salmon only a few thousand yards, while others will swim for thousands of miles to get there. When they leave the ocean and enter the freshwater stream, they quit eating. Their stomachs are no longer needed and begin to disintegrate internally, leaving more room for developing eggs and sperm. They nourish themselves with the fat stored in their tissues. These fish have to swim upstream, fight against the current and jump repeatedly to get over waterfalls, rapids and dams. Some varieties from Idaho must travel 900 miles upstream and climb nearly 7,000 feet before they reach their spawning grounds. During the journey, bears, otters, eagles and other predators will eat whatever salmon they can catch. A large percentage of the fish die before spawning. Only the fittest and luckiest of them can complete the journey. The survivors are exhausted by the time they arrive at their spawning grounds, but many still have some energy left for reproduction. Once there, the females lay eggs, and the males fertilize them. This mating process can take a day or two. After spawning, their bodies deteriorate rapidly and the salmon die. What a journey! Do the fish know in advance the horrors they will have to encounter? Why would any reasonable fish with foreknowledge undergo such suffering? They must not know what is coming. Something is driving them.

Arthur Schopenhauer (1788–1860), a German philosopher, discusses of the lengths that different species will go to in order to birth and/or raise the next generation. He suggests animals are driven by a Universal Will, focused on ensuring the survival of the species.

Colossal seals called sea-elephants used to live on Three Kings Island near New Zealand. (During the nineteenth century, they were mostly exterminated for their oil.) They swam together in groups, always on the watch for lurking predators. The females birthed their young on the shore. And then for seven to eight weeks, as the mothers suckled their young on land, the males formed a circle around them to prevent them from entering the sea in search of food. When the females attempted to enter the sea, the males stopped them by biting them. It seems harsh, but there was a reason. For those seven to eight weeks, none of the seals would enter the sea. The entire community would undergo a communal fast on land, so that the young did not enter the sea before they were able to swim well enough to avoid the predators.[195]

Schopenhauer writes about wild duck, whitethroats and other birds that will fly in front of a hunter's feet, flapping about when he approaches their nest. They pretend their wings are broken to lure the hunter away from their young and towards themselves instead. Does and hinds will induce hunters to pursue them, sparing their young from harm. Swallows have flown into burning houses to save their young or to die with them.[196] These are selfless actions these animals take in order to preserve their babies.

Human Sacrifice for the Good of the Species

Humans are no different. We too will suffer and risk our safety and well-being for our young, except we have foresight.[197] We know the sacrifices associated with childrearing beforehand, so we can logically conclude that it makes no sense to have children. Why would anyone do it? Why invest hundreds of thousands of dollars and thousands of hours of service to what often become ungrateful children? We freely choose to exchange our happy, carefree days of romance, fun and irresponsibility for sleepless nights, dirty diapers, loss of freedom and boring soul-killing careers. Fun becomes a lost memory. The ceaseless drudgery of our daily jobs and of the raising of a selfish child supersedes any inclinations we might have had to satisfy our own needs. To varying degrees, we parents live exhausted lives. And when our children cross the threshold into adolescence, many of us then become subject to a barrage of lies and outright contempt from our maturing offspring. Why would any rational creature knowingly begin this process? Why would we willingly trade away our youthful carefree lives for nearly twenty

---

[195] Arthur Schopenhauer, *The World as Will and Idea*, trans. R. B. Haldane and J. Kemp, vol. 3, ch. XLII,

[196] Schopenhauer, Ch. XLII.

[197] I am making the assumption the animals do not have foresight of the risks and hardships they will undergo. I could be wrong here. But that doesn't affect my point.

years of drudgery? We are, like the salmon, undertaking the torturous journey to the spawning grounds that ends in certain death. It makes no sense, at least on the individual level. But that is the point. Despite all we have been told, nothing makes sense on the individual level. We try to form some intelligible meaning out of our lives, coming from this viewpoint of self, but there is none for us there. The meaning exists on a higher level—we too are working to preserve our species.

The Mystery of Death and Our Limits of Understanding

Suppose a young person close to us dies. How do we explain this to ourselves? A Hindu might think that it is no problem, as the dead will certainly come back through Reincarnation. They were here to do something, to endure some ordeal, but they have completed their task and will return with a new task. A Christian, unfortunately, has no good explanation, except that "God works in mysterious ways," which is in essence admitting that Christian theology doesn't address this problem. It cannot explain the greatest mystery of all, death.

I suggest a different interpretation, which is: "who says we should have the capacity to understand? Where did that idea come from?" Just because we can make rocket ships does not mean we can understand life and death. The meaning exists on a higher level, and we cannot attain that level of understanding, unless perhaps we trip into a mystical state, which I believe some of us do. Very few of us. I think Arthur Schopenhauer was one of us who did. He wrote that we can attain absolute knowledge through mystical experiences, but we cannot explain it to others.

Nonetheless, he did try to explain it in his writings, and perhaps he was able to relate the answer to the tragic death of a child. The answer may sound brutal—the child and I and you, as well, are of no importance. Your child, your sadness, in the real scheme of things, are ultimately insignificant. So, there is no point fixating on it. But let's let this go and return to his main points.

We Exist to Reproduce

According to Schopenhauer, people do not exist to be happy, rather we exist to propagate the species.

> *The life of the individual is at bottom only borrowed from the species…Procreation is the highest point; and after attaining to it, the life of the first individual quickly or slowly sinks, while a new life ensures to nature the endurance of the species, and repeats the same phenomena.*[198]

The individual really has no importance at all in the grand scheme of things. Rather it is only the species that matters. We exist to procreate. Then we can die.

This "alteration of death and reproduction is the heartbeat of the species."[199] It is the heartbeat of all species. Schopenhauer called this force of the species, "the Will," and this Will in each of us is greater than our individual desires. We may enjoy the peaceful evening at a restaurant with our spouse, but our duty to raise our children properly comes first; and so we forego years of pleasant nights on the town. The Will is greater than our desires.

Some may see a parallel between the Will and God, maybe even confuse the two, but I need to clarify, the Will is not God. The Will does not know or care about anything. Instead, the Will is like gravity or magnetism. It is merely a law of nature. It just is.

At first look, some trends seem to refute this concept of the Will. As I write this, we are experiencing a decades-long tendency of increasing numbers of women not having children. An article in the *Harvard Business Review* states that among successful corporate career women in the forty-one to fifty-five age bracket, 42% are childless. But as the author states,

---

[198] Schopenhauer, vol. 1, 214.
[199] Schopenhauer, vol. 3, 312.

> *These women have not chosen to remain childless. The vast majority, in fact, yearn for children. Indeed, some have gone to extraordinary lengths to bring a baby into their lives. They subject themselves to complex medical procedures, shell out tens of thousands of dollars, and derail their careers—mostly to no avail, because these efforts come too late. In the words of one senior manager, the typical high-achieving woman childless at midlife has not made a choice but a "creeping nonchoice."*[200]

The Will is always there. But it must compete with the career, social and financial pressures that these women are experiencing. And for this reason, sometimes the Will is suppressed, until it is not. And then for many of these women, it is too late. Their aging bodies will no longer produce children. But the Will is always there, and the regret that some older childless women feel is a manifestation of the Will.

Why else would a sea-elephant refrain from eating for several weeks? Why do people and animals sometimes sacrifice their own lives for those of their offspring? It is the same story. Forces within us are stronger than our own desires for pleasure, sustenance or even survival. The will of the species is stronger than the will of the individual.

Time Erases Everyone

The individual is of little importance to the species. People die all the time, and the species continues. Memories of individuals persist in the hearts of the survivors, but in turn these survivors die and eventually all memory of an individual is lost. Plato was right.

> *Man is real, men are fleeting moments in the phantasmago-ria of life.*[201]

As with Ecclesiastes,

---

[200] Sylvia Ann Hewlett, "Executive Women and the Myth of Having It All," *Harvard Business Review*, April 2002, https://tinyurl.com/y6oenwsl.

[201] Will and Ariel Durant, *Age of Voltaire* (Simon & Shuster, 1965), 586.

For the wise and the foolish both die. The wise will not be remembered any longer than the fool. In the days to come, both will be forgotten.[202]

Many great individual achievements are remembered for a time, until they are replaced by greater achievements, or are just plain forgotten. We may still enjoy Mozart now, but he lived only 250 years ago. The songs of Caesar's day are lost, and there surely were great musicians then. We do still read the plays of the ancient Greeks, but most ancient works have been lost forever. The Athenians of the Golden Age lived 2,400 years ago, but what of the literature from the ancient civilizations that predate the Greeks? Almost all of classic literature, art and music are lost, just as ours will be in time as well. It is shortsighted to think that Shakespeare will be remembered forever. Even today, educators are removing Shakespeare from the curriculums. Soldiers, statesmen and explorers who were remembered for a few hundred years are well on their way to being forgotten. This is how change happens. Just as the elements slowly wear down statues until only faint semblances remain, so time dims humanity's memory of great individuals until they are forgotten—eclipsed by newer, more meaningful replacements.

This forgetfulness is an ancient and timeless truth. The writer of Ecclesiastes, 2,300 years ago captured it:

We don't remember what happened in the past, and in future generations, no one will remember what we are doing now.[203]

Though Ecclesiastes lamented that all our human endeavors are fleeting, practical ancient treasures like the wheel, the shovel, the hammer, chains and cement continue to enrich our lives. Nobody knows who invented these things. These creations have been continually improved upon throughout the ages. Memory of the original breakthrough moment and of the first creator is lost. Still the products of the genius of humankind endure to enhance the lives of all of us who follow. The species is

---

[202] Ecclesiastes, 2:16 (New Living Translation).

[203] Ecclesiastes, 1:11 (New Living Translation).

evolving, and our lives are better due to those who came before us, even though we don't know who they are.

Morality in the Shadow of the Will

So then, if the only thing that matters is the Will and if we are of no consequence, then why even have morality? If the fool and the wise man are equally forgotten, what is the point of living virtuously?

Schopenhauer offers a profound answer: morality lies in transcending our fleeting selves through compassion. As we humans all share in this struggle of the species to survive, we are all part of the whole, we are humanity. To be human is to suffer. Small sufferings at first for most, but as we age the suffering increases until our bodies are in perpetual pain. And the grief of losing those we love weighs on our souls as well. Our morality is grounded in our shared experience of suffering, as we are all driven by the same universal Will. It is all about compassion for others. When that barrier between the other and myself has been breached and I can feel their pain as my own, that is compassion, the true foundation of morality. This can come from recognizing that the suffering of others is just like the suffering we, too, endure.

For example, helping someone in distress is moral because we recognize their suffering as like our own, transcending our individual ego. Living a life to please ourselves is empty. Living a moral life based on compassion is fulfilling. So, if the wise man and the fool are equally fleeting, what is the point of living a moral life? Besides aligning us with the Will, living a life based on compassion fulfills us, and what more can you ask for than to be fulfilled?

Final Comments

Our lives are fleeting, but humanity continues on. In the grand scheme, we individuals are of little importance. We can continue to live in ignorance of this truth and live the lie of self-importance. But what's the point? We will just encounter frustration after frustration as we repeatedly rediscover that our self-aggrandizing schema does not conform to reality. Things just don't always go our way. It never was about us anyway.

But there is a better way to live. What if we just surrendered to the truth that our lives are brief and, frankly, meaningless? What if we dropped our individual focus and instead adopted the point of view of humankind itself? How would we live then? Just a thought for now. We will go into this concept in more detail in later essays.

Wrapping It Up

- Groups affect our outlooks more than we think. In order to belong, we must put aside our individual thoughts and sometimes ignore our conscience and adopt the thoughts and morality of the group. The power of the group over the individual is clearly seen when you consider the unethical things people will do for their company in order to fit in and succeed in their jobs.

- Good people in bad groups can do horrible things. Consider the collective madness of the Nazis, which drove what may have been otherwise good people into committing diabolical acts of mass murder.

- Groups can be powerful. The weak will often unite into groups to protect against and defeat strong individuals.

- The Medieval Church used to provide a moral guideline for people. But as the centuries passed, humanity broke away from the Church. We in the West are living in relatively unprecedented times in which there is no overarching religion to guide people.

- Many theories exist about where morality comes from. It may come from God or from natural selection or from angels and demons. In any case, morality serves humanity. It is a set of rules for individual members to follow to ensure the survival of the group.

- Nietzsche wrote that in the post-pagan era, our era, people have adopted a morality of the oppressed, Herden-Moral, based on humility, kindness and love, whereas the Romans before them maintained Herren-Moral, a morality based on strength, bravery and mastery. He said that our current morality, Herden-Moral, leads to mediocrity and suppresses individual excellence.

- Bees have different moral schemas for different orders of honeybee society. Workers work and will only kill drones and not other workers; drones don't work or kill and queens will only kill other queens. The orders have different roles and different rules.

- Statesmen and nations operate by a different set of morals than individuals. They must engage in actions like deception, conquest or violence for the greater good of the state. Soldiers must kill to maintain a strong state; whereas, workers must not deceive or kill. These different standards of morality have been recognized and discussed by political thinkers throughout history.

- The species is the mother of all groups; and, to the species, the individual is of little importance. Individuals come and go, and all that concerns the species is that it continue, reproduce and evolve.

- According to Schopenhauer, what matters is the "Will" of the species, which is stronger than individual desires. We all die and are all forgotten in time. Both fools and the wise are equally of no consequence over time. All that matters is survival of the species—in our case, humanity.

❧ Let's be smart for once and see life as it truly is and stop living the lie of self-importance and agency. We are not in charge of our thoughts, our moralities or our fates. The group controls all of that. The group is the real master here, not you, and only the group matters.

❧ True morality is based on compassion we can develop for each other, as we all suffer together as manifestations of the "Will" or humanity or the species, whatever you want to call it.

PART 2

An Exploration of Truth across Historical, Mystical and Philosophical Dimensions

I tried to rattle your cage in Part 1. I did my best to explain to you that everything you think you know is, for the most part, not true. Nothing is for certain.

Well, what good is that? It doesn't enhance your life one bit to walk around unsure of everything.

In the next group of essays, we are going to look at a few more topics, mostly related to religion, history and whatever it is that lies beyond the reach of our senses. The purpose for visiting these topics is to encourage you to reconstruct your worldview based on a different, more functional, foundational postulate.

Assuming you are successful in this transformation of thought, you will see the world more clearly. You will have a deeper appreciation of your part in the long chain of human affairs that we call history. You will understand what really is important. And you will know what to do about it.

Essay 8
Religion –The Dilution of Divine Truth through Human Weakness, Time and Power

The rejection of a priestly caste who claimed to be exclusive custodians of a private hot line to the sacred was, in my opinion, a great step forward in the emancipation of mankind, and we have the mystics—among others—to thank for this achievement.
— Abraham Maslow

Some Introductory Comments

To this point, I have done my best to convince you that we don't know half as much as we think we do. Our brains are not wired to experience reality as it really is. We filter out those things that don't fit into our schemas. And for those things that do make it into our minds, we distort their meanings to reinforce our beliefs because we need what we "perceive" to reinforce our beliefs. It is in our nature.

We belong to groups that further skew our perspectives. We unconsciously believe in science, which treats only the material aspects of the world around us, totally missing the more important reality and the context for everything. All of these things limit our perception of the actual world. We are clueless, as Voltaire (1694–1778) realized when he wrote:

> *It does not seem likely that the first principles of things will ever be known. The mice that must be in some little holes of an immense building know not whether it is eternal, or who the architect is, or why he built it. Such mice are we; and the Divine Architect who built the universe has never, that I know of, told his secret to one of us.*[204]

Voltaire continually belittled religion and for good reason. Consult any atheist and you will hear a litany of reasons to dismiss organized religion. But religion and the original teachings of the mystics from which the religions arose are two different things—often atheists confound the two. In this essay we look closer at religion, mysticism and truth. Perhaps the secrets Voltaire despairs of never knowing are in there somewhere.

Playing the Game with No Rule Book

Throughout the centuries, we humans have turned to God and religion to guide us. Embracing the spiritual realm can give us the meaning we need to live fulfilling lives. Saint Augustine (354–430 CE) wrote that "because God has made us for Himself, our hearts are restless until they rest in Him."[205] For a moment, let's suppose he was right. How would you go about connecting with God like that? I don't think the ability to do so is intuitive. I think we need some direction.

Our brains have very little programming at birth. We know how to identify our parents, suck at the tit and ingratiate ourselves with others so that we may be loved and cared for. Other than that, we are born into

---

[204] Voltaire, in letter to Frederich the Great, August 26, 1736, in Durant and Durant, 444.

[205] Saint Augustine, *Confessions*, Book 1 (Classic Books America, 2009), ch.1.

this world clueless. No swimming skills, no typing skills, can't change a tire. Most important, we cannot fathom why we are here and what we need to achieve.

Neither of those big picture topics matters to the infant. But at some point in our lives, the questions do present themselves. At some point, we need to know why we are here and what we are supposed to do. As adults, we need to find something to live for, don't we?

What we need, in essence, is a rule book that we can follow or a framework on which to drape our lives. At the same time, society needs a way to restrain our darker natures and a way to unify us so we are not fighting against each other. For many of us religion provides all of these things. (I know. Some of you are repulsed by religion. Don't worry, this essay and the next will put religion through the wringer, just like earlier essays shredded science.)

Ideally, religion tells us how to live and what to live for—in short, it gives us meaning. It has provided the basis for unity and order in society to different extents throughout history. We'll look at unity and order later; for the moment let's address meaning.

During childhood, countless voices repeatedly impressed upon us what we must do in order to have a successful life. We were taught the "right" way to live, as opposed to the way those "other people" did things—you know, the drug addicts, prostitutes and criminals. If you were a middle-class American man in the 1950s through the 1980s, you were taught to get a college degree, a good job, a wife, a mortgage, a child and then retirement, in that order. It was the formula for success. Life was preconfigured for those of us who were willing to buy into the plan.

During my college years, I thought that those who adhered to this prescription led dull and unfulfilling lives. Just looking at the older generations, it was plainly obvious their lives were not for me. I thought these adults on the "correct path" were falling far short of their potential and, more than that, they never had any fun. I could never take their advice, and I wouldn't take it. Like automatons, most of the students at my college bought into it without asking why. I would sit in smug judgement, mostly isolated from the rest of them. I could never understand why anyone would want such a tedious and unsatisfying life.

My observations correlated with what American social philosopher Eric Hoffer (1902–1983) observed:

> *When people are free to do as they please, they usually imitate each other.*[206]

It is understandable, isn't it? We are all looking at each other hoping the other person knows what is going on, because we certainly don't. I didn't have a clue, but at least I knew that the majority were even more clueless than I was.

As I saw it, you have to know what is most important first, then you can devise a plan to get there. My problem was that I did not know what was most important. What eighteen-year-old does? For that matter, does anyone?

If you reject the rules of the game that are handed to you, you have to fill the void. You have to figure it out on your own. If you continue on your own path without guidance for a decade or more, you will likely remain clueless, dismissive and resentful, and you will probably be relatively poor and unfulfilled. Meanwhile the majority who listened to their parents will be making good money, living in big houses, driving new cars and having children. Superficially, it will appear that they are winning the game, and you are losing it badly.

But, over time, for many, these bright and shiny indicators of success will reveal themselves as chains that the outwardly successful have willingly bound themselves with, and from which they cannot escape. Many suffer spells of spiritual emptiness and, finding little room to maneuver, cannot reorient their lives to remedy their predicament. They find themselves shackled with mortgages, debts, jobs, spouses

------

[206] Eric Hoffer in Paul O'Brien, *Great Decisions, Perfect Timing* (Divination Foundation, 2015), 38.

and children that they cannot leave. On top of that, their bodies are starting to fail. It is becoming too late to try a new direction.

What good is this type of winning if you neglect your soul and find yourself unfulfilled and unable to do anything about it?

Those of us who questioned society's prescribed path found ourselves grappling with uncertainty about our life's purpose and the direction we should take. We could have listened to older people. But most of them were clueless too. Fools who live to be old are not wise. They are just older fools.

This is not an easy game, and life is a game whether we recognize it or not. Many choose to believe life is not a game and insist that they will not play the game, but that is just another way to play. And it is a sure path to losing.

We were placed into this world with a limited time to accomplish something. But how can we live a successful life when we don't know what success is? Should we try to be like Napoleon, Howard Hughes, Steve Jobs or Mother Theresa? Were they fulfilled? And is the point to be fulfilled?

Imagine an isolated Brazilian tribe, untouched by the modern world, coming across a game of Scrabble. What would they do with it? They might plant the tiles in the ground or wear them as jewelry. Perhaps a shaman would use the tiles in sacred divination rituals. A rule book came with the game, but its instructions were inaccessible as the tribe didn't read or write. Now suppose that the Scrabble game appeared in other isolated cultures around the globe, it would likely be used in completely different ways by each of them. Nothing is obvious—and the tribes are left creating some sort of significance for the game. That is how I see life. Metaphorically, for the game of life, our different human societies have been given the same game pieces, a game board and no intelligible instructions. Each society is left to develop the game differently. Different objectives, different things to strive for, different meanings—all to be derived by the group. And they pass their made-up rules—I guess we could call them customs, traditions and creeds—down to succeeding generations, so they can play at Scrabble (I mean, life), too.

The twelfth-century Mongols had different objectives and rules than the eighteenth-century French aristocracy, and these had different objectives and rules than monks in tenth century Cluny, France. Were the Mongols right? They honed their killing prowess. Maybe the French aristocrats were right in developing their capacity for clever talk and seduction. Or, perhaps the monks in Cluny were right, living lives of constant prayer. Perhaps none of them were right. As I see it, no society grasps the truth of what it is supposed to achieve or how its members should devote their energies, but they act like they have it all figured out. Because we have no comprehensible rule book for life, we are as clueless as the hypothetical Brazilian natives, who have the game pieces and even the directions, but do not know what to do with them.

This is where religion steps in. We have been told that religion is the definitive rule book. We have been taught that some Higher Power has provided us with divine scriptures, that is, the rule book. God has communicated with humankind and given us direction and meaning. Except, which of God's rule books is the right one? If you are a Christian, then the rule book is the four gospels and a handful of letters written by Saint Paul. Never mind that the Christian Bible was formed by factional church councils with their excommunications, purges, and book burnings. Never mind that this same convention of politicians, driven by doctrinal purity and power, excluded and condemned dozens of other texts, which they decided were not of the true faith.[207] Wasn't Mohammed the latest prophet? He came after Christ. Or perhaps

---

[207] I am referring to the Council of Nicaea, First and Second Councils of Constantinople, Council of Chalcedon, Council of Ephesus, and others—there are so many. If you read the history of the Catholic faith in the fourth and fifth centuries, you will likely conclude, as I did, that the bishops were politicians more than men of God. They fought over whose ideas should form the canon. The losers in these fights for ideological purity often faced loss of Church office, excommunication, exile, public condemnation, destruction of "heretical texts," imprisonment and occasionally death. This need for ideological purity reminds me of the Bolsheviks, except that the Bolsheviks were far more blood-thirsty than the Bishops.

Swedenborg was the latest prophet. He came after Mohammed. Or maybe it Bahá'u'lláh, who came after Swedenborg. Or maybe it was Joseph Smith, who came after Bahá'u'lláh? All of them said they were the latest and greatest word of God. So, whose book do we follow?

Some of us, whether by learning or by impulse, question everything. Educated by Jesuits, I was taught that you must question and fight your faith in order to strengthen it. As the twelfth-century monk Abelard wrote,

> *The first key to wisdom is assiduous and frequent questioning ...For by doubting we come to inquiry, and by inquiry we arrive at the truth.*[208]

Sounds good, but I don't believe Abelard either. If you question the faith, then you are questioning God's rule book. And who are we, lowly creatures that we are, to even think of questioning God?

Can we ever know with certainty that we have stumbled upon the answers to the riddle of life, or that others have? How would we know? We wouldn't. But, believe me, we don't have God's rule book now.

Suppose it were possible. Suppose for a moment that we were among the wiser ones who actually did understand. It would take most of our lives to gather that wisdom. By that time much of our energy and time would have been squandered. Once we started to understand how to play this game of life, we would be old, with the game almost over.

Why can't we be born knowing what some of the old have already figured out? What kind of nasty game is this? Perhaps it is a cosmic joke played on us by an evil God. As Julian (331–363 CE), the once-revered Roman Emperor, wrote,

---

[208] Peter Abelard, "Prologue," *Sic et Non*, in Will Durant, *Age of Faith*, 939.

Is it not. . .excessively absurd, that God should forbid men. . .the knowledge of good and evil? For what can be more foolish than one who is not able to know what is good and what is depraved?[209]

Fools we are, all of us. We are born to lose this game of life. Martin Luther saw it even worse. Not only are we born to squander our lives in ignorance, the vast majority of us are pre-destined to burn in hell forever. According to Luther, that is how the game was designed by God. How can that be?

Religion as a Rule Book

Many throughout the centuries have believed that they have independently stumbled upon the answer, and some of them wrote rule books for the rest of us to make our lives easier. Prophets and Gods like Jesus, Lao Tse, Mohammed, Ramakrishna, Swedenborg, Bahá'u'lláh, Joseph Smith and others have written or spoken to enlighten us. If they were right and if we follow their teachings, we can avoid years of directionless effort that gets us nowhere. Then we don't have to lose the game entirely. Perhaps that is why most of us turn to a particular religion.

Still other reasons account for people joining a religion. Most of us are born into a creed and never leave the community of believers. Others join so that they can be part of a community. Some marry into a religion. Some want to better themselves. Others join to fit in and cultivate a respectable reputation. Some even do it to further their careers or to cultivate connections with exclusive social circles. To outsiders, some religious people seem to be deeply peaceful. Their religion appears to provide them with meaning, perspective, significance and a lifestyle that fulfills them; and so, these outsiders decide to try it.

---

[209] Julian the Apostate, "The Arguments of The Emperor Julian Against the Christians, trans. Julian Willis Nevins" (Williams and Norgate, 1873), 31, https://tinyurl.com/23utejx8. In case you didn't catch this, he is referring to the Adam and Eve being cast out of the Garden of Eden for eating of the Tree of the Knowledge of Good and Evil. Although Julian was poking fun at the Judeo-Christian god and not God himself, his arguments still work today in this Christian world, even though his pagan gods are long dead.

Of course, nobody lives up to the ideals of their religion, but we try and find a peace in knowing we are progressing on the path to God or Perfection. Catholicism is very gentle on us when we fall short. We can fail again and again, and we will always be allowed back into the arms of the Mother Church. That is reassuring. The Church provides ritual, which for many, can be a profoundly spiritual event. Catholics know the deep sense of relief that comes after confession. It is the strangest thing, unfathomable to outsiders. After telling the priest your moral failures and shortcomings, this lightness and refreshing feeling arises, as if you are starting anew, unburdened of all of your unfortunate failings of the past. For outsiders it is easy to ridicule, but having undergone confession many times, I know, it truly feels like God, Himself, has forgiven you and you are sinless. As historian Will Durant wrote, religion offers the "consolations of faith," it brings "comfort. . .to souls shivering in the immensity of mystery, or the loneliness of grief, or the harsh fatality of defeat."[210] Indeed it can.

Avoiding the Question

Many of us, even if we rejected the "wisdom" of our elders and sought a different meaning, at some point, eventually, after years of struggle, slip into line. I know I did. As a youth I was obsessed with finding the "meaning of life," to the point that most of my peers found me strange. I had a deep conviction that there had to be a reason we are here. Once I knew that reason, I figured, I would know what to focus my efforts on. I was fixated on this for years, but eventually everyday life intervened. Most of those eccentric seekers, like me, at some point, are forced to deal with day-to-day reality. We all have rents or mortgages to pay, big bosses to avoid, childhood scars to overcome and romantic disasters to address. It is easy to get entangled into the game that ensnared everyone else. I sure did.

---

[210] Will and Ariel Durant, 160.

I set a goal to make enough money to retire and I worked at it, day in and day out, focusing on achieving material success. When you become material minded like that, thoughts about meaning are crowded out, as they cannot help you achieve your goals. There I was. I had joined the predominant schema. I became a man of the world, and I got good at it.

Then came retirement. When you retire, you have time, entire days, weeks and months, and the question presents itself: "What should I do?" Or even better: "Why would I do that?"

Really, what do retirees do? And why? Retirees don't have to work to pay their bills. They are done with that. So, theoretically, retirees are free to do what is important. But just what is important? Many have their "pet causes," which are often political or humanitarian. Feeding the hungry, indoctrinating the children with their ideology, helping people on the other side of the world get access to fresh water. But is this really that important?

At some point, when faced with forty additional hours to fill each week, the questions probably arise: *What am I trying to accomplish here in retirement? What is going to make me happy? Am I just trying to stay busy?* Many are doing just that. If you stay busy, you won't have to confront the questions that have remained unanswered, the questions that you have been avoiding for the past five decades while you were distracted by the tedious demands of your working life.

If you think about it, this is exactly what Western society has been doing, at least since the establishment of the Church of Rome—avoiding the real questions. Focusing on diversions, anything, but not the void that is staring us in the face. In fact, even during early church times in the fourth century, much of the energy of the Christian leaders in the Roman Empire was wasted in nonsense arguments over whose faith was correct, whose scriptures should be abolished and which bishops should be excommunicated. The emperor Constantine the Great, the emperor who made Christianity the faith of the Roman Empire, prohibited the assemblies of heretics and the confiscated their public properties. Roman soldiers were sent to attack heretic churches. Armies of rival monk sects fought with weapons. The famous saints Cyril (375–444) and John Chrysostom (347–407) participated in the persecution of people who believed differently. All of this nonsense was totally missing the point of the religion and also conveniently provided a diversion so people could easily avoid the real questions that Christianity was supposed to answer.

Peakers and Non-peakers

At the beginning of every known major religion was a solitary individual who had one or a series of mystical experiences. These individuals touched God, communed with the Universe, experienced the Unity of all people and things, however you want to put it. These individuals were rebels, in essence, as they went their own way and trusted their own experiences rather than those of the existing religion, society and institutions around them.

According to the famous psychologist, Abraham Maslow (1908–1970), all of these religious visionaries experienced the same thing, a peak experience in which they communicated with the Divine. Of course, their interpretation of what they saw was defined by their time and culture.[211] What to Jesus Christ was communion with God his Father was to Gautama Buddha the Great Nothingness of the Universe. Same thing but seen through the lens of different social and individual schemas.

It takes two types of people to create a religion. A lone visionary who experiences the Infinite, whatever you may call It, and an organizational type, who codifies and institutionalizes the teachings. The organizational types who follow the visionary revere the visionary as a prophet, a guru or a god. The visionary's utterances are sacrosanct. For every Jesus Christ, a Saint Paul (or a group of followers) is required, who puts it all together into an organization with a proscribed canon and rituals. Joseph Smith, the prophet of Mormonism, had Brigham Young. The idea, of course,

---

[211] Abraham Maslow, *Religions, Values and Peak-Experiences* (Penguin Books, 1994), 20.

is to provide a path for the rest of us to follow so that we can attain the same spiritual heights and experience the Infinite or God.

But I don't believe anyone has succeeded in forging this path.

Truth Is Ineffable

The problem is, our language is limited, especially when it comes to describing the profound euphoria associated with Divine revelation. Our language cannot communicate ecstasy. Can you communicate the feeling of an orgasm to a virgin? Hell, our language cannot even communicate how to swim. You can read all the books in the world on swimming; it does not mean you can swim. When you hit the water the first time and your lungs fill with water, you will instantly realize the limitations of language and books.

Al Ghazali (1058-1111) was a Sunni Muslim philosopher, theologian and mystic, who lived mostly in Bagdad and Damascus. In his autobiography, he wrote:

> *I recognized for certain that the Sufis are assuredly walking in the path of God…In the prophetic [the mystics] the sight is illumined by a light which uncovers hidden things and objects which the intellect fails to reach…The prophet is endowed with qualities to which you possess nothing analogous, and which consequently you cannot possibly understand. How should you know their true nature, since one knows only what one can comprehend? But the transport which one attains by the method of the Sufis is like an immediate perception, as if one touched the objects with one's hand.*[212]

---

[212] From Al-Ghazali's autobiography, in William James, *Varieties of Religious Experiences* (Longman, Green & Co., 1917), 395–397.

Osho[213] addressed this in The Mustard Seed:

The kingdom of heaven cannot be explained directly, immediately. It is impossible. Unless you enter it there is no way to say anything about it. Whatsoever is said will be wrong. The truth cannot be said. Then what are Jesus, Lao Tzu and Buddha doing continuously, for years? If the truth cannot be said, what are they doing? They are trying to explain something to you which cannot be explained, through some symbols which you know; trying to explain the unknown through the known. This is the most difficult thing in the world—parables, myths, stories.[214]

Or maybe, it can be said quite simply: "It is just like a blind man asking what light is like. How can you ask what light is when you are blind?"[215]

Of Krishnamurti (1895-1986) whom we will meet later, a biographer wrote,

He was fueled by a burning desire to share the realization he himself attained. Yet he discovered early on…that the inexpressible could never be communicated through language; he could teach to the end of his days, he could theorize, intellectualize, convince, cajole or bully his audiences, but, ultimately, the fire he aimed to ignite could not be contained in words or concepts, no matter how inspired the speaker.[216]

And what is worse is that the disciples of these enlightened individuals who have glimpsed the truth, unintentionally dilute it due to their

---

[213] Osho is the Indian guru, previously known as Bhagwan Shree Rashneesh. Osho founded a commune in Oregon in the 1980s with tens of thousands of members. The local Oregonians hated him and his followers and used the law to banish him from the country. If you haven't heard of Osho, I strongly suggest you watch the Netflix series, *The Big Country*, a documentary on this tragic episode in history.

[214] Osho, *The Mustard Seed (Osho International foundation, 1975)*, 11.

[215] Osho, *The Mustard Seed*, 12.

[216] Roland Vernon, *Star of the East: Krishnamurti—the Invention of a Messiah* (Sentient, 2002), 198–199.

limited understanding. And the generations that follow further distort and water down the remaining fragments of wisdom, until finally the message is lost and you end up with institutionalized religion.

This incapacity to communicate Truth is like a law of physics; perhaps you can call it the Law of Spiritual Truth. Truth cannot be conveyed using language. Throughout the centuries, many have tried to break the law that I just proposed. Thousands of books have been written to convey "the Truth," but the possessors and readers of these books can only progress slightly, barely an inch further along the path towards whatever spiritual endpoint they are seeking. Especially when the writers haven't even found Truth themselves. The number of exceptional spiritual adepts in our history is small, with hundreds of times more writers on spiritual topics than actual adepts.

Christopher Isherwood (1904–1986) is one, a writer, not an adept. He was deeply immersed in Eastern religion. In his book on Ramakrishna, he described a state of consciousness that mystics and saints achieve,

> *samadhi - known as the fourth state of consciousness, because it is neither waking, dreaming nor dreamless sleep. But it is impossible for me to say anything very explicit about it. Like all but the merest handful of people alive in the world today, I have never come anywhere near experiencing it. And even those who have experienced it have had great difficulty in speaking of their experience. One may say, indeed, that it is by definition indescribable. For words deal with the knowledge obtained by the five senses; and samadhi goes beyond all sense-experience. It is in its highest form a state of total knowledge, in which the knower and the thing known become one...Outwardly, samadhi appears to be a state of unconsciousness, since the mind of the experiencer is entirely withdrawn from the outer world...But, in fact, samadhi is a state of awareness unimaginably more intense than everyday consciousness.*[217]

---

[217] Isherwood, *Ramakrishna and His Disciples (Vedanta, 1965), ch. 6.*

But now that we have read his description of the indescribable, can we understand it? I don't think so.

Peak Experiences and Mysticism

Maslow is famous for his studies of peak experiences. Unfortunately, the term "peak experience" has morphed over the decades and now means different things to different people. Others have called the rush from skydiving or winning a lottery a peak experience, but this is something different from what I am writing about here. In this essay, I am using Maslow's definition of peak experience, which is a mystical experience.

So, what is a peak experience? It is hard to describe, but I can try. A peak experience is something that alights upon you like a butterfly. It happens rarely and you cannot force it. It is relatively short, maybe lasting minutes or up to an hour. When you are in one, you feel this all-encompassing feeling of love, of a sense of unity with all people and perhaps all things. You love them all. No problems reside in this state. The world is wonderful, beautiful, perfect, and you are part of it. You experience a sense of certainty that you never experience outside of a mystical state. You understand everything. You have no thought of yesterday or tomorrow. You can view your day-to-day life from afar, objectively; and it is beautiful, sad and comic all at the same time. In my own experiences, I often felt the profound vastness of time, the great sweep of history and my insignificant place in it.

The same sense of love, of awe, of reverence, of perfection, of certain knowledge are reported by everyone who has had such an experience, whether called "peak" or "mystical." It is for this reason that most religions are at heart, the same. Different people describe this same experience differently, and hence we have different religions; but all the great religions started with lone mystics who had a peak experience. It all followed from there.

According to Maslow, in his essay "Religions, Values and Peak-Experiences," everyone can have peak-experiences, but peak-experiences frighten most of us and we fight them off, suppressing or denying them when they occur. Most of us are fearful of losing control, of our emotions taking over or of going insane. If we have peak experiences, we may explain them away as moments of craziness.

In this regard, Maslow breaks humanity into two types: those who can have peak experiences, "peakers," and the rest of us, which includes those who may have them but, by using various mechanisms, resist them. This second group, the majority, are the "non-peakers." The problem is that organizational types are usually "non-peakers." They are rational. They make order out of chaos. They create the structured whole from the incomprehensible utterances of the visionary.

The organizers of religions, non-peakers, are trying to preserve the precious truths of the peaker. But they invariably cannot fathom the deeper meaning behind the visionaries' vain attempts at relating what they know. Although peakers often will try to communicate the ineffable in stories, non-peakers still garble the underlying meanings when they write the stories down. So we have two problems here. The peakers' experiences cannot be conveyed accurately in words and the non-peakers cannot understand the truths even if they could be conveyed in words.

How Religion Falls Short

Organized religion, then is an attempt to communicate the ecstatic visions of the visionary, the peaker, to the non-peaker—something that cannot be done. And thus we end up with soulless theology that brings us no closer to God. We revere the prophet and lose the divine vision. Our religions become forms of idolatry or fetishism; this has been the curse of every large religion.[218] The original meaning gets lost in the menagerie of words, symbols and rituals. People adhere to these trappings as if they were sacred, but they are not. By nature, religious institutions become hostile to mysticism, even the authentic original mystical experience upon which the religion was based. Once the doctrine has been settled, new ideas or prophets are not needed.

---

[218] Maslow, 24.

Religious institutions tend to divide, after a time, into two camps. One camp contains the peakers (mystics) and privately spiritual people, and the other camp is composed of non-peakers, those who

> *worship little pieces of wood rather than what the objects stand for, those who take verbal formulas literally, forgetting the original meaning of these words, and, perhaps most important, those who take the organization, the church, as primary and as more important than the prophet and his original revelations.*[219]

The non-peakers end up running the religions, and usually the mystics are then branded as heretics and persecuted. This was demonstrated by Fyodor Dostoevsky in his Grand Inquisitor parable in The Brothers Karamazov. In the story, Jesus had returned to Seville during the Spanish Inquisition. The people recognized Him and worshipped Him as He passed. But the authorities arrested Him and condemned Him to death. The Grand Inquisitor visits Jesus in jail. The inquisitor knows who He is, but he nonetheless rejects Him, because the Church is doing a fine job without Him. He would just cause problems if He remained alive.

> *Why, then, art Thou come to hinder us? For Thou hast come to hinder us, and Thou knowest that. But dost thou know what will be to-morrow?. . .to-morrow I shall condemn Thee and burn Thee at the stake as the worst of heretics. And the very people who have to-day kissed Thy feet, to-morrow at the faintest sign from me will rush to heap up the embers of Thy fire.*[220]

So what is the point? The major religions today are caricatures of what their original prophets could possibly have envisioned. The prophets were radicals who had a personalized relationship to the Divine. They rebelled against the religious institutions of their day. And in every case, institutions loosely based on their teachings, arose to direct the devotees.

---

[219] Maslow, 25.

[220] Fyodor Dostoevsky, *Brothers Karamazov, ch. 5.*

Yet these institutions missed the point completely, becoming just as oppressive as the religions the original prophets rejected.[221]

Jesus's Teachings Sullied by Non-Peakers

Maslow tells us that

> *Transcendent experiences seem to occur more frequently in people who have rejected their inherited religion and who have then created one for themselves (whether they call it that or not).*[222]

Jesus of Nazareth was one of these, a peaker. He communicated with God outside of the prescribed Jewish religious practices. According to the gospels, Jesus taught that it was not necessary to rely on the Jewish priests and rituals to have a relationship with God. People could communicate with God directly, just as Jesus did. The elaborate Jewish religious requirements, rituals and customs were getting in the way.

This is true of any religion. When prayers or rituals are repeated mindlessly, they cease to have any meaning. Religion for many throughout the centuries has been reduced to "thoughtless, habitual, reflex-like, absent-minded, automatic responses, which are dubbed 'religious' by many people"[223]—the non-peakers. This is called "religious formalism," where our attention is directed to the outward trappings of religion but completely misses the point, which is developing a deeper, ongoing, life-changing experience of God. Religious formalists are the ones who attend worship regularly, say all the words you are supposed to say, and adhere to all the visible aspects of the religion, but remain untouched inside.

---

[221] This appears to be a "group thing" rather than a "religion thing." Communist revolutions have the same pattern. Wonderful ideology. A state is created based on it, perverts it, oppresses the people, and a perversion of the revolutionary thought becomes the new establishment. Rinse and repeat.

[222] Maslow, 34.

[223] Maslow, 34.

Religious formalism is found in all religions, as it is a common characteristic of non-peakers; and non-peakers dominate and rule the world. It is rare, but the peakers can change the world when the non-peakers don't kill them first. But, as we all know, sometimes after peakers are murdered, they can inspire even greater change.

The Very Early Church

So using that peaker/non-peaker context, let's take another look at the beginning of the Christian religion. We will see how non-peakers took the original message of Jesus and transformed it.

Forty days after Jesus died, the Church of Jerusalem was established. This was the first Christian church in the world. For a time, the apostles remained in Jerusalem as part of that community. James, the half-brother of Jesus from Joseph's prior marriage, was the first primary leader of the Church of Jerusalem. After the martyrdom of James, Jesus's cousin, Simeon, became the second head of the Church. The first fifteen bishops in the Jerusalem church were all circumcised Jews. The Church united the law of Moses with the doctrine of Christ. Jesus and his apostles were Jews, after all. When people talk of the early Christians, I believe they are talking about people who met Jesus, and these were the people in the Church of Jerusalem. They were renegade Jews.

Initially, the Church of Jerusalem was considered the standard of orthodoxy for the teachings of Jesus. Distant churches frequently appealed to the authority of the Church of Jerusalem and contributed money for its upkeep.

In the year 50 CE, Paul and Barnabas met with James, Peter and John, the leaders of the Church, and received permission to preach to the pagans in the empire and to present Jesus's message without the Mosaic Law portion. Paul and Barnabas then fostered large Christian communities in the great cities of the empire, such as Antioch, Ephesus, Corinth and Rome. As these Christian communities grew, the status of the community in Jerusalem diminished. The original Jewish converts, later called Nazarenes, were eventually looked down upon by the other communities, and their Mosaic beliefs were eventually no longer tolerated.

The Nazarenes claimed that Paul was an imposter. Followers of Peter and Paul fundamentally disagreed with each other, as followers of Peter practiced the Mosaic Law and followers of Paul did not.

Paul believed that Christ was resurrected in a spiritual form, not a material body. His idea of resurrection was, like Clement of Rome's (the only other first century Christian writer whose writings we have), that the spiritual body arose from the decay of the natural body. He did not believe that Jesus returned into his material body after his crucifixion. He had never seen the canonical gospels, "nor is there any reason to believe he had ever seen a gospel in which Jesus denied being a spirit, after the resurrection."[224] Jesus was able to communicate with the apostles after His death through supernatural means. Paul's and Clement's writings make no mention of miracles, or even of a virgin birth. That came later in the second century.

In 70 CE, in response to the Jewish uprising, the Romans destroyed the Temple in Jerusalem. The Nazarenes were forced to leave the city and settled in Pella, a town beyond the Jordan, where the Nazarene Church languished for more than sixty years in solitude and obscurity.

So what happened to the Nazarenes? They were the original followers of Christ after all. As Gentile Christianity grew, the Nazarenes' Jewish practices and semi-orthodox beliefs were increasingly unacceptable to the prominent Church leaders, and they were marginalized. After the Council of Nicaea (in the fourth century), their gospel, the Gospel of the Hebrews, was suppressed by the Church. By the fifth century, the Nazarenes faded away most likely due to assimilation and persecution by both Rabbinic Jews (for accepting Jesus) and Christians (for adhering to the Jewish law). The Gospel of the Hebrews was just one of many gospels and epistles that were lost to history.

---

[224] Judge C. B. Waite, *History of the Christian Religion to the Year Two Hundred (C. V. Waite, 1881), 29.*

Lost Early Christian Writings

Saint Paul's letters represent the earliest sacred Christian writings that we recognize today. They were written during his missionary work in the mid-first century CE. The four gospels that we are familiar with (Matthew, Mark, Luke and John) came much later. Before them, the early Christians had many gospels about Jesus, but they have been largely forgotten today. Some writings were found in a cave at Nag Hammadi in 1948. Of these, some were used as kindling to ignite fires, but most ended up in the hands of religious scholars. Other gospels no longer exist or exist only in fragments. In the first century, the *Gospel of Paul, the Recollections of Peter* and the *Oracles or Sayings of Christ* were written. We only know of these lost gospels from the writings of early Church fathers, such as Origen, Tertullian, Justin Martyr and Eusebius, who refer to them.[225]

One of the most well-known gospels in the second century is the Gospel of the Hebrews, which has been lost to history, its author unknown.[226] It couldn't have been written after 125 CE,[227] and it was the primary gospel of the second century with the Nazarenes using it for over 300 years. The Gospel of the Hebrews contains no references to the immaculate conception of Jesus. But some miracles did appear in the Gospel, such as healing of the sick. The more radical miracles, such as changing water into wine and raising Lazarus from the dead do not occur until later Christian writings. The Gospel of the Hebrews did include the resurrection of Christ in a material body and the doctrine flowing from it. This was the first instance known of material bodily resurrection, and the Catholic Church has upheld it ever since.[228] There were many other largely forgotten and lost gospels and epistles from the second century

---

[225] Waite provides these and other details from early Church fathers' writings.

[226] We know of the contents of the Gospel of the Hebrews from fragmentary quotes found in the early church fathers. Jerome claimed to have translated the Gospel of the Hebrews from Hebrew or Aramaic into Greek and Latin, but those translations have not survived.

[227] Waite, 62.

[228] Waite, 77.

before the four gospels we are familiar with were written. The writings of the second century include the Second Epistle of Clement (the third bishop of Rome),[229] the Epistles of Peter the apostle, the writings of John the apostle, the Epistle of James and the Epistle of Judas.

Authorship of the Christian Gospels

So the four Christian gospels we are familiar with were not written until well after all the apostles and anyone who knew the apostles had died. No mention of these gospels is recorded in any of the Christian writings until 170 years after Jesus's death. Assuming the apostles were the same age as Christ and assuming one of them lived to the age of eighty years, then it would be ninety years after that octogenarian's death that writings appeared in the names of those apostles. Until that time, several other gospels were used by Christian communities in the first and second centuries.

Judge Charles Burlingame Waite (1824–1909) wrote an exhaustive study of the writings of the early church in *History of the Christian Religion to the Year 200*, which I have already referred to. In it, he quotes Bishop Faustus in a fifth century correspondence with St Augustine:

> *As we have proved again and again, the writings are the not the production of Christ or his apostles, but a compilation of rumors and beliefs, made long after their departure, by some obscure semi-Jews, not in harmony even with one another, and published by them under the name of the apostles, or of those considered the followers of the apostles, so as they give the appearance of apostolic authority to all these blunders and falsehoods.*[230]

There you go. Non-peakers formed the Christian religion. Over the centuries following Jesus' death, generations of non-peakers systematically rejected the authentic doctrines of Christ's earliest followers,

---

[229] The First Epistle of Clement was written at the end of the first century but was very popular in the second century.

[230] Waite, 342, in "On the Manichean Heresy," *Works of Augustine, Book 33.*

pushed out early Christian texts like the Gospel of the Hebrews with their canonical Gospels, and set up the orthodox theology, rituals and hierarchical Church that endure today.[231]

Since its embrace by Constantine the Great, the Church has strayed from its original mission. One sign of such drift is the great lengths to which the Church has gone to persecute and silence those with "wrong" beliefs. Gibbon in The Decline and Fall of the Roman Empire makes it clear that far more followers of Christ were killed by the Church than were ever killed by the Roman pagans. Attacking those who disagree is a far cry from Jesus's teachings of love and compassion.

Roger Bacon on Church Depravity

In 1271, about sixty-three generations after Christ walked on the Earth, the Church had deviated considerably from Christ's original message. Roger Bacon, a medieval English philosopher, a Franciscan friar and one of the earliest advocates for the scientific method, described the lamentable condition of the Church in his day.

> *More sins reign in these days than in any past age. . .the Holy See is torn by the deceit and fraud of unjust men. . .Pride reigns, covetousness burns, envy gnaws upon all; the whole Curia is disgraced with lechery, and gluttony is lord of all. . .If this be so in the Head, what then is done among the members? Let us see the prelates, how they run after money, neglect the care of souls, promote their nephews and other carnal friends, and crafty lawyers who ruin all by their counsel. . .Let us consider the Religious Orders; I exclude none from what I say; see how far they are fallen, one and all, from their right*

---

[231] One can consider it shameful that humanity has polluted the original message; and although there were probably some selfish reasons this was done, there were also good reasons. To spread the word of God and grow the community of believers, it is necessary to have a clear message. Many of the gospels of the first centuries of Christianity were similar to the four gospels we know today. But some of them were radically different, and some communities professed contrasting ideas about Jesus and God. If you are trying to spread a doctrine that you think is a blessing to humanity, do you just let anyone believe what they want? Once again, I don't think so.

state; and the new Orders [the Friars] are already horribly decayed from their original dignity. The whole clergy is intent upon pride, lechery, and avarice; and wheresoever clerks [students] are gathered together. . .they scandalize the laity with their wars and quarrels and other vices.[232]

Rediscovering Jesus's lost Message

The main points Jesus of Nazareth was trying to make have been lost. The non-peakers who tried as best they could to continue His legacy and spread His message botched it all up. They didn't get it. So now we have the parables of Jesus, many of which have been rendered incomprehensible to us. They have been written down, translated and interpreted by "non-peakers."

Eckhart Tolle, I believe, is one of our modern-day enlightened ones, a peaker and communicator of the first degree. It appears that he understands many things in the Christian gospels that never made that much sense to me.

The Kingdom of Heaven is one of them.

Tolle's message focuses on accessing this Kingdom by calming the mind and breaking free from constant thinking. Most of us have to endure a constant stream of thinking, which usually is complete nonsense. If we try to meditate and to listen objectively to the thoughts as they appear, not getting lost in them, just witnessing them, we will realize that the majority of them are not even worthy of our attention. They are just noise. They come and they go. Addressing our thoughts objectively, we can realize that we are not our thoughts. We can watch them drift in and out and be amused by them rather than identifying with them and being controlled by them.

Meditation is much like defragging a hard drive. Many of these thoughts need to appear, so they can be stored somewhere in your brain where

---

[232] Roger Bacon, *Compendium Philosophiae* (1271), in Durant, *Age of Faith*, 1,013.

they belong. After a while, most thoughts have been processed and not many thoughts are left. The space between thoughts increases until there is silence. For me, it takes about twenty-five minutes to notice that the thoughts are becoming sparse. It is here in between the sparse thoughts that a glimpse of an eternity can be felt in a single second. Perhaps this is what the Bible meant, where it says "Be still and know that I am God." Through stillness you can become aware of the vastness of the great silence, which is God.[233] But what major Western church teaches that?

Matthew 25 includes a well-known parable of the ten virgins.

> *Then shall the kingdom of heaven be likened unto ten virgins, who took their lamps, and went forth to meet the bridegroom. And five of them were foolish, and five were wise. For the foolish, when they took their lamps, took no oil with them: but the wise took oil in their vessels with their lamps. Now while the bridegroom tarried, they all slumbered and slept. But at midnight there is a cry, Behold, the bridegroom! Come ye forth to meet him. Then all those virgins arose, and trimmed their lamps. And the foolish said unto the wise, Give us of your oil; for our lamps are going out. But the wise answered, saying, Peradventure there will not be enough for us and you: go ye rather to them that sell, and buy for yourselves. And while they went away to buy, the bridegroom came; and they that were ready went in with him to the marriage feast: and the door was shut. Afterward came also the other virgins, saying, Lord, Lord, open to us. But he answered and said, Verily I say unto you, I know you not. Watch therefore, for ye know not the day nor the hour.[234]*

We have been taught that the bridegroom is Jesus in the afterlife, and the oil is the Holy Spirit. To be successful in this life, we must be like the wise virgins and live a holy life with the Holy Spirit. Those who do

---

[233] "Eckhart Tolle for Christians," *Todd Wright Now*, toddwrightnow.com/2010/02/eckhart-tolle-for-christians_01.html, accessed January 1, 2023. Thanks to Todd Wright for sharing his thoughts.

[234] Matthew 25, 1-13 (American Standard Edition).

not live holy lives will not be rewarded with everlasting life in heaven. But according to Tolle, what if the oil represents the consciousness you can get by being still and experiencing God? The five careless women were living unconsciously in the world and had no oil. They didn't experience the silence. The bridegroom is the prize, the experience you can get by being still, the experience of being here NOW. The wedding feast that the five virgins missed was enlightenment. Jesus was trying to tell us to be conscious. To sit still and experience God NOW. God can be with us NOW. We do not have to wait for the second coming.

Think of the hundreds of millions of people who have waited for the second coming of Jesus and the Last Judgement. It hasn't come. They were looking in the wrong place—outside, not inside.

Jesus, the man, was exceptional. His message was lost. That's all.

Tolle says,

> *These are parables not about the end of the world [the second coming] but about the end of psychological time [which is the coming of stillness]. They point to the transcendence of the egoic mind and the possibility of living in an entirely new state of consciousness.*[235]

In Matthew, Jesus is said to have warned us:

> *Watch therefore: for ye know not on what day your Lord cometh. But know this, that if the master of the house had known in what watch the thief was coming, he would have watched, and would not have suffered his house to be broken through. Therefore be ye also ready; for in an hour that ye think not the Son of man cometh.*[236]

We have been taught that this passage is about how we need to remain always ready for Jesus' second coming, for we do not know when it will happen. According to Tolle, that was not Jesus' point at all. It is not

---

[235] Tolle, *79.*
[236] Matthew 24, 42–44, American Standard Version.

about Jesus' second coming. God can enter into our lives at any minute. We can live better lives if we are open to God's presence and can identify It when It appears. It may appear in the kindness of strangers, the loving caress of our spouse, the love you feel when you reassure your child. If we are not conscious, we will likely miss the presence of God in our lives.

How are we, especially me, your writer, to know what Jesus really meant? I suppose we should not try to apply reason to things of the Spirit. But the teachings of the Christian doctrine have many unresolved problems, which makes me think that the traditional teachings are missing Jesus' original point. Throughout the centuries, the non-peakers have so damaged His original meanings, that we have this tangled theology. Perhaps Tolle, a peaker himself, was able to decipher it.

Martin Luther, the Non-Peaker Prophet

During the Reformation, Martin Luther, a non-peaker, wrangled what remained of Christ's message into something altogether different. And the remnants of his radical thinking remain today enshrined in Protestant institutions and beliefs. For hundreds of years in the later medieval period, the Catholic Church had been laughably corrupt. The bishops, cardinals and popes were held in a similar contempt as politicians are today. Higher church positions were purchased. They were considered a lucrative investment by the rich, as church offices brought great financial returns and prestige.[237]

Before we get to Luther, we need some context.

Let's talk purgatory.

We discussed earlier how non-peakers have changed the messages of the original mystics, creating the dogmas we have today. Well, purgatory was an invention of Christian non-peakers. Christ never spoke of it,

---

[237] That these purchased positions could be kept for life was not guaranteed. It was political. Higher Church authorities could replace appointees at any time. I suspect as long as monies flowed from the bishops and cardinals to the higher-ups, their positions were more likely to be maintained.

nor did Paul in his letters. In the fifth century, Augustine wrote of a purifying process for souls that were not fully sanctified. It was an abstraction then, not part of the Church's established dogma. About seven hundred years later, in the twelfth century, the term "purgatory" was finally coined when theologian Peter Lombard wrote about it. And it became official Catholic doctrine in 1274 with the Second Council of Lyon.

In medieval times, people believed that purgatory was a place of intense fiery suffering, although the inmates were nevertheless full of joy knowing they were eventually heaven-bound. After death, souls might spend decades or even centuries in torment in purgatory before moving on to heaven. Generally, it was a place to avoid, if you could, but it did beat hell.[238]

From the thirteenth century on, it was increasingly believed that prayers and masses in one's name were thought to lessen the time one's soul would reside in purgatory and make one's time in purgatory less harrowing. The rich, upon dying, would bequeath cash to monasteries or churches so that masses would be conducted for the safe conduct of their souls in the afterlife. This process of bequeathing cash in exchange for masses was a significant source of income for monasteries and churches. Better yet, buying plenary indulgences allowed people to bypass this purgatory altogether. In the early sixteenth century, representatives of the Church were selling indulgences, which were "get-out-of-purgatory-free" passes. If one purchased a full (plenary) indulgence, the purchaser could bypass otherwise unavoidable suffering in the afterlife (in purgatory) on their way to heaven.

Indulgences had been around for a long time. But as the Church needed money to pay for the construction of Saint Peter's Basilica in Rome, which started in 1506, it expanded its network of authorized preachers

---

[238] The Catholics have since repackaged the concept of purgatory. It is no longer a place, more of a state, and it is marked more by joy, mercy and hope than suffering now. Most Protestant denominations don't have a purgatory in their theology.

and agents to sell indulgences. The German Dominican Friar, Johann Tetzel (c. 1465–1519) was probably the most famous for this. He was an inquisitor for the Church in Poland and Saxony, but later became the Grand Commissioner for indulgences in Germany. He traveled the German territories preaching and selling indulgences. He was famous for the catchy phrase "As soon as the coin in the coffer rings, the soul from purgatory springs." Indulgences were inexpensive, going for whatever the market would bear but, in most cases, probably less than the cost of a lamb. Usually, they were purchased for those who were already dead, so that the departed could avoid suffering in the afterlife.

The following snippet from a Tetzel sermon brings it all alive to me. I can see people making these types of arguments today.

> *Don't you hear the voices of your wailing dead parents and others who say, "Have mercy upon me, have mercy upon me, because we are in severe punishment and pain [in Purgatory]. From this you could redeem us with a small alms and yet you do not want to do so…We have created you, fed you, cared for you, and left you our temporal goods. Why then are you so cruel and harsh that you do not want to save us, though it only takes a little?"*[239]

They sold indulgences for the living as well. According to Luther, Tetzel was preaching that once you had an indulgence, you had license to sin for the rest of your life. The following is from Luther's writings:

> *After Tetzel had collected a large sum of money in Leipzig, a certain nobleman came to him and asked whether he would be able to grant him indulgence for the sin he was about to commit.*

Tetzel agreed, took the money, and as he left Leipzig,

> *the nobleman, attacked him on the way, smeared his skin thickly with blows, and then let him go back to Leipzig empty [handed]*

---

[239] Mark Konnert, *Medieval to Modern: Early Modern Europe* (Oxford University, 2017), 103.

> *after he had reported how this was the sin he had intended to commit.*[240]

Martin Luther, a Catholic priest at the time, had issues with the hypocrisy of the Church's teachings and practices. But it was the selling of indulgences that spurred him to action, leading him to nail the Ninety-Five Theses onto the door of the Castle Church in Wittenberg in 1517. Nailing theses for debate onto church doors was a common practice at the time. It was an invitation to debate other academics. Luther did not intend to spark the breakup of the Church with this action. He merely wanted the Church to stop selling indulgences.

Luther asked in his eighty-first thesis, if Christ's message was love and forgiveness, then why

> *does not the pope empty purgatory for the sake of holy love and of the dire need of the souls that are there [since he redeems a]…number of souls for the sake of miserable money with which to build a church?*

As expected, Luther was met with opposition to his ideas, which only hardened his position against the Church and its unwillingness to confront its own hypocrisy and corruption. Too much money was being made by the higher clergy. Like the other groups I described in an earlier essay, the Church had become just another group that had lost hold of its original purpose and instead strove to keep the good things going—in their case, maintaining power over people's lives and a generous income for its leaders. Fortunately for Luther, powerful provincial political leaders were not happy with the Church reaping all that indulgence money when it could have gone into their own pockets. The local leaders protected Luther; and only because of them, did the Reformation take place. It was a political thing. And it was a money thing.

---

[240] Martin Luther, *Dr. Martin Luther's Complete Writings, Reformation Writings,* Volume 15 (Concordia Publishing House, 1899), 363.

We have no evidence that Luther was a peaker. He wrote or spoke of nothing indicating that he received Divine illumination. Instead, Luther's writings and the Lutheran Church carried Christianity further away from Jesus's original message—both that lost message (stillness and communion with God) and the retained message (loving and cherishing others).

Luther asked why did the people need priests and a hopelessly corrupt church to inform them what God's intentions were? Instead, he claimed that the Truth was to be found in the Bible—specifically in his German translation of the Bible, which he made available at an affordable price. The hierarchy, rituals, customs and traditions of the Church only got in the way. Now anyone could read the Bible and interpret it for themselves. In his hometown, Wittenberg, during his lifetime, over 100,000 copies of his New Testament were printed. It became the best-selling book in Germany.[241] People no longer needed priests and the Catholic Church to provide the Word of God. The people could now find it for themselves in their own Bibles.

And so, Martin Luther opened a Pandora's Box when he claimed that people can know God's will by reading the Bible. The problem is that anyone can interpret the Bible however they want. If people truly followed Luther's basic idea of religious freedom, religious anarchy would take hold, as there would be thousands of home-grown leaders, each preaching different ideas about God and religion. Of course, that is exactly what happened. Religious anarchy reigned for a short time. Some of the sects became radical, communist and anti-authority. Peasant rebellions broke out across Germany. As the temporal powers of the time would not stand for anyone questioning the social order, there followed the persecution and murder of adherents of some of these sects. Finally, some stability was reached when a religious-political system emerged in which the ruler of a region would determine the religion of its inhabitants.

---

[241] Will Durant, *The Reformation* (Simon & Schuster, 1957), 369.

One could argue that the Anabaptists embraced Martin Luther's idea of religious freedom more than any other major group. As a result, they were hated by almost all of the other Christian sects and governmental authorities as they were spiritual anarchists.

The Anabaptists were a loose congregation of sects in sixteenth century Germany, Switzerland, Austria and the Netherlands. They held tightly the right to choose their own religious beliefs, rather than having to comply with whatever doctrines the political leaders forced on the people. Adults, rather than infants, were baptized when they were ready to submit to God, hence their name—Anabaptists[242]. They were pacifists. They would not serve in any army or government nor take any dispute to the courts. Many were socialists and tried to bring back their vision of the early Christian communities that shared all belongings. Roundly hated by the institutional churches and governmental authorities, they were hunted down, exiled and killed. The Mennonites and the Amish faiths descend from the Anabaptist lineage.

It wasn't just the Anabaptists who were problematic to the authorities. Luther's radical ideas were a contributing factor to the German Peasants' War of 1524 to 1525. Luther sided with the authorities and condemned the rebellion in his pamphlet entitled "Against the Robbing and Murdering Hordes of Peasants," urging the princes to crush the revolt, which of course they did, killing about 100,000 peasants.

In response to the anarchy that followed Luther's rebellion against the Church, Luther backtracked on his initial ideas of freedom of religion. He now emphasized the importance of a fixed church structure and obedience to Lutheran church authorities, as well as to secular authorities. This shift helped transform Lutheranism into a more defined theological system. Despite these changes, Luther continued to stress

---

[242] Ana is Greek for "again" and *baptizein* is German for to baptize. So the term meant rebaptizers. It was a perjorative name given to them by their enemies. They referred to themselves as the Brethren, God's people, saints, and there were other names as well.

that the Truth was in the Bible and not in the contrived sacraments and institutions of the Catholic Church.

Luther replaced some Church teachings with some very bleak teachings of his own, which became the canon of most early Protestant movements and some current churches today. According to Luther, we are born depraved and corrupt due to Adam and Eve's tragic mistakes in the Garden of Eden.

> *We are all sinner by nature—conceived and born in sin; sin has poisoned us through and through; we have from Adam a will, which continually sets itself against God.*[243]

All people are therefore deserving of an eternity of hell. We are powerless to change our ultimate fates. There is nothing we can do to save ourselves from hell. Performing good deeds will not help us. But God, through His grace, has chosen some souls for salvation and the rest of us to be damned to hell.

Whereas the Catholic Church taught that people can earn their way to heaven through faith and good works (or buy their way in), Luther taught that all people except the elect few were doomed at birth. Nobody knew who was doomed and who was elect, and there was nothing you can do about it. According to Luther, our spiritual lives have been predestined by God. We have no free will regarding our spiritual lives.[244]

> *God, in this world, has scarce the tenth part of the people; the smallest number only will be saved. The world is exceedingly ungodly and wicked.*[245]

---

[243] Martin Luther, *Table Talk*, 244.

[244] John Carroll, *the Wreck of Western Culture, Humanism Revisited* (ISI Books, 2008), 54-55.

[245] Martin Luther, *Table Talk*, 91. What is amusing is what he wrote in the next topic on natural medicine, in XCII: 'Tis wonderful how God has put such excellent physic in mere muck; we know by experience that swine's dung stints the blood; horse's serves for the pleurisy; man's heals wounds and black blotches; asses' is used for the bloody flux, and cow's with preserved roses, for epilepsy, or for convulsions of children.

Humans have no freedom, yet we are responsible and must pay the penalty.[246] Australian professor John Carroll described Luther's message as:

> *I shall so bury you under your own guilt, your own pitiable weakness, your total dependency on the Lord God, that I shall have you living on your knees in prayer. You are nothing. You are nobody. I shall fling you back into the spiritual dungeon where your thinking faculty has no chance of creating the illusion in you that you have some control over your own destiny. It is down there in the dark, where the light of neither reason nor law shines, where only God can help you, that you may find grace. All is determined. Your fate is set.[247]*

This stark divergence from Jesus' original teachings of a loving and forgiving God demonstrates how profoundly spiritual messages can be transformed over time by those who lack direct mystical experiences. It is very sad to me—but it is the story of humanity.

The Quakers, a Religion of Peakers

A hundred and fifty years after Martin Luther, George Fox, a seventeenth-century mystic and founder of the Quaker movement in England created a religious movement with no hierarchy, no priests and no churches. Early Quakers recognized that God's light shines, or can shine, in all people, and it only follows that all should be treated equally. (By the way, this is typical Peaker administrative ineffectiveness—no hierarchy.)

Quakers hold that God is not more in one place than any other. For this reason, they have no need of churches. The Quaker house of worship is merely a room with many benches to sit on. It has no altar, for God does not need rituals or offerings to be satisfied. God does not come from some place but is everywhere and is present in the souls of all men. God's spirit needs only a responsive, open soul, and He can be found

---

[246] John Carroll, 56.

[247] John Carroll, 57–58.

there. Each member of the Quakers is to be a priest unto God. Quaker meetings do not have set prayers like most Christian religions. Instead, Quakers gather in stillness until the Holy Spirit inspires someone to rise and speak as guided by God.

The Quakers and their mystical approach to God were not well received by other Protestants. They originally called themselves the Religious Society of Friends. They received the name Quakers by those who hated them, as "in consequence of their apparent convulsions which they labored under when they delivered their discourses, because they imagined they were the effect of divine inspiration."[248] Their refusal to take oaths[249] and their pacifism was unsettling both to the public and to English King Charles II's (1630–1685) government. As a result, the House of Lords enacted an act against the Quakers that included fines or exile from the realm. Some were exiled to plantations in the New World. According to Fox,

> *their meetings were daily broken up by men with clubs and arms and their friends thrown into the water, and trampled underfoot until the blood gushed out, which gave rise to their meeting in the open streets. A relation was printed, signed by twelve witnesses, which says that more than four thousand [and] two hundred Quakers were imprisoned.*[250]

After the passing of King Charles, James II (1633–1701) granted the Friends liberty to practice their religion.

It is estimated that by 1680, 60,000 Quakers were living in England and Wales, about 1.2% of the population. According to the familiar

---

[248] John Foxe, *Foxe's Book of Martyrs*, Section 26.

[249] Unlike others of the time, Quakers refused to swear to God, "take oaths," to affirm the truth of a statement. In seventeenth-century England, taking oaths was common, such as swearing allegiance to the king, testifying in court, or affirming loyalty to the Church of England. Quakers refused to take oaths because doing so implied that their word was not trustworthy without invoking God's name, which was contrary to their commitment to absolute truthfulness at all times.

[250] Foxe, Section 26.

pattern, though, most of those who followed George Fox either were not able to completely grasp his message or were overly affected by their own self-interest. As a result, over the centuries Quakerism was inevitably transformed. In the nineteenth century, schisms within the movement began to appear, so now there are at least four different Quaker bodies, some of which are much closer to traditional evangelical Christianity. Partially as a result, the movement shrank considerably. By 1860, only 13,859 Quakers remained in England and Wales, about 0.07% of the population.

What is interesting about the Quakers is that the religion was meant to be a society of peakers. The problem is that most of us are *not* peakers. We miss the fundamental message of the peaker founders. When non-peakers inevitably take over, the religion risks becoming just another human group, drifting from its original vision and getting caught up in human problems, often splitting into pieces.

It doesn't matter which religion or what century, mankind has always had the problem that the great majority of us are non-peakers and don't understand the roots of spirituality. We non-peakers cannot compare to the superstars of divine communion, like Jesus, George Fox or Buddha. It is just beyond us. Religions, created by and for non-peakers, provide a simplified rule book and give a semblance of meaning to our lives. The peakers can always find their way on their own.

I have noticed this same phenomenon in today's Catholic Church, I have noticed that there are two types of attendees at Sunday mass. The first group are those who attend on Sundays during the most crowded masses. These are the majority of Catholics. They are good people. They have lives to live, pressing financial concerns, problems to resolve, yet still a part of their lives is their devotion to their faith. They say the prayers, maybe even sing the songs; but their devotion can only go so deep as they are unable to take it any further. Religion to them, for the most part, is ritual, shared beliefs and moral code. This is the many.

The second group are the more spiritual Catholics who stress their connection to God, rather than their connection to the Church. They read spiritual classics and steadfastly pursue their relationship to God as the primary concern in their lives. To some of these, the ritual is very important. They spend hours in prayer or meditation. Their devotion to God is intense. These are the few. You find them frequenting the masses that few people attend or they may skip services altogether.

This is human nature. A small minority have an acute spiritual sense. Even Saint Augustine recognized this dichotomy. He said that only a small percentage of a congregation was truly pious, whereas the rest merely regurgitated the prayers and aped the other formalities. And it is not just a Catholic thing. It is a human thing.

I am not disparaging the majority here. They are experts in other things, just not God. Not all people have the same capacity for matters of the spirit. I believe that in all facets of human competence there is a sort of Gaussian distribution, with very few people being incredibly evolved or sophisticated in any particular topic, very few having no capacity at all for the topic, and the great majority in the middle, with a middling capacity for competence in the subject. This applies to running, mathematics, spirituality and, really, anything. It follows then, that very few of us can truly be peakers.

Many of us have been trained in the doctrines and ceremonies of our religions, but few of us really touch God, know that it is possible or even see the need to experience it. Very few of us become saints or adepts because few of us were born with the spiritual sensitivity to be so. Only a small percentage of us have a great desire to touch God, and of those, only a portion of them are able to actually do it.

> *The essence of religion is eternal, but it is only the men of genius who can grasp it. The religion of the majority has to be simplified and coated with sugar.*[251]

---

[251] Colin Wilson, *Religion and the Rebel* (Riverside, 1957), 133.

And in these days of constant overstimulation with televisions, radios, internet, texting and social media, few empty, silent moments remain in our lives and, therefore, much less opportunity to hear the whispers of God.

The World Teacher, the Ultimate Peaker

I have mentioned before that the great truths that the peakers experience is ineffable. They cannot convey what they experience. Yet religions still form around them to guide the rest of us, so that we can follow their paths and reach God. The essence of their message is lost; and as a result, religions can only lead us so far. So what happens when the new Jesus appears, the new World Teacher? Can it work? The World Teacher actually was here in the early twentieth century, and it ended badly. The story of the world teacher is sad to me. But first for context, we will start with the movement itself that predated the World Teacher.

Helena Blavatsky (1831–1891) was a Russian immigrant to the United States with what many today regard a dubious past. She claimed to have travelled for seven years in Tibet and studied under certain Himalayan masters, referred to as the Great White Brotherhood of Masters. The Brotherhood had received such a rigorous esoteric spiritual training that they had attained supernatural powers. These Masters were tasked with preserving the world's ancient spiritual knowledge and watching over humanity to guide its evolution. Some of these Masters were Buddha, Lao Tse, Confucius, Abraham, Moses, Solomon, Jesus, Plato, Cagliostro and Mesmer.

The Masters would approach those who were deemed worthy and use them as instruments to disseminate their ideas. They would communicate with them telepathically. Having studied with the Masters, Blavatsky served as their messenger, relaying wisdom to humanity through inspired writings. One of these communications was Blavatsky's book *Isis Unveiled*. She claims that she did not write large parts of the book but rather they simply appeared during the night as she slept. Other sections were dictated to her while she was in a trance, where the Master would take over her body and write for her. This was a big help, as *Isis Unveiled* ran a thousand, two hundred pages.[252]

The critics panned the book, dismissing it as "discarded rubbish" (*New York Sun*) and a "large dish of hash" (*Springfield Republican*). Many critics simply ignored it. But the book was not written for the haughty literary establishment. It was written for passionate truth seekers. *Isis Unveiled* provided a deep need for answers at a time when table raising, seances and spiritualism were all the rage.[253]

After the book was published, Blavatsky and two Americans inadvertently launched the Theosophy movement in New York City in 1875. The movement was not planned, but people had become excited after hearing Blavatsky speak and created a study group that evolved into the Theosophical Society. According to Colonel Henry Steel Olcott (1832-1907), one of the founders, the movement was not to be so much a spiritual movement, but a scientific movement intended to bring forth psychic phenomena and occult knowledge.[254]

Overall, though, the movement was centered around a set of beliefs, including that many of the world's religions originated from a single ancient religion, the "secret doctrine," which was allegedly known to Plato and early Hindu sages. Throughout the centuries, while men have been burning libraries and killing sages and prophets, spiritual beings, whom the Theosophists called the Ancient Masters, have been preserving ancient teachings. The Masters understood and explained miracles, the afterlife, and psychic phenomena. The Theosophy movement aimed to share the Masters' teaching with humanity and develop members' spiritual growth through study, prayer and meditation, with the hope that some might one day connect directly with the Masters—but that rarely happened.

---

[252] Granted, I am a slow writer; but, at my pace, for me to write 1,200 pages, it would take me forty-four years. So you have to admit, she must have had some sort of help.

[253] Peter Washington, *Madame Blavatsky's Baboon* (Schocken Books. 1993), 53-54.

[254] Washington, 55.

To the elite few in the Theosophy movement, either these revealed messages would appear directly on paper or materialize in the form of automatic writing by an individual in a trance. Many of these messages were handed to recipients from Blavatsky herself, who received them from the Masters, while others just appeared apparently without the assistance of a human helper. The leaders of the movement understood the importance of controlling access to the Masters.[255]

Unlike many religions, which had sacred texts and decades of tradition, Theosophy was non-sectarian. There was no established doctrine. The rules of the Society were careful to state that a member could believe whatever they wanted to. The Society's objective was not to teach doctrine but to conduct "scientific" research into all doctrines. Still, the Society borrowed primarily from Eastern religions and the occult and took very little from Christianity, Judaism or Islam. Of course, this organization, like all other movements encountered the same old problems associated with groups: internal dissent, division, scandal, etc. The Theosophists were no different from any other successful organization in this way.

When it first started, the Society's lack of doctrinal coherence made for a loose community that attracted people of many disparate beliefs. The Theosophy Society, according to Peter Washington, tended to attract "the neurotic, the hysterical, the destructive and the downright mad."[256] The permanent residents at its Adyar community in India in the 1880s and 1890s were a "quarrelsome collection of minor English aristocrats, rich American widows, German professors, Indian mystics and hangers-on of every description."[257]

---

[255] Washington, 126. Whether the Masters is a true concept or not, I cannot say. But it seems fishy in retrospect that most or all of these messages from the Masters came from the leaders of the movement.

[256] Washington, 70.

[257] Washington, 55.

In 1909, a leader in the movement, Charles Leadbeater[258] (1854–1934), noticed a dirty and unkept fourteen-year–old Indian boy, Jiddu Krishnamurti (1895–1986), who had an extraordinary aura. He determined that this boy was destined to be the next incarnation of the World Teacher that humanity had been waiting for. He believed that this World Teacher had previously taken the bodily form of Jesus Christ 1,900 years earlier and was destined to lead humanity to the next spiritual level. Leadbeater took charge of the boy, cleaned him up and taught him spiritual principles.

Annie Besant (1847–1933), then President of the Theosophical Society, agreed with Leadbetter. She believed that the unleashing of the World Teacher was the culmination of Blavatsky's teachings and the achievement of Theosophy's long-term goal, which was that "earth will be a heaven in the twenty-first century." The Wisdom of God had been retrieved and was once again to be revealed to the world through the divine representative Krishnamurti.[259]

Krishnamurti met with one of the Masters, Koot Hoomi, every night for fifteen minutes of instruction.[260] He was very good at communication with Masters, until one day, decades later, he accidentally walked through one of them and they declined to ever appear to him again.

After only two years, in 1911, Leadbeater described the first hint of the spiritual force manifesting. Krishnamurti was handing out certificates to new members, when

> *All at once the Hall was filled with tremendous power, which was so evidently flowing through Krishna[murti] that the next member fell at his feet, overwhelmed by this marvellous [sic] rush of force. I have never seen or felt anything in the least like it; it reminded*

---

[258] Leadbeater had a questionable past. Before discovering the Indian boy, Leadbeater had been thrown out of the Theosophical Society for his sexual instruction of young men. But he was readmitted prior to this discovery of the World Teacher.

[259] Vernon, 165.

[260] Washington, 128–129.

one irresistibly of the rushing mighty wind and the outpouring of the Holy Ghost at Pentecost. The tension was enormous, and everyone in the room was most powerfully affected. It was exactly the kind of thing that we read about in the old scriptures, and think exaggerated; but here it was before us in the twentieth century. After that, each one prostrated himself as his turn came, many of them with tears pouring down their cheeks. [261]

Krishnamurti began to see himself objectively and speak of himself in the third person. As Krishnamurti said in an interview in 1928,

As the river enters the sea and loses itself in the sea, so Krishnamurti has entered into that Life which is represented by some as The Christ, by others as The Buddha. . .Hence Krishnamurti as an entity fully developed has entered into that Sea of Life and is the Teacher. [262]

Annie Besant created the Order of the Star in the East, a group within the Theosophical Society, whose purpose was to prepare the world for Krishnamurti's mission. By 1928, there were 45,000 members of the order. But the Theosophical Society became progressively more troubled with power struggles, disputes, self-seeking, schisms and bitterness. Although many Theosophists never bought into the idea that Krishnamurti was the World Teacher, most did. And to Krishnamurti's followers, the coming of the Lord was at hand.

His very presence projected a spiritual force that so enraptured the spectators that it made little difference what he said, or whether it was understood or not. [263]

---

[261] Mary Lutyens, *Krishnamurti: The Years of Awakening* (Farrar, Straus and Giroux, 1975), 6.

[262] Interview with Krishnaji, London, England, June 10, 1928, *International Star Bulletin, August 1928, in Vernon, 166.*

[263] James Santucci, Foreword to Govert Schuller, "Krishnamurti and the World Teacher Project: Some Theosophical Perceptions," Theosophical History Journal/Occasional Papers, Volume V, (James Santucci, 1997), iv, https://tinyurl.com/2d6fg4d4.

Krishnamurti spoke each night at the Order of the Star summer gatherings every year in Ommen, Netherlands. Geoffrey Hodson (1886–1983), considered the second-best clairvoyant in the Theosophical Society after Leadbeater, attended Ommen in 1927 and wrote about the powerful experience of hearing Krishnamurti speak.

> *As he speaks, the spirit of the Christ descends, as a great collective inspiration, into the hearts and minds of all. It draws nearer and nearer in a great ring-shaped cloud of golden light. It hovers over our heads, descends still lower, slowly and gently, like a warm summer rain, till all are enwrapped in its beauty, its peace and all-compelling love.*

The voice is silent.

> *Night after night, as he ceases to speak, a miracle occurs. Two thousand seven hundred people remain perfectly still. In that silence the splendour of splendours is revealed to the inner eyes. The figure of the Lord appears above the head of Krishnaji. The silence deepens. We are enfolded in His embrace, filled with tenderness and compassion as He draws near.*[264]

In 1927 and 1928, Krishnamurti's speeches got bolder and more rebellious, causing problems with many of the older leaders of the organization. He began to reject the path that the Theosophical Society had been teaching. He thought focusing on the Masters was a distraction from their true calling. The older members did not want to reject him, but they refused to listen to his new message. They attempted to haggle, accepting some parts of his teaching, if he would accept parts of their ideology.[265] "Krishna thought they were the blind seeking ever deeper

---

[264] Geoffrey Hodson, "Camp-Fire Gleams, an account of the camp fire meetings of the Order of the Star in August 1927," Thus Have I Heard: A Book of Spiritual and Occult Gleanings from the Teachings of the Great (Theosophical Publishing House, 1929), reprinted from The Herald of the Star, https://tinyurl.com/29g2oo6m

[265] Vernon, 173–174.

blindness."[266] Lady Emily Lutyens (1874–1964) wrote that his words left many followers "naked and alone, their foundations shattered."[267]

The next year in 1929, at an annual summer gathering in Ommen, Netherlands, he gave a shocking speech to about 3,000 followers, where he completely abandoned the tradition and teachings of the Theosophical Society. This speech was to turn the Theosophical Society upside down.

> *Truth, being limitless, unconditioned, unapproachable by any path whatsoever, cannot be organized; nor should any organization be formed to lead or to coerce people along any particular path. If you first understand that, then you will see how impossible it is to organize a belief. A belief is purely an individual matter, and you cannot and must not organize it. If you do, it becomes dead, crystallized; it becomes a creed, a sect, a religion, to be imposed on others. This is what everyone throughout the world is attempting to do.*
>
> *If an organization be created for this purpose, it becomes a crutch, a weakness, a bondage, and must cripple the individual, and prevent him from growing, from establishing his uniqueness, which lies in the discovery for himself of that absolute, unconditioned Truth.*
>
> *Organizations cannot make you free. No man from outside can make you free; nor can organized worship, nor the immolation of yourselves for a cause, make you free; nor can forming yourselves into an organization, nor throwing yourselves into works, make you free.*
>
> *So you will see how absurd is the whole structure that you have built, looking for external help, depending on others for your comfort, for your happiness, for your strength. These can only be found within yourselves.*[268]

---

[266] Vernon, 174.

[267] Lady Emily Lutyens, *International Star Bulletin*, September 1928, in Vernon, 177.

[268] Krishnamurti, Dissolution Speech, August 3, 1929, *Krishnamurti Foundation Trust*, kfoundation.org/dissolution-speech, accessed January 1, 2025.

And with this speech, he dissolved the Order of the Star and the following year, he cut his ties to Theosophy.

This speech left his followers with an uncomfortable dilemma. If you believed he was the World Teacher, then you had to accept what he says. But if you accepted what he said, then you had to leave the Theosophical Society, because it would be hindering you from achieving the very goal that led you to joining the group in the first place. If there was no path, as the World Teacher claimed, then the Theosophical Society was wrong, because they maintained up to this point that there was a path and that they provided it for humanity.

Or you could believe that the World Teacher was wrong or perhaps Krishnamurti was not the World Teacher after all. But if you believed that, then much of what the Theosophical Society had been communicating for decades was wrong, and you should then leave the group, because they have been misleading everyone.

Still, how was one to know what was true and what was not? Now we are back to the original problem and to why people joined the Theosophical Society in the first place—to have a path and to have some sense of certainty that they were on the right path.

The uproar from the speech was considerable and many left the Theosophical Society as a result. A group needs its members, and the Theosophical Society membership declined substantially and never recovered.[269] Hodson wrote, "After arrival in Australia, I became aware of the influence of the teachings of Krishnamurti upon the membership of The Theosophical Society. One Lodge had just sustained severe losses in the resignation of some of its most talented and promising students." Many just left. "These ex-members had arrived at the conclusion that Theosophy was valueless, was indeed a hindrance in the process of self-illumination and the fulfillment of life."[270] This is exactly

---

[269] The Theosophical Society continues to this day, albeit broken up into several splinter organizations.

[270] Geoffrey Hodson, "J. Krishnamurti and the Search for Light," *Theosophy*, 1935,

what Krishnamurti said. You don't need a group. You don't need the Theosophical Society. Find Truth within yourself.

Others continued within the Theosophical Society, even though the World Teacher told them that it offers them nothing but "a crutch, a weakness, a bondage, and must cripple the individual, and prevent him from growing."

As Annie Besant, the President of the Theosophical Society stated a few months later in the General Report of 1929, "Personally I acknowledge Him as the vehicle of the World Teacher in our world, but I cannot, of course, in any way bind the Society, which has no creed, leaving absolute Freedom to every member to belong to any religion or to none, each member being responsible to himself alone for his beliefs and unbeliefs."[271] And they did have differing beliefs.

Hodson thought that the World Teacher did manifest a few times briefly in Krishnamurti's body; but, having spoken to Krishnamurti's doctor, he learned that the physical and psychological strain of his being the World Teacher was just too much.[272] And he dropped the mission. He just wasn't up to it.

Although Krishnamurti severed his ties to the Theosophical Society, he continued to speak and write books until his death in the 1986. As Hodson wrote in a pamphlet in 1935:

> *Here…is a question put to him in various forms more than once: 'I have listened to your talks for several years, but to be frank, I have not yet grasped what you are trying to convey.'…Krishnamurti says, 'All that I am trying to do is to help you to discern for yourself*

---

https://tinyurl.com/22pvwse3, accessed January 1, 2025.

[271] Annie Besant, "Letter from the President," *General Report of the Theosophical Society,* 1929.

[272] Govert Schuller, "Krishnamurti and the World Teacher Project: Some Theosophical Perceptions," *Theosophical History Occasional Papers,* Volume V, 1997 (James Santucci, 1997). See the section on Hodson.

that there is no salvation outside of yourself, that no Master, no society can save you.[273]

If you follow the World Teacher's advice, how do you know if you are on the right path? There is nobody there with you, no system, texts or creed to keep you from straying. In general, people are encouraged by congregating with others thinking similar thoughts and enduring similar trials. It is easy to give up when you are on your own. It is easy to doubt yourself, as you don't know whether the path you are on is pure fancy or madness, or maybe it really is the path to God. You just cannot know. At least with the group, you can fool yourself into thinking you are on the right path, because the others, people you respect and trust, are thinking the same thoughts and doing the same things you are.

Krishnamurti was special. He was a peaker. Having reached an elevated state, he might be able to make his own way in the spiritual world alone, but a large percentage of the members of the Theosophical Society were not peakers and could not make it alone. And the vast majority of the rest us cannot make this journey alone either. Cyril Scott (1879-1970) wrote that because Krishnamurti had reached an advanced state of consciousness and evolution, in his modesty he failed to see that those around him were not at his level; and his teachings, which were appropriate for someone at his level, were not applicable to those around him.[274]

> *As an old man he complained that not a single person, despite his sixty years of work, had actually lived the teachings and attained the liberation of which he spoke.*[275]

Perhaps he should have read Maslow before killing his religion.

Can you see that? The Peaker speaks, the non-peaker is clueless. That is how it goes.

---

[273] Hodson, "J. Krishnamurti and the Search for Light."

[274] Schuller, 12–13.

[275] Vernon, 199.

There were many explanations of what happened with the World Teacher Project. One view is that Krishnamurti was indeed the World Teacher, but he was rejected, as was Jesus and Buddha before him. The people were not ready to hear his message. Radha Burnier (1923–2013), a later editor of *The Theosophist*, wrote that Krishnamurti did his job as World Teacher, but that the people lacked the insight to accept his message, as they were not ready.[276] I think she is right. I think that non-peakers will never be ready for a message like that. Non-peakers need a religion, a rule book, to follow.

Those that took Krishnamurti's word and tried the solitary path, according to Hodson, became lost.

> *During the seven or more years of Krishnamurti's later mission[277] I have seen many promising lives rendered tragically fruitless, many hopes destroyed, and many good servants of humanity lost to that service...Religion, philosophy, ethics, and even morals—on all these they have turned a scornful back...I have seen noble-hearted, pure-minded men and women, both young and old, throw over their previous moral restraint, cast aside that discipline of life without which there can be no happiness. I have watched them cease from a service to those less fortunate than themselves, which hitherto had made their lives noble and fruitful. All this they do, as they suppose, at the bidding of Krishnamurti.[278]*

I believe that Krishnamurti did not understand the people around him at all. There were thirty thousand members of the Order of the Star in the East, most of whom likely received something meaningful from belonging to this organization.

At Ommen, they were no longer Crazy Uncle Charlie or Hysterical Auntie Annie, isolated from their families and communities by their

---

[276] Radha Burnier, "J. Krishnamurti," *The Theosophist* 107/6 (March 1986), 203, in Schuller.

[277] Krishnamurti taught for fifty-seven years after leaving the movement. Hodson wrote this in 1935, when Krishnamurti had only taught for seven of those years.

[278] Geoffrey Hodson, "J. Krishnamurti and the Search for Light."

eccentric occult interests. At Ommen, they were understood. There they found community. They probably weren't mystics like Krishnamurti was. Maybe what was meaningful wasn't so much about advancing along the solitary path to the Infinite but rather about being with others who shared the spiritual path with them. They belonged to this communion of seekers of truth. That is why they were there listening to Krishnamurti.

The Many Paths of Ramakrishna

Religions do serve a purpose for most of us. As we discussed previously, they miss the great revelation of the original spiritual superstar, but they do retain some elementary truths that are useful to both the individual and society, even to the peaker. Once you are armed with the basics, you can take off on your own personal journey. That is what the Hindu saint Ramakrishna (1836–1886) did—many times.

In the 1850s, while the northern and southern states of the United States were trying to avoid a civil war though compromise, Ramakrishna was a priest in India in a temple dedicated to the goddess Kali. Ramakrishna was profoundly religious and from childhood on would have ecstatic experiences of God. Ramakrishna was obsessed with spiritual practice. The people of the town thought that he was too obsessed with religion and became impatient with him; others thought he was a fool. He would weep for hours at a time, imploring Kali to reveal herself. After many days of meditation, when she did not appear he became deeply depressed.

He recounted,

> *I began to think I should never see Mother. I was dying of despair. In my agony, I said to myself: "What's the use of living this life?" Suddenly my eyes fell on the sword that hangs in the temple. I decided to end my life with it, then and there. Like a madman, I ran to it and seized it. And then - I had a marvelous vision of the Mother, and fell down unconscious. . .It was as if houses, doors,*

temples and everything else vanished altogether; as if there was nothing anywhere! And what I saw was an infinite shoreless sea of light; a sea that was consciousness. However far and in whatever direction I looked, I saw shining waves, one after another, coming towards me. They were raging and storming upon me with great speed. Very soon they were upon me; they made me sink down into unknown depths. I panted and struggled and lost consciousness.[279]

After this experience, Ramakrishna was unable to function for a time. A doctor was called for, but to no effect.

His nephew was worried about him.

I saw how Uncle's chest and eyes were always red, like those of a drunkard. He'd get up reeling from the worshipper's seat, climb onto the altar, and caress the Divine Mother, chucking her affectionately under the chin. He'd begin singing, laughing, joking and talking with her, or sometimes he'd catch hold of her hands and dance...I saw how, when he was offering cooked food to the Divine Mother, he'd suddenly get up, take a morsel of rice and curry from the plate in his hand, touch the Mother's mouth with it and say: "Eat it, Mother. Do eat it!" Then maybe he'd say: "You want me to eat it - and then you'll eat some afterwards? All right, I'm eating it now." Then he'd take some of it himself and put the rest to her lips again, saying: "I've had some. Now you eat."[280]

Ramakrishna experienced God, but he did not do it by following the traditional forms of worship. He broke custom, just like other prophets do. Normal practitioners thought he was a madman, just as they do with other prophets. But it became clear to the perceptive that Ramakrishna was not a madman but a saint. Perhaps all saints are mad. (But not all madmen are saints.)

---

[279] Christopher Isherwood, *Ramakrishna and His Disciples*, (Vedanta Press, 1965), ch. 6..
[280] Isherwood, ch. 6.

Years later Ramakrishna plunged himself into several other mystical practices, some of which were Hindu: Vaishnavism, Shakta Tantrism, Advaita Vedanta. He also tried Islamic Sufism and Roman Catholicism. By means of these various practices, Ramakrishna had similar experiences of the ultimate reality of the universe. He experienced a vision of "the great yogi" Jesus embracing him and disappearing into his body.

Ramakrishna saw God in everything and everyone and he taught that all paths lead to the same end, God. Like Jesus Christ, he spoke in parables. God is like a mother with a handful of sick children, each with a different illness. For each then, there should be a different cure. So it is with different races of man, each with a different history, schema and temperament, each of which needs its own path to God. That's why we need so many religions. He compared

> *the many aspects of God to the different parts of the elephant that the blind men touched, or to the different colours of the chameleon seen at different times by different men—and taken always by their ignorance to be the only aspect, the only colour.*[281]

Union with God, the Universe or Nothingness (whatever they choose to call it) has been the goal of every true mystic. The Buddhists call it nirvana; the Christians, the mystic union; the Hindus, samadhi.[282] People of different religions who have touched God conceptualize it differently, being constrained by language and culture. This fits neatly with Maslow's claim that all of the prophets (or mystics) experienced the same thing, but that their cultural conditioning led them and their followers to describe it differently.

Although he wrote and spoke about how the many creeds can lead one to God, Ramakrishna was a peaker and was not one to follow the rules or observe the decorum of any creed. He did it his own way, as did Moses, Jesus, Mohammed, Buddha and Krishnamurti. Peakers are

---

[281] Isherwood, ch. 13.

[282] Isherwood, ch. 6.

trailblazers. They do not follow the well-worn paths. They do not fear authority. They have no care for authority. Their focus is on the Prize.

The themes of Ramakrishna and Krishnamurti may on the surface appear to oppose one other. Ramakrishna suggests that all religions lead to God. Krishnamurti suggests that you must cast aside religion and venture alone to reach God. Yet, I don't think they contradict at all. They are not talking about the same thing. The major religions all point vaguely in the direction of God; but as some point, if you are to really experience God, you have to leave convention behind and venture on alone. And the Prize? That is something that only some of us can attain—only the peakers.

The rest of us, the non-peakers, will have to be content with the religions we have, as imperfect as they are. They were created for non-peakers. For the peakers, religions can serve as a good starting point from which one must jump into the unknown.

Major Religions Focus on the Wrong Thing

Of the visionaries who were the original spark of the major religions, most spoke and wrote of the oneness of humanity, the oneness with God or the Universe. This oneness, this unity, is the apex, the ultimate great prize we can attain. Yet the major religions mostly ignore this in their scriptures, traditions and rituals.

It is only the minority sects in these religions that are primarily concerned with the mystic path. The Catholic mystics, the Jewish Kabbalists, the Muslim Sufis, the Hindu Sadhus and the Buddhist Jhana experience mystical visions and write about them. Mainstream religious thought, rituals, and all the rest are completely devoid of mystical teachings—that is, the teachings that the originators of the religions tried to communicate.

Instead, most of the major religions[283] are focused on how to get some sort of personal reward—such as heaven for Christians and Muslims,

---

[283] Judaism is our exception. Judaism teaches us of the love of God for his people. Additionally, the Jewish religion alone stresses the common mission of and common fate

a better life in a future birth for Hindus, and liberation from the cycle of birth-suffering-death-rebirth for Buddhists. These religions provide a path for an individual to earn the reward. Their teachings reinforce the fact that we are all individuals in this world, and that our individual fates are of our own making.

This individualistic orientation is probably necessary to make the religion appeal to the majority of the people on a level at which they can relate. Religions are made for the masses, not for the adepts, not for Krishnamurti or Ramakrishna. To be understandable to and appeal to the masses, a religion must meet people where they are. For most of us, our main concerns are for our own well-being.

Always a Religious Dark Age

Theodore Parker (1810–1860), a New England Unitarian minister, agreed that religions do, at some point, provide good direction for people. But he explained in a sermon how humanity outgrows its religions. Our different religions that were formed during our progression through the centuries have been instrumental in our spiritual development. But these religions remained static, while Humanity grew spiritually. We continue to evolve, so that the religions no longer lead us forward but rather have become outdated. They serve only to retard us from progressing further.

An example: our primitive worship, reverence and fear of the elements no longer seem relevant. The great majority in society today look with disdain on such religions, as they can contribute little value to our modern lives. We feel the same for the Aztecs' worship of the sun and rain gods and their human sacrifices. Those practices are considered primitive and are no longer used, as we have evolved far beyond that stage. According to Theodore Parker, the same can be said for Islam,

---

of its people. Unlike the Catholic, Protestant, Muslim, Hindu and Buddhist experience, where individuals are rewarded and punished individually, the fate of all Jews is often bound together. It is unique in this way.

Christianity, Hinduism, and the rest. He preached that "the story of the flood has strangled a world of souls. The miracles of the New Testament no longer heal, but hurt mankind."[284] Mankind has progressed beyond this type of thought, but the churches continue to teach the same outmoded ideas over and over, leading many to abandon religion.

The simple stories of biblical miracles are useful for children, as it suits their mentality. But,

> *to learn boys [sic] lessons, and be amused with boys [sic] stories, —this helps the boy, but it hinders the man. Long ago we got from these helps all that was in them. To stay longer is a waste of time. Look at the men who have been doing this for ten years; they are where they were ten years ago.*[285]

Rather than

> *study the diagrams of God writ on the heavens in points of fire. . .[man is] told to keep counting his fingers. . .and all piety is wiped out of his consciousness, and he hates God and God hates him.*[286]

To stay longer in these religions is a waste of time. To continue to teach traditional religious doctrine only serves to drive more people away from God.

These childish stories and rituals disgust the well-educated and powerful and they link religion to superstition and unbelievable fantasy, so that people want to have nothing to do with it.

> *Philosophers. . .many of them have turned away in disgust from the folly that is taught in [religion's] name. Of all the great*

---

284 Theodore Parker, "Of Piety, and the Relation Thereof to Manly Life," *The Collected Works of Theodore Parker: Sermons, Prayers*, https://tinyurl.com/2bq6g9el.

285 Parker, "Of Piety, and the Relation Thereof to Manly Life," 8.

286 Parker, "Of Piety, and the Relation Thereof to Manly Life," 8.

philosophers of this day, I think no one takes any interest in the popular forms of religion.[287]

The tendency of humanity to outgrow old religions, rituals and dogmas has been going on since the beginning of religion itself. This is why new ones seem to crop up every few thousand years.

Why is it that other fields, such as science, accounting, management and law advance in their capacity to solve problems, while religion, if anything has stood still? Why is it that we are still reading books for religious inspiration that are thousands of years old? If we believe that humanity is evolving, then where is our religious evolution? Shouldn't we have newer, more evolved, holy scriptures? It appears we have been living in a religious dark age. But one can argue that this has been true for most of human history. This recurring stagnation of religious thought can only be broken by the arrival of a visionary prophet who ushers in a new era of spiritual enthusiasm and progress.

Our traditions are many centuries old. Islam, the youngest of the major religions is about 1,400 years old! Assuming a generation lasts twenty years, that is seventy generations of people mouthing the same beliefs and performing the same rituals. Christianity, of course, is older, over 2,000 years old (100 generations), voicing pretty much the same prayers, performing the same rituals, believing the same things. I suppose if it works, why fix it? But religion isn't working. We are no closer to the Ultimate Reality that the messiahs and prophets originally experienced. That is the problem. You would think that people would be ready for new revelations!

So why is religion lagging when it comes to progress?

Perhaps it is not.

It usually takes centuries for new religions to become major religions.[288] We have no reason to think that the major religion of the future has not

---

[287] Parker, "Of Piety, and the Relation Thereof to Manly Life," 9.

[288] You may come up with exceptions. The Protestant faiths (Society of Friends, Latter

already begun, that it is still in its early stages. Perhaps new prophets have already appeared. Maybe we just haven't recognized them. Maybe, just like with Jesus and Mohammed, very few people listened to them. After all, it is common knowledge that any so-called new prophet is a fake.

The Continuation of Revelation

In the nineteenth century, Joseph Smith (1805–1844) found tablets with new, more modern books of the Bible. His church, based on those tablets, the Church of Jesus Christ of Latter-day Saints has grown and continues to grow. Many non-believers think Joseph Smith was a fraud, a charlatan, a swindler, exactly what they said about Jesus. But if Joseph Smith was right, then his religion, less than 200 years old, is a newer religion for a newer, perhaps more evolved, people. Christianity was probably much smaller 200 years after Christ died than the Church of Jesus Christ of Latter-day Saints is now. It took Christianity about 300 years to really catch fire.

Many new "lesser" religions have emerged in the last century and a half, such as Christian Science, the Unitarian Universalists, Unity, and many other New Age churches, plus lesser-known movements such as A Course in Miracles, whose writings were dictated from Christ in 1965. The *Urantia Book* is supposed to have materialized out of the spiritual plane at some point between 1924 and 1955. And then there are Jim Jones, David Koresh and probably hundreds of other prophets.[289] The number of new religious movements established throughout the centuries is countless, and it is possible that one of these will be the religion of the next eon. We cannot know what the future holds.

Day Saints, Seventh Day Adventists, Lutherans, Methodists, etc.) grew very quickly, but they can be considered offshoots of the root religion, Christianity. When it comes to wholly new religions, I think my statement for the most part holds.

[289] I am not claiming these guys are necessarily right. How would I know? I am only reporting what their followers claim about them. They are or were seen as prophets.

Who Picks the Winning Religions?

So, then the obvious next question is: what explains the success of the great religions in attracting followers when there were so many competing belief systems? Certainly, in the beginning, for all religions, many people became adherents because they saw the spiritual benefit of doing so. But, Hinduism apart, [290] the largest religions were able to gain critical mass because they obtained official support from the state. This support gave them a huge advantage over other faiths. I wonder, can a new religion really spread significantly without a state forcing it on the people?

Wrapping It Up

- We come into this world with no instructions, no guidebook, to show us the way in life. We initially pick up clues from our families and society at large.

- At some point, many of us see that that is not enough and may even be the wrong path.

- We need structure and solace in our lives, and we are looking for that missing guidebook. Religion is supposed to provide all of these, and for many it does.

- Our great religions were based on mystics who encountered the Divine. That would include Jesus, Moses, Mohammed, Buddha, Zoroaster, etc.

- Mystical experiences with God cannot be communicated in words, even though mystics have tried.

- Mystics, aka peakers, are not known to be good at constructing or administering religious organizations. They are good at connecting with God.

---

[290] One can point to Protestant denominations, such as Mormonism, which have spread and become large without state actors pushing it. But they are just sects of a major religion, Christianity. A new religion would be wholly foreign to what we have today.

- Almost all of the followers of the original mystics were non-peakers, who could never experience God nor understand what the peaker was trying to explain. These followers created the religions we have today—the dogma, rituals, hierarchy, etc. Our religions were created by non-peakers for non-peakers, which most of us are.

- The true messages of the many Messiahs and Prophets are quickly lost after they die. The religions we have now are missing the integral truths that the peaker on which the religion is based was trying to communicate. The religions devolved into empty shells—dogma, ritual and hierarchy lacking that divine communion which had originally led to the explosion of the movement.

- An example is that the four Gospels on which Christianity is based were written 170 years after Jesus' death. The writers had never even met the apostles. The early Jesus movement in Jerusalem was denigrated, shunted aside and eventually forgotten by the Church. Most of the original writings from the early years after the death of Christ were lost. The ideas on which Christianity was based were filtered through generations of men. The religion was created by politicians in clerical garb over the centuries.

- Martin Luther, who sparked the Reformation, was not a peaker, and his teachings of fire and brimstone took the original message further from its original essence.

- We receive an incomplete and distorted message from our religious institutions. These defective religious teachings might be beneficial for us, but still they are not the messages of Truth the original peakers tried to communicate.

- Krishnamurti taught that one cannot use religions or churches to find God. It is an individual quest, and religions will only hold us back.

- Ramakrishna taught that any religion will do. You can experience God from the starting point of many different religions, but from that starting point, you must venture on alone.

- There is Truth to be found. Some have found it, but only through an individual journey. Religions cannot help with that.

- Throughout the centuries, as humanity evolves spiritually, religions become stale and people need some new message to take them further.

- Though fresh prophetic voices occasionally spark new religious movements, many self-proclaimed prophets fail to gain traction and are frequently perceived by the masses as mentally unsound or misguided.

- History tells us that it is usually the state that decides which religions become dominant.

- It takes centuries for revolutionary new religions to arise. We might be witnessing the nascent stages of the next great spiritual movement without even realizing it.

Essay 9
Reason is the Devil's Whore

Reason is. . .the chief prostitute of the devil, a lousy, filthy, and disgusting prostitute that ought to be trampled on and destroyed, both she and her companion wisdom. It would be a good thing to make her detestable by throwing filth in her face, for abominable wretch that she is, she only deserves to be placed in the dirtiest place in the house, the privy.
— MARTIN LUTHER[291]

We Know Nothing

He burst into tears. "I don't know what to do with my life. I'm forty-four years old and I have no idea if I'm doing the right thing." The tears flowed and his body shook. I grabbed his hands and squared up opposite him.

---

[291] Alfred Baudrillart, *The Catholic Church, the Renaissance, and Protestantism, lectures at the Catholic Institute of Paris, January to March 1904,* (Kegan Paul, Trench, Trubner & Co., 1907), 269.

"Andrew, no one knows if they're doing the right thing. No one. Whatever story you've been telling yourself about how you've failed, whatever 'should' you've been carrying about having had it all figured out by now…well, all that's just bullshit."[292]

By now, I suspect you have guessed my purpose in writing these essays—it is my way of suggesting to you that we as human beings do not know anything about what is most important and are on our own when it comes to making our way through life. We may know how to make rocket ships and really good music, but where does that all fit within the greater overarching framework of meaning? Indeed, what are we supposed to be doing and are we doing that? Or are we merely distracting ourselves with our toys and games until we die, having accomplished nothing of any real importance?

What we think we know about the world is often false, or at least unproveable. Most of our knowledge has come from the groups we belong to, which by their nature shape our minds with distorted perceptions of reality. Science is imperfect and only addresses part of our experience and misses the larger and more important part—the essence that animates living things. And religions, although useful, have lost the essential message that the original prophets were trying to communicate.

So where do we turn? If you want to avoid religion, as increasing numbers of us are now doing, there is always philosophy. But Western philosophers have been trying for thousands of years to untangle the meaning behind our lives and still have no answers, except, oh yes, the conclusion that there is no answer. Philosophy is a fool's game. As Osho, the Indian guru, said, philosophy is "just a toy, a toy to stop the baby crying."[293]

Again, this is nothing new. Over 2,400 years ago, Socrates was aware of this same incapacity to understand the world. Of course, nothing has

---

[292] Jerry Colonna, *Reboot: Leadership and the Art of Growing Up* (Harper Business, 2019), 137.
[293] Osho, *The Secret of Secrets*, 212.

changed. Plato's Apology has him saying, "He knows nothing, and thinks that he knows. I neither know nor think that I know."[294] I've condensed the idea to, "I know only that I know nothing."

Even philosophy, a discipline dedicated to understanding meaning, concludes with ignorance.

But we do know one thing. We know that we will certainly die. The only thing we can know is the one thing that we would rather not know and often choose not to. We create all sorts of mental constructs to obscure this knowledge, to distract us. Believe in them and you can conveniently forget about death. There is heaven. There is reincarnation. Our spirits leave the body and exist somewhere. Of course, nobody knows whether any of these ideas are true. These mental constructs are not based on facts and cannot be proven to be true—but they might be true.

I saw a profound cartoon that I should describe here.[295] It was a play on evolution. In it was a fish in the ocean, and it was thinking, *eat, survive, reproduce.* There was also an amphibian, thinking the same, *eat, survive, reproduce.* A lizard and a monkey, both thinking the same thing. Finally, comes a human, who was instead thinking, *what's it all about?* The cartoon shows how silly we are or at least people like me are. We have deluded ourselves, thinking that since we can figure out some things, we should be able to figure out all things. This is a common fallacy.

Perhaps our thinking capacity is just inadequate to the task of understanding our place in the world. Like the cartoon suggests, we are animals, gifted with more complex minds, but still animals, directed by the same Universal Will to eat, survive and reproduce. Perhaps we live only to maintain the species. Period. If so, to question the meaning of it all is ludicrous.

As Schopenhauer said, we are all directed by the Will of the Universe. The same Will that directs the animals to eat, survive and reproduce

---

[294] *Apology by Plato*, trans. Benjamin Jowett (Project Gutenberg, 2008).

[295] Cartoon by Patrick Hardin, knowyourmeme.com/memes/eat-survive-reproduce, accessed Nov. 24, 2023.

directs us, too. We do what we are commanded to by the Will without even knowing it.

If Schopenhauer is right, our individual lives have no discernible meaning. Maybe the Will possesses its own set of meanings and philosophies for us, but why should that be fathomable to us humans? We are on a different plane entirely from the Will.

This is similar to what I understand probably being incomprehensible to the cells in my thumb. The cells in my thumb may understand some things, such as how to stay alive and replicate, but not how to use algebra in story problems. Just like the cells of my body are outclassed by the entirety of me, individual humans are just tiny insignificant parts, outclassed by the whole of Humanity. We can never understand the greater reality. Individually, we are of a different order, a menial one, and should not be expected to understand the workings of Humanity and the Will.

Remember as we discussed earlier, the Will is not God. The Will is just a law of nature, like gravity. It is just a blind, non-rational force driving living beings.

Everything I wrote here follows a clear train of thought, that is, if we can assume there is no God, then, without God there is ultimately no purpose in life. We are just animals with brains. We can choose from a hodgepodge of half-baked ideas to believe, but nobody knows anything with any authority. We know deep inside that, no matter what philosophical ideas we cling to, we are probably wrong and we don't have a clue how to live. Only a God, who is all-knowing, can give us real Truth. (That is, assuming we can understand it.) For this reason, we must have religion.

Society Needs Religion

Despite all that, the human mind is wired to try to make sense of everything. So, it is no surprise that the members of every society need a system of meaning to explain their place in the universe and why things happen as they do. Until recently, religion has provided meaning for Western societies. Talcott Parsons (1902–1979) noted in his introduction to Max Weber's *Sociology of Religion:*

> *There is no known human society without something which modern social scientists would classify as religion. . .The existence of the supernatural order is taken seriously, in that many concrete events. . .are attributed. . .to [it], and men devote an important part of their time. . .to regulating their relations with [it] as they conceive it. . .Religion is as much a human universal as language.*[296]

Not everyone will be content with their inherited religions. That is to be expected. But as long as most of us adhere to the basic values of our inherited religions, societies can continue to function. Unbelief can lead to destructive activities, such as crime, addiction, loss of trust in a society's institutions, and it eventually will weaken and destroy any society.

Reason vs. Religion

When a society rejects religion, religion is replaced with reason. In 1875, a lecturer proclaimed:

> *This is a sad, a very sad age, full of dead and dying faiths; full of idle prayers sent out in vain search for the departing gods. But oh! it is a glorious age, full of the golden light which streams from the ascending sun of science!*[297]

From the time of Constantine in the fourth century until at least the sixteenth century, the large majority of Western Civilization believed that God was at the epicenter of the universe. The universe did His bidding. The Church and the kings were created by God to

---

[296] Talcott Parsons, "Introduction" to Max Weber, *Sociology of Religion*, (Beacon, 1963), xxvii-xxviii.

[297] Dr. F. R. Marvin, "Lecture on Mediomania and Insanity," New York, 1875, in Helena Blavatsky, *Isis Unveiled* (Aryan Theosophical, 1919), 82.

rule humanity. Then, in the sixteenth century, Humanism arose with a very different thesis. Mankind became the center of the universe, not God. It was theorized that humanity could use reason to create a heaven on earth, and we have been trying to ever since.

Today perhaps the majority assume that reason is the only way to understand the world and solve human problems.[298] It seems inconceivable to many of us that reason need not necessarily be the foundation of our perspective on the world. It wasn't for centuries. People have lived and can live lives not based on reason.

It seems unfathomable to us now. How can you live a life without reason?

Mysticism, is by nature, anti-reason. Mystics discover truth directly through sudden divine intervention (such as Saul of Tarsus) or by inward contemplation (like the Buddha). The truths of Jesus were not deduced or induced with reason; nor were the truths of Mohammed. It is said that these truths were obtained directly from God. Certainly, reason had no part in them.

Often these truths were associated with a philosophy of living and became religions. These religions that sprang from the great mystics are not open to question because they have come from God. Who would dare question God?

Well, believers in reason would. That is where Martin Luther comes in. He argued that there was no point in using reason to try to comprehend God. Human reason is limited and can never understand the immensity of God. If you apply human reason to Christianity, you are forced to conclude that either there is no God, or that God is unjust. Take a look around. Why is it that so many of the unjust appear to prosper while many of the just suffer? Reason will tell you that this is evidence that

---

[298] This wasn't the first time. Reason was at the center of Western thought in ancient times. According to Socrates, you can use reason to save your soul, and you can use reason to find Truth. Plato's works are all about Socrates using reason to solve problems.

the world is not following any divine plan. No benevolent god would allow this. As John Carroll so eloquently wrote:

> *In her presumption she [Reason] seeks to measure God, thus reducing his authority. . .Once reason is given the authority to investigate the ways of God, the battle is over. Its authority is already equal to that of God.*[299]

This is why Luther called "Mistress Reason" the "Devil's whore. . .She is seductive, deceiving, offering a moment of pleasure in order to seize the whole soul."[300]

This distrust of reason didn't only reside in the Christian world. Five hundred years before Luther's condemnation of reason, Al Ghazali (c. 1056–1111), a Sunni Muslim philosopher, theologian and mystic, wrote: "Reason leads to universal doubt, intellectual bankruptcy, moral deterioration and social collapse."[301]

One can easily apply reason to the religious institutions of humanity and find them lacking. Reason will always find fault with them and proclaim itself superior. Atheists and agnostics often do this and then confound religions with God. *If the religion has such a horrid history of hypocrisy, greed and murder, then it is certainly all based on lies—God would never permit His religion to be so fraudulent. Therefore, God cannot exist.*

But the religion is not God. It is a system of ideas built around a partial understanding of God. It was built by flawed people. The skeptic is confusing God with the system built around God, only pointing out the shortcomings that many are already aware of—the religion is flawed. I mean, really, what Catholic priest will tell you that God chose a man

---

[299] John Carroll, 54-55.

[300] John Carroll, 54-55.

[301] Al-Ghazali, *Tahafut al-Filasifa* (The Destruction of Philosophy), in Will Durant, The Age of Faith, 332.

who ordered the massacre of thousands of civilians, the Butcher of Cesena, to be pope?

When they criticize the theology, they are again confounding God with a flawed human intellectual system based on an incomplete understanding of God. *Since purgatory was made up centuries after Christ but now is part of the Catholic theology, it is certainly contrived, and therefore God, Himself, must be an invention, not a reality.* Again, this misses the mark. They are confusing the theology with God Himself.

Reason cannot directly address God or the original revelations of Jesus and the other great mystics. Those truths come from a place that logic cannot reach. It is like trying to apply three-dimensional geometric reasoning to four-dimensional objects. It just cannot be done.

The Adventures and Arguments of Simon Magus

You may recall the name of Simon Magus (first century CE) from the Acts of the Apostles, a Christian canonical work. Simon was a famous miracle-worker during the time of the apostles and famous for attempting to purchase his way into becoming an apostle of Jesus.

Clement I (35–99 CE), the third bishop of Rome, wrote in his *Recognitions* about some remarkable events that involved Simon Magus and the apostles of Jesus. In his account Simon and Peter appeared together before Emperor Nero more than once, each claiming that the other was a wizard. Nero had seen Simon's miracles. Simon could make statues laugh and walk. He turned stones into bread. He could appear and disappear magically. He could float in the air. Peter, on the other hand, could heal the sick and raise the dead. Both were extraordinary people who performed these miracles with the help of unseen forces, perhaps even of God Himself. Once during an interview with Nero, Simon, angry at Peter, exclaimed, "Let great dogs come forth and eat him up." Suddenly great dogs appeared and rushed at Peter. But Peter stretched out his hands in prayer, showing a loaf of bread that he had blessed; and the dogs, seeing it, disappeared.[302] In a later meeting of Nero, Simon and Peter, this time with Saint Paul as well, Nero didn't know who to believe was truly sent by God and who was a wizard. Simon proposed jumping from a tower and flying to prove his superior power.

> *Simon goes upon it, and commences flying in the air, attended by his angels. Peter, looking steadfastly at him, prays to the Lord to stop him. His prayer is answered, and Simon falls headlong . . .and perishes.* [303]

Nero had Peter and Paul imprisoned for three days while he waited for Simon to rise from the dead, as Simon claimed he had done before. But Simon never returned among the living. (If you read the history of magicians, you will notice that they rarely die well.)

Prior to Simon's death, he and the apostle Peter debated on the nature of God over a three-day period. A representation of the remarkable conversation was also provided in Clement's *Recognitions*.

Simon powerfully reasoned against Peter's Christian claims. He claimed that Peter's god was weak because man "was not able to remain such as he [God] had intended him to be." Certainly, God did not intend man to fail in the Garden of Eden. Shouldn't God have known he would fail in advance if He was all-knowing?

Also, Peter's god could not be good, Simon asserted, if he

> *gave a law to the first man, that he should eat of all the trees of paradise, but that he should not touch the tree of knowledge; and if he should eat of it, he should die. Why should he forbid him to eat, and to know what is good and what evil, that, knowing, he might shun the evil and choose the good?*[304]*. . .But truly, if man was*

---

[302] The story is from the *Acts of Peter and Paul*, paraphrased from Waite, 126–7.

[303] Ante-Nicene Christian Library, vol. 16, 263–273, in Waite, 127.

[304] This is what Julian the Apostate argued centuries later. I quoted Julian in an earlier essay.

> *to be injured by this means, why did he place the cause of injury in paradise at all?*[305]

So Simon concludes,

> *it was still possible for me to infer from those evils which are done in this world, and are not corrected [by the creator], either that its creator is powerless, if he cannot correct what is done amiss; or else, if he does not wish to remove the evils, that he is himself evil; but if he neither can nor will, that he is neither powerful nor good.* [306]

If you don't like this archaic language, let me restate the argument: Peter's god was stupid for not foreseeing that humanity would fail in the Garden of Eden. And his god was either powerless, as he could not correct the evils and suffering of this world, or he was evil by allowing suffering and evil to prevail upon the world, or both. Simon's reasoning holds even until today.

And that is reason talking.

The Arguments of Voltaire

This argument becomes even better when applied to Luther's predestination. How is it that the always-present, all-knowing God knew in advance what Adam and Eve would do, and knew that humankind would therefore be damned and destined to hell for an eternity? If He knew all this in advance, why would He create humans? What kind of God is that?

In the eighteenth century, Voltaire used his pen in his war against the Church.

> *... what kind of God does the Christian theology offer?*
> *A tyrant whom we should hate.*
> *He created men in 'his own image',*

---

[305] *Clementine Recognitions*, Book 2, ch. 54.

[306] *Clementine Recognitions*, Book 2, ch. 54.

only to make them vile;
he gave us sinful hearts
to have the right to punish us;
he made us love pleasure,
so that he might torment us with frightful pains
...eternal.[307]

Over and over again, Voltaire critiqued the Church:

He had hardly given us birth when he thought of destroying us. He ordered the water to engulf the earth. He sent his son to atone for our sins; Christ died, but apparently in vain, for we are told that we are still stained with the crime of Adam and Eve; and the Son of God, so acclaimed for mercy, is represented as waiting vengefully to plunge most of us into hell, including all those countless people who never heard of him.[308]

In the light of reason, the Christian God doesn't look so good.

Even the religious today base much of their worldview on reason. Although people profess to belong to religions, in many cases, their associations are much like belonging to the Rotary Club or the Lions. People are born into the religion and it becomes for many part of their identity or their social circle. But do they really believe in the religious dogma? Some do. But I think, if it really came down to it and you asked really hard questions, many would not agree with the dogma—it is not reasonable.

The Requisite Leap of Faith

So, the problem with Christianity is that it does not make logical sense. As discussed, why would an all-knowing, all-powerful, all-loving God allow there to be evil in the world? Why would this God allow good people to suffer at the hands of evil people, who appear to never have to

---

[307] Voltaire, *Epitre a Uranie* (1732), in Durant and Durant, 53.

[308] Voltaire, "Le Pour et Le Contre" (1722), in Durant and Durant, 39.

face punishment in this life for their misdeeds? This is the central paradox of Christianity. You can add to it many logical inconsistencies, some of which I addressed earlier. This was an issue that the Danish philosopher, Soren Kierkegaard (1813–1855), explored. Christianity is not rational. It is not logical. People whose thought processes are primarily rational cannot believe in Christianity unless they compartmentalize their faith separately from their approach to everything else. To be a Christian, according to Kierkegaard, one must take a leap of faith. One must put aside rationality and just believe. Interestingly, in many cases, it is the converts who are the most fervent believers. They had to, at some point, make a decision to toss rationality aside and just believe.

Religion and Social Order

It should be obvious that religion has tamed the wild soul of humankind so that we may live and work together; and for this reason, our religious foundation should not be upset. This has been known for centuries. The great Islamic philosopher Averroes (1126–1198) wrote that the mature philosopher will neither utter nor encourage any word against the established faith[309] because faith is the foundation of social order.

As much as they worked to destroy the influence of the Church on French society, the philosophes of the French Enlightenment were well-aware of the need for faith. Voltaire, for all the damage he caused to the reputation of the Church, wrote:

> *In a word, gentlemen, all men are not philosophers. We are obliged to hold intercourse and transact business and mix up in life with knaves possessing little or no reflection, with a vast number of persons addicted to brutality, intoxication, and rapine. You may, if you please, preach to them that the soul of man is mortal. As for myself, I shall be sure to thunder in their ears that if they rob me, they will inevitably be damned.*[310]

---

[309] Will Durant, *The Age of Faith*, 336.

[310] Will and Ariel Durant, 748.

Yet even though these philosophers understood the value of religion, they couldn't help themselves. The hypocrisy of its leaders, the logical inconsistencies of its doctrines, the hypocritical history of the Church—they had to destroy it. Through an unending stream of criticism and ridicule, they started a process that inevitably, over time, eroded the very underpinning of society. From their writings can be traced the thinking that led to the French Terror of the revolutionary period, the rise of nihilism, anarchism, atheism and subsequently the twentieth century regimes of terror and mass murder.

The theory of the divine right of kings had still prevailed up to the French Revolution. According to the theory, God still played a part in human history through His appointed kings. The French King Louis XVI (1754–1793) was enthroned and sustained by God's guiding hand. The sentencing of King Louis XVI to death by the National Convention cast God from the world of men. God's representative had been judged by men, and he was no longer deemed sufficient as the arbiter of right and wrong. Man was now the judge. God no longer had a place in the governance of man.

Killing the king was not all. The Hébertists,[311] a radical Jacobin faction that dominated French politics from 1793 to 1794, led a movement to thoroughly de-Christianize France. Their war on Christianity included the deportation and execution of Catholic clergy, the closing of churches, the destruction of religious monuments and relics, and the outlawing of religious education and public and private worship. A law in 1793 subjected priests and any who harbored them to death on sight.

---

[311] The Hébertists were educated middle class radical ideologues who supported the revolutionary ideals using the most draconian methods of the state and mob violence, including, as historian Stephen Schama put it, "unrelenting surveillance, denunciation, indictment, humiliation and death." Their allies in radicalism, the sans-culottes, were urban, working-class, violent partisans who dominated France from 1792 to 1795. The sans-culottes supported the Hébertist faction into prominence through mob violence and threats. The Hébertists and sans-culottes were so radical that they considered Maximilien Robespierre to be too moderate.

If the Hébertists had their way, the divinity of God was to be replaced by the divinity of the people. God was to be replaced by human ideals, initially, by Reason. And later they added Justice and Equality to create the new pantheon. Everyone knew that the will of the people corresponded to Reason and Nature.[312] The French naively believed that a free people would be infallible and always be guided by Reason.

But what happens when revolutionary factions disagree on how to proceed? They hadn't thought out that one. When the revolutionaries disagreed, it became necessary to label the other faction "counter-revolutionaries" and murder them so that the exalted human values of Reason, Justice and Equality could reign. Jean-Paul Marat (1743–1793), a well-known journalist and politician of the Revolution, exclaimed,

> *They question my right to the title of philanthropist. Ah, what injustice! Who cannot see that I want to cut off a few heads to save a great number?*[313]

After all, if utopia is really just around the corner, who can object to a short reign of terror along the way? It's just a small number of killings, and then we will achieve the goal of paradise for everyone. They always say that.

French existentialist Albert Camus (1913-1960) in his profound book *The Rebel* examined the historical and rational steps we took to justify murder for the sake of the coming utopia. What started with critiques of the Church led to the killing of the King, the remaking of society and finally the justification of murder for the sake of sacred human ideals.

The French Revolution not only transformed the political landscape of Europe, but it also reshaped philosophical thought, as intellectuals had to address the consequences of replacing divine authority with human ideals. It was a political revolution, but a revolution in thought as well. We never went back to how it was before.

----

[312] Albert Camus, *The Rebel: An Essay of Man in Revolt* (Vintage Books, 1956), ch. 6.
[313] Camus, ch. 6.

While the revolutionaries justified murder in the name of Reason, Justice, and Equality, their actions raised profound questions about the nature of history, progress and morality. These questions reverberated beyond France, influencing thinkers in Germany and elsewhere who sought to understand the Revolution's place in the broader story of human progress. One such thinker was Georg Wilhelm Friedrich Hegel (1770-1831), whose philosophical system provided a framework for interpreting the Revolution as a necessary, if violent, step toward the realization of a higher ideal. His philosophy can get hopelessly abstract, but it relates to what we are talking about.

Hegel's philosophical system centers on the ongoing development of Geist (Spirit or Mind) as it unfolds through human history. For Hegel, human consciousness and freedom develop progressively as societies evolve. This development is manifested in our religion, philosophy, art, and political institutions.

As humanity creates increasingly rational social and political structures—what Hegel calls "the State"—we become more self-aware and free. Hegel saw history as a process moving toward greater human freedom and self-understanding. While his philosophy is complex and open to interpretation, the core insight is hopeful: humanity is progressing toward forms of life and social organization that better support human flourishing, rational freedom, and mutual recognition.

And from the perspective of this future paradise, present and past history can be judged. In other words, the interim bloodletting doesn't matter, only the final goal matters. (This sounds familiar.) As our institutions, that is, the State, serves as the major vehicle to bring this vision into reality, the individual is of little consequence. Individuals come and go, but the Absolute perseveres, matures and becomes self-aware.

Many have used Hegel to justify removing those individuals who stand in the way of progress, as if they were cancerous cells that can be surgically excised. If the fate of individuals does not matter and it is really all about the progress of the whole, then murder of individuals in service of progress is justified. It follows logically.

This type of thinking became the bedrock of much political theory in the nineteenth and twentieth centuries and probably continues into today. Here we have the rationalization of murderous totalitarian states in the service of great human ideals.

Addressing the threat of nuclear annihilation during the Cold War, Che Guevara (1928–1967), the well-known Argentine revolutionary, wrote: "we must proceed along the path of liberation even if this costs millions of atomic victims."[314]

Mao Zedong (1893–1976) shocked his audience when he flippantly said:

> *Let's contemplate this, how many people would die if war breaks out. There are 2.7 billion people in the world. One-third could be lost; or, a little more, it could be half…I say that, taking the extreme situation, half dies, half lives, but imperialism would be razed to the ground and the whole world would become socialist.*[315]

Individual lives don't mean much to idealists. We can find thousands of quotes from powerful idealists to this same effect. Idealists are willing to sacrifice thousands or millions if they think it will lead to them to achieving their lofty ideals for humanity. This is because, in their minds, people are no longer creatures of God. Instead, people have become creatures of The State. According to Camus, man has become a tool, a means, for these leaders to usher in the world of the future. But in reality, as Camus tells us, all people have value and should be treated with dignity and compassion.

---

[314] Ernesto Che Guevara, "Tactics and Strategy of the Latin American Revolution," *Che Guevara Reader: Writings on Politics and Revolution*, ed. David Deutschmann (Ocean, 2003). First published in Verde Olivo, October 9, 1968, after Guevara's death.

[315] Mao Zedong in Jung Change and Jon Halliday, *Mao: The Unknown Story* (Alfred A. Knopf, 2005), 428.

Stalin, Mao, Hitler, Pol Pot and many lesser-known leaders have killed millions in their alleged pursuits of the perfect. Politicians are willing to lie, break laws, jail allies of their enemies or have their enemies killed because, after all, "we are going to do great things if we can gain (or retain) power."

Today's Dystopian Future and Saving the Planet

In the twenty-first century, we are living in a more negative age. I have noticed that we have stopped dreaming of a brighter future. Rather than reach for the Utopian ideals of the twentieth century, we dream of avoiding the cataclysms that humanity may face in the future. The oceans are dying. The atmosphere is warming up. Farmland continues to deteriorate. Pollution increases. Animal species are dying out and so on. The root source of these threats appears to be excess human population. But is anyone paying attention to this problem? It is much easier not to.

In an interview, television writer Dennis Kelly said,

> *We're sleepwalking into something very difficult…I knew we were coming up to 7 billion and it seemed like no one was talking about this. We were all talking about the environment, but we weren't talking about the obvious thing, which is that the pressures on the environment are largely caused by…having a large population.*[316]

We have known for decades that excess population is problematic, ever since Paul Ehrlich released his book *The Population Bomb*. Published in 1968, when there were 3.5 billion people on the planet, the book popularized the problems associated with human overpopulation. Ehrlich and his book were so popular, he even appeared on the Johnny Carson show. He predicted mass famines in the 1970s and 1980s and the starvation of hundreds of millions due to overpopulation and the

---

[316] Dennis Kelly, "An interview with Dennis Kelly about Utopia, the show too bleak for TV," interview by Chris Schultz, *New Zealand Herald*, April 20, 2017, nzherald.co.nz/entertainment/an-interview-with-dennis-kelly-about-utopia-the-show-too-bleak-for-tv/ZRRENODBS4PVECSNYP6UFUVGE4/, accessed January 1, 2023.

underdevelopment of agriculture to feed the ever-growing mass of people. Ehrlich had many suggestions to lower population, such as adding infertility drugs to the water supply, taxing parents with children or instituting a Federal Department of Population and Environment, which should take whatever steps necessary to reduce the U.S. population. It will be so bad, Ehrlich thought, that we would need to perform triage on the starving countries. Countries, such as India that were hopelessly unable to feed themselves should be cut off from food aid entirely.

Ehrlich's predictions were a bit overstated and what he predicted did not come to pass. Up until publication of his book, the world's population had been growing at an accelerating rate; after its publication, the rate of growth slowed. But, despite the deceleration, the planet's population continues to grow. The problem is still with us. By 2024, the world's population had reached over 8.1 billion people, more than double what it was when Ehrlich's book came out in 1968.

At some point it seems that there will be too many people on the Earth. When that happens there will be shortages of energy, natural resources and food. Only the rich will have access to resources, while everyone else will suffer. This type of inequality can be destabilizing and lead to civil war and revolution. It is said that it only takes missing nine meals for a population to become desperate, violent and revolutionary. It is hard to shake the feeling that we are heading towards a breaking point, where the world shudders under the impact of overpopulation. It's easier to look away, pretending that the collapse won't hit in our lifetime.

So today, the Utopian idealists of the twentieth century have given way to the anti-dystopian crusaders of the twenty-first century. Rather than bringing about a perfect world, today idealists strive to avoid catastrophe. It is as if our entire worldview has been turned upside down.

Where did this shared dystopian mentality come from? Fear-mongers have always been with us. The end of the world has always been around the corner, at least as far back as the Jewish prophetic revelations of

Armageddon. And we haven't stopped worrying. We've just been stacking end of the world scenarios on top of each other—from fears of a nuclear exchange in the 1950s, to overpopulation in the 1960s, to global cooling in the 1970s, to global warming since the 2010s. Ideas of a dystopian future have always haunted the Western mind, but as they pile ever higher in our minds, little room is left for hope.

Nobody knows how the planet will respond to the changes brought about by the growing mass of humanity. There is a tipping point somewhere, where cataclysmic change occurs, but nobody knows where it is. It could be triggered by a war. Perhaps the radiation and other pollutants in the oceans will reach a dangerous threshold, killing off the oxygen-producing organisms in the oceans, leading to a massive decline in oxygen in the atmosphere. Really, anything can happen. Western culture has highlighted several dystopian scenarios in newscasts, articles and films. According to this line of thought, at some point, the majority of humanity will suffer—perhaps we will lapse into civil wars for scarce resources or perhaps die from plague. But all popular scenarios share the same result—mass die offs and a future world where it will be difficult to survive.

Bombarded with post-apocalyptic movies, novels and news that only confirm the worst imaginable future, it is hard especially for the younger generations to have hope for the future. It's clear that we must avoid this catastrophe if we can.

The Gaia Theory

James Lovelock, an independent English scientist, presented the Gaia theory in his 1979 book, *Gaia: A New Look at Life on Earth*. The Gaia theory views Earth as a single organism that is self-regulating, like any other animal.

> *My Gaia theory sees the Earth behaving as if it were alive, and clearly anything alive can enjoy good health, or suffer disease.*

> *Gaia has made me a planetary physician and I take my profession seriously, and now I, too, have to bring bad news.*[317]

Lovelock, along with Al Gore, was instrumental in promoting the climate change movement. In 2006, Lovelock wrote in the UK newspaper *The Independent:*

> *Before this century is over billions of us will die and [the] few breeding pairs of people that survive will be in the Arctic where the climate remains tolerable.*[318]

In an interview in 2009, he said,

> *I think it's wrong to assume we'll survive 2°C of warming: there are already too many people on Earth. At 4°C we could not survive with even one-tenth of our current population. The reason is we would not find enough food, unless we synthesized it. Because of this, the cull during this century is going to be huge, up to 90 per cent. The number of people remaining at the end of the century will probably be a billion or less. It has happened before: between the ice ages there were bottlenecks when there were only 2,000 people left. It's happening again.*[319]

---

[317] James Lovelock, "The Earth is about to catch a morbid fever that may last as long as 100,000 years," *The Independent Commentators,* January 16, 2006, independent.co.uk/voices/commentators/james-lovelock-the-earth-is-about-to-catch-a-morbid-fever-that-may-last-as-long-as-100-000-years-5336856.html.

[318] "Gaia scientist James Lovelock: I was 'alarmist' about climate change," *NBCnews.com,* April 23, 2012, https://tinyurl.com/2yvfklon.

[319] James Lovelock, "One last chance to save mankind," February 11, 2009 interview, *About the Earth,* abouthearth.wordpress.com/2009/02/11/lovelock-interview-one-last-chance-to-save-mankind. Lovelock later dismissed the entire basis for global warming concerns in his BBC television interview, discussed by Marc Moano, *Climate Depot:* "Take this climate matter everybody is thinking about. They all talk, they pass laws, they do things, as if they knew what was happening. I don't think anybody really knows what's happening. They just guess. And a whole group of them meet together and encourage each other's guesses." https://tinyurl.com/2944lf6c.

What are we supposed to do with that? I guess it doesn't matter, as it is ultimately the call of the authorities. The question is, will they even consider their moral codes when they make decisions for all of us? And which moral code am I even referring to? The morals of a statesman or the morals of a worker—our morality? To wrestle with that, let's try some difficult questions about what we'd do in a crisis. Then we will get back to Lovelock's bleak vision of the future.

Some Moral Thought Experiments

Consider this thought experiment: Suppose you are driving down a city street and you see a person step right in front of your car. You cannot slow down in time to avoid hitting and killing this person. You can swerve to the left and hit an oncoming car and kill that driver and possibly yourself. You can swerve to the right and hit and kill two pedestrians. Assuming that no matter what you do, someone is going to die. What do you do?

Most people would answer, kill as few people as possible. Others may want to answer that it depends who the targets are. If the person in the road appeared sweet and kind and the people on the sidewalk looked unsavory and dangerous, perhaps some might consider hitting the unsavory-looking people and saving the sweet one. No matter the reasoning, there is no good answer here. You are going to kill someone. In some cases, such as this traffic scenario and the existential crises we are facing, we are forced to make the least-worst decision. How are we going to do that?

A second thought experiment: Suppose you were a passenger on a cruise ship that sank, and you were a lucky one who got on a lifeboat. Suppose the lifeboat was designed for ten people and there were twelve people on the boat and it was taking on water because of the added weight from the extra two people. What do you do? The rational decision is that two people must leave the boat and drown. Otherwise, all of the people in the boat will drown as the raft sinks. Again, what do you do? Perhaps you ask for volunteers willing to lose their lives for the sake of the others. What if nobody volunteers? Then what do you do? What is the rational response? I could be wrong, but I believe the rational response is to throw out the people who are least likely to live long anyway: the old or the sick. Or it could be to throw out the people on whom nobody depends. If a breadwinner of a family is sacrificed, the entire family could be thrown into poverty. So, I guess that means children or single, childless people. You could sacrifice yourself, but what if you had a family that relied on you? If you die, your children would grow up poor and without a father (or mother). They might not get that quality education that you had planned for them. I guess you have to determine what is most important first. Then you can base your decision on that. In any case, it appears the rational decision will result in the death of at minimum two people. But again, what criteria do you use to decide such a case? Many would have different solutions, using different reasoning processes.[320] I would hate to be on that boat. Imagine all twelve people in a raw panic, yelling, fighting and pleading over who lives and who dies.

These scenarios are difficult ones with no good choices to make, only bad choices. You can have great intentions; you could even be Jesus Christ or the Buddha and you would still be forced to make a bad choice, because all options here are bad.

Sometimes bad actions appear necessary to achieve goals, while acting morally is supremely ineffective and doesn't serve the larger good. When faced with these choices, many of us would be tempted to do evil for a good end. It appears that most successful politicians follow this principle.

Here's an example of the quandary that comes up all too often. You are running for mayor of a small rural town. Your opponent, the

---

[320] This exercise reminds me of the sinking of the *Titanic*, when passengers did face this choice. Most of the men went down with the ship, and those men who survived probably lived in private shame all their lives. What a terrible moral decision to have to make! The decisions of the dead men and the shame of the living men were all driven by the social mores of the time, which included protecting the women and children.

incumbent, takes donations from developers who want to replace the farmland and woodlands in the town with housing developments and big box stores. You are sure he is getting paid by the developers for his help getting projects approved, but you don't have any evidence. If you are elected, you will maintain the town's rural character and keep it from becoming another cookie cutter suburban town. This is important to you and your friends. You are behind in the polls. You are going to lose. You have hired people to dig up dirt on your opponent, and they couldn't find anything except something about his daughter. She has been running with the wrong crowd, doing drugs, and even turning tricks to support her drug habit. It would be morally wrong to bring the daughter into the race, to run an ad attacking her decision-making and attributing it to your opponent. Still, you know an apple doesn't fall far from the tree.

That's all you got. If you don't do that, you will surely lose the race and the town will lose its character. You know your goal, maintaining the town's character is morally the best choice. So what do you do? Smear the daughter and her father and maybe win the race and save the town? Or do you maintain your moral code, lose the election, and watch your town become part of the suburban sprawl. I am sure plenty of politicians have faced similar situations, where those who chose to run the clean campaign lost. Their ambitions and dreams all came to naught because they wouldn't play dirty.

On the other hand, many of us do choose the ethically questionable path from time to time in our daily lives. A little evil here, a little white lie there, to get what we want. For example, lying on a resume to get a higher paying job so you can send your child to a better school—that could be considered noble. You could cheat clients to help your company become more profitable so you can be promoted and better provide for your family. Great ends, right? But what do you become in the process? The means we choose shape not only our self-perception but also the person we ultimately become.

It comes down to this simple thought experiment: If you could save a billion people by killing one person, would you do it? Suppose you knew by some magical means that your neighbor is going to be responsible for the deaths of over a billion people. Would it be morally correct to murder your neighbor and save a billion people? This is a tough question, one that I don't want to answer myself. But please, stop for a moment and try to answer it.

If your answer is yes, you would kill a single person to save a billion; then for you, a morally right outcome justifies the use of immoral means, such as murder, to achieve it.

Applying Morality to the Apocalypse

Now let's return to the problem that appears to be facing humanity. If you believe that our future holds a massive extinction event for humanity, as Lovelock predicted, then shouldn't we try to stop it? If you had the power to enforce measures to prevent these catastrophes from happening, would you? Probably. The question is, how far would you go? Would you create and release a pathogen that would kill perhaps half the population of the world? That would certainly solve the problem. If you killed half the population, perhaps that is better than allowing a Lovelock's scenario where there is a massive die off with only a few thousand remaining in a depleted world.

This situation is just an extension of the lifeboat dilemma: if you could save the world by killing someone, would you do it? We are just adding a few zeroes to the equation.

Whether it is only one murder or millions, murder is clearly immoral and so is the murderer. The counter argument is that saving the world is a good and moral outcome. Or is it? What kind of world is being saved if murderers are allowed to decide when and if murder is justified and then go free?[321] I can only imagine French and Russian societies during their revolutionary bloodletting. Those were not happy places.

---

[321] Although I am sure these arguments are common knowledge, I paraphrased from

Have you noticed a similar theme here? We have a goal that appears to be more important than individual humans; and in order to achieve it, we must be willing to murder those people who are standing in the way of our goal. This is what the anarchist bombers did in the late nineteenth century. This is what the communists and Nazis did in the twentieth century. Same methods, different goals.

Enforced Sterilization as a Solution

But maybe we need not go as far as murder.

In the 2013 British television series *Utopia*, a better potential solution to the problem is presented. A group of powerful people deliberately introduce the deadly "Russian Flu" throughout the world. They then provide vaccinations to protect the fearful population from this deadly influenza, but they have designed the vaccine to sterilize almost all of humanity. All of this is done to benefit humanity in the long run, to alleviate the suffering that would likely occur during the great culling by starvation that Lovelock spoke of.

In an interview, the writer of *Utopia*, Dennis Kelly, said,

> *The question is really simple and it's one that follows her [a main proponent of the sterilization program] through her life and the question is this: If I stop doing this [advancing the sterilization program], what's going to happen? What about the billions that live in the future? She might be right. When our resources run out, what is going to happen? Phosphates will last another hundred years, the best estimate is three hundred years. Without phosphates, we don't have food to support eight billion people, never mind the 12 billion that will be there.*[322]

Perhaps mass sterilization would be the most humane method, that is, if we believe we still have time before these impending catastrophes

---

gotquestions.org/ends-justify-means.html, November 17, 2023.

[322] Dennis Kelly, "Utopia writer Dennis Kelly defends violent scenes," interview by Kev Goeghegan, BBC News, June 17, 2014, bbc.com/news/entertainment-arts-27886003

occur. Sterilization addresses the problem while allowing people to continue to live. You don't have to kill anyone. The population will slowly decline, and the problem will resolve itself.

John Holdren (1944–), along with Paul and Anne Ehrlich, whom I mentioned before, discussed using forced sterilization to address human overpopulation in their 1977 textbook, *Ecoscience: Population, Resources, Environment*. So, this is not a novel idea. Forced sterilization has been used in many countries in the world at various times, including Israel, Canada, China, Germany, Peru, Mexico, South Africa, Sweden and the United States. In several of these situations, certain ethnic or other specific groups were targeted, which makes one think the motives were not completely about overpopulation.

Certainly, something must be done about the impending crisis. An organization that promotes awareness of the population problem shares some inspirational quotes from its board of directors:

> *The human population can no longer be allowed to grow in the same old, uncontrolled way. If we do not take charge of our population size, then nature will do it for us and it is the poor people of the world who will suffer most.*[323]

But how do we take charge of our population size?

Here is another one.

> *As the soaring demand for food, water and energy is exacerbated by climate change, it is no longer legitimate to leave policies for lowering birth rates off the policy agenda.*[324]

I wonder what they have in mind.

---

[323] Sir David Attenborough, *Population Matters*, populationmatters.org/our-patrons, accessed January 1, 2025.

[324] Sara Parkin Obe, co-founder of the Forum of the Future, *Population Matters*, populationmatters.org/our-patrons, accessed January 1, 2025.

Reason's Response to the Impending Disaster

John Stuart Mill (1806–1873), an English philosopher, is known for popularizing Utilitarianism, a philosophy that can help us decide which actions are best to take. It is very easy. Whatever causes the most happiness and the least pain for the greatest number of people is the best action to take. Applying Utilitarianism to the lifeboat problem is simple. Two people die and ten live. (Well, it is not that easy—just which two have to die?)

By addressing our population problem with the Utilitarian perspective, the writers of *Utopia* found a winning solution in mass sterilization. Sterilization creates the most happiness and least pain. That's perfect. Consider the other possibilities. If we do nothing, overpopulation will lead to tremendous suffering and death. An alternate course of action, murdering billions of people to lower population, would cause great suffering and turn the perpetrators into inhuman beasts. That would be a terrible choice. Mass sterilization would lead to suffering as well, but much less than mass starvation or mass murder. Many would suffer disappointment at not being able to raise children. We might encounter economic problems, a decline in our standard of living, and political unrest. [325] But none of these problems associated with mass sterilization can compare to the suffering that would have been if nothing were done. So, forced sterilization is a rational response to the impending crisis.

Culling Humanity's Flaws

The scenario we just looked at raises interesting ethical questions. Is forced sterilization ethical? In the twentieth century, many in Western Civilization thought so. If it is justified to sterilize a population in order to save humanity in the long run, then wouldn't it also be justified

---

[325] With the advent of artificial intelligence and humanoid-type robots, it is possible that there may not be work for the majority of people anyway. The great productivity gains of artificial intelligence and inexpensive robots actually make this sterilization argument more persuasive as the economic arguments against population decline melt away.

to forcibly sterilize criminals, people on welfare, alcoholics and drug addicts or people with hereditary mental and physical illnesses in order to improve our breeding stock? One could argue that these elements act as a drag on society. They take from society but do not give back as much as they take, making all of us poorer and less secure.

Madison Grant's popular book, *The Passing of the Great Race*, published in 1916, made this point:

> *It is highly unjust. . .to burden the responsible. . .but still overworked, elements in the community with an ever-increasing number of moral perverts, mental defectives, and hereditary cripples.*[326]

It was commonly believed in the early twentieth century that socially undesirable traits were genetically inherited. It was expected that children of addicts, criminals and the physically or mentally ill would likely have the same deviant characteristics as their parents. In 1918 Anna Blount, a physician, wrote in the *Birth Control Review,*

> *There they are, a motley group, from the gay, lighthearted moron, who cannot make an intelligent plan, even to do mischief; to the doddering idiot, the crafty paranoiac, the wretched epileptic, the moral imbecile, the chronic criminal with hereditary taint, and even the village ne'erdowell. What do they cost us, in wealth, in labor and in misery? They must be eliminated. Eugenics makes birth control imperative. . .But whatever the means this stream of human waste must be deflected from the meltingpot. . .In that day, we shall see a race of American thoroughbreds, if not the superman.*[327]

Such calls for forced sterilization were popular in the United States and Europe during the early twentieth century. They were part of the

---

[326] Madison Grant, *The Passing of the Great Race or the Racial Basis of European History,* (Charles Scribner's Sons, 1916), 45.

[327] Anna E. Blount, M.D., "Large Families and Human Waste," *Birth Control Review,* vol. 2, number 9 (September 1918), 3.

progressive movement, a time of idealist belief in progress toward a better future. Through institutional reforms, such as jail reform, labor reform, better food standards and a plan to weed out transgenerational genetic defects, it was believed a better future was assured. Eugenics even became an academic discipline at many universities and colleges. The American Breeder's Association established a subcommittee on eugenics in 1906, which included Alexander Graham Bell, Luther Burbank and Stanford president David Starr Jordan as members. The organization's goal was to study human heredity, specifically with the purpose of improving humanity through selective breeding. This could be done by eliminating inferior blood from the gene pool. Other supporters of the eugenics movement included W. E. B. DuBois, Theodore Roosevelt, H. G. Wells, Helen Keller, Winston Churchill, Oliver Wendell Holmes, Jacques Cousteau, Herbert Hoover and John Maynard Keynes. Margaret Sanger, another backer, founded Planned Parenthood to push for legal contraception for poor immigrant and minority women.

To eugenicists charitable feelings were a force for evil. In Margaret Sanger's *Birth Control Review*, Edward East wrote that

> *well-intentioned philanthropy and social service is nothing but a brutal gesture to posterity.*[328]

It was harmful in the long run to help the "deviants;" instead humanity would all be better served if they were just eliminated. Margaret Sanger presented the argument clearly:

> *We are now in a state where our charities, our compensation acts, our pensions, hospitals, and even our drainage and sanitary*

---

[328] Edward M. East commenting on H. Adye Prichard, "Propaganda — As I See It," *Birth Control Review*, vol. 14, no. 4 (April 1930), 109. More information on the *Birth Control Review* can be found at www.hli.org/resources/sangers-birth-control-review-part-i/, as was posted on November 21, 2023.

> *equipment all tend to keep alive the sickly and the weak, who are*
> *allowed to propagate and in turn produce a race of degenerates.*[329]

It is estimated that 64,000 people in the United States were forcibly sterilized between 1907 and 1963. Some states sterilized imbeciles for much of the twentieth century. Between the 1930s and the 1970s, approximately one third of the female population of Puerto Rico was sterilized. Native American women were sterilized without their knowledge when they gave birth. The Supreme Court ruled in 1927 that the State of Virginia could forcibly sterilize individuals under the Virginia Sterilization Act of 1924. Later, when the Nazi's were on trial for war crimes in Nuremburg, they justified their mass sterilizations (over 450,000) by citing the efforts in the United States as their inspiration.

There is scientific merit in eugenics theory, that is, in deciding who gets to breed and who doesn't. Cattle ranchers keep only the best bulls and cows for reproduction. The rest of them are sent to the slaughterhouse. Luther Burbank, a pioneer in agricultural science developed more than 800 varieties of plants using selective breeding. Why would this not also apply to humanity? Madison Grant wrote in his book *The Passing of the Great Race:*

> *Mistaken regard for what are believed to be divine laws and a*
> *sentimental belief in the sanctity of human life tend to prevent*
> *both the elimination of defective infants and the sterilization of*
> *such adults as are themselves of no value to the community. The*
> *laws of nature require the obliteration of the unfit, and human*
> *life is valuable only when it is of use to the community or race.*[330]

Margaret Sanger wrote:

> *To meet this problem [of dysgenics] as a great scientist has recently*
> *pointed out, we need not more of the fit, but fewer of the unfit. The*

---

[329] Margaret Sanger, "Birth Control and Women's Health," *Birth Control Review*, vol. I, no. 12 (December 1917), 7.
[330] Grant, 44–45.

propagation of the degenerate, the imbecile, the feebleminded, should be prevented.[331]

More from Madison Grant:

[Eugenics] is a practical, merciful, and inevitable solution of the whole problem, and can be applied to an ever-widening circle of social discards, beginning always with the criminal, the diseased, and the insane, and extending gradually to types which may be called weaklings rather than defectives, and perhaps ultimately to worthless race types.[332]

Eugenics was heavily influenced by racial theories. The northern white European races were considered the most intelligent and most virtuous of races. The Eastern European, Southern European, Latin, African and Asian races were considered inferior and should not temper the purity of the gifted races. Racial mixing was unacceptable. So, the U.S. clamped down on immigration from these groups with the Immigration Act of 1924, severely restricting immigration from Eastern and Southern Europe and banning Asians outright.[333] All of this was based on scientific studies of race.

It is said that Hitler was an active reader of Sanger's *Birth Control Review* and eugenics was foundational to the Nazi ideology. As we all know, the Nazis not only sterilized hundreds of thousands, but they also killed millions of the handicapped, "deviants," occultists, races and ethnic groups they found inferior. After the destruction of the Nazi regime and the revelations of the death camps, the popularity of eugenics took a big hit. Eugenics became associated with the racism and murderous authoritarianism. In response, eugenics societies changed their names (for example, the American Eugenics Society became the Society for

---

[331] Margaret Sanger, "The Eugenic Value of Birth Control Propaganda," *Birth Control Review*, vol. V, no. 10 (October 1921), 5.

[332] Grant, 46-47.

[333] Mexican quotas were not reduced as the country needed cheap labor.

the Study of Social Biology) and moderated their beliefs. Yet much of the ideology continued.

Today, for the most part, eugenics is considered in poor taste, immoral, and frankly taboo because of past abuses. Some proponents of eugenics today declaim the old racist ideologies. As one wrote, just because past attempts went astray, does not mean the idea is inherently evil. They no longer call for sterilizing inferior races, the unintelligent, the criminal, the insane or the alcoholic. Instead, some believe that prenatal tests should be performed, and would-be parents should decide to kill their unborn children if they have physical or mental defects.

Rational Arguments Against Eugenics

You may be wondering how I strayed so far from Simon Magus and the killing of the King Louis XVI all the way to Margaret Sanger and eugenics. This chapter is about reason. If you follow reason, you can end up in some very precarious places—like murder and eugenics.

To the French subject who believed in progress and who applied reason to the political and social realities of the day, killing the oppressors (the monarchs, the nobility and the clerics) was a legitimate way to bring progress to humanity. Killing was therefore good.

If you use reason—and only reason—and if the assumptions about population growth and environmental catastrophe are correct, then both forced sterilization of humanity and eugenics targeting people with undesired characteristics would be among the best solutions for guaranteeing the future of the human race. The problem with this rational approach is that the assumptions about population and the environment may not be right.

And reason itself is only one way to view a situation and develop a response. It is not always the best way. There are other methods.

Let's deal with assumptions first. The arguments about overpopulation are not new. They were not discovered in the 1970s. In the 1920s and

1930s people were warning about overpopulation. In 1931, H. G. Wells wrote,

> *The world is already too full. . . Unless a solution is found, life will come to mean a world without animals, for we shall not be able to support even squirrels. There will be no open country, no streams, cataracts, and woods, no independent travel——and still the increase will continue.* [334]

In the *Birth Control Review*, in 1926, Frank Hawkins wrote:

> *With an increase of fifty percent in agricultural efficiency and a utilization of all tillable areas America can raise food for only 208 million people.* [335]

Hawkins failed to predict the agricultural revolution which greatly increased the Earth's capacity to make food. Of the almost 400 million people in the United States today, a smaller percentage is starving now than at any time since the pilgrims landed in Massachusetts. In fact, in the United States and many other nations, a larger problem than starvation is obesity, the very opposite. In California, millions of acres of the nation's best farmland lie fallow because the water, which would have been used for irrigation, is instead diverted into creeks and rivers to support native fish species. We have no food problem here. The predictions of global food shortages never came to pass. The thinkers of the 1920s and 1930s missed the green revolution. [336] (I understand it is difficult to predict revolutions.) Their assumptions were dead wrong, which means their suggested means were unnecessary.

---

[334] "H. G. Wells Speaks on Birth Control," Birth Control Review, vol. XV, no. 11 (November 1931), 317, lifedynamics.com/wp-content/uploads/2023/01/1931-11-November.pdf. No author has been attributed to this article.

[335] Frank H. Hankins, Ph.D. "Does America Have Too Many Children?" *Birth Control Review*, vol. X, no. 2 (February 1926), 60.

[336] The Green Revolution occurred from the 1960s to the 1980s, primarily in developing countries, and involved massive increases in farm productivity through the use of high-yield crop varieties, chemical fertilizers and pesticides.

Regarding exponential growth, the United Nations has recently predicted that the world population will peak at 10.3 billion, and then begin to decline. Presently, the only regions that are experiencing large increases in population are Sub-Saharan Africa and Pakistan. Birth rates are down across most of the world. Do you remember Italians used to have large families? Most young Italians do not have siblings or cousins anymore. In 2020, the Italian birthrate had fallen to its lowest level since the country's unification in 1861. The Pope calls the problem a tragedy, saying, "The demographic winter is a real problem."[337] In 2020, the United States birthed fewer babies than is has in four decades, when its population was much less. In Japan the number of people under fourteen has been dropping for forty years. Losing 400,000 people in 2020, China had its first population decline since the famine of the late 1950s.[338] According to a study published in The Lancet in 2020, by the end of the century, Italy and China are projected to lose 50% of their populations due to declining birthrates.[339] China would lose between 600 and 700 million people.[340] So the assumptions of impending doom from overpopulation may all be wrong.

Instead, perhaps we might encounter problems associated with low birthrates. There won't be enough younger workers to support the relatively larger number of retirees. Societies will be top heavy, with more takers than givers. In the United States, in the 1960s there were six people of working age for every retiree. In 2022, the ratio was 3 to 1. It is projected that by 2035, it will be 2 to 1. The young could bristle at a system that plunders their wages to feed the elderly. Declining birthrates

---

[337] Sam Raskin, "Pope Francis calls declining birth rate in Italy a 'tragedy,'" *New York Post,* December 26, 2021, https://tinyurl.com/y24ldlwt.

[338] Darrell Brickner, "Bye, bye, baby? Birthrates declining globally—here's why it matters," *World Economic Forum,* June 15, 2021, https://tinyurl.com/2yy2oau3, accessed January 1, 2025.

[339] Vollset et al, "Fertility, mortality, migration, and population scenarios for 195 countries and territories from 2017 to 2100: a forecasting analysis for the Global Burden of Disease Study," *The Lancet,* 2020, vol. 396, issue 10,258, 1,285–1,306.

[340] Brickner.

can lead to political instability and potentially violence. In addition, those countries with high birth rates may invade or take over countries with declining populations. After all, history is all about demographics.

I suppose you can still make the argument that although population growth is slowing, it is still growing. The peoples of the world are becoming more prosperous, which means they are directly and indirectly consuming more energy. And much of the energy that we use generates CO2 in the atmosphere, which will eventually reach a tipping point leading to catastrophic consequences in the climate. We may not have the luxury of waiting eighty years for the population to decline substantially.

But then again, we have heard this urgency over and over. According to a 1989 Associated Press article,

> *A senior UN environmental official says entire nations could be wiped off the face of the Earth by rising sea levels if the global warming trend is not reversed by the year 2000. Coastal flooding and crop failures would create an exodus of "eco- refugees" threatening political chaos, said Noel Brown, director of the New York office of the UN Environment Program, or UNEP. He said governments have a ten-year window of opportunity to solve the greenhouse effect before it goes beyond human control.*[341]

As you can see, predicting the future, as these dystopian thinkers attempted to do, is impossible really. In this case Mr. Brown was just plain wrong. But he wasn't alone. Millions believed this. Like most of us do, he assumed that events follow linearly, extrapolated historical trends combined with "known" science, and still he missed it. Brown's prediction should have been relatively easy, because it was just a linear extrapolation, and nothing new interfered with the linear course of events. Perhaps climate science was just not that accurate back then.

---

[341] Peter James Spielmann, "U.N. Predicts Disaster if Global Warming Not Checked," *AP News*, June 29, 1989, https://tinyurl.com/y2tdhbyf, accessed January 1, 2025.

Generally, predicting the future is a fool's game because nobody can account for the black swan events that come out of nowhere and radically change the course of history. The future plays out predictably until out of nowhere a black swan event bursts onto the scene. Who would have predicted that a global pandemic would bankrupt hundreds of thousands of businesses in the U.S.? Or that the Agricultural Revolution would transform agriculture? Or there'd be a Reformation, Bolshevik Revolution, or Spartacus Rebellion? There have been thousands of black swans in history. Things can change abruptly and usually we have little to no visibility before it happens. The future is often not a linear projection of the present. So why should we have any faith in any predictions of the future?

So, if we cannot have that much faith in our predictions of the future, then why would we take drastic action to prevent a scenario that is unlikely to occur. This is my reason-based counter-argument to sterilization.

So how did the Western World progress from "Love thy neighbor" to "sterilize the masses?" "Love thy neighbor" is not reason-based, but the argument for sterilization is. Reason can take you strange and inhumane places. It isn't as beneficial as people think it is. As Pascal wrote,

> *Anyone who chose to follow reason alone would have proved himself a fool.*[342]

And that anyone may be Western society.

The Inner Voice

Reason is not the only way to address the world and our problems in it. We also have knowledge that is innate, guidance that comes from within—from the inner voice.[343] This internal knowledge comes not

---

[342] Blaise Pascal, Pensées (Penguin, 1972), 40.

[343] This is not new news. A long line of medieval theologians has written about this for centuries.

from our personal experience. We need not study textbooks to learn how to breathe, suckle or walk. Most of us know there is a greater reality out there, regardless of what we call it. We know we should avoid death. We know that happiness is good. Many of us know who we should marry the moment we first meet our future spouse. That is the inner voice speaking. It isn't reason that informs us of these things. It is innate knowledge, innate wisdom.

According to the German Romantics, following the inner voice is our duty. The romantic hero will follow the inner voice in defiance of tradition, authority and social pressures and pursue its direction regardless of personal consequences. I consider the signers of the Declaration of Independence to be romantic heroes. They signed the Declaration knowing it was treason against the English Crown. They knew that if captured that they would be tortured to death. Their possessions would be seized by the English. Their families would suffer and become impoverished. They had a lot to lose. It was not a rational decision to throw in with the signers of the Declaration. These men are true romantic heroes. They believed and acted on their beliefs against the greatest empire in history, knowing full well that they might suffer terribly for it. And indeed, many of them did. Nine of the fifty-six signers died from wounds suffered fighting in the Revolutionary War. Five others were captured by the British as traitors and tortured as traitors and then promptly executed. Two had sons die in the war. Twelve had their homes ransacked and burned. Eight more had their homes looted by the British or Tories. Several died in poverty. One of them, Thomas Nelson, Jr., in the Battle of Yorktown, upon learning that the British had taken over his house for their headquarters, urged the Americans to artillery the house. They did, destroying the home, and Nelson later died bankrupt. They were not rational men. A rational calculation would be to do nothing, to let others take the risk. And if the risktakers won, everyone would share the spoils of liberty anyway, risktakers and the rational non-actors alike. The rational response would have been to do nothing.

Romantic Arguments Against Eugenics

Now, let's take on the rational argument for eugenics. Instead of rebutting premises or logic, I think the best method to counter the eugenics argument is to approach it from an entirely different perspective—one that views life as sacred. This is not a provable or rational premise, but it resonates innately with most people. Life itself possesses an inherent value, period!

This reverence for life is often described as a sacred or inviolable principle. It's a fundamental belief that doesn't necessarily require logical reasoning or rational arguments to support it. In fact, some argue that this respect for life is embedded into the human psyche, hardwired into our very being.

The concept of the sanctity of life serves as a basic premise upon which our moral systems are built. It is a core component of our internal moral compass, influencing our decisions and actions, usually without us even noticing.

The cold logic of using sterilization to better society conflicts with our innate principle of respecting life. Our instinctive rejection of eugenics confounds some of us, defying logic that seems convincing. We lean on reason in our ethical discussions, but ultimately our most profound moral decisions come from a more visceral bond with all that lives.

The Nobel prize winner, Albert Schweitzer (1875–1965), made the sacredness of life a cornerstone of his philosophy. At one point, Schweitzer was considered the most famous man living, primarily due to his philosophic outlook. "To the man who is truly ethical all life is sacred."[344] We should never destroy life unless it is unavoidable. He wrote:

> *The elemental fact, present in our consciousness every moment of our existence, is: I am life that wills to live, in the midst of life that wills to live. . .The essence of the humane spirit is: Preserve life,*

---

[344] Albert Schweitzer, *Albert Schweitzer: An Anthology* (Beacon, 1947), 262.

promote life, help life to achieve its highest destiny. The essence of Evil is: Destroy life, harm life, hamper the development of life. [345]

So, at what point should we treat humans as things? That is a fundamental question that eugenicists dodge. Eugenicists won't ask the question, they just dream, conspire or act, blindly pursuing their vision of utopia—all the while viewing people and populations as things to be manipulated like clay.

This conflict between the sanctity of life and the cold reasoning behind eugenics highlights the real problem: the potential for rational thinking to override our innate moral instincts. While Schweitzer's philosophy anchors us in the intrinsic value of all life, eugenicists' reliance on logic to justify their actions demonstrates how rationality can override morality and can seduce our leaders into performing brutal acts on the rest of us.

Rationality is a tool that can be used to further our ends. We should use it to get things done, but once we start to overlook the sacredness of living things in the name of efficiency, we need to take a step back and reflect. Rational thinking can easily go too far and become inhumane. Most likely all of the twentieth-century dictators' programs that resulted in millions of deaths were the result of rational thinking. Their assumptions might have been wrong, but their thinking was still rational. If only we could always remember Albert Schweitzer and always keep in the front of our minds his dictum that "all life is sacred" and allow that idea to temper all decisions. Then perhaps we could avoid making asses of ourselves and harming others with decisions that are logically sound but ethically deficient.

The Moral Bankruptcy of Unabated Logic

Let me tell you a love story. A long time ago in a faraway land there was a king who was beloved by all, or at least that is what they tell us. And being the king, he could do anything he wanted because nobody could punish him. This king was intensely attracted to his neighbor's wife, and

---

[345] Albert Schweitzer, *Out of My Life and Thought* (Johns Hopkins University, 1998), 156–157.

even slept with her. She liked being with the king. But her husband could become a problem, so he had to die. Then everything would turn out for the best. Well, this cuckold husband was a soldier; and conveniently for the king, a war was going on. He asked the cuck's commander to put him in the front lines where he would most certainly be killed. And Uriah the Hittite was killed. And then King David married Bathsheba.

Imagine, if you could commit a crime, such as murder, thievery or rape, and you knew that you would never be punished for it. If that were true, then wouldn't it be logical to do the crime? It is the reasoned approach.

I want that.
If I do this, I will get that.
And there are no possible negative consequences to doing this.
Therefore, I should do this (even if it is murder),
and I will get that, which is what I want.

I am not suggesting that rationality be abandoned. Pure logic is amoral. It is just a tool, like a hammer. You can use a hammer to build a house or murder people. The hammer is not moral or immoral. It is just a hammer. What really matters is the intention behind the use of the hammer, which boils down to the premises.

Rationality is Only a Tool—It is the Premises that Matter

It isn't really rationality that is the problem. It is the premises behind the logical reasoning. Schweitzer still used logic. His logic was based on his premise that life is holy, and nothing compares to that. The atheist's premise might be that God's church must be perfect. The sterilization argument is based on premises that: (1) we know what the future will be if we do nothing, (2) the survival of the human race is most important, and (3) it is best to cause as little pain and death as possible. I suppose that there could have been other lines of reasoning to the Lovelock bleak scenario. Elon Musk seems to have one: establish a colony on Mars before the Earth destroys itself.

After We Kill God, We Still Need a Church

David Hume wrote that philosophy, logic and science cannot prove the existence of God or the immortality of the soul; only direct intuition can prove these beliefs. And without these beliefs, there can be no moral order, and therefore no civilization can survive.[346]

We are living in such a society now—one based on reason. For generations we have become increasingly reliant on reason, to the extent that we cannot imagine what it would be like to live otherwise. And, wherever you look, it appears the foundations of Western society are cracking—precisely from our over-reliance on reason.

In revolutionary France, the radicals were aware of the necessity for religion at the same time they were removing all traces of Christianity from the country. Almost all of them hated the Church, and a large number of them were atheists. A new religion was needed to provide a common moral framework and shared values to cement French society. Some argued that the Revolution itself was a cause great enough to bind the French people together. But nationalism is not a religion. It has no spiritual element in it. It has no supernatural entity that establishes and maintains order in the universe. The French radicals realized that they needed a real church to bind the people and create order.

French Revolutionary Attempts at Religion

In place of the deposed Christian religion, a couple of attempts were made to form a French national church, both of which failed after their main backers were guillotined.

In 1793, one of the more radical French revolutionary parties, the Hébertists, established the Cult of Reason. (The word "cult" at that time had nothing to do with the modern definition of cult.) The Cult of Reason was the Revolution's first attempt at a revolutionary church.

---

[346] Durant, *The Age of Faith, 332.*

Most members of the Hébertist faction were members of the cult, as were their allies, the working-class, urban sans-culottes.[347]

The Cult of Reason was an attempt at a church without God. An argument can be made that it was an atheist church, although most of its sponsors were Deists[348]. Deists believed God was the creator of the universe and set the universe up to operate using the natural laws of physics, but God was not involved in human affairs. Deists believed in few, if any, Christian doctrines. The point of the "religion" was to strive for the perfection of mankind through the attainment of Truth and Liberty. It was based on the supreme values of Reason, Nature and Truth. Essentially, God and the supernatural were thrown out to be replaced with these human sublime values.

Reason was not worshipped. Instead, worship was reasonable, rather than based on a biblical fables and superstitions.[349] Antoine-Francois Momoro, a main proponent of the Cult of Reason, explained that

> *there is one thing that one must not tire telling people. Liberty, reason, truth are only abstract beings. They are not gods, for properly speaking, they are part of ourselves.*[350]

About 2,000 Catholic churches were transformed into Temples of Reason, including the Notre Dame in Paris. The Festival of Reason, which occurred on November 10, 1793, was created to spread the Cult of Reason beyond the Hébertists and sans-culottes to the rest of the French population. A few accounts are still available of the Festival, the one great religious event during the religion's brief tenure. The Festival of Reason was not supposed to be a religious event. The festival had

---

[347] The sans-culottes were working class radicals of Paris. Their name comes from that fact that they wore pants and not knee-breaches.

[348] Many of the American founding fathers were deists, including Franklin, Payne, Washington, Jefferson, Madison and Monroe.

[349] Charles Lyttle, "Deistic Piety in the Cults of the French Revolution," *Church History*, vol 2, no. 1. (March 1933), 23.

[350] Emmet Kennedy, *A Cultural History of the French Revolution*, (Yale University, 1989), 343.

been scheduled elsewhere but was hastily moved to Notre Dame. The opera provided most of the musicians and singers. Similar celebrations were held in the provinces, many of which were highly improvised and less extravagant.

If you were present at Notre Dame's Festival of Reason, you would have seen in front of the altar an artificial mountain decorated with trees and grottoes and topped with a columned structure labeled "To Philosophy." On the mountain were effigies of Voltaire, Rousseau, Franklin, and a small altar halfway bearing a torch of Truth. After music played, maidens in white dresses with tricolor sashes and flaming torches proceeded up the mountain to honor the effigies and altar. A woman dressed like the Goddess of Liberty appeared in the peristyle to receive their homage. The enthusiastic crowd then escorted the performers to the National Convention, where it was declared that Notre Dame would become "The Temple of Reason," celebrating reason over superstition.[351]

Maximilien Robespierre (1758–1794) and others felt that this farcical celebration would only give additional ammunition to the enemies of the Revolution. He dissuaded most members of the Assembly from attending the event. And that was the story of the much-maligned Festival of Reason.

But it appears that most accounts (in English, at least) are from critics. They should be taken with a grain of salt. These detractors claimed that the attendees had a field day, one even claiming that the actress representing Liberty was a courtesan. One contemporary wrote that he "did not attend the more than scandalous scenes which took place in the Church of Notre-Dame, where an actress of the Opera was incensed as a divinity, and I must say, at least half of the conventionnels refused to attend."[352] Thomas Carlyle, a hater of all things associated with the

---

[351] Lyttle, 24–25.

[352] Pierre Toussaint Durand Maillane, *Histoire de la Convention Nationale* (Baudouin Freres, 1825), 181–182, in Rodama: a blog of 18th-century & Revolutionary France, May 15, 2019, rodama1789.blogspot.com/2019/05/the-fete-de-la-raison-at-notre-dame.html.

French Revolution, wrote in 1837, "And the dancers, I exaggerate nothing, the dancers nigh bare of breeches, neck and breast naked, stockings down, went whirling and spinning, like those Dust-vortexes, forerunners of Tempest and Destruction."[353]

The slander and ridicule at the time were so bad that Robespierre denounced the Cult of Reason as "aristocratic atheism."[354] Even today, a large number of articles on the Cult of Reason focus on the licentious accounts, rather than on the mundane reality of what really happened.

Many thought that the French people had degenerated into animals during the revolutionary years. Gouverneur Morris (1752–1816), the American ambassador to France at the time, described revolutionary-era French character as "volatile, debauched, ferocious, and incapable of self-restraint."[355] They no longer had the Church to guide them. Robespierre realized that for smooth governing, the people must be virtuous, and this could come only by guiding them with a religion that was based in God. He liked to quote Voltaire: "If God did not exist, it would be necessary to invent him."[356]

Robespierre used the religious issue to publicly denounce many of the radicals not in his camp. Eventually he was able to send the de-Chrisitianizers to the guillotine in March 1794, just four months after the infamous Festival of Reason. Included among the dead were Hébert and Momoro. With their deaths, the Cult of Reason lost its most influential leadership and effectively ceased to exist. It was then replaced by Robespierre's deistic Cult of the Supreme Being, which

---

[353] Thomas Carlyle, *The French Revolution: A History*, Book 3, ch. 5, sec. IV, archive.org/details/frenchrevolution0000unse_x1w5/page/n7/mode/2up?q=breeches, accessed April 11, 2025.

[354] Lyttle, 26.

[355] Theodore Roosevelt, *Gouverneur Morris* (Arlington House, year unknown, but preface written in 1898), 162.

[356] I know it may seem surprising, but Robespierre, who is mostly remembered for executing his political enemies by guillotine, had a deep faith in God. He was repulsed by the atheistic reputation of the Cult of Reason.

worshipped the Supreme Being shorn of the "superstitions created by the Church." Robespierre preached the immortality of the soul, along with French revolutionary themes. His religion also had a grand festival, this time with Robespierre on the altar as the high priest. In his speech at the Festival of the Supreme Being, Robespierre said:

> *The day forever fortunate has arrived, which the French people have consecrated to the Supreme Being. Never has the world which He created offered to Him a spectacle so worthy of His notice. He has seen reigning on the earth tyranny, crime, and imposture. He sees at this moment a whole nation, grappling with all the oppressions of the human race, suspend the course of its heroic labors to elevate its thoughts and vows toward the great Being. . .Our blood flows for the cause of humanity. Behold our prayer. Behold our sacrifices. Behold the worship we offer Thee.*[357]

Revolutionary Paris was a special case in history. Rarely has a people experienced such a prolonged and complete chaotic breakdown of the way things used to be. November 1793 to May 1794 was a time of unrelenting instability, uncertainty, fear and rage. The revolutionaries had just murdered their King. The government had closed down the churches and its religious schools. All of France's frontiers were being attacked by royalist enemies. Civil war raged in the provinces. The people were beset by an unending stream of rumors of counter-revolutionary conspiracies by royalists and Catholics. And then there was the Terror—arbitrary arrest, public executions and riots in the streets. The country was wracked by economic collapse, and many were enraged and devastated by the loss of friends and family. With all that turmoil, perhaps it makes sense then that up to 500,000 people were said to attend the cult's inaugural event in Paris.[358] But adherence to the cult was political as well as regional. Support was centered in Paris. Robespierre's followers were more likely to join in, while his

---

[357] Robespierre, speech at the Festival of the Supreme Being, 1794, historyplace.com/speeches/robespierre.htm, accessed January 1, 2025.

[358] Many were coerced into attending.

opposition remained critical, some mocking his role as a high priest. In that hyper-political environment, to align with the cult would imply aligning with Robespierre, which his many opponents could not do.

Needless to say, the religion failed to capture the public's devotion. Robespierre, although a great speaker and writer, did not possess the charisma needed to ignite religious fervor in the hearts of the people. Nor did he have the time. The cult effectively lasted about two months and ended when Robespierre was arrested and executed by his enemies. After his death, supporters dropped away as it was dangerous to appear to be associated with him.

It takes decades for a successful religion to amass a tradition, a culture and a large following. The Cult of the Supreme Being only had a little over two months.

But the question is, were these cults really religions? The founders had hoped that they would be. But they died before they could attain critical mass.

The Way of the Future

It seems people are always trying to start religions. Most attempts just never make it out of obscurity. For example, just recently, in 2017, *Wired* magazine ran an article about a new church that is forming, which is called the Way of the Future. This church is to focus on a god based on Artificial Intelligence (AI). It's founder, Anthony Levandowski (1980–) said in an interview:

> *What is going to be created will effectively be a god...not a god in the sense that it makes lightning or causes hurricanes. But if there is something a billion times smarter than the smartest human, what else are you going to call it?*

He makes some good arguments:

> *There are many ways people think of God, and thousands of flavors of Christianity, Judaism, Islam...but they're always looking at*

something that's not measurable or you can't really see or control. This time it's different. This time you will be able to talk to God, literally, and know that it's listening.[359]

Levandowski says that like other religions, his church will eventually have a gospel, a liturgy and probably a physical place of worship. None of these has yet been developed.[360]

Religion vs. Spirituality

Should we consider Levandowski's church a religion? Wouldn't his church be purely intellectual? How would spirituality fit into such a church?

Perhaps it is time to discuss the difference between religion and spirituality. How do we separate them out? Certainly, many different views are held on this. As I see it, religion is a set of rites, traditions, hierarchy and stories about our relationship to the supernatural world. The framework of religious thought comes from outside of us, for example, from holy books, traditions or church decisions. Religion provides needed structure for our personal lives. And it happens to make societies run more smoothly as well. But a religion need not have much spirituality in it. Instead, a lot of thinking goes into religions in an attempt to make them palatable to a rational mind. And, as most people are non-peakers and rarely connected to the non-material spiritual world, the spiritual content has mostly been stripped out of religions.

Spirituality, in contrast, is based on the individuals' private relationship with God or the supernatural. So spirituality is indeed very individual. Spiritual people understand their own relationship to God in their own way, whereas the religious share the same understanding as taught by their tradition. Spiritual peak experiences touch us so deeply that

---

[359] Mark Harris, "Inside the First Church of Artificial Intelligence," *Wired*, Nov 15, 2017, wired.com/story/anthony-levandowski-artificial-intelligence-religion.

[360] Levandowski became preoccupied with other more pressing issues, so he closed the church in 2017. In 2023, he reopened it.

once we experience them, we are never quite the same. We gain more perspective. We develop depth in our understanding of ourselves and the world around us. Unlike in religion, spirituality offers no shared rules for what to believe or how to live. We learn our personal rules as we proceed. Spirituality is based in love for all as opposed to religions, which usually are based in compliance and fear.

Perhaps the difference is most simply stated by Deepak Chopra (1946–),

> *Religion is belief in someone else's experience. Spirituality is having your own experience.*

Religion is a group thing, whereas spirituality is an individual thing.

But spirituality is not always good for society. Whereas religions teach us to conform in ways that enhance society or at least the society of the church, peak experiences can lead people into individualistic, even anti-social, behavior. Jesus, Mohammed and Buddha, driven by their own communications with the Divine, broke all kinds of religious rules and were rejected by the greater society for doing so.

Rationality, as mentioned before, can attack, judge and destroy religions. Religions contain dogmas that a thinking mind can grasp and that a keen rational mind can shred. Religions are easily targeted by rationality, as they describe a worldview which can be challenged. Spirituality is completely foreign to rationality. It is not rational, does not attempt to present a coherent argument, and thus cannot be challenged by rationality. Spiritual experience offers nothing to argue with. Nothing for the sharp knife of rational thinking to rip. I suppose a thinker can call it hogwash and leave it at that, but that is not a reasoned response, just a judgement. Knowledge gained from mystical experience cannot be proven or disproven. Our senses cannot perceive anything associated with the experience. No deduction or induction is involved. It is just knowledge from within or from the supernatural realm, however you want to describe it.

Schweitzer was a mystic. He wrote:

No one can give a definition of the soul, but we know what it feels like. The soul is the sense of something higher than ourselves, something that stirs in us thoughts, hopes and aspirations which go out to the world of goodness, truth and beauty. The soul is a burning desire to breathe in this world of light and never to lose it—to remain children of light.[361]

This is deep. This non-rational type of thinking, this is what spirituality is all about. Rational thought cannot touch this.

So let's briefly return to the eugenics argument. The rational argument for sterilization was strong. But there are rational counterarguments, such as I have provided, and they work; but they, too, can be countered. Spiritual argument is unassailable. How can you counter the argument that life is sacred and all our actions should follow from that basic truth? No rational argument exists to be made either for or against it. It is innate knowledge. The only way for the rational mind to deal with any arguments based on this truth is to ignore them or dismiss them. You cannot address them head on with critical thinking. Or, I suppose you can embrace the darkness and deny the truth of the sacredness of life. But by doing so, your mask will be removed, and all will see you for what you are.

Intellectual vs. Intuitive

Perhaps a larger view of this split is in order. Rather than compare religion and spirituality, why not compare the sources of religion and spirituality, as both are just the products of their respective sources. Religion is a product of the intellect, whereas spirituality is a product of that other part of us that we can never fathom. Perhaps it is the soul. Perhaps it is the unconscious mind. Maybe they are the same thing. Maybe they are somehow related.[362]

---

[361] Albert Schweitzer, *Reverence for Life: Sermons 1900-1919* (Irvington, 1973), 78.

[362] Many traditions, including some esoteric approaches, and thinkers including Carl Jung and Paramahansa Yogananda, link the unconscious mind and the soul. They explain

Intellect and soul are separate ways of perceiving and understanding reality. Each captures a completely different representation of the world around us. Both provide us important information we need to survive and thrive in the world.

Arnold Toynbee (1889-1975), the British historian, wrote that

> there is a distinction between the two facets of truth…In the Human Psyche there are two organs: a conscious, volitional surface and a subconscious, non-volitional abyss. Each of these two organs has its own way of looking at, peering through, the dark glass that screens Reality from Man's inward eye and, in screening it, dimly reveals it; and therefore each mode of imperfect apprehension calls its finding "the Truth." But the qualities of the two different facets of a latent unitary truth are as different as the nature of the two organs of the human psyche that receives these 'broken lights.'[363]

The physicist J. Robert Oppenheimer (1904–1967) wrote about the very same thing:

> These two ways of thinking, the way of time and history and the way of eternity and timelessness, are both parts of man's efforts to comprehend the world in which he lives. Neither is comprehended in the other nor reducible to it. They are, as we have learned to say in physics, complementary views, each supplementing the other, neither telling the whole story.[364]

Lawrence Leshawn (1920–2020), in his book *The Medium, the Mystic and the Physicist* also explores these two different means of perceiving and

---

that there is a link between the soul and the unconscious or subconscious mind, that the stirrings and remembrances of the soul reach our conscious selves through the pathway of the unconscious mind.

[363] Arnold J. Toynbee, *An Historian's Approach to Religion*, (Oxford University, 1956), 27, in Lawrence Leshan, *The Medium, the Mystic and the Physicist, Toward a General Theory of the Paranormal*, (Arkana, 1974), 57–58.

[364] J. Robert Oppenheimer, *Science and the Common Understanding*, (Simon & Schuster, 1964), 6, in Leshan, 58.

understanding the world. The material, sensory-based, rational approach is great for designing rocket ships, organizing your daily calendar and generally functioning in the world. The intuitive, mystical approach is more useful to achieve a sense of serenity, a joy in living, a feeling of being fully at home in the world. It brings a deeper understanding of truth and develops our fullest ability to love.[365]

Perhaps you can say, the intuitive approach is akin to strategic thinking, while the sensory rational approach is akin to tactical thinking. When you apply the wrong type of perception to a problem, it doesn't work. Many hopeless mystics can never function effectively in the modern world. Running a profitable business, navigating an airport, or cooking from a recipe could be disastrous without a rational orientation. The person who is limited to only rational thinking may be completely competent in the material and social worlds, run profitable businesses, never miss a plane and be an expert cook but may be ultimately unsatisfied because life lacks meaning and their soul feels empty.

Ideally, we want to be fully integrated, to have both modes of perception and cognition working for us, each in its own sphere. Then we can be competent in the world and have a meaningful context in which to use our competency.

But the problem with most modern people (and perhaps most people of the past few hundred years) is that we operate solely within the rational sphere and give little to no mind to any stirrings not based in our senses or rational thinking. Most of us push these inklings down, cover them up, ignore them, as they are often threatening. They do not fit into our rational understanding of the world. As I wrote in an earlier essay, these are the non-peakers—these are most of us. And because we block the unconscious from entering our lives, we are much more likely to never experience the oneness of a mystical experience.

---

[365] Leshan *60*.

The Peakers' Experience

Remember the man who escaped Plato's cave? He was a peaker. He was able to free himself, leave the one-dimensional world of the cave and experience the fuller reality outside. He was a changed man due to his new knowledge. He wanted to share his new truth with the others who only knew the shadow reality of the cave. Mystics, or peakers, are like that man. For a short while, they remove the blinders of the material world and enter the world of the Spirit. The cave inmates, then, are like the rest of us, who continue to experience a unidimensional life solely through senses and logic.

The peakers have experienced a more complete reality than the rest of us. Most of them keep silent about it to avoid ridicule or loss of prestige. That is the easier route. But some peakers take on a mission to share their experience with others, no matter what the cost to themselves. These are often the prophets of new religions.

So, again, what is it that peakers experience? Words cannot adequately convey the intensity of the experience. But many have tried. These descriptions of mystical experiences are unique, as they are filtered through the peaker's schemas. Their descriptions are tempered by the peaker's personal outlook, their society and their historical time. But if you can see beyond the limitations of the peakers' schemas, you will notice that stories of peak experience share commonalities across all religions, cultures and eras.

William James, an American founding father of psychology, addressed mystical experiences in his *Varieties of Religious Experience*, a series of lectures on the various aspects of religion, delivered from 1901 to 1902. In his lectures, he quotes from several acquaintances who have had mystical experiences.

Here's one account:

> *These highest experiences that I have had of God's presence have been rare and brief—flashes of consciousness which have compelled me to exclaim with surprise—God is here!—or conditions of exaltation*

and insight, less intense, and only gradually passing away. I have severely questioned the worth of these moments. To no soul have I named them, lest I should be building my life and work on mere phantasies of the brain. But I find that, after every questioning and test, they stand out today as the most real experiences of my life and experiences which have explained and justified and unified all past experiences and all past growth. Indeed, their reality and their far-reaching significance are ever becoming more clear and evident. When they came, I was living the fullest, strongest, sanest, deepest life. I was not seeking them. What I was seeking, with resolute determination, was to live more intensely my own life, as against what I knew would be the adverse judgment of the world. It was in the most real seasons that the Real Presence came, and I was aware that I was immersed in the infinite ocean of God.[366]

And another from a Canadian psychiatrist:

Directly afterward there came upon me a sense of exultation, of immense joyousness accompanied or immediately followed by an intellectual illumination impossible to describe. Among other things, I did not merely come to believe, but I saw that the universe is not composed of dead matter, but is, on the contrary, a living Presence; I became conscious in myself of eternal life. It was not a conviction that I would have eternal life, but a consciousness that I possessed eternal life then; I saw that all men are immortal; that the cosmic order is such that without any peradventure all things work together for the good of each and all; that the foundation principle of the world, of all the worlds, is what we call love, and that the happiness of each and all is in the long run absolutely certain. The vision lasted a few seconds and was gone; but the memory of it and the sense of the reality of what it taught has remained during the quarter of a century which has since elapsed. I knew that what

---

[366] J. Trevor, "The Autobiography of J. Trevor," in William James, *Varieties of Religious Experience* (Green & Co., 1917), 389.

> *the vision showed was true. I had attained to a point of view from which I saw that it must be true. That view, that conviction, I may say that consciousness, has never, even during periods of the deepest depression, been lost.*[367]

Another wrote,

> *The One remains, the many change and pass; and each and every one of us is the One that remains. . .This is ultimatum.*"[368]

It doesn't get more mystical than that.

You don't have to be a saint or a prophet to have a mystical experience. Ordinary people have them. But how do you know you have experienced a mystical experience and not just some hallucination or drug experience? Below are eleven defining characteristics of a mystical experience.[369]

1. You feel a conscious unity. Your boundaries and your individual identity vanish. You feel as if you are one with everything and everyone around you.

2. Your sense of time changes. You no longer perceive time as you did, but as a stream of eternal present moments. You feel a part of time.

3. Your sense of space changes. Space becomes endless. Your identity is gone. Your ability to separate your surroundings into separate elements disappears.

4. As you no longer see the world from your own perspective, you are seeing it as a whole, objectively, and it is perfect.

5. You feel an awe, perhaps gratitude, at your insignificance as just a small part of the vast universe, and that you get to play a part in all of it.

---

[367] Dr. R. M. Bucke, *Cosmic Consciousness: A Study in the Evolution of the Human Mind* (Citadel, 1901), cited in James, 391.

[368] James, 378–379.

[369] I paraphrased these characteristics from Mateo Sol, "9 Signs You've Had a Mystical Experience," *Lonerwolf,* lonerwolf.com/mystical-experience, accessed January 1, 2024. In doing so, I dropped one and added a few.

6. Having experienced this miracle of consciousness, you feel a new respect for the sacredness of life.

7. You are filled with overwhelming love for all people and everything.

8. Your everyday sense of individuality creates a duality in your thinking. There is you and there is that; but once you become merged with everything, your thinking changes. You find paradoxes, for example, something is both here and absent, both human and divine. In understanding these paradoxes, you experience mind-blowing realizations.[370]

9. You cannot describe the experience with words. You can try; but it usually, if not always, appears trite. Words cannot give the experience the justice it deserves.

10. The experience doesn't last. You get perhaps minutes, perhaps an hour or more. But you have to go back to everyday life.

11. The experience is life-changing. Death is no longer as scary as it was. Your prior ordinary beliefs and ambitions, which you once held to be so important, lose their meaning. You may want to try to bring as much of the mystical experience as possible back into your day-to-day life.

To those of you who have not had a peak or mystical experience, you are missing something intensely profound and meaningful. The good news is that there are ways to increase the chance that you may have one.

Pursuit of peak experiences reminds me of the days of my youth when I was seeking love. Whenever I tried, I could never find it. I was always left alone and disheartened. Love always found me when I wasn't actively looking. It is the same with mysticism. Yet, just like you can change basic habits that will make you more likely to meet your soulmate, you can establish practices in your life that will increase the chances that you may be struck by a peak experience.

---

[370] I never experienced this one, so I find it difficult to describe.

Despite Maslow saying the experiences could not be induced, his students often had them, perhaps because they were actively thinking about them.[371] This fact made Colin Wilson (1931–2013) believe that you could force a peak experience. He published his last book on this topic in 2009, *Super Consciousness: The Quest for the Peak Experience*. According to Wilson, if you have a period of unbearable tension that is suddenly dropped, in that time of relief, you might encounter your peak experience. For example, Russian roulette is likely a great peak experience inducer.[372] (I am not suggesting you point a gun to your head. Don't do it.)

Wrapping It Up

- Although societies need religion to promote order, religions do not offer spirituality, just doctrines, hierarchy and practices. Religions instill values from sources outside of ourselves, such as tradition or holy writings, which we often struggle with and doubt. On the other hand, spirituality gives us a personal irrefutable meaning through direct contact with the Divine.

- Rationality cannot fathom mystical experiences and can only scrutinize religions, which are very different. Under the lens of rationality, religions become convoluted stories, silly rituals and heinous histories of abuse. Religions by nature are flawed and the sharp knife of rationality carves them to pieces. In contrast, rational argument cannot assail arguments based on intuition or spiritually acquired knowledge.

- Rationality is a dead end that leads to efficient, but often heartless and destructive thinking. Thinking purely rationally, other people can become disposable objects that either help or stand in the way of achieving our objectives. Rational thinking can lead

---

[371] My guess is that the constant bombardment of information from cellphones and the internet so clutter our minds that we are not able to enter into peak experiences as much as we did in past centuries.

[372] Colin Wilson, "Maslow, Sheldrake and Peak Experience," *Critique: A Journal of Conspiracies and Metaphysics*, January 8, 2019, https://tinyurl.com/2c6cuvdv.

to rationally rigorous but morally questionable outcomes, such as murder, eugenics or mass sterilization to reach a desired end.

❧ Attempts have been made to replace traditional religion with reason-based alternatives, such as the Cult of Reason during the French Revolution. They have not lasted.

❧ Though in the twenty-first century we may no longer realize it, rational thinking is not the only way to think, or even the best way to think. Intuitive knowledge is a different approach to the problems of the day.

❧ Life is sacred. This understanding of the sacredness of life is an intuitive truth that perhaps we all share. It is also one that is strongly reinforced through mystical experience.

❧ From the postulate that life is sacred, rational arguments for eugenics or sterilization can be overcome.

❧ Peak experiences or mystical encounters provide insight beyond rational understanding. People try, but these experiences cannot be communicated adequately in words, as they are so much more profound than our words can express.

❧ While peak experiences cannot be forced, certain practices may increase the likelihood of having them.

❧ Rational thinking is useful to navigate the world and accomplish our goals. Intuitive perception is useful to give purpose to life and to establish a general framework of meaningfulness. The complete person utilizes both types of knowledge, but most in today's world live only in the sensory rational mode and may be competent, but unfulfilled and empty inside.

Essay 10
The Profound Depths of History: From Mystical Insights to the Evolution of Consciousness

If you didn't know history, you didn't know anything.
You were a leaf that didn't know it was part of a tree.
— MICHAEL CRICHTON

A Mystical Understanding of History

There are two types of knowledge—the left-brained, analytical type, that relies on the senses, and the right-brained intuitive type, which just comes to you. When it comes to history, what do we have? We have books, verbal traditions and artifacts. Left brain thinking relies on these and mostly uses analytical thinking—along with some creativity (made-up stuff) in there—to understand the past. The other way to gain knowledge…well, it just comes to you as dreams, intuitions or mystical experiences.

Newton's famed apple falling from the tree led to that "aha" moment and his new law of gravity. Einstein valued periods of unstructured reflection. He would allow his mind to wander freely exploring new connections that would emerge spontaneously. This type of free thinking can work for the historian as well. It seems that the great visionary historians of the twentieth century, Arnold Toynbee (1889–1975) and Oswald Spengler (1880–1936) used their right brains extensively, and it came out in their writings. Toynbee described ten different mystical experiences he had experienced regarding history in Volume 10 of his *A Study of History.*

Toynbee and the Vast Tide of History

Toynbee was not shy about sharing his mystical experiences.

> *In London in the southern section of the Buckingham Palace Road, walking southward along the pavement skirting the west wall of Victoria Station, the writer [that's Toynbee] once, one afternoon not long after the date of the First World War…had found himself in communion, not just with this or that episode in History, but with all that had been, and was, and was to come. In that instant he was directly aware of the passage of History gently flowing through him in a mighty current, and of his own life welling like a wave in the flow of this vast tide…An instant later, the communion had ceased, and the dreamer was back again in the everyday cockney world which was his native social milieu.*[373]

As we shall see, this mystical sense of timelessness greatly influenced his approach to history.

Mystical Experience – the Story Remains the Same

I suppose I had a similar experience.

When I was in my early twenties, I spent the night with my brother and some of his friends at the beach. We had all eaten psilocybin mushrooms, something I had never tried before. My brother and his

---

[373] Toynbee, *A Study of History, Volume X, (Oxford, 1954), 130-140.*

friends got high and wandered off, but I felt nothing. My memory is sketchy of what happened next, but the mushrooms did work. I only remember the end of the experience. It was about four a.m. when I found myself lying in the sand, face down with "O Que Será," a song by Milton Nascimento and Chico Buarque, repeating in my mind. It might be the most profound song ever written. It certainly was to me that night. But let's get back to the beach. There I was, lying down. The haunting trumpets and the mournful foreign voices repeating over and over. They seemed to echo the vastness of everything; yet, at the same time, the sad, limited nature of our lives, that no matter what we try to do, we are trapped in our time and constrained by our fates. I viewed my life from a timeless spirit's perspective. I saw how I was young and how I would fall in love in my youth, marry, have children, work, dream of things, and then die, and how my father was playing out the same pattern before me, and how his father had played it out before him, and so on, back through the generations. It was then that I realized our profound connection to history, how we are all living the same story, generation after generation, over and over again. And to me it appeared so sad. What seems so exciting and important to us is in reality so small and insignificant from this greater perspective. We all die, and everything about us will be forgotten. This transcendent vision of our lives is so beautiful, as this is our story that we repeat, generation after generation. We each take our turn in this dance of life, then fade away; and the next generation takes our place, repeating our dreams, struggles and triumphs once again, just as we repeated the story of our parents. That is when I understood that history, all of human history, was my story. As we all share in this sacred ritual of living, we are all family. It is this—our common dreams, loves, failures, fears and deaths—that makes us human. And when we forget our shared story, our commonness, we fool ourselves with our self-importance. It is really all about "us," not "me." It was then that I fell in love with history—not as a retelling of names and dates, but as our story.

Perhaps our relationship to history can be compared to the relationship of ocean water to the ocean wave. The present, and all the people living in the present, are like the water molecules on the crest of an ocean wave as it rolls into shore. An instant passes; the wave moves on towards its destination. And new group of water molecules takes its place as the crest of the wave. Meanwhile, those who were formerly at the crest of the wave have been left behind, forgotten, just like our never-ending stream of forbearers, left behind in the stillness of the past.

It Was All Done Before

My profound experience is not that unusual. It has been experienced before, countless times. Toynbee felt it. So did Rosalind Murray a writer who happened to be Toynbee's wife. Murray wrote a poem that appears in Volume X of Toynbee's *A Study of History*. In an introduction to the poem, Toynbee wrote of "a sense of personal communion with all men and women at all times and places, which outranges the gamut of an historian's prose, but is articulate in a poem which was already familiar and dear to the writer of this Study at the time when that ineffable experience travelled through him."[374]

Here's the poem:

> *Men laughed in Ancient Egypt, long ago,*
> *And laughed beside the Lake of Galilee,*
> *And my glad heart rejoices more to know,*
> *When it leaps up in exultation too,*
> *That, though the laugher and the laugh be new,*
> *The joy is old as is the ancient sea.*
>
> *Men wept in noble Athens, so they say,*
> *And in great Babylon of many towers,*
> *For the same sorrows that we feel today;*
> *So, stranded high upon Time's latest peak,*
> *I can with Babylonian and with Greek*
> *Claim kinship through this common grief of ours.*

---

[374] Toynbee, vol. 10, 40.

The same fair moon I look upon to-night,
This shining golden moon above the sea,
Imparts a richer and more sweet delight
For all the eyes it did rejoice of old,
For all the hearts, long centuries grown cold,
That shared this joy which now it gives to me.

Whate'er I feel I cannot feel alone.
When I am happiest or most forlorn,
Uncounted friends whom I have never known
Rejoicing stand or grieving at my side,
These nameless, faceless friends of mine who died
A thousand years or more e'er I was born.[375]

History Repeats Itself – Nothing New

Just as Rosalind Murray wrote, history tells the same old stories over and over again. New faces, old stories. We can think about it abstractly, but perhaps it might hit home a bit more if I relate a story that happened a long time ago that could have happened today. I am going to relate an eyewitness account of the Fourth Crusade (1202–1204 CE). First, I will set the scene, so you have some context. Then the eyewitness account. What you read in it—it could have happened yesterday in any war zone.

The Fourth Crusade – More of the Same

The story of the Fourth Crusade is laughable and tragic. The crusader armies' original plan was to recapture Muslim-controlled Jerusalem for the Christian world. On their way to Jerusalem, the crusaders passed through Constantinople, the capital of the Eastern Roman Empire, which had deposed its emperor seven years before. Constantinople had 500,000 inhabitants, making it one of the largest cities of that time. Before they reached the city, the crusader leaders entered into

---

[375] Poem by Rosalind Murry found in Toynbee vol. 10, 40.

an agreement with a Byzantine prince sent out to meet them. They would help him restore his father as emperor in Constantinople. And in exchange, the Byzantine royal family, after returning to rule, would supply money and military aid to support the crusade. According to plan, the crusaders then defeated Byzantium and restored the prince and his father as co-emperors. And the money flowed to the crusader leaders. Everything was working perfectly. A few months later the people of Byzantium again deposed the father and son and replaced them with someone else. Now, as the Byzantine prince and his father were no longer in power, they could no longer pay the crusaders as agreed. So the crusaders returned to Byzantium and attacked it to get what was coming to them. The new Byzantine emperor lined up for battle with his army, grossly outnumbering the crusader army, but he lost his nerve and fled without fighting. The Byzantines then restored their old emperors, the same ones the crusaders had installed on the throne, but the crusaders did not stop fighting. They were angry. They sacked and plundered the city.

A historian wrote,

> *For three days they murdered, raped, looted and destroyed on a scale which even the ancient Vandals and Goths would have found unbelievable. Constantinople had become a veritable museum of ancient and Byzantine art, an emporium of such incredible wealth that the Latins were astounded at the riches they found. Though the Venetians had an appreciation for the art that they discovered (they were themselves semi-Byzantines) and saved much of it, the French and others destroyed indiscriminately, halting to refresh themselves with wine, violation of nuns and murder of Orthodox clerics. The Crusaders vented their hatred for the Greeks most spectacularly in the desecration of the greatest Church in Christendom. They smashed the silver iconostasis, the icons and the holy books of Hagia Sophia and seated upon the patriarchal throne a whore who sang coarse songs as they drank wine from the Church's holy vessels. The estrangement of East and West,*

which had proceeded over the centuries, culminated in the horrible massacre that accompanied the conquest of Constantinople. The Greeks were convinced that even the Turks, had they taken the city, would not have been as cruel as the Latin Christians.[376]

We will see about that last statement later.

The snippet that follows is an eye-witness account by Nikitas Khoniatis about an unfortunate event that occurred during this sack of Byzantium by the crusader army. Much of the best history is from personal narratives, where the reader can envision the experiences and empathize with the writer who lived through them. Khoniatis was one of a party of refugees trying to make a dangerous escape from the city of Byzantium during the war.

One of their number, a girl, was kidnapped before their helpless eyes by Frankish soldiers. Our writer was making a hopeless attempt to rescue her. After all, he had no power, no weapons. He was just another refugee.

Our chief anxiety was for the women, so we had put them in the middle of our party with a cordon of men outside and had instructed the girls to smear their faces with dirt [in order to conceal their sexual attractions from the Frankish soldiery's eyes]. . .We were bound for the Golden Gate; but, when we had got about as far as the church of Mocius the Martyr, a barbarian. . .snatched a beautiful girl from among us. She was a judge's daughter. . .and her father, whose stamina had been broken by old age and sickness, had slipped and fallen in a puddle and was now lying there crumpled up, lamenting aloud and plastered with mud. He kept on looking at me as if he were expecting at least some show of assistance from me, and he began to call upon me by name to do anything that I could to help him to retrieve his daughter. So I turned back there and then, without more ado, and started to follow at the kidnapper's heels, weeping and denouncing at the top of my voice the crime that had

---

[376] Speros Bryonis, *Byzantine and Europe*, 1967, Harcourt and Brace, 152.

just been committed. As I went, I made supplication to any passing soldiers of the Frankish army who were not altogether ignorant of our [Modern Greek] tongue—trying to induce them to come to the rescue and taking some of them by the hand, till I had managed to work upon the feelings of some of them so far as to prevail upon them to form a posse for the pursuit of that lecherous beast. I led the way with my posse behind me; we arrived at the villain's billet; and then he pushed the girl inside and took his stand at the gates in a truculent posture. . .When my companions told him with some vigour to give the girl back, his first reply was an insolent refusal. Two imperious passions—lust and rage—had him fast in their grip; but, when he saw that the men were losing their tempers, and heard them threatening him with impalement for misconduct aggravated by contumacy, and when he was convinced that they were really in earnest, he reluctantly yielded and gave the girl up! [377]

The point of this anecdote is to convey that what happened in the past was real then; but you can imagine, this can still happen today. The nature of humanity, and the things we do, remain constant in history. The same people who exist today could have existed centuries ago. How many times in history has this exact same event taken place? It is still taking place today in our modern wars. Over and over again. The wheel keeps on turning. Same old stories, but with new faces and new gadgets.

120 Generations of Cyclical History

Ecclesiastes, certainly my favorite book in the Old Testament, was written sometime between 450 and 200 BCE, which is about 120 generations ago. Around that time, Socrates, Alexander the Great and Scipio Africanus walked the Earth. Since then, nothing really has changed. The truths remain the same:

---

[377] Toynbee, *A Study of History*, Volume 10, 133-134, where he quotes from Nikitas Khoniátis, *Narrative of Events after the Capture of the City*, Immanuel Bekker's edition (Weber, Bonn, 1835) 779-782.

What has been will be again,
what has been done will be done again;
there is nothing new under the sun.
Is there anything of which one can say,
"Look! This is something new"?
It was here already, long ago;
it was here before our time.
No one remembers the former generations,
and even those yet to come
will not be remembered
by those who follow them. [378]

Our Insignificance in the Greater Story

In that never-ending cycle of the generations of humanity, then, any individual, even you, is of little consequence. We live our lives. We affect the lives of others around us. Our dreams, our choices, ripple forward, minutely altering humanity's trajectory. And then we die. Those that continue to live will remember us. And when they die, so will any lingering memories of us die with them.

Years ago, I was presenting these ideas during a seven-minute Toastmasters speech, and my audience found this concept depressing. Really? Did they really think their lives mattered? Every thought we have, every desire we have, every action we take, has been thought, desired, acted upon countless times throughout the ages. In light of that, why should we matter? It is amazing to me how we are able to maintain such fantasies about our importance.

Even the famous among us, our politicians, athletes and movie stars, not to mention writers, will all be forgotten in time—most of us within a generation or two after our deaths. For a very few of us, our names will be remembered, perhaps our achievements, but knowledge of who we

---

[378] Ecclesiastes 1:9-1:11, *The Bible*, New International Version.

really were will vanish.[379] We all know who Alexander the Great was, but do we know whether he liked to tell jokes or sing songs? Or what type of people really bothered him? No. We don't have a clue about his actual person. All that remains are some stories of things he did, usually written by people who never met him.

Throughout the course of human history, it is not just individuals, but even societies, cultures and nations also, that are born, struggle, thrive, die and are forgotten. Most history has been forgotten and lost.

Even the Great Cities are Forgotten

The city of Nineveh was mentioned in the Book of Genesis, where it says Nimrod built it. It became the capital of the Assyrian Empire. The Book of Jonah describes Nineveh as an "exceedingly great city of three days' journey in breadth,"[380] whose population was more than 120,000.

Nineveh was the largest city in the world for about fifty years, until the year 612 BCE when it was brutally sacked by its former subject peoples. When Xenophon (c. 403–355 BCE) passed the city with his Greek soldiers 250 years later, the city was abandoned and the people living nearby didn't know anything about it, not even its name.

Xenophon described the great ruins as

> *a large undefended fortification near a city called Mescila…The base of this fortification was made of polished stone in which there were many shells. It was fifty feet broad and fifty feet high. On top of it was built a brick wall fifty feet in breadth and a hundred feet high. The perimeter of the fortification was eighteen miles.*[381]

---

[379] The reader might counter that this last statement contradicts nearly every paragraph in these essays, as I have countlessly referred to individuals and societies in the past that are still remembered. But, alas, their time will come as well. From the great civilizations of Ur, Sumer and the Nile, how many great athletes, painters, and master craftsmen do we still remember? I think none.

[380] In the book of Jonah, God sent the reluctant Jonah to the wicked city to preach to the Ninevites of their coming destruction if they did not repent.

[381] Xenophon, *The Persian Expedition*, Book 3, Chapter 4 (Penguin Books, 1949) 118.

Xenophon never realized that the city he passed was once the heart of the great Assyrian empire.

In the 1,500-year span covered in Gibbon's *Decline and Fall of the Roman Republic*, tens of thousands of cities, communities and peoples who lived, thrived, loved and suffered perished and have been forgotten, even by historians—the very people who are supposed to remember. Tens of thousands of towns and cities have been abandoned to dust. Today, it is as if these peoples and communities never existed.

If towns, cities, even great cities like Ninevah were forgotten by succeeding generations, why would we think we would be remembered by posterity?

History Constrains and Determines Who We Are

When a baby is born into a family, it is born into a world of the physical, mental, emotional and spiritual. All of these components contribute to forming the child's outlook on the world: The home and the family's possessions. The family's relationship to other people, to the government, to their employers, to their god. The family's beliefs about life and their destinies. All of these factors influence how the child thinks, what the child thinks is possible and ultimately who the child becomes. The family's historical experience is a large determiner of the destiny of the child. But not the only influence.

On a larger scale, we are born into the human family, schooled in our collective history, infused with our society's political philosophies, religious beliefs and general worldview, all of which combine to shape our identity and approach to living.

Our legal systems, our financial systems, our governments, our cities, our buildings, our machines, our languages, our sciences, our mathematics, our religious systems—everything devised by humanity that existed at the time of our birth—was handed to us by previous generations. These gifts from the past comprise the external and interior worlds that we navigate. Our minds are formed by and constrained by these inherited systems.

The actions of those who came before us provide the backdrop of our lives. History, then, is integral to our individual stories. It surrounds us in everything we see. It forms the majority of our worldview, of our thoughts even, although we may not realize it.

If you have ever tried to meditate, you probably noticed that your mind won't stop thinking, at least for the first fifteen minutes. If you were able to record your thoughts, I bet that the majority of them would be linked to history. Thoughts of Jesus, Allah, driving, voting, eating cheeseburgers, what you should wear tonight, the moles eating your cucumber plants, the latest plot of a TV series, the basketball game. All of these reflections are tied to the innovations of other people, most of whom are no longer alive. Someone wrote the holy books, invented the car, developed democratic institutions, conceived the cheeseburger, etc. That is what I mean by mentally constrained—there's hardly anything we can ponder that hasn't been shaped by our collective past. Very few things you can think of exist outside of our shared historical legacy, other than any mystical experiences we might have been blessed with.

We think we have free will. But, as you can see, our will is constrained by our historical context. In ancient Nineveh, slavery was the poor person's fate. Today, even the poor can strive to become a senator, a computer gamer or an astronaut, but only because earlier generations have opened those doors of possibility.

In this way, all of us who inhabit, have inhabited or will inhabit this world are inextricably linked to one another. We all affect one another. What the dead have done constrains what we can do. What we do constrains what the as-yet-unborn will do. We can only do what our history allows. The American historian David Mccullough (1933–2022) summed it up when he said, "History is who we are and why we are the way we are."[382]

---

[382] This quote is cited at the University of Memphis History Department webpage,

Meaning and History

I suppose many of you found high school history class to be tedious. For many it was just memorization of names and dates that felt pointless as a teenager. Some say that history is biased, as indeed written history is. And, here, I am saying that history is very important. It has formed our worlds and our minds and our trajectories in life. But we are talking about different things.

What Do I Mean by History?

When we are not clear with our words, we can get confused. For example, the word "love" has many meanings and using the term can confuse people. The love of a friend, a child, a soulmate, a hobby, a new car, a place, a vocation—these are profoundly different qualities. If I, an older man, told a younger woman that I loved her, I might mean it as a father loves a daughter, but she could well interpret it as I am hoping to marry her.

Well, "history" has a similar problem. History means different things to different people. To keep it clear, I have come up with three different terms for history. My three types of history are written history, ancestral history and absolute history.

Written History

Written history, as you read in books, is to some extent contrived. Unlike chemists and physicists, historians cannot set up and observe events repeatedly until they get it right. Historical events only happened once. And most likely, a long time ago. Historians are left with only fragments of information, which must be put together into some

---

although they do not cite where it came from. https://www.memphis.edu/history/about/history_is.php, accessed October 20, 2024. It is also found at the University of Illinois History Department website. Given McCullough's prolific career as a historian and author, it's likely that he used this phrase or variations of it in multiple speeches, interviews or writings over the years. The consistency with which it's attributed to him across various sources suggests that it's a sentiment he expressed frequently.

kind of unified story. So historians impose a narrative structure on the story, which may not have ever existed in reality. In real life, thousands of trends, events and movements are all occurring at the same time. The historian ignores almost all of them and focuses on just a few that are considered to be significant. And no historian can view historical events with a neutral mind. Each historian will put the fragments together to tell a different story to some extent corresponding to their own personal worldview. And as we know, history is written by the winners. Of course, it is biased.

So, in this essay am I referring to these somewhat accurate, but somewhat inaccurate, history books when I speak of history? Not at all. I use anecdotes from written history often. But that is the extent of it.

Ancestral History

Another kind of history fundamentally contributes to who we are as people. I call it ancestral history, which is really a shared cultural memory of a people. Ancestral history contributes to the mental and emotional environment we live in. We carry ancestral history within us. Nations carry ancestral history with them. Peoples don't forget. Ask the Irish what they think of the English. They haven't forgotten the centuries of abuse. Or ask the French what they think of the Germans. They suffered humiliating invasions over and over again. Their youth were slaughtered. Their towns and cities were destroyed. Ask the descendants of American slaves what they think about white America. Ancestral history lives within us, regardless of what is written in books.

Where does this kind of history come from? It can originate from the narratives of our family repeated to us when we were children. It may come from films, television shows and podcasts that portray people who look like us or talk like us. Also, some sort of supernatural connection shared by families, peoples or nations may be at play. I don't know. But ancestral memories are strong and can cause us to behave in ways that seem irrational to outsiders. These ancestral histories, biased, individualized and usually not written in books, are what shape our individual and communal worldviews, more so than the histories we read in school. Ancestral history is powerful. It tempers our perception of the world. A negative ancestral history can keep a group down.

In my own case, my father's family was of Mexican descent. In the American society of the 1940s, 1950s and 1960s, Mexicans were considered less human and of less value than white people. Remember, they were sterilizing Mexican women in California in the 1960s. This racism still persists in some parts of the United States.

In the 1930s, my Mexican grandfather was in the hospital for tuberculosis. He died in a hospital after they took all his ribs out on one side in an experimental procedure. But that didn't kill him. It was the blood transfusion. They gave him the wrong kind of blood. Did this happen to Caucasians, too? Perhaps. But for those who were shunned as "dirty Mexicans," who lived on the other side of the tracks from the whites, it was easy for them to believe that an unfortunate death like that only happened to people like them. From this story and many other familial stories of poverty, hardship and disdain from the greater white society, it would be easy to unknowingly pick up the unconscious belief that you are less than other people. To our kind, the doors to success, ease and security can appear closed, when they might really be open.

Regardless of race or nationality, if you believe the doors to wealth and power are closed to you, they will be. If you believe that they are not, then they won't be. If you come from a group that carries historic memories of hardship or oppression, it is natural that these ancestral memories can develop into limiting beliefs for you. And you can live a lifetime never even knowing these deep-seated beliefs are there and, if you do, you probably won't realize where they came from.

Deep-seated beliefs, shaped by ancestral history, are carried forward through generations, often silently influencing how we see ourselves and our place in the world. The powerful, unwritten force of ancestral history molds our identities and communal bonds, for better or worse.

Absolute History

Finally, there is absolute history, which is human history as seen from the perspective of the heavens. Absolute history encompasses all that transpires both on the earth and beyond. Absolute history is objective truth. It is what actually happens and is rarely recorded correctly in books as written history or in the memory of peoples as ancestral history.

Absolute history is without beginning and without end. While we live, we are afloat in the current of time. And absolute history is the ongoing story we play a part in. The story is great, and we are small. It outlives us. We die, and the current continues.

Does History Have Meaning?

The big question is, can any pattern be found in the absolute history of humanity? In the big story? Throughout the centuries, the Western tradition has had many different views of absolute history, but the three basic views of history are cyclical, linear and chaotic.

The Ancient Greeks' Cyclical History

Ancient Greek writers like Plato, Pythagoras and Thucydides claimed that there were patterns in history and that they repeat. Pythagoras believed that the world was repeatedly destroyed and then restored. The same events would occur during each regeneration. Similar people from different ages would do the same thing forever. He thought that there was no beginning of time, but that the universe was eternal in the past. Aristotle also believed history to be cyclical since he saw cycles everywhere in nature. Even Ecclesiastes says everything is cyclical.[383] These philosophers found the cycles meaningful in their own philosophies, but they did not envision humanity progressing towards any ultimate goal.

---

[383] I found a good treatment of this in Ashley Brydone-Jack's thesis, "A Christian Philosophy of History: St. Augustine and The City of God," 2017, https://tinyurl.com/2ogvysbj, accessed January 1, 2024.

Augustine's Linear History

Saint Augustine wrote his book *The City of God* as an attempt to explain why God allowed Alaric the Visigoth to sack Rome in 410. Many in Augustine's time blamed Christianity for downfall of Rome. As they saw it, the gods had forsaken Rome because the pagan temples had become abandoned as the empire had become Christianized. Augustine took more of an overarching view of the situation. Rather than merely respond to the specifics of the downfall of the Roman State, he reexamined history in general and how this event fit within the entire framework of history.

Breaking with the ancient observations, Augustine claimed that history is linear and not cyclical. Instead, the story of history is the story of the redemption of humankind after our pivotal failure in the Garden of Eden. Humankind's redemption plays out over thousands of years, over hundreds of generations as documented in the Bible—from Adam to Noah to Moses to Jesus himself.

And today, in the Christian tradition, we continue to play a part in this linear evolution. Historical events flow towards this ultimate goal of redemption—the Final Judgement, which will send the worldly to hell and the godly to heaven. This view of linear absolute history is deeply embedded in Christianity. If you think about it, Augustine's concept of history being linear is logical, orderly; and it serves as a convenient framework for Christian theology. It is a fundamental belief underpinning Christian doctrines, although many practitioners may not realize that they have adopted this historical viewpoint.

A Materialist View of History

With the advent of science in the seventeenth century came the materialist view of the world, where people and animals were seen as machines, with no spirit or soul.

Let's assume for a moment that we are materialists. That is, we believe that the only things that exist are made of matter and that science is the only way to describe our world. We could then say that there is no spiritual world. That God is a myth for weak people who need consolation during difficult times. There is no ultimate meaning out there. Seeking ultimate meaning is a fool's quest, when science has most of it already figured out, or at least will someday.

Now, how would a strict materialist view history? It would lack ultimate purpose.[384] Change occurs, but not progress if progress means a broad movement toward a deeper spiritual communion with God (or the Universe, whatever you want to call it). In strict materialism, no such end exists, as spiritual goals, nay, everything of the spirit, are rejected.

If materialists believed in the spiritual world, then there could be an end goal, but materialists don't go there. According to the materialist theory of evolution, we are the product of random mutations and natural selection. Humans are here by chance, not design. From this perspective, humanity doesn't matter. You don't matter and I don't matter.

I suppose a materialist could believe in natural laws that pertain to human societies. Perhaps like people, societies are birthed, develop and die, but to no great end. The stories of societies, just like the stories of individuals, would be random and meaningless. We live, we die, we are buried and we are forgotten. And mostly, nothing matters. History is aimless, meaningless and heading nowhere in particular.

Humanity's Need for Meaning

I have a hard time believing that absolute history is aimless. Most of us believe there is some point to it, even if they don't know what it could be.

---

[384] There are many flavors of materialism, and I don't want to get us lost in the weeds here. If I explain them all, then we will lose the point I am trying to make. When I speak of materialists I am speaking of reductive materialists. An obvious criticism is that Marx is a historical materialist, and Marx did see meaning in history. His end goal was social and economic equality through political systems, but not spiritual evolution.

Throughout history we have continued to identify patterns and create systems for everything we come across. Ancient cultures devised the constellations of stars we know today, such as the Big Dipper, the Southern Cross and others.[385] They are just stars, points of light in the sky, but our ancestors grouped some of them and called them constellations, which we accept regardless of how arbitrary these groups are. In natural sciences, we developed a system to classify animals as fish, mammals, birds, and the rest—we all accept it as gospel. We have named different types of rocks and grouped them into families, just like we did for animals and plants. As our tools got better, we developed systems for subatomic particles, and new classifications will continue to be developed in the future. (These groupings could have been done differently. They are arbitrary, but that is another story. The systems are widely accepted now and challenging them is a waste of time.) Everywhere you look, our understanding of the world is based on a set of patterns and generalizations crafted by our forebears, handed down to us and accepted as building blocks of truth.

In the same way, throughout the centuries philosophers of history have tried to make sense of our past, looking for a greater meaning. We are always searching for a better understanding of our environment and of ourselves; so it only makes sense that people have developed well-thought-out perspectives on absolute history.

Perhaps a greater meaning lies hidden; but if history has no pattern, then we have to accept that history consists of nothing more than an arbitrary succession of random occurrences. And this view conflicts with our human need for order. Things must make sense. We must find patterns. Our minds cannot handle the idea that our existence is futile. And so, the story of humanity must make sense. We must believe in some sort of order and purpose to our long history.

---

[385] As should be expected different cultures differed on the construction of the different constellations; and, of course, they had different names, images and legends associated with them. For example, the Southern Cross might include the dimmer stars or might not, depending on the culture considered. The Indigenous Australians saw it as an eagle.

Imagine that there were no purpose and that history were merely aimless. To accept this would be an affront to humanity itself. We would be left with no point in living. We might as well kill our neighbors and take their things. Why be moral when you can be rich? If there is no grand significance to history, then nothing we do matters.

Fortunately for me, Hegel believed that there was a meaning to history.

Hegel and a Return to Linear History

In the early nineteenth century Hegel's philosophy transformed human history into a meaningful narrative of human progress. In the previous centuries, history had not been a popular topic for philosophers. After Augustine in the fifth century, not much was written on the topic until Hegel.[386]

Hegel became famous as a lecturer at the University of Berlin. Students from all over Germany came to study under him. He lectured on aesthetics, the philosophy of religion, the philosophy of history and the history of philosophy.

Hegel adopted the linear view of history from the Medieval period. But rather than history being a story of humanity's spiritual evolution and eventual redemption at The Last Judgement, Hegel emphasized the linear development of human freedom. Hegel's system is just as conceivable as Augustine's system.

Hegel is very difficult to read. When trying to read Hegel, it is hard not to feel stupid. Take any page of his; and if you have my limited intelligence or something close, you will have to read it perhaps five

____

[386] Well, there was one in between. Jacques Bossuet wrote in *Discourse on Universal History* in 1681 that to understand the procession of empires and religions through time was "to comprehend in one's mind all that is great in human affairs and have the key to the history of the universe." Why? According to Bossuet, God determines what happens, often as punishment for evils performed. So, if you understand history, then you understand everything. His book came out right before Newton's scientific discoveries. Bossuet did have the attention of Europe briefly until the scientific outlook crept in and dominated and cleared out all references to the Divine.

times, slowly, working a pencil and paper on the side to fool yourself into thinking you understand what he wrote. But you won't. I am not alone here. According to Arthur Schopenhauer,

> *Should you even intend to dull the wits of a young man and to incapacitate his brains for any kind of thought whatever, then you cannot do better than give [him] Hegel to read.*[387]

Indeed, Hegel is tough!

Hegel believed that human history is not just a series of random events. Rather, it has meaning and leads towards some definite end. (In fact, Francis Fukuyama in his 1992 book, *The End of History and the Last Man*, wrote that we have already reached that end.) Hegel claimed that change in human societies over time is not random or accidental. If we study the past, we can identify the pattern that is unfolding. History is the story of the progress of freedom, meaning personal freedom from restrictions, the ability to do what one wants. It is not necessary for people to be mindful of this progress as they live their lives. Instead, he said, as we pursue our everyday needs and desires, we are unconsciously moving the whole—humankind—towards freedom of the Spirit. Our actions are "the means and instruments of a higher purpose of which [we] know nothing."[388] This is true not only of the masses of people, but also of the rare great ones who play crucial roles in historical events. They too pursue their own private goals, but these happen to coincide with the continued development of freedom.

---

[387] This quote can be found all over the internet, but I could not find the source. Here is some more comic Schopenhauer on Hegel for which I could find the source: *The World as Will and Idea*, Volume 3 (Boston Ticknor, 1887), 22. "If I were to say that the so-called philosophy of this fellow Hegel is a colossal piece of mystification which will yet provide posterity with an inexhaustible theme for laughter at our times, that it is a pseudo-philosophy paralyzing all mental powers, stifling all real thinking, and, by the most outrageous misuse of language, putting in its place the hollowest, most senseless, thoughtless, and, as is confirmed by its success, most stupefying verbiage, I should be quite right."

[388] Hegel, 25.

Before I wrote that an individual's freedom is constrained by society. Hegel's writings say the same. Our laws, traditions, religions and institutions limit what a person can do or say. But Hegel adds that our freedom is actually promoted through those constraints. Arbitrary freedom, doing anything we want without restrictions, is ultimately unfulfilling and ruinous for ourselves and society. Our institutions don't allow us to drive as fast as we want or to kill our neighbors for fun and profit. Instead, they provide a structure which guarantees our security and prevents us from destroying ourselves and others. Our institutions provide an environment in which we can exercise our freedoms and thrive, and thereby enhance society as a whole. This is the freedom that Hegel focuses on, true freedom, which is acting in accordance with ethical and reasonable principles. As human societies evolve and freedom progresses, individuals will be able to enjoy freedom in a way that benefits everyone.

The Spirit of History

Hegel wrote about the *Weltgeist*, often translated as World Spirit, but I am calling it the Spirit of History in these essays.

The actions of individuals, cultures and states make up the Spirit of History. Is the Spirit a conscious spirit, like a god? Is it a law like the Law of Gravity? Or is it just a philosophical way of explaining the trajectory of history? Hegel's writing is so abstract, it is not clear. There have been many differing interpretations of just what he meant by the Spirit.

He describes the Spirit in different places as the rational unfolding of history, the collective consciousness of humanity or the self-realization of the Absolute through human institutions and culture. As a result, scholars and philosophers have different opinions of what he meant—some see the Spirit as a metaphysical force, others as a secular process of historical development, and some even lean toward a theological reading.[389] (What that means, really is, you are free to interpret Hegel as you wish.)

Baruch Spinoza (1632-1677) saw God as a single substance pervading all reality in the entire universe. He claimed that there is a connection between all things because we share the same spirit. Hegel's Spirit is not that.

Hegel's Spirit pervades human consciousness and animates human actions individually, but you can really see it in larger groups like nations, especially when you take the historical perspective. You can say it is a tendency for improving our institutions so that we can live freer lives. But it is more; it is indeed a spirit that pervades all people. It is something we all share. And the Spirit drives our history.

Hegel's Spirit of History is much like Schopenhauer's Will, which we spoke of in an earlier essay. Although both have different purposes— Hegel's Spirit drives us towards freedom, Schopenhauer's Will drives us to procreate—both are universal forces that manifest themselves through humans and are an intrinsic part of our nature.

History unfolds through a process of conflict and transformation with the leading edge of freedom moving from one civilization to another— from ancient Greece to Rome to modern Europe—often leaving behind cultures that have fulfilled their role.

So where is humanity going exactly? Hegel tells us that the Spirit of History is guiding us toward an ultimate state of self-awareness, where individuals and societies fully embody freedom and ethical ideals. It's headed toward an end where the world works in a way that makes sense, where people and their governments and cultures are guided by clear, fair reasoning and everyone is truly free to thrive. I cannot imagine anyone thinks we are in that society today.

---

[389] But then, who says that you have to accept all or none of what any philosopher says. You take what you like and go from there. For example, Isaac Newton had some great ideas on physics, but his ideas on religion have generally been discarded.

States, Religion and the March of Freedom

Hegel considered the state to be the true "historical individual." When thinking about the progress of humanity, rather than consider the billions of individuals roaming the planet, we should instead examine the states of different peoples. We can track states a lot easier than billions of individuals. To best understand a state, no element is more significant than its religion.

According to Hegel, as we trace the parade of leading states throughout history, we will see that humanity's religions progress towards the ultimate truth, mirroring the progress of the Spirit of History towards our ultimate freedom. Each state that was dominant in its time can be represented as a stage in the historical progress of the Spirit.

So, why then, if a state is the highest form of the Spirit of History, would it decay? According to Hegel, by the time a state has reached its apex—fully expressing a particular stage of freedom—times will have changed, there will be a conflict and another state will become the world leader, the vanguard for the unfolding of the Spirit of History. The old state, having fulfilled its mission, loses vitality and declines. Through this ongoing process, where states emerge, develop and give way to new forms, the development of freedom and reason advances.

The Spirit of History's Progression through the States

In his lecture series on the philosophy of history, Hegel devoted one lecture to each of several example eras that show the progress of the Spirit. I suppose it can be summed up in this quote:

> *The Eastern nations knew only that one is free; the Greek and Roman world, only that some are free; while we know [today] that all men absolutely. . .are free.*[390]

Ancient China and India were ruled by one man, who arbitrarily determined what people should do and what was acceptable in society.

---

[390] Hegel, 19.

Only the ruler was free. To the monarch, the people were mere objects. In ancient Persia, the ruler still made the rules but was bound by religious principles. The Persians allowed subject peoples more freedom to practice their own religions. You may remember the Persian king, Cyrus the Great, releasing the captive Jews and helping to rebuild the great temple in Jerusalem.

In Ancient Greece, humankind advanced the cause of freedom substantially, at least for the wealthy. But resources and technologies were limited in those times. So, in order for there to be a democracy in Athens, for example, it was necessary that there be tribute states and slaves so the wealthy would have leisure to contemplate and engage in politics.

Despite the progress made in ancient Greece, the freedom to think differently remained constrained by societal norms, including customs, traditions and established institutions. But this was progress compared to ancient China, India and Persia.

Freedom progressed further in Rome, where the power of the territorial governors was limited (at least in theory) by law, which allowed for the rights of the individual citizen to be recognized. The needs of the individual remained in conflict with the needs of the state, and the individual had to obey. From this conflict came stoicism, in which individuals were resigned to conforming to the demands of society, while at the same time looking inward for fulfillment.

Christianity led humanity closer to freedom by emphasizing the spiritual aspect of individuals. Humans were made in the image of God and thus had intrinsic value as individuals. Christianity also presented the idea that humans should not just live in the world, but act to change it for the better. Christian morality was based on love, forgiveness and charity, a huge step beyond the Roman theology.

As the Church in the Middle Ages attained more power and authority, it inserted itself between God and humanity. People had to adhere to the doctrines and customs of the Church or suffer persecution. The Christian spiritual revolution morphed into a strict adherence to dogma and a slavish devotion to relics, icons and ceremonies. Freedom took a step backwards until the Reformation came, which introduced a direct link between God and individuals. Luther's new doctrine said that any person could now communicate with God. The original message of Christianity was recovered, for a brief while, until some of the more extreme sects, such as the Anabaptists, were presenting too much of a challenge to the established authorities. In response, Luther, the Calvinists and some other Protestant sects took control, setting themselves up as the new rule givers, replacing the Catholic Church as the spiritual authority. The general direction through all this was still towards liberation of the human spirit. It was then, and still is now, just an erratic process.

The progress of humanity has to be viewed from a high level. If you look too closely, your attention can be diverted by the repression of unauthorized Christian sects, the Holy Inquisition, the Crusades, the World Wars, and countless other tragedies. These were setbacks to the Spirit of History's unfolding freedom, yet they fueled its progress. From a long-term point of view—according to Hegel—overall progress in the advance of freedom can be seen. It is much like the stock market. The market fluctuates every day. Sometimes it goes down for days, weeks or even months in a row. But, overall, over a larger time horizon, it moves only up. The small variations up and down are just noise in the general upward trajectory. All downward variations eventually result in some sort of correction to the upside.

In a similar way, history progresses toward greater freedom not in spite of conflict and regression, but through them, as each crisis paves the way for a deeper realization of freedom. It took the Greek and Armenian genocides to bring forth international law against genocide. It took the horrors of World War I to bring about the Geneva Convention which codified "ethical" standards in war, like humane treatment of prisoners of war and a ban on poison gas.

A look at the history of the major Western cultures, at least from Constantine's era to the present, does show that people have enjoyed progressively more freedom, taking huge steps forward with the Reformation and the French Revolution. But perhaps Hegel was examining too small a historical dataset to derive a reasonable theory to hold for an eternity. Perhaps he was extrapolating from too small a sample. Hegel was alive during the French Revolution and Napoleon's wars. He saw the beginnings of the unification of Germany. He saw the overthrow of kings under Napoleon. But he missed the communist revolutions and their totalitarian governments that erased personal freedom in Eastern Europe and Asia. He missed Stalin, Mao and Hitler. Twentieth century Europe regressed into a nightmare with its dictators, civil wars and genocides. But these were merely setbacks in humanity's overall advance toward freedom. It seems likely that during the twentieth century, the vanguard of the Spirit of History had moved to the United States. Compared to war-torn Europe, the United States *was* the land of freedom.

They Don't Like Hegel Anymore

William H. Dray (1921–2009), in *The Philosophy of History*, wrote

> *the construction of speculative systems of history is. . .somewhat out of fashion. . .Hegel's philosophy of history is nowadays usually regarded, even by those who have never read a word of it, as a paradigm of how not to theorize about the past.*[391]

Hegel has been criticized by nearly everyone in the philosophy world, even his followers. Bertrand Russell (1872–1970), an English super-heavyweight philosopher, claimed that almost all of Hegel's doctrines were false.

Philosophers object to Hegel's system of history because they state that he just made it up. They call it *a priori*, which to them is a pejorative term. *A priori* refers to "before experience," that is, something that comes from within, rather than being based on what we perceive with

---

[391] William H. Dray, *Philosophy of History* (Prentice Hall, 1964), 2.

our senses, which philosophers call *empirical*. Hegel belongs in the same camp with Plato, who based most of his ideas on *a priori* knowledge.

Hegel had the audacity to assume that actual history must correspond to his reasonings. Apparently, this is untenable to philosophers. But really? Finding patterns in nature and claiming that there appears to be a system? That is unacceptable? That is precisely what many famous philosophers have done. It is the nature of philosophy.

If one is able to create philosophical systems from observing patterns in nature, as many philosophers have, why would you not think that one can do the same for patterns of history? Newton had the audacity to think that physical phenomenon would correspond to his mathematical reasoning—a claim no less sweeping than Hegel's theories. Was he being intolerably arrogant too?

Others have criticized Hegel for only including some cultures and not others. What about the Aboriginals, the African nations, the Islamic world? They assert that the facts he considers significant are just those facts that help confirm his theory. I suppose Hegel could respond by stating that he was only looking at the most advanced cultures at the time. He only picked one for any given era. So, while some cultures were in retrograde, or perhaps not developing spiritually at all, those cultures that he selected were at the vanguard of the liberation of the Spirit.

When Hegel wrote about his idea of cultures being the manifestation of the many individuals, he used the word "state," which many took to mean government. From this they inferred Hegel meant that governments are expressions of the Spirit of History, justifying them in whatever they do. These critics then criticized Hegel saying that many authoritarian governments based their terror on Hegel's idea that they were serving the Spirit of History as they ruined the lives of their subjects. I suppose this is about the same as blaming Christ for the Inquisition. Just because others misinterpreted Hegel's works and used them to justify evil does not mean that his works are evil or wrong. It is said that communism is an outgrowth of Hegel's theories, but these same people do not remark that the early Christians were early progenitors of the communist movement as well.

From a Belief in Progress to a Belief in Decay

Before Hegel's philosophy of the progress of freedom, French economist Anne Robert Jacques Turgot, in a 1750 Sorbonne lecture, described history's march toward perfection.

> *The human race, viewed from its earliest beginning, presents itself to the eye of the philosopher as a vast whole which, like every individual being, has its time of childhood and progress. . . .Manners become gentler; the mind becomes more enlightened; nations, hitherto living in isolation, draw nearer to one another; trade and political relations link up the various quarters of the globe; and the whole body of mankind, through the vicissitudes of calm and tempest, of fair days and foul, continues its onward march, albeit with tardy steps, toward an ever-nearing perfection.*[392]

Perfection. This is exactly what people believed was possible. They really believed we were on our way towards perfection—until the 1850s, when it all began to fall apart. According to Albert Schweitzer, writing in the 1920s, philosophy used to provide meaning for people. And, in Europe, it did. Europe had a difficult time with religion, where rulers, claiming that God chose them to rule, had for centuries dictated what subjects had to believe. The Enlightenment and the French Revolution to a large extent brought an end to that. And, as belief in religion waned, Europeans turned to philosophy.

It is hard for us moderns to believe, but philosophy used to be important to people. People used to get excited about philosophical systems. In post-French Revolutionary Europe, people looked to philosophy to guide ethical behavior, reform oppressive systems and give life meaning. It was a secular roadmap for moral and social progress.

---

[392] Turgot, "The Successive Advances of the Human Mind," lecture, Sorbonne Université, December 11, 1750, found in Will and Ariel Durant, *The Age of Voltaire*, 775.

As the centuries passed, philosophy also lost its grip on people. Since then, much of philosophy has devolved into pedantry. It wastes its energy arguing about trivial points in difficult, indecipherable language. It has fallen by the wayside, and few people pay attention to it anymore.

Meanwhile in the United States, religion continued to provide meaning for many Americans, and Americans have continued to be much more religious than Europeans. A 2017 study found that 76% of American Christians believed in God with absolute certainty, while only 23% of European Christians did. In fact, more Americans who do not identify with a religion (27%) believe in God with absolute certainty than do European Christians (23%).[393] But American religiosity has been in decline for decades. A 2024 study found that 62% of American adults identify as Christian, whereas in 2007, the number was 78%.[394]

Today many of us believe in facts rather than theology or philosophical systems. We have dropped our idealism and become pragmatic. That which we can perceive has become our reality. And that is all there is to it. But facts don't have any profundity. They have no grand meaning behind them. It used to be we believed in human ideals and strove to perfect ourselves and society. Now we shrug, muttering, "It is what it is."

We have lost belief in human moral progress and replaced it with the idea of social decline. Today, we see the world very differently than Turgot did in 1750. Now we believe that as nations evolve, they grow, mature and finally collapse. They often start out vigorous, warlike and unsophisticated. They conquer nations around them and establish national boundaries. Then, as generations pass, these nations become wealthy. Their warlike spirit dissipates and wealth and culture grow instead. When these nations become wealthy enough, many no longer have to work, and they acquire the luxury to think for themselves. With

---

[393] Jonathan Evans, "U.S. Adults are More Religious than Western Europeans," Pew Research Center, Sept. 5, 2018, https://tinyurl.com/2xk8mkhj.

[394] Gregory Smith, et. al., "Decline in Christianity in the U.S. has Slowed, may have Leveled off," Pew Research Center, Feb. 26, 2025, pewresearch.org/religion/2025/02/26/religious-landscape-study-executive-summary/.

wealth comes decadence and the degradation of the original shared national schema, and with that comes factionalism and national decline.

Oswald Spengler popularized this theory in *The Decline of the West*, which was published in 1918. He wrote that Western Civilization as a whole was entering an age of skepticism, the last stage of civilization, and that there was no way out of it. What would follow would be the end of Western civilization and ultimately younger more vigorous civilizations would gain from our demise.

You can say Spengler believed history was cyclical, but within a framework of chaos. He believed that there is no purpose in these cycles of civilizations.

> *'Mankind'. . .has no aim, no idea, no plan, any more than the family of butterflies or orchids. 'Mankind' is a zoological expression, or an empty word.*[395]

Spengler was not a believer in human progress. This grim vision took hold in the United States after World War I, when American idealism foundered and sank into the mire of an inescapable pessimism.

For the Americans, entering World War I was the last gasp of American idealism. Americans eagerly volunteered to fight "The War to End All Wars," believing that President Wilson's post-war League of Nations would end pointless European wars and usher in an era of world peace. We still believed in progress then and were led by our progressive president, Woodrow Wilson. Unfortunately, the war delivered on few of his promises. Instead, millions were murdered and mutilated in World War I for nothing. Wilson's idealistic visions were hijacked by our vengeful and self-seeking European allies. It was all for nothing, and it was this war that killed the American belief in progress for at least a century.

What would it be like to have an entire society believe in human progress? We cannot know. But if you think about the literature and

---

[395] Oswald Spengler, *The Decline of the West*, vol. 1 (Alfred A. Knopf, 1926), 21.

philosophy of the twentieth century objectively, perhaps then you can see it. The twentieth century, that is, post-World War I, was a century of pessimism. Art no longer tried to express timeless truths or beauty, but the fleeting emptiness of existence. Twentieth century literature was full of stories of powerless men being mere cogs in a great machine, living frivolous, insignificant lives, where nothing mattered. Existentialism preached the meaninglessness of life. As there is no afterlife, we all die in the end, and that's it. And as there is no ultimate meaning in life, you have the freedom to create your own trivial meaning, so just come up with a hobby and let that fulfill you. That is hardly hopeful. The twentieth century was a time of despair. And this despair has spilled into the twenty-first century. But this fall into despair is a subject for another book.

Collapsing Civilizations

So, what happens when a civilization collapses? There are different definitions of collapse, I suppose. A nation can become weak and be conquered like the Western and Eastern Roman Empires, or it can just implode on itself as people quit cooperating and become progressively more violent, less skilled and less wealthy.

Written history does not provide us with clear-cut examples of a culture imploding. This phenomenon appears to be a creature only of science fiction and futuristic speculation. Although some believe it is happening now in the West.

What usually happens is that a society weakens itself through in-fighting, declining respect for institutions and the erosion of the original values that once made the society great, such as hard work, military prowess, self-sacrifice. Once weakened, the society then becomes unable to defend itself from more vigorous outsiders. This seems to happen often in history. Examples of this storyline are all too common. Name any great kingdom or empire of the past, and they probably followed this trajectory. You want examples? How about Rome, where Romans would no longer serve in the military. The Byzantines were another example, where they could hardly field an army when the crusaders sacked Constantinople. A city of 500,000 to 700,000 souls could only field an army of 7,000 to 10,000 soldiers. Perhaps they were more concerned about chariot races than the well-being of their nation.

The conquering cultures often will absorb some of the fallen civilizations' institutions and achievements. But much, if not all, of the dying civilizations' literature, music, political systems, philosophy and other accomplishments are lost.

Toynbee also wrote of collapsing civilizations in his *A Study of History*. Toynbee places most of the blame for the collapse on the elites that rule them. During a society's growing phases, the elites are often of great benefit to their societies as they are able to overcome the problems that the society faces, such as external enemies, internal disorder or class exploitation. They set up institutions that help to maintain a self-sustaining society. These institutions may include religion, law-making bodies, tax collectors, military, media, unions, courts, police, agencies that monitor and regulate health, food, labor, etc. The people are happy to be ruled by the elites, who are so instrumental in keeping things running. But at some point in a society's lifespan, the "creative minority," the elites, become less effective at solving problems and become instead more concerned about enriching themselves and maintaining their position at the top. Toynbee called this transition one from the "creative minority" to the "dominant minority." The dominant minority uses social institutions to maintain their positions and to silence or eliminate opposition. This oppression by the elites leads to internal discord. Their hijacking of social institutions leads to a loss of respect for these same institutions that had in the past served society. Society then divides into factions that in their struggle against each other break down social institutions further. But this disintegration of a society does not necessarily happen in one lifetime. Historically it has taken centuries.

It is possible that the inevitable fall of Western Civilization will be different. Most of the dystopian literature and movies of the past decade have been based on an implosion of society. If they are any indication, our fall may not be gradual like that of prior societies, but sudden, violent and catastrophic.[396]

Is the West Collapsing?

Our Western world has become very complex and is thoroughly, at all levels, reliant on fossil fuels. Our population has exploded. We were only able to reach this state of growth, abundance and complexity due to our use of fossil fuels. We use fossil fuels to transport food and other goods. We use fossil fuels to make electricity. We use fossil fuels to make fertilizer.

As the decades pass, it becomes more and more difficult to extract natural resources as they become harder to obtain and their declining quality make them harder to refine. We have already used up the oil that is easy to access. If you remove fossil fuels, food production and distribution of goods plummets. Without fossil fuels, store shelves will be emptied and our modern world will collapse. Hundreds of millions will starve to death, and millions more will die in violence triggered by shortages. Even worse, once money can no longer be made from the manufacture of goods, capital will flow to destructive ventures, which profit from destroying everything we have created. Ventures such as cybercrime and trafficking of arms, drugs and humans. Armed mercenary services will thrive, hastening the destruction of polite society and everything we have built. Yes, the demise of the Western World could be sudden and violent. And then comes the Mad Max dystopia. Need I describe it? A world devolved from the American society we know into a sparsely populated world of anarchy, rule by violence, loss of knowledge and scarcity.

Let's just hope the science fiction authors are wrong, or, if they are right, that at least we don't have to live through the horror.

----

[396] Some very thoughtful ideas on this topic can be found at https://tinyurl.com/ y2mx5ocf, April 10, 2020.

The Tragedy of Lost Civilizations

As you read this you might be thinking, "Why does he have to get so negative?" Well, here's my answer. It is too easy to assume that the future will mirror the past. That is small-minded thinking. Change does not always come gradually. Sometimes it is catastrophic and sudden. Still, these types of changes need not be ruinous for the individual. Augustine and many millions of others lived through the end of the Western Roman Empire. Most people survived. Some even thrived. Institutions rise and then they fall. That is just the way of history. It is only a matter of time before our society faces its demise. It may be next year; it may be a thousand years from now. But it will happen eventually. Our form of social organization may well be forgotten, but others will arise to continue the story, as the Spirit of History continues to evolve through us. Remember, the story is not about us or our society. It is about the progress of Humanity itself.

This relentless march of Humanity into the future does sometimes leave great destruction in its wake. The destructive elements among us do great damage and hurt a lot of people. Our creations, the work of generations of people are trampled on, burned, melted down and forgotten. And Humanity moves on. As ugly as it is, we must face it. This is our story. And this is precisely the legacy of the Spirit of History.

The Snowman

When I was about ten years old, I lived in the countryside outside Portland, Oregon. In the winter we would get good wet snows perfect for building snowmen. I remember one day after a snowstorm, my little sister, my mother and I took a walk on our country road to the little store about a mile away. It was closed. We built a snowman there. And we admired our creation. But we then became increasingly unnerved by a four-wheel-drive Jeep across the street that was skidding and sliding as it was peeling out in the snow. Back and forth it went. The windows were rolled down. We could hear the people inside laughing, hollering and enjoying themselves. They were probably really drunk, but I wouldn't have known that back then. They aimed at us, paused, and then bore down on us, or rather, on the snowman. We ran away. At some point I stopped, turned around, and watched as they ran over our snowman, back and forth, back and forth, laughing. I was shaken—truly in shock. We could do nothing but escape. I had never seen or imagined people so callous and uncaring. We were frightened and would have been helpless if they would have come for us. That is what I feared they would do. I will never forget this. Up to then, I had thought my parents could protect me, but then I realized they couldn't. I had thought that adults were nice to each other, that they cared about each other's well-being. But that day I encountered people who weren't like that. They were evil. It was then that I first learned that destructive forces exist in this world that have no concern for the pain and devastation they leave in their wake.

I know. . .it was just a snowman. A snowman and a frightened boy amount to nothing in the greater scheme of things, even in the smaller scheme of things. Who cares? But we had created that snowman. We were proud of it, and we had hoped it would stand for a time so that others could appreciate what we had done.

Perhaps that is why I feel so strongly about the loss of cultures. To me, the snowman was our creation, just like a culture is the creation of generations. People come together. They put their energy into something. They identify with it. It is theirs. They expect it to endure. And then some brutes arrive and destroy everything. The perpetrators can care less for the suffering they inflict on others. And often, after the destruction, murder and plunder, nothing is left. The culture is dead and forgotten. To me, this is tragic. All of that work, that genius, that love, that whimsy, all of it, gone forever. But Hegel and Toynbee would just say that it is just part of the historical process.

The End of Constantinople

Rape, pillage, and wanton destruction is common after a city is conquered. It continues today. We read about the sack of Constantinople in 1204 by the crusader army. It happened twice more. The last time was in 1453, when Constantinople, the last bastion of the Roman Empire, was destroyed by Mehmet II and his Ottoman army after a fifty-three-day siege. The city had been an imperial capital of the Roman Empire from 330 CE when Constantine founded it. It stood for 1,100 years as the Roman capital city. And then the civilization was gone. The sack of Constantinople may be the greatest loss to Western civilization in history, worse than the burning of the library of Alexandria or the sack of Rome.[397]

Here is an eye-witness account:

> *Nothing will ever equal the horror of this harrowing and terrible spectacle. People frightened by the shouting ran out of their houses and were cut down by the sword before they knew what was happening. And some were massacred in their houses where they tried to hide, and some in churches where they sought refuge.*

> *The enraged Turkish soldiers. . .gave no quarter. When they had massacred and there was no longer any resistance, they were intent on pillage and roamed through the town stealing, disrobing, pillaging, killing, raping, taking captive men, women, children, old men, young men, monks, priests, people of all sorts and conditions. . .*

> *Old men of venerable appearance were dragged by their white hair and piteously beaten. Priests were led into captivity in batches, as well as reverend virgins, hermits and recluses who were dedicated to God alone and lived only for Him. . .Tender children were brutally snatched from their mothers' breasts and*

---

[397] Paraphrased from a quote from Encyclopedia Britannica, ascribed to historian J.J. Norwich.

girls were pitilessly given up to strange and horrible unions, and a thousand other terrible things happened. . .

Temples were desecrated, ransacked and pillaged. . .sacred objects were scornfully flung aside, the holy icons and the holy vessels were desecrated. . .Saints' shrines were brutally violated in order to get out the remains which were then thrown to the wind. Chalices and cups for the celebration of the Mass were set aside for their orgies or broken or melted down or sold. . .Immense numbers of sacred and profane books were flung on the fire or torn up and trampled underfoot. The majority, however, were sold at derisory prices, for a few pence. Saints' altars, torn from their foundations, were overturned. . .

When Mehmed (II) saw the ravages, the destruction and the deserted houses and all that had perished and become ruins, then a great sadness took possession of him and he repented the pillage and all the destruction. Tears came to his eyes and sobbing he expressed his sadness. "'What a town this was! And we have allowed it to be destroyed!" His soul was full of sorrow.[398]

His sorrow must have been for the destruction of the city and its artifacts, but not for the people who made the city what it was. The vast majority of the survivors in Constantinople were still forced to become slaves.

The Walls of Nineveh Destroyed

Sometimes cultures obliterate their own pasts. I wrote earlier about Xenophon's ancient account of the fleeing Greek soldiers chancing upon the walls of Nineveh thousands of years ago. The gates still stood when I started these essays. But just recently in 2016, two of the gates were destroyed by ISIS (Islamic State of Iraq and Syria) militants, who consider some pre-Islamic imagery to be sacrilegious. We do not

---

[398] This eyewitness account appears in C. R. N. Routh, *They Saw It Happen in Europe 1450-1600,* (Basil Blackwell, 1965).

learn; we repeat. In the same year, ISIS vandalized Mosul's Museum of antiquities, destroying ancient statues, and ransacked Mosul's library, burning more than 100,000 old books and manuscripts, some of which were recognized as historical rarities by the United Nations Education, Scientific and Cultural Organization (UNESCO). They also destroyed historic Shiite mosques and shrines. But it isn't just extremists who obliterate the past. Governments do, too. In 2021, stretches of the same wall were demolished to make way for new roads.[399]

Why would they do this? Some say that ISIS actively annihilates ancient artifacts to cleanse history of all traces of any past that is not Sunni Islam. Similarly, the Taliban recently defaced the sixth century, 165-foot-tall Buddhas of Bamiyan. They are removing all traces of any civilization that is not their own.

Iconoclasts

Radical Islam is not alone in demolishing priceless historical relics in their own lands. They were merely repeating what others have done before them, over and over again. In the Eastern Roman Empire, for a period of about eighty years, 726 to 843 CE, the "iconoclasts" destroyed sacred images. This movement was directed by the emperors and was eventually sanctioned by the heads of the Church. They saw images of Christ or the saints as idolatrous, violating the Second Commandment: "Thou shalt not make thee any graven image. . .Thou shalt not bow down thyself unto them, nor serve them."[400] They argued that images, being physical representations, could only represent God in a material form. Icons could not convey what is really important, the spiritual essence of God, which exists beyond the physical realm. Icons confused people. They had to go. During this period, centuries-old paintings and mosaics were whitewashed; statues were destroyed. Because monks opposed the removal of icons, monasteries were razed and many monks

---

[399] https://thearabweekly.com/3000-year-old-wall-destroyed-nineveh-iraq.

[400] Deuteronomy 5.8-9, King James Version.

were punished and humiliated. How did this end? A new empress decided icons were valuable and it stopped right there.

Christian Protestant fundamentalists have done it as well and for the same reason. During the Protestant Reformation in the sixteenth century, the Calvinists destroyed paintings, stained glass windows, sculptures and saintly relics in churches. The French revolutionists did it, too, in the 1790s. I recently visited Avignon and found the heads had been lopped off the statues that adorned the churches. It happened again during the Spanish civil war in the 1930s. Many Catholic churches and convents were burned. We humans seem to do this from time to time. It is part of the process.

Genocide is the Rule

Not only is the socially sanctioned widespread destruction of our historical artifacts more common than we want to believe, so is recurring obliteration of entire civilizations and races. I understand that this is a part of our history. But I don't like it. To me, it seems the greatest evil of all to remove from the face of the planet all remembrance of a people.

Erasing Jewish History

Sometimes this obliteration of a culture is done as a matter of policy. During World War II, in Lublin on their way through Poland, Nazi soldiers ransacked the library at the Jewish Theological Seminary. They collected the books and piled them high in the market square and set them aflame. This act, in its own way, was as destructive to the Jewish culture as mass murder. It was the collection of knowledge from the wisest of many generations of rabbinical teachers. Now it is lost forever. No group's identity can survive without a past, and the annihilation of Jewish identity is exactly what the Nazi's intended. They followed this same pattern of destruction throughout Europe. This was German policy: to seize the land and urban properties, eliminate the local population, and replace it with their own people. In some areas they stripped Jewish cemeteries of their headstones. The Nazis were intent on literally erasing the Jewish people from the landscape and from history.[401] This Nazi brutality was just another instance of a repeating murderous pattern of humanity's shared history.

Biblical Genocide

We are appalled by genocide, but genocide is not that unusual; and it didn't first appear in World War II. It seems to be an inherent feature of "civilization." In ancient times, when cities were nations in themselves, conquerors would often kill nearly everyone in a rival city and enslave the rest. In fact, the Hebrew Joshua's conquest of Canaan can be considered a genocide. Variations of the same pattern have reappeared throughout the centuries: kill the male inhabitants, take their stuff, rape the women, take some as wives and enslave the rest. In the case of Canaan, it was simpler. God commanded Joshua to kill all the people and even their livestock as well.

> *Now go and attack Amalek, and utterly destroy all that they have, and do not spare them. But kill both man and woman, infant and nursing child, ox and sheep, camel and donkey.*[402]

And he did it.

> *So Joshua conquered all the land: the mountain country and the South and the lowland and the wilderness slopes, and all their kings; he left none remaining, but utterly destroyed all that breathed, as the LORD God of Israel had commanded.*[403]

I know, scholars now believe that the Hebrews did not kill everyone in Canaan, even though the Bible says they did. They say that people used to write in extremist language back then. It doesn't matter though.

---

[401] Brendan January, *Genocide: Modern Crimes Against Humanity*, (Twenty-First Century Books, 2007), 27-28.

[402] 1 Samuel 15:3, New King James Version.

[403] Joshua 10:40 New Kings James Version.

The point is that genocide has been with us forever. It is even in our holy books.

Colonial Genocide

Genocide and cultural genocide were common during the colonial era. The European colonial powers took land and established their colonies. Natives were viewed as subhuman, which made it much easier to justify killing and enslaving them. For the most part, most of the natives on the North American continent were killed by soldiers, settlers and the diseases introduced by contact with the whites. In order to eradicate native cultures, their children were forcibly educated in the English language and in European ways as late as the 1960s.[404]

In keeping with the Christian and Hegelian views of moral progress, we would like to think we have evolved beyond genocide. Unfortunately, it has remained common in the twentieth century and into the twenty-first century. Notable examples include the Turkish genocide of the Armenians and the Greeks, the German genocide of the Jews and the Romani, the genocide of Christians in some Middle Eastern and African countries, the Rwanda Hutu's genocide of Tutsi, and there are many more. The list is depressingly long.

Turkish Greeks and Armenian Genocide

The Greeks thrived on the coast of Asia Minor (Turkey) for centuries, starting around the time of Homer, 800 BCE. In the fourth century BCE, Alexander the Great marched through the center of Asia Minor, conquered the Persian Empire and took control of the area. Alexander died soon thereafter. His successors, the Greek Seleucids, ruled Asia Minor until the Romans defeated them in the second century BCE. Rome governed with a hands-off policy for centuries; and over those centuries, Asia Minor became progressively more Hellenized, with

---

[404] I am speaking in generalities here. Not all colonists saw Native Americans as sub-human. Eliminating Native Americans was not a common policy, but was applied in varying degrees in various places.

the Greek language becoming supreme. But the history of the area is complicated and difficult to summarize. Many nations had a piece of Asia Minor throughout the centuries. One major player was the Greek Byzantine Eastern Roman Empire, which ruled an ever-shrinking area in Asia Minor as the centuries progressed.

After the conquest of modern-day Turkey in the fifteenth century by the Ottomans, the Greeks remained in Asia Minor, free to live as they chose. The Ottoman Empire had a reputation for tolerance with minority populations. In 1912, there were an estimated 1.8 million Greeks in Turkey, about 18% of the population. Asia Minor had such a rich history of Greek culture, but few Greeks remain there now. Since then, the Ottomans wiped them out. According to the Austrian consul, in a report to his foreign minister, Ottoman official Rafet Bey stated in November 1916, "We must finish off the Greeks as we did the Armenians."[405] In another conversation a few days later, Bey told the consul, "Today I sent squads to the interior to kill every Greek in sight."[406]

Hundreds of thousands of Greeks were sent by foot to the interior of Turkey in work brigades. Many were massacred. Many died of starvation. Nothing has been heard of them since. They vanished from history.

The same Austrian foreign minister also wrote:

> *The strategy implemented by the Turks is of displacing people to the interior without taking measures for their survival by exposing them to death, hunger, and illness. The abandoned homes are then looted and burnt or destroyed. Whatever was done to the Armenians is being repeated with the Greeks.*[407]

---

[405] Manus Midlarksy, I, *The Killing Trap: Genocide in the Twentieth Century*, (Cambridge University Press, 2005), 342-3, as found at https://military-history.fandom.com/wiki/Greek_genocide#cite_note-17, accessed January 1, 2024

[406] Midlarksy.

[407] Midlarksy.

Some Greeks were forcibly converted to Islam. Greek Orthodox churches, monuments and sacred relics were destroyed. Of course, it is never so simple. The Turks had entered the First World War in league with the Central Powers alliance—Germany, Austria-Hungary and Bulgaria. The Greeks and Armenians were seen as potential enemies within. Whether the Greeks and Armenians were a threat or not, the result was the same: the obliteration of a people and their culture from a geographic region.

If you are lucky enough to travel to Cappadocia in the center of Turkey, you will find huge caves dug into the sandstone rock. When I visited, I knew that Greeks had once lived there. The Christian frescoes were a dead giveaway. Cappadocia was an important monastic center from the fourth to the thirteenth century. Christians escaping Roman persecutions in the fourth century had carved into the rocks and mountains underground dwellings, monasteries and even cities. Cappadocian Christians are even mentioned in the First Epistle of Peter as enduring persecution. But there are no signs of any Greeks there now. When I asked locals why had people lived in caves and when did they live in the caves, they didn't know. When there is genocide, history gets forgotten. And that is often the point.

Raphael Lemkin, One Man's Crusade

Genocide troubled Raphael Lemkin (1900–1959) so much that he devoted his working life to ending this cycle of cultural annihilation. His story shows how one person can influence the moral evolution of humanity. His life's work continues to affect our world today, even though his name has long since been forgotten. It starts in the Ottoman Empire...

The Ottoman Empire's Minister of the Interior, Mehmad Talaat Pasha (1874–1921), was the principal architect of The Armenian Genocide, which also took place before the Greek genocide we spoke of earlier. In that government action,[408] over one million Armenians were murdered.

---

[408] A sad but amusing anecdote of Talaat found in *Totally Unofficial: The Autobiography*

As World War I was ending, and Turkey's alliance had lost the war, Pasha realized that the Allied Powers (France, Britain, the U.S.) would hold him accountable for what he had done, so he fled Turkey. He settled in Germany under an assumed name. A tribunal in the post-war Ottoman government tried him in absentia and found him guilty and condemned him to death. But Germany refused to extradite him. It appeared he was going to get off scot-free for the murder of over one million Armenians. But in 1921, a young Armenian, Soghomon Tehlirian, tracked him down and assassinated him, screaming, "This is for my mother!" Tehlirian was one of the few survivors of the Armenian genocide. He had been saved because the body of his dead mother had fallen on him, shielding him from the bullets of the Turkish army. The young man was charged by German authorities with the murder of Pasha. The story made international news and the trial brought the Armenian genocide to the world's attention. As many Armenian witnesses had recounted their horrific stories in court, the trial was transformed in the public mind into a trial of the Turkish perpetrators. The jury acknowledged that Tehlirian had acted justly, but they could not condone murder. Instead, he was acquitted due to "insanity."

While this story was in the news, a young Jewish student in Poland, Raphael Lemkin, asked one of his professors why Talaat wasn't arrested for the massacres and put on trial. The professor responded that there was no international law that allowed for an arrest of such a man.[409]

---

of Raphael Lemkin, Raphael Lemkin and Donna-Lee Frieze, (Yale University Press, 2013), 184-185: "When [Henry] Morgenthau [Sr.], [the American ambassador to Turkey who tried to save the Armenians in 1915 from their Turkish murderers] was talking to the minister of the interior, Talaat Pasha, endeavoring to prevent deportations of the Armenians to the death camps, Talaat Pasha interrupted him with an 'innocent' question: 'By the way, Mr. Ambassador, on some of the Armenians we found insurance policies, and even reassurance policies from companies in the American city of Hartford, Connecticut. Since they are Turkish citizens, could you help the Turkish government to cash these policies?'"

[409] If you are thinking there is a contradiction here: Talaat Pasha left Turkey to flee the law but the professor said there is no law that prosecutes for crimes like his-- no international law at the time. But after the war, the allies set up military tribunals and he was prosecuted

"Consider the case of the farmer who owns a flock of chickens. He kills them and this is his business. If you interfere, you are trespassing." This made little sense to Lemkin. He asked, "Why is a man punished when he kills another man? Why is the killing of a million a lesser crime than the killing of a single individual?"[410] His professor explained that there were no international conventions against genocide. In fact, the word genocide hadn't even been invented yet, even though it had been practiced for thousands of years. Many years later, Lemkin himself was the one who coined the term genocide.

During World War II, this man, Raphael Lemkin, after having read Hitler's *Mein Kampf*, managed to escape the joint German and Russian occupation in Poland. He ended up in America. He had tried to convince his family and friends to flee Poland, but they didn't believe his warnings. They perished. He was successful saving his own life but lost forty-nine relatives to the Holocaust.

In the United States, he served on the faculty at Duke, Rutgers and Yale. He devoted his life to establishing an international law against genocide. He proposed to criminalize genocide-type crimes during the Paris Peace Conference of 1945, but his proposal was turned down. He met stiff opposition from the British and some other countries. In America, the American Bar Association warned a Senate subcommittee that the Genocide Convention could be applied to lynching blacks.[411] Lemkin left his professorship and worked full time lobbying various United Nations (UN) delegations and national governments to get a Genocide Convention approved by the UN. During this long struggle, he lost his health and lived off loans from friends. For lack of payment, he was kicked out of hotels. His clothes were seized. He was yelled at by proprietors in the middle of the night. Lemkin gave everything to his cause. He was eventually successful when in 1951 the UN put in

---

under Ottoman Law.

[410] January, 23-24.

[411] Douglas Irvin-Erickson, *Raphael Lemkin and the Concept of Genocide* (University of Pennsylvania Press, 2017), 204.

place his Convention on the Prevention and Punishment of the Crime of Genocide. That day, after the United Nations meeting, journalists found him sitting motionless, tears running down his face.[412] It took six years, but he did it.

Lemkin's story is an example of how humanity can evolve morally in response to its darkest moments. The UN convention on genocide would never have come into being had it not been for the barbaric genocides of the previous years.

The Murder of National Cultures

Thanks to Lemkin, genocide has been formally defined in international law. The authorities did manage to water down his definitions; but overall, he was successful. Genocide is defined in international law as "deliberate acts committed with the intent to destroy national, ethnic, racial, or religious groups by killing them, causing serious harm to them, imposing measures to prevent them from having children, stealing their children, or otherwise deliberately inflicting conditions that will destroy the group."[413]

Lemkin describes a nation as being, above all, a group of individuals who share a collective mind and think of themselves as belonging to the same group. They share an ancestral memory. They share culture, which is composed of languages, arts, mythologies, folklores, collective histories, traditions, religions, ancestry and a common geographical location.[414] It need not be all of these, though.

---

[412] Lemkin's story is truly inspirational. I heartily recommend previously cited autobiography, *Totally Unofficial*.

[413] From Article II of the Convention of the Prevention and Punishment of the Crime of Genocide, by the United Nations. https://www.un.org/en/genocideprevention/genocide.shtml, accessed Jan. 1, 2024.

[414] Irvin-Erikson, 66.

Spengler took it further when he wrote that peoples are not defined merely by linguistic, political or zoological traits but are fundamentally "spiritual units" or "units of soul."[415]

And it is through major events and a people's reaction to them that the souls of a nation are bound together.

> *The great events of history were not really achieved by peoples; they themselves created the peoples. Every act alters the soul of the doer.*[416]

For example, the resilience, determination, and fierce individualism that define the American spirit were shaped by the harsh realities of the western frontier, including conflicts with Native American tribes, the demands of hunting and preserving food, and the relentless challenges of extreme weather. There was no guarantee of survival. The settlers survived by their wits. And add to that the response of the American revolutionaries to British tyranny. They had the audacity to challenge the authority of their king and the mightiest military power of their time. The revolution fostered a strong sense of equality among men (initially white), a belief in a classless society based on merit, and an enduring anti-authoritarianism that prioritized individual rights. It was these events and the reactions of these early Americans that bound the American people together, creating a shared ancestral memory that has become essential to the nation's identity. Events are what bind a people with their shared ancestral memory. What makes a population a people, a nation, is "the inwardly lived experience of 'we.'"[417]

As I wrote previously, cultures are created by those who are alive now and those who have lived before. Every person living in a nation, to some degree, contributes to its culture. The language, traditions, myths,

---

[415] Spengler, *The Decline of the West*, vol II, (Alfred A. Knopf, 1928), 169. What is even cooler is that on page 82, he wrote that "persons are not bodies but units of force and will." Very profound, but placed here in the notes because it is a distraction from the point I am trying to make.

[416] Spengler, vol. II, 165.

[417] Spengler, vol. II, 165.

libraries and churches, the overall cultural pattern of the group are "the shrines of a nation's soul."[418]

And it is our cultures, to which we all contribute, that in turn shape the composition and trajectory of humanity.

Whereas murder involves killing one person, genocide usually involves killing many people, but the underlying purpose is to kill a culture. Lemkin wrote:

> *When a nation is murdered, its culture goes too. The dead cannot write literature. Through its culture, the life of a nation continues, when the physical life of individual members is finished.*[419]

To destroy a culture is to erase the creation of generations of people. To blot it out, to make it disappear. It is an utter rejection not just of one person, but of the millions of people, living and dead, who composed such a culture. This is pure evil.[420]

Destroying cultures hurts all of us. As Lemkin wrote in his famous book, *Axis Rule in Occupied Europe,*

> *The world represents only so much culture and intellectual vigor as are created by its component national groups. Essentially the idea of a nation signifies. . .original contributions, based upon genuine traditions, genuine culture, and well-developed national psychology. The destruction of a nation, therefore, results in the loss of its future contribution to the world.*[421]

Each culture is unique, both with its good and bad points; but overall, all cultures are components of the rich tapestry of humanity. They all point to possibilities, what a society could be. Sure, dominant cultures

---

[418] Lemkin and Frieze, 172.

[419] Lemkin and Frieze, 27.

[420] There are so many arguments for why this is evil, and I really want to stick to my line of thought, so I am not going to explore this. If you are not convinced it is evil and you made it this far, that is all right, just keep on reading.

[421] Raphael Lemkin, *Axis Rule in Occupied Europe,* (1944), 91.

drive the Spirit of History's progress, but all cultures enrich humanity's legacy, so their loss diminishes us all.

The Tibetan Genocide

The more thoughtful purveyors of cultural genocide have found a way to murder a culture in a way that perhaps the world may not notice. They do it slowly. There may be periods of intense bloodshed and destruction; but overall, it is a quiet process. Rather than a bloody rage spanning a few years, it can be quietly done in a few generations. That is what is happening in Tibet right now.

In an interview, the leader (in exile) of Tibet, the fourteenth Dalai Lama (1935–), said just recently,

> *The Tibetan civilization has existed for ten thousand years; and in some areas of the Tibetan plateau, human habituation existed for as many as thirty thousand years. And today's situation of Tibet is the most serious crisis in the entire history of the nation. During the Cultural Revolution [in the late 1960s to early 1970s], some Chinese officials made a pledge that within fifteen years the Tibetan language must be eliminated. So they burned books, such as the three hundred-volume Tibetan canon of scriptures trans-lated from India, as well as several thousand volumes written by Tibetans themselves. I was told that the books would burn for one or two weeks. Our statues and our monasteries were being destroyed.*[422]

Traditionally the second most prominent authority in Tibet is the Panchen Lama. The Panchen Lama, like the Dalai Lama, is both a temporal and spiritual leader. The tenth Panchen Lama (1938–1989) was enthroned in 1949 in the middle of the Chinese civil war that resulted in the establishment of the Communist People's Republic of China. The Panchen Lama supported the Communist government, while the Dalai Lama did not. In 1959, the year the Dalai Lama fled to

---

[422] Douglas Carlton Abrams, *The Book of Joy*, 149-150.

India, the Panchen Lama became chairman of the Chinese government's Preparatory Committee for the Tibet Autonomous Region.

In 1962, the Panchen Lama, after touring Tibet, submitted a petition to Zhou Enlai, the premier of the People's Republic of China. Although his petition praised the doctrines and policies of the Chinese government, he expressed his concerns about the Chinese actions in Tibet. From this document we learn of some of the terrible happenings that were part of the Chinese "democratic reforms" campaign.

The Panchen Lama reported that massive destruction had been carried out:

> *Innumerable Buddhist images, sutras, and shrines have been burnt to the ground, thrown into rivers, demolished, or melted. There has been a reckless and frenzied destruction of monasteries and shrines. Many Buddhist statues have been stolen or broken open for their precious contents.*[423]

Tibetans' religious sentiments had been intentionally insulted by using holy Buddhist scriptures for toilet paper and as an inner lining for shoes.

Monks and nuns who refused to renounce their religion were subjected to fierce public humiliation and often imprisoned. Almost all others were forced to secularize so that monasteries were virtually depopulated. Many were extremely spiritual and otherworldly lamas, who had no understanding of the demands of Chinese. They were too involved with the spiritual plane to be concerned with worldly matters; but as they resisted reeducation they were imprisoned as reactionaries.[424] The Panchen Lama reported,

> *Before Democratic Reform in Tibet. . .in the whole of Tibet . . .there were a total of about 110,000 monks and nuns. Of those, possibly 10,000 fled abroad, leaving about 100,000. After*

---

[423] Warren Smith, "Panchen Lama's 70,000 Character Petition," 1997, 12. www.rfa.org/english/news/tibet/warrensmithbooks/Warren5A.pdf, accessed January 1, 2024.
[424] Smith, 11.

democratic reform was concluded, this number of monks and nuns living in the monasteries was about 7,000, which is a reduction of ninety-three percent.[425]

In 1964, at twenty-six years of age, the Panchen Lama called for Tibetan independence. Ironically, he was declared an enemy of the Tibetan people by the Chinese government. He, too, was publicly humiliated and then imprisoned. (He was released in 1977 and eventually was considered "rehabilitated." He rose to high position in the Chinese government, before dying in 1989 at age forty.)

The next Panchen Lama was six when he was recognized by the Dalai Lama as the Panchen Lama. He was immediately seized by Chinese authorities in 1995 and put into "protective custody." He hasn't been seen by Tibetans since. In that same year, Chinese officials, after declaring themselves "arbiters of Tibetan custom," chose their own Panchen Lama, complete with a sacred ceremony. The Chinese government even has its own religious school for reincarnated Buddhas. On the topic of the Chinese finding and selecting reincarnated Buddhas, the Dalai Lama said,

> *The very fact that the Chinese are trying to select is totally senseless. Can you imagine some sacred Hindu tradition being performed by a Communist who does not even believe in religion. How can it be possible?*[426]

China does not take the prize in cultural annihilation, though. It is easy for us to blame "those other people," like the Chinese. Unfortunately, we should recognize instead that genocide is something that human societies tend to do in every age. It just doesn't seem to stop.

---

[425] Smith, 12.

[426] Newsweek staff, "The Day of the Living Buddhas," *Newsweek*, March 5, 2000, https://www.newsweek.com/day-living-buddhas-156733

The Loss of Knowledge

Aristarchus of Samos wrote in the fourth century BCE that the planets revolve around the sun, a heliocentric model which Galileo had to rediscover many centuries later. Aristarchus's work is now lost and only known through secondary sources. So are many books written by Julius Caesar and Sulla, as well as the Emperor Claudius's book on dice games and Eudemus of Rhodes's fourth century histories of arithmetic, astronomy and geometry and about two-thirds of the works of Aristotle. Marcus Terentius Varro, a contemporary of Julius Caesar, wrote a famous work describing Roman institutions and religion, *Antiquities of Human and Divine Things*, which still existed in the fifth century, but has since been lost. These are just some of the thousands of valuable lost works from ancient times that we know once existed.

Something similar will happen to our more recent achievements in Western Civilization when our culture collapses. Imagine most of Shakespeare lost, all of Plato, Mozart, Tchaikovsky; the American Constitution; the works of Madison, Newton, Einstein, Darwin, Adam Smith, Saint Francis; the impressionist paintings; Rembrandt; Michelangelo; even Miles Davis and Led Zeppelin, all of it lost forever. It is inevitable. Our material and intellectual worlds are here now and then gone forever. Everything has a finite lifespan, even art, music, religion and ideas.

Our Responsibilities to Future Generations

Who owns Shakespeare's works today? We all do. Who owns the music of Michael Jackson, Louis Armstrong or Bob Marley? Technically, someone might own the rights; but really, we all own the content. A musician records a song, releases it into the world and it becomes part of our reality. We can play it whenever we want. Some of these songs repeat in our heads and won't stop. By writing a hit song, the musician gives the world a gift that affects all of us in some way. It's the same with literature, art, architecture, scientific discoveries, anything created by people. Once brought to light, the creation is added to our collective lives, our collection of possibilities; and it will persist, affecting other works to come even after it is lost and forgotten.

Theodore Parker, the great Unitarian minister, transcendentalist thinker and abolitionist sermonized on this topic:

> *The wisdom that this generation shall develop, foster, and mature will not perish with this age; it will be added to the spiritual property of mankind, and go down bequeathed as a rich legacy, to such as come after us. . .a property which does not waste, but greatens in the use.* [427]

He continues,

> *At death the. . .greatness becomes public property to the next generation. The piety of Jesus of Nazareth did not die out of mankind when he gave up the ghost; the second century had more of Christ than the first; there has been a perpetual increase of Socratic excellence ever since the death of the Athenian sage...This is a remarkable law of Providence, but a law it is...So the great men of antiquity continue to help us—Moses, Confucius, Buddha, Zoroaster, Pythagoras, Socrates, Plato. . .* [428]

The sermon continued,

> *Into our spiritual labors other men shall enter, climb by our ladder, then build anew, and so go higher up towards heaven than you or I had time or power to go. There is a spiritual solidarity of the human race, and the thought of the first man will help the wisdom of the last. A thousand generations live in you and me.* [429]

All of the great achievements of humanity have been the result of human genius, suffering, diligence and hard work. Most have been given to us

---

[427] It is ironic, that this very sermon he wrote is a case in point. Parker's sermons are a blessing to those of us who read them.

[428] Theodore Parker, "Sermon II, Of Truth and the Intellect," *Ten Sermons of Religion*, 14.

[429] Parker, 24.

as our birthright from the generations before us. Some, achieved in our lifetimes, have become an integral part of our shared experience. We take them for granted, but these works of the human spirit are precious. We made them. They belong to us.

It is our responsibility to preserve and to pass the creation of all of us, our civilization, onto future generations. It was the previous generations' gift to us and our gift to our children. It is our duty to preserve our Western culture's accomplishments for the generations to come. So how does the inevitable annihilation of our culture fit with our responsibility to preserve and pass on our civilization? I know, history demands from time to time that civilizations be destroyed and lost forever. It will happen here as it happens everywhere. Let us hope we never see it.

But even after a culture has been destroyed, its ideas often linger—through a merging of conquering and conquered peoples, refugee communities or rediscovery. Still with its destruction, its living vitality dissipates, and this loss diminishes humanity's "rich tapestry."

The Painful Truth

The recounting of these horrific instances of cultural annihilation and genocide leaves me with a crushing loss of faith in humanity and the world in general. Genocide, to me, stands as the most abhorrent of all crimes. It obliterates the works, not to mention the masterpieces, of an entire culture—the collective creation of thousands to millions of individuals over countless generations. During these outbreaks of unthinkable barbarity, the destroyers devolve into merciless savages, embodying the darkest aspects of human nature. Without realizing what they are doing, they destroy our shared legacy. I feel very emotional about this. The wrongness of it all—it is just too much.

The problem is that here I am inserting my personal subjective feelings into the problem at hand. That snowman did a number on me. Remember, I said the individual is of no consequence. Our perspective on the world is inherently limited, akin to that of mice—tiny beings in a vast, complex universe that extends far beyond our comprehension. We do not matter. I suppose that includes me and my thoughts and feelings. Still, I cannot fathom why the process of history must be so murderous and horrible. But it is. And who can know the mind of God, or the Spirit of History? I think none of us can. We are mere infinitesimal bits of Humanity. It doesn't matter what we individuals think. It is all about the big picture—the evolution of the Spirit of History through cycles of creation and destruction.

Perhaps the depth of this pain stems from my (and our) deep-rooted bond with our civilization and with humanity in general. We are all fundamentally invested in the fate of our species. Imagining our civilization wiped out or the death of humanity brings to me the deepest sense of bitter sadness. I am sure all of us would experience a deep, heartfelt sorrow if humanity's end were near. Our common history and collective future bind us in ways that become painfully clear when confronted with the possibility of our total destruction.

The death of any culture is just a dress rehearsal for the death of our own culture. Maybe that is why I feel so strongly about genocide.

I just cannot put together the pieces that I have presented in this essay. There is not a coherent whole here. The ideas appear to be at cross purposes. It seems impossible to me to bask in history (as I would a hot bath), to revere it like I would a god, while at the same time being aware of the occasional outpourings of brutality that societies occasionally inflict on each other. How can you love that?

To truly understand history is to embrace its mysterious dual nature—its creations delight us, while its destructions devastate us, driving us to preserve what remains.

I guess we have to accept that a part of the historical process involves the destruction of cultures—wholesale murder, the worst thing I can imagine—but I guess that is how it works. It isn't about me and what I like and abhor. It is about the bigger picture. And that is the entire point.

Wrapping It Up

Do me a favor, and please read these points slowly.

- There at two types of knowledge: the analytical type and the intuitive type. A complete person operates from both, often to the displeasure of others.

- History can be understood through both analytical and intuitive/mystical approaches. Great historians like Toynbee and Spengler often incorporated their mystical experiences into their understanding of history. Mystical experiences, like mine on the beach, reveal history's timeless unity, connecting us all to our shared march of humanity.

- History is not random. There are cycles in it, but it is not primarily cyclical either. In the grand scale, it is linear, though its occasional brutal episodes can obscure the fact that we are progressing.

- History portrays the mostly linear progressive evolution of consciousness. It can be seen as the story of the Spirit of History's maturing towards self-realization, with humanity serving as the vehicle for this awareness. As our societies evolve, we gain greater freedom to explore and live according to our deepest aspirations. Our civilizations, cultures, and institutions are the temporary vessels housing this evolving spirit.

- Our history is like the glue that binds us together. All of us benefit from and are constrained by our common past. Our thoughts, actions and possibilities are limited by the historical context we're born into.

- History is not just a series of isolated events, but the shared story of humanity's journey through time. It permeates the core of our being. We carry the Spirit of History with us in our souls.

- We are part of the ongoing historical process. What we do influences future generations, just as what the dead have done influences us.

- We individuals repeat the same cycles of life as our ancestors did, and our descendants will do the same after us. Our lives are not unique. We are playing out the same drama over and over throughout the generations. Nothing is new under the sun.

- Historical events, even from centuries ago, have parallels in modern times, further illustrating this cyclical nature of human experience.

- History created the societies we live in, the stories we tell ourselves, and the technology we use. History created the environment within which we live our lives.

- Our civilizations are the product of the accomplishments of millions of our forebearers. Although imperfect, our civilizations are masterworks in progress. They must be preserved and passed down to succeeding generations.

- But even when destroyed, many ideas of our cultures persevere through intermarriage of cultures, diaspora and rediscovery.

- In the larger course of things, we individuals are unimportant. The real story is the story of humanity. It is our great overarching human project, whether we are aware of it or not. We all contribute to it. We are all players in the great story; but after we are gone, humanity will continue to play out its story.

- Rare individuals like Rafael Lemkin can help push the Spirit of History forward.

- We cannot understand the Spirit of History. Its progression through time sometimes involves a brutal sacrificing of us individuals and our civilizations, along with some of our greatest achievements.

- But while cyclical collapses disrupt progress, they fuel renewal, advancing the Spirit of History's linear march towards greater consciousness.

- Yet still, we are the living embodiment of the Spirit of History. History is us.

Essay 11
We Are All Here Together: Speaking with the Dead, Ramblings of the Madman, and the Soul of the World

Ye are all leaves of one tree and the drops of one ocean.
— Bahá'u'lláh

All Is Not Lost

Even if a society is destroyed, along with all of its literature, art, architecture, political systems, religions and everything else, its accomplishments may not be lost forever. According to a long series of thinkers, the achievements of humankind do not only exist in the material world. They are stored, like library books, in some sort of supernatural repository for the benefit of the rest of us. I know, you are thinking, where is he going with this? Well, read on. This is going to get very interesting.

Ralph Waldo Emerson and the Over-Soul

Most adults have heard of Ralph Waldo Emerson, and if you have made it this far in the book, you probably know quite a bit about him. Emerson was a well-known preacher, poet, essayist, philosopher and speaker. He lived in New England from 1802 to 1882, advocated for the abolition of slavery and remains one of the most influential writers of the nineteenth century. He is most remembered for his inspiring quotes. In fact, a large number of today's self-improvement books contain quotes from Emerson, such as:

- The only person you are destined to become is the person you decide to be.

- Dare to live the life you have dreamed for yourself. Go forward and make your dreams come true.

- Our greatest glory is not in never falling, but in rising up every time we fall.

- Do not go where the path may lead, go instead where there is no path and leave a trail.

Unfortunately, even though they sound like Emerson and are attributed to Emerson, Emerson didn't write any of the above statements.[430] But he did write these:

- God will not have his work made manifest by cowards.[431]

- It is easy in the world to live after the world's opinion; it is easy in solitude to live after our own; but the great man is he who in the midst of the crowd keeps with perfect sweetness the independence of solitude.[432]

---

[430] The problem is that Emerson wrote in the language of his time, which is not our language of today. These quotes falsely attributed to Emerson say essentially what he was conveying, but in our modern style. If you want to find them online, just type the quote into your browser and you will find them all over the place, especially in websites of famous quotations.

[431] Ralph Waldo Emerson, *The Essay on Self-Reliance*, (The Roycrofters, 1908), 31.

[432] Emerson, *The Essay on Self-Reliance*, 19.

❧ Nothing is at last sacred but the integrity of your own mind.[433]

Emerson covers the same themes as those made-up quotes. And it is for these kinds of sentiments that he is famous. Even today, I was reading a paragraph in Brendon Burchard's *High Performance Habits*, which is remarkably similar to Emersonian thinking.

> *The main motivation of humankind [is] to be free, to express our true selves and pursue our dreams without restriction—to experience what may be called personal freedom. Our spirits soar when we feel unencumbered by fear or the weight of conformity. When we live our truth—expressing who we really are, how we really feel, what we really desire and dream of—then we are authentic; we are free.*[434]

Despite all his fame, the most important points that Emerson tried to make have mostly been forgotten by time. If you spoke of how all the experiences and thoughts of the dead still exist in some metaphysical sense and that we can all somehow tap this information. . .if you said this to average people on the street, they would think you absolutely looney. And if you were a writer, you would be discredited by critics as a goofball. But this is what Emerson wrote about quite a bit. Earlier, we spoke about how the divine essence of the prophets' messages were lost to succeeding generations. Instead, cheap, easily accessible facsimiles of their great truths were passed down. Exactly the same has happened with Emerson. Popular culture has completely missed the mark on Emerson. But what's new? Fortunately, in Emerson's case, we actually have his writings, so we can see what it is he was trying to express.

According to Emerson, every thought, every emotion, every experience ever entertained throughout history is accessible to all of us and continues to influence us all. It is well-known that we can access the thought and experience of famous individuals in books, on the

---

[433] Emerson, *The Essay on Self-Reliance*, 30.

[434] Brendon Burchard's *High Performance Habit*, (Hay House Publishing, 2017), 274.

internet and at lectures. But what about the contributions of the rest of humanity? Emerson wrote:

> *There is one mind common to all individual men.*
> *Every man is an inlet to the same and to all of the same...*
> *What Plato has thought, he may think;*
> *what a saint has felt, he may feel;*
> *what at any time has befallen any man, he can understand.*
> *Who hath access to this universal mind is a party*
> *to all that is or can be done,*
> *for this is the only and sovereign agent.*[435]

This bank of thoughts, emotions and experiences exists in some supernatural realm we cannot perceive with our senses and scientific instruments. Emerson, along with his fellow Transcendentalists, called it the Over-Soul. Through it, all humans, regardless of time or place, are linked to one another.

The Transcendentalists

The Transcendentalists were a group of radical Boston-area thinkers who were active from the mid-1830s up to the civil war. They were born into a world of New England conformity. (Remember, the Puritans had settled the Massachusetts area Two hundred years earlier.) Religious doctrines and social morays were dictated by society, and all but outcasts and madmen obeyed. Exterior and interior worlds were formed by the prevailing conservative standards of the time and place. The Transcendentalist movement broke away, partially in reaction to that constricting societal straitjacket. The enhanced individuality that we Americans enjoy today comes in large part from that historical fissure.

To Transcendentalists, truth comes from within, not without. Their view is that dogma and traditions limit people from being what they

------

[435] Ralph Waldo Emerson, "History," *Emerson: Essays* (Humphries, 1899), archive.org/details/emersonessays00emergoog/page/n12/mode/2up. Emerson wrote this in a prose essay, but it just seems clearer when arranged as a poem, so I put it in poetic form.

can be. Dogma and traditions fashion people to be near identical in thought and aspirations. Dogma and tradition are the constraints of history upon our spirits. (Hegel would have loved this.)

If only individuals would attend to the Divine spark within, they could break free, or transcend, and live unique fulfilling lives that hopefully would benefit all of humanity. For example, Beethoven followed his inner wisdom, breaking many of the traditions of formal composing and gave to Humanity his gift, his Fifth Symphony. (You know the one: Da da da dummm!). Beethoven's works are a product of bottom-up thinking rather than top-down thinking. Rather than be constrained by the rules of how music should be (top-down), he followed his spirit (bottom-up) and wrote compositions that we still enjoy hundreds of years later.

The Transcendentalists believed that the truth of religion does not come from tradition or historical facts but emanates from the soul. By cultivating self-reliance and intuition, we can tap into this collective consciousness, the Over-Soul, and gain spiritual insight and realize our unique potential. If we attend to our souls, we can experience religious truth, master our unique gifts and become one with God.

The God of the Transcendentalists is fundamentally Christian, but without the fire and brimstone dogma of earlier Puritan generations.[436] Still, they, like their Puritan forebearers, believed that they were trail-blazing the way for humanity, demonstrating what religious life could be for those who might follow. The Transcendentalists dreamed of a new "City on a Hill." Some of them even tried to establish a utopian community, Brook Farm, to be a shining light in the darkness for all the world to emulate. Many famous Transcendentalists were involved in the experiment. Nathaniel Hawthorne later wrote about it in a short novel. Unfortunately, it did not work out as planned.

The Transcendentalists were influenced by the German Romantics. Both groups believed strongly in the power of the unconscious mind

---

[436] In fact, Transcendentalism is an offshoot of the Unitarian Church, which itself evolved from the Puritan religion.

and the need for individuals to follow their own unique paths. You may remember Henry David Thoreau spent a much-publicized night in prison for refusing to pay a tax to fund President Polk's war with Mexico. (He would have stayed longer but someone anonymously paid his taxes.) This was Thoreau bucking social pressures and living according to his own authentic beliefs. Other famous Transcendentalists include Theodore Parker, Margaret Fuller and William Henry Channing. Many of them transitioned into abolitionists during the ante-bellum period.

Soul and the Over-Soul

Emerson wrote on the soul and its relationship to the Over-Soul:

> *The soul in man is not an organ,*
> *but animates and exercises all the organs;*
> *is not a function, like the power of memory, of calculation,*
> *of comparison, but uses these as hands and feet;*
> *is not a faculty, but a light; is not the intellect or the will,*
> *but the master of the intellect and the will;*
> *is the background of our being, in which they lie.*[437]

According to Emerson, our souls are filled and animated by the Over-Soul, which is the collective soul of all people past and present. "Man is a stream whose source is hidden. Our being is descending into us from we know not whence."[438] The soul of every person, both living and dead, is unified in the Over-Soul.

When people act from their souls, their unique brand of Truth from their higher self becomes evident:

> *When it breathes through his intellect, it is genius;*
> *when it breathes through his will, it is virtue;*
> *when it flows through his affection, it is love.*[439]

---

[437] Emerson, "The Over-Soul."

[438] Emerson, "The Over-Soul."

[439] Emerson, "The Over-Soul."

As Emerson explained, God is also connected to the Over-Soul, so that by connecting to the Over-Soul, we are indirectly connecting to God.

> *Within man is the soul of the whole;*
> *the wise silence;*
> *the universal beauty, to which every part and*
> *particle is equally related,*
> *the eternal One.*[440]

Each one of us, then, is a unique manifestation of God.

Emerson sparked a huge scandal when he proclaimed in a 1838 commencement address at Harvard Divinity School that Jesus was not any more divine than we can be.

> *[Jesus Christ] saw with open eye the mystery of the soul. . .he lived in it, and had his being there. Alone in all history, he estimated the greatness of man. . .He saw that God incarnates himself in man. [Jesus] said, in this jubilee of sublime emotion, 'I am divine. Through me, God acts; through me, speaks. Would you see God, see me; or, see thee, when thou also thinkest as I now think.*[441]

Often after our athletes perform an extraordinary feat, they will point to the sky, which I think gives the credit of their accomplishment on the field to God, not to themselves. This follows the Transcendentalist idea that our brilliance flows from God.

> *When I watch that flowing river, which, out of regions I see not, pours for a season its streams into me, I see that I am a pensioner; not a cause but a surprised spectator of this ethereal water.*[442]

Or in modern, less poetic, terms: our souls are receivers of God's essence. When we are at our most effective, we are merely letting God's energy flow through us.

---

[440] Emerson, "The Over-Soul."

[441] Ralph Waldo Emerson, commencement address to Harvard Divinity School, 1838.

[442] Emerson, "The Over-Soul."

These ideas about Over-Soul are infused into parts of our schema, even though most of us just haven't given it a name, like Emerson did.

The other day, I heard Lex Fridman say on a podcast:

> *Where do ideas come from?...Tell me one scientist or artist that can tell you where their good ideas come from...It's never systematic. It's always, like...you're like channeling, you're a receiver, an antenna or something. Where is that coming from?*[443]

Could he be referring to the Over-Soul without knowing?

Complicated Lives Block Out the Over-Soul

Why don't we always act from this higher source? The problem is that we are flawed creatures. Our emotional and mental preoccupations prevent us from receiving as much of the Divine inspiration of the Over-Soul as we could. Emerson wrote,

> *The influence of the senses has, in most men, overpowered the mind to that degree, that the walls of time and space have come to look real and insurmountable.*[444]

We can all be Godlike, if we heeded our souls, but we don't. Instead, we are numbed by constant stimulation. We pursue our selfish desires. We act to shelter our fragile egos. All of this overpowers the gentle whispers of our souls. We don't hear them anymore, and we become stupid or brutish or we sleepwalk through life. We are certainly nowhere near the God-like potential that we could be. We create circumstances that require others to suffer so that we can achieve our ends. Ultimately, all suffering results from people not heeding the Divine guidance of their souls.

Since I was a child, I have viewed Divine inspiration (Emerson called it influx) as akin to a shower head. We stand under the shower and

---

[443] Lex Fridman, quoted in *Joe Rogan Experience* #1824, July 27, 2024, https://www.youtube.com/watch?v=5zlEvwmVOhA.

[444] Emerson, "The Over-Soul."

hope to be bathed in the clear water of the Divine. But as we age and our lives become complicated, the flow of Divine water through the shower head becomes impeded by minerals and grunge, that have lodged in the showerhead, so we receive little or none of the Divine flow. Our selfishness, our lies and our warped perspectives all serve as the metaphoric grunge preventing our reception of Divine inspiration. This is the common lot of humankind. Our psychological shortcomings stunt us spiritually. We have so much potential, and we unknowingly waste it because we haven't figured out how to remove the muck or prevent it from building up in the first place.

> *What we commonly call man, the eating, drinking, planting, counting man, does not, as we know him, represent himself, but misrepresents himself. Him we do not respect, but the soul, whose organ he is, would he let it appear through his action, would make our knees bend.*[445]

Indeed, all of us share the Over-Soul. When we meet others, rather than judge their physical, mental or emotional states, we should instead recognize them for what they are, unique manifestations of God, just like we are. We are all One in that way.

Feuerbach and the Soul of the World

If this concept of Over-Soul is true, then shouldn't the concept have been accessible to other people of other times?

Actually, it has been—over and over again in history.

At the same time Emerson was writing, Ludwig Feuerbach (1804–1872), a German philosopher, and follower of Hegel, wrote that Reason is the same in all people. It is universal and infinite. Thinking is not performed by individuals but by the species acting through the individual. [446] (I believe he means more than Reason here.)

---

[445] Emerson, "The Over-soul."

[446] This is the problem with thinkers, they all use different terms, sometimes referring to

> *In thinking, I am bound together with, or rather, I am one with—*
> *indeed, I myself am—all human beings.*[447]

For Feuerbach, thinking is performed through us by the spirit of the universe, or God.[448] Sounds familiar, doesn't it? This is just like Emerson's Jesus: "I am divine. Through me, God acts; through me, [God] speaks."

Certainly, in this realm of limited time and space, we are individuals. But at the same time, the whole idea that we are individuals is an illusion. We are instead a part of this Great Spirit that animates all of it. It has no limitations of time or space. We should always be aware of our dual nature.

Spirit is immortal, while we individuals are here briefly, playing only a small part in Spirit's never-ending unfolding. So what is history then? History is the story of the evolution of this Spirit—of its maturing.

To Feuerbach, the right way to believe in immortality, then, is to have

> *a belief in the infinity of Spirit and in the everlasting youth of*
> *humanity, in the inexhaustible love and creative power of Spirit,*
> *in its eternally unfolding itself into new individuals out of the*
> *womb of its plenitude and granting new beings for the glorification,*
> *enjoyment and contemplation of itself.*[449]

---

the same thing, and sometimes not. This is especially the case when you are dealing with writers in languages foreign to us, because then we have to rely on what the translator "thinks" the writer is writing about.

[447] *Gesammelte Werke*, ed. Werner Schuffenhauer (Akademie Verlag, 1981), 18, cited in Stanford Encyclopedia of Philosophy online.

[448] Feuerbach changed his thinking dramatically during his career. All references to Feuerbach here are to his earlier writings.

[449] Ludwig Andreas Feuerbach, *Thoughts on Death and Immortality from the Papers of a Thinker*, trans. J. A. Massey (University of California, 1980), 137, pdfcoffee.com/feuerbach-thoughts-on-death-and-immortality-pdf-free.html, accessed April 1, 2025.

If we are to entertain the thought that all people are truly one creature, we must accept that God is the animating Spirit itself, which means, we are God.

Individually, then, we are nothing. But together we are everything.

To be spiritually virtuous would then involve a mystical approach, submersing oneself into the Sprit. God is not the creator and director of the history as Christianity might claim, but rather, God is "a prolific artist who lives in and through it."[450]

So, although Hegel spoke of the Spirit of History actualizing itself through human events, it was Feuerbach who took it further and made it pointedly theological. Now we are talking about God, rather than the abstractions of Hegel. God lives through us.

Collective Unconscious and the Over-Soul

Sigmund Freud (1856–1939) is the one who made popular the belief in an unconscious mind. Before that, it was thought that all decisions were made consciously. Thanks to Freud, now many believe that the unconscious mind makes decisions and the conscious merely justifies them with rationality. (As you probably know, Freud also believed that the basic impulse that determines our decisions is sexual.)

Freud hand-picked Carl Jung (1875–1961) to be his successor to promote his radical ideas. Jung was Sigmond Freud's protégé for several years until he broke away to pursue his own ideas. Jung expanded upon Freud's ideas about the unconscious mind, but he dropped the sexual part.

Jung believed that our unconscious mind's deepest motivation is to integrate all the parts of ourselves, to become a whole person. As individuals, we need to establish an understanding of our suppressed

---

[450] "Ludwig Andreas Feuerbach," untitled article, *Stanford Encyclopedia of Philosophy*, December 9, 2013, revised September 20, 2023, plato.stanford.edu/entries/ludwig-feuerbach/#EarlIdeaPant, accessed Jan 1, 2025.

dark sides in order to become whole. Jung realized that dreams allow the unconscious to speak plainly, exposing both our unconscious tendencies and the desires we keep buried. For example, when we repeatedly sabotage ourselves, dreams can show us why. He practiced psychoanalysis on patients and on himself for decades, using dreams and other methods to bring integration. He wrote many books, most of which are in German professorial style, which means they are difficult to understand.

Like Emerson, Jung also wrote of the Over-Soul, but he used different words:

> *The true history of the mind [the collective unconsciousness] is not preserved in learned volumes, but in the living psychic organism of every individual. . .Aren't we the carriers of the entire history of mankind?*[451]

The history of humanity is stored inside all of us.

His most significant theory was that of the collective unconscious, which he described as the "deepest layer of the psyche, containing the experiences, fears, memories and all cognitive perceptions shared by all human beings on earth."[452] Sometimes Jung talked as if the collective unconscious should be considered God. [453] This sounds exactly like the Over-Soul and many scholars have since likened Emerson's Over-Soul to Jung's collective unconscious. For example, social psychologist William McGuire called Emerson's essay "History" "a regular parade of Jungian ideas and instances." [454] Citing Emerson's descriptions of "the one mind

---

[451] Carl Jung, *The Collected Works*, ed. Reid, Fordham and Adler (Princeton University, 1958), 11:35, in Neil B. Yetwin, "Thoreau, Jung, and the Collective Unconscious," *Thoreau Society Bulletin*, no. 265, Winter 2009.

[452] Jung in Yetwin, 9:42.

[453] Leon James, "A Comparison of Keywords in the Dynamic Psychology of Jung, Swedenborg and Freud," *Journal of Psychology and Clinical Psychiatry*, vol. 3, issue 3, August 8, 2015, medcraveonline.com/JPCPY/a-comparison-of-keywords-in-the-dynamic-psychology-of-jung-swedenborg-and-freud.html.

[454] Jung, in Yetwin, 9:42.

common to all men" and "this universal mind," Edward F. Edinger (1922-1998), an influential Jungian analyst, declared that the essay "describes clearly what Jung has termed the collective unconscious."[455] Except that Emerson died before Jung started writing.

It is odd that Jung's thought was so like that of Emerson, when he did not know anything about him. Which leads one to think that perhaps they both picked up the concepts elsewhere. And, in fact, they did.

Varro's Soul of the World

Jung and the Emerson are relatively modern. Nobody knows precisely how Emerson came up with the Over-Soul. But his ideas have been around for centuries. It is believed that the concept comes from a mashup of a variety of sources such as Swedenborg, the Hindu Vedas and others. But as far as I know, none of the Transcendentalists mentions Varro. But, they were well read in the classics, and I am convinced that the Transcendentalists read Saint Augustine's *City of God*, in which Augustine discusses Varro's ideas.

Marcus Terentius Varro (116–27 BCE) was a contemporary of Caesar and Pompey. He commanded one of Pompey's armies against Caesar in the Roman Civil War. He was also a very prolific writer. Many of his writings are mentioned by others in their books and letters, but most of his works have been lost to history. One of his major works, *Antiquities of Human and Divine Things*, described the culture and institutions of Rome and the Roman religion. Unfortunately, it is one of the books that was lost. We learn about Varro's ideas from Saint Augustine, who in his *City of God* spends quite a number of pages refuting Varro's ideas on religion—ideas that were in the now lost *Antiquities of Human and Divine Things*.

As we don't have Varro's original text (I am sure the Christians burnt every copy they could find), we have to trust that Saint Augustine was somewhat fair in stating Varro's view of the spiritual world. It appears

---

[455] Jung, in Yetwin, 9:42.

that much of Varro's discussion of religion describes the various gods and goddesses, but then he drops some radical deism. Augustine wrote:

> *The same Varro, then. . .says that he thinks that God is the soul of the world. . .and that this world itself is God. . .Here he seems, in some fashion at least, to acknowledge one God.*[456]

According to Augustine, Varro wrote that there are three grades of soul in universal nature. The first grade is that which nourishes living things with the power of life. The second grade of soul is our ability to sense things.

> *The third grade of soul is the highest, and is called mind, where intelligence has its throne. This grade of soul no mortal creatures except man are possessed of. Now this part of the soul of the world, Varro says, is called God, and in us is called Genius.*[457]

I want to interpret this last bit, for my own sake. I get tripped up on words often when I read writers from the past, so I need to simplify it:

> *The third grade of the soul, the greatest, is the universal mind, which is God. People can access this universal mind, and when we can, it is called Genius.*

Is this not the Over-Soul or Collective Unconscious we were just previously discussing? I think it is.[458]

Augustine wrangled hard, as he was wont to do, with Varro's Soul of the World claim.

---

[456] Saint Augustine, *City of God, Book 7*, Part 6, newadvent.org/fathers/120107.htm, accessed January 1, 2025.

[457] Saint Augustine, *City of God*, Book 7, ch. 23.

[458] Back to Emerson for a second: If you have read Emerson, you know that he has sentences of gold within a multitude of throwaway paragraphs. I don't think Emerson was capable of writing concise bullet points like business and military leaders do today. Emerson was not that clear on exactly what the soul is and what the soul is not and what the relationship between God and the Over-Soul is. Varro, on the other hand, was very clear about the Soul of the World, or at least Augustine's interpretation of Varro was clear.

> *And when. . .he says that Genius is the rational soul of every one,
> and therefore exists separately in each individual, but that the
> corresponding soul of the world is God, he just comes back to this
> same thing—namely, that the soul of the world itself is to be held
> to be. . .the universal genius. . .For if every genius is a god, and
> the soul of every man a genius, it follows that the soul of every
> man is a god.*[459]

Arguing for Varro, my response would be, no, the soul of every man
is a unique manifestation of God and together all souls comprise the
collective consciousness, which is one facet of God.

Swedenborg's Influence

It could have been Varro, through Augustine, who planted this seed in
the minds of Emerson and Jung. On the other hand, perhaps the main
reason that Emerson and Jung came up with this same concept is that
they were both familiar with the writings of Emmanuel Swedenborg
who lived about 100 years before Emerson and about 190 years before
Jung. Both Emerson and Jung revered Emmanuel Swedenborg.[460] They
didn't use his terminology, but my guess is that Swedenborg's ideas
greatly influenced their work.

In his Harvard address of 1836, Emerson praised Swedenborg.

> *There is one man of genius who has done much for this philosophy
> of life, whose literary value has never yet been rightly estimated. I
> mean Emanual Swedenborg. . .he saw and showed the connection
> between nature and the affections of the soul.*

---

[459] Saint Augustine, *City of God*, Book 7, ch. 13.

[460] In 1850, Emerson published an essay on Swedenborg as part of his seven-lecture
collection, entitled *Representative Men*. The other subjects of his writings were Plato,
Montaigne, Shakespeare, Napoleon and Goethe. Jung is quoted praising Swedenborg in his
autobiography, *Memories, Dreams, Reflections*. "I admire Swedenborg as a great scientist
and a great mystic at the same time. His life and work has always been of great interest
to me and I read about seven fat volumes of his writings when I was a medical student."

Scholars have differed on the effect of Swedenborg on Emerson's thought, but Clarence Hotson declared "Swedenborg had more influence on Ralph Waldo Emerson, directly and indirectly, than any other author."[461]

Remember Emerson writing about how the soul is a receptacle of heavenly influence? Here is Swedenborg on this topic.

> *All things inflow with man, so that man is only a recipient organ. . .As the eye is a recipient of light, the ears recipients of sound. . .so the understanding is a recipient of the light of heaven or of wisdom, and the will is a recipient of the heat of heaven, thus of love. There is nothing in man but the faculty of receiving.*[462]

I have written of Emmanuel Swedenborg in an earlier essay, but perhaps it is time to give a little more information about the man. Swedenborg was a respected eighteenth-century Swedish inventor, scientist and philosopher. He resembled Benjamin Franklin in that he investigated and published books on a variety of subjects, enlarging human knowledge in science. He was offered the chair of mathematics at the University of Uppsala; but he turned it down, since his best work at the time was in geometry, chemistry, and metallurgy. In some of his work, he anticipated the existence of neurons, the existence of the endocrine system, the function of the pituitary gland and the organization of the nervous system—discoveries that would be made much later. He became internationally known for his writings on the smelting of copper and iron. He also wrote philosophy books, trying to integrate philosophy with natural science. Up until a transformative experience, Swedenborg was merely a successful scientist who furthered human knowledge.

---

[461] Zuber, Devin, "The Sage and His Mystic: Ralph Waldo Emerson and Emanuel Swedenborg," Accessed on January 1, 2025 at newchurchhistory.org/articles/dz2002.php.

[462] Emanuel Swedenborg, "Conversations with Angels," *Collected Minor Works,* (Swedenborg Foundation), swedenborg.com/wp-content/uploads/2013/03/swedenborg_foundation_minor_works.pdf.

In 1745, at age fifty-seven, he went through a six-month period of intense dreams. He kept a dream journal and worked at interpreting his dreams much like Carl Jung did almost 200 years later.

During this period of intense dreams, which biographers consider a religious crisis, he underwent a transformation of character. He recognized and abandoned earlier personality traits of egotism, ambition, selfish pride, scientific vanity and lust. He was amazed how his arrogance had left him, along with a loss of sexual desire. He was becoming saintly.

It is said that his transformation became complete one night when he was dining in a private room in a tavern. The room darkened and the feeling in the room shifted. A man appeared who warned him not to eat too much. This frightened Swedenborg, who hurried home. He was awakened in his sleep by a dream of this same man. This time the man told him that he was the Lord, and that he would reveal spiritual truths to Swedenborg and that he would guide him in what to write. Following this, he was able to converse directly with spirits, which he continued to do nightly for the next twenty-seven years. He wrote over forty volumes describing what he learned, some of which were published and many of which were left in manuscript form at his death.

Explaining his new vocation, he wrote:

> *It has been granted me, now for several years, to be constantly and uninterruptedly in company with spirits and angels, hearing them converse with each other, and conversing with them. Hence it has been permitted me to hear and see things in another life which are astonishing, and which have never before come to the knowledge of any man, nor entered into his imagination. I have there been instructed concerning different kinds of spirits, and the state of souls after death—concerning hell. . .concerning heaven. . .and particularly concerning the doctrine of faith.* [463]

---

[463] George Trobridge, *Swedenborg, Life and Teaching* (Swedenborg Foundation, 1955), 83–84.

Swedenborg's claims may appear unbelievable on the surface. At first glance, he may seem to be just another charlatan in a long line of religious conmen. But what was his motive? Swedenborg did not intend to start a church. He had a speech deficiency and could not lecture to crowds. He had no desire for power, notoriety or wealth. He just wrote what he learned in his nightly mystic states.

Think about it.

> *The Lord created us to be capable of communicating with spirits and angels while still living in our bodies, as people actually did in the earliest times. After all, we are one with spirits and angels. In fact we ourselves are spirits clothed in flesh.*[464]

Angels and spirits are merely the souls of people who have already lived and died. They are everywhere around us, much like the flies pestering me as I write this.

Swedenborg and Christianity

Swedenborg was fundamentally a Christian, and all of his beliefs are based on the Bible. Except, he would not accept the Epistles of Paul nor the Acts of the Apostles as legitimate. He also did not approve of many books of the Old Testament.

He diverged from mainstream Christian thought in the following ways: He did not believe in a Trinity. He denied that angels and demons were different beings than humans. They were just the spirits of humans that had already died. He denied predestination. He denied that Christ intervened to take away our sins. He denied justification of faith, which means he believed you cannot get to heaven by merely confessing your belief on your deathbed. He believed we have free will and the final judgement whether we ultimately end up in heaven or hell is a decision we make for ourselves.

---

[464] Emanuel Swedenborg, *Secrets of Heaven* (Swedenborg Foundation, 2008), paragraph 69.

He must have been convincing, as a number of well-regarded writers have been influenced by Swedenborg. These include such famous names as: Balzac, Baudelaire, William Blake, Jorge Luis Borges, Elizabeth and Robert Browning, Carlyle, Coleridge, Dostoyevsky, Arthur Conan Doyle, Emerson, Hegel, Goethe, William James, Jung, Kant, Robert Frost, Schelling, Schopenhauer, D.T. Suzuki, Tennyson, Whitman and Yeats. Other notable people influenced by Swedenborg include Helen Keller, Johnny "Appleseed" Chapman and Franklin Delano Roosevelt.

Consciousness Beyond the Physical

Jung and Swedenborg had a lot of ideas in common. Both believed that consciousness extends beyond the physical body. Swedenborg wrote that consciousness does not reside in the organs of the physical body. Instead, all consciousness and meaning reside in the psychic-body (which Jung would call the Collective Unconscious). Jung wrote that any potential thought or feeling we could have is already contained in the Collective Unconscious. We merely need to access it. Jung explicitly designated the Collective Unconscious as infinite and divine.[465]

Jung admitted that he had only an obscure and unclear idea of the Collective Unconscious. It could not be directly observed in ordinary consciousness. He used indirect methods such as spontaneous word associations, active imagination, and the analysis of dreams and religious symbols. His methods worked and formed the basis of Jungian analysis practiced today.

Swedenborg, on the other hand, had obtained passage into this Collective Unconscious. Every night for twenty-seven years, Swedenborg would enter the Collective Unconscious, where he would communicate with spirits of people who had already died. He spoke with people he had known while they were living. He spoke to long-dead authors whose

---

[465] James.

books he had read. Jung had communicated with the dead as well, but I don't think he received the extensive schooling that Swedenborg got.[466]

Swedenborg was directly conscious of what Jung called the Collective Unconscious. whereas Jung could only dimly perceive it.[467]

> *Jung dimly realized that the psychic world of the Collective Unconscious is the immortal world of the afterlife into which every human being enters upon death. Jung held that the Collective Unconscious is where all of humanity is congregated, unconsciously to us while we are on earth, but consciously in the afterlife.*[468]

Why is This Important?

Why do I spend so much time on this subject of Over-Soul, Collective Unconscious, the Soul of the World, and Swedenborg's Spiritual World of Eternity? It is because I believe that these concepts are fundamentally true. As I have written earlier, humans can never know the Truth. But some of us can have glimpses. Jung had them. Swedenborg was a true exception. He was able to pass into the spiritual world and directly learn from the entities that are out there.

It is also reassuring that these concepts were not invented by some lunatic. People have been thinking these concepts for thousands of years in very diverse places. For space reasons I did not mention that besides Varro, Emerson and Jung, these concepts are found in the Indian holy writings, the Vedas, which feature the world-animating spirit, Brahma. Plotinus, the third century founder of Neoplatonism, wrote of the Universal Soul. He wrote of mystical union with the One. The Roman emperor Julian (the Apostate) was deeply influenced by Neoplatonism. Teilhard de Chardin, a twentieth century priest and archeologist, also wrote on this topic, but he used the term the Noosphere. These ideas

---

[466] James.

[467] James.

[468] James.

of the unity of all minds, souls or whatever you call them have been around in various forms for centuries.

Morphic Resonance

Rupert Sheldrake, whom I referenced in earlier essays, was a contemporary English author and biologist who took these ideas even further into a more unified theory of morphic resonance that is actually backed by scientific experiments.

Sheldrake has written more than ninety scientific papers and nine books. His books have been published in twenty-eight languages. He is considered among the top 7.5% of researchers, based on number of citations of his work. His theories are controversial. He questions materialist thinking and scientific dogmatism. In 2013, he gave a TEDx talk on "The Science Delusion," which, among other things, questions the materialist worldview—that is, that the universe, animals and people are unconscious machines, as discussed in one of my earlier essays. Two materialist critics objected to the talk and were able to pressure TED to take the talk out of circulation. Sheldrake's TEDx talk was eventually reinstated, relegated to a corner of the website and stamped with a warning label. His Wikipedia page has also been subject to controversy and eventually censorship. As of this writing, Sheldrake continues to write and publish.

The concept of morphic resonance is like that of Over-Soul and of the Collective Unconscious. It is the concept that people's minds resonate with one another and therefore are linked.

According to Sheldrake:

> *Magnetic fields extend beyond the surfaces of magnets. The Earth's gravitational field extends far beyond the surface of the earth, keeping the moon in orbit. Solar radiation extends far beyond the surface of the sun. The morphic fields of our minds do the same,*

extending far beyond our bodies, and we do it through intention and attention.[469]

This explains why people who are focused on their goals are more likely to meet success than those who give them less mental energy. Successful people often talk about the power of the mind being the key to their success. Even though they may not have conceptualized morphic fields, they have experienced their power. Focus on something and you get it.

He explains that our memories are not necessarily stored inside our brains, but rather our brains are more like cellphones. They broadcast, but they also receive. We broadcast to, and receive from, the human morphic fields or the Over-Soul or Collective Unconscious, whatever you want to call it.

Morphic fields are not limited to humans. Each species has its own morphic field. This accounts for the unique instincts of different types of animals. Each individual in a species inherits a collective memory from past members of the species. Morphic fields also contribute to the collective memory, affecting other members of the species instantaneously and into the future. This means that new patterns of behavior can spread more rapidly that we would expect. Rather than learning new behavior only by seeing or learning of others doing the same, individuals in a species can learn unconsciously from others who are thousands of miles away. "For example, if rats of a particular breed learn a new trick in a Harvard lab, then rats of that breed should be able to learn the same trick faster all over the world, say in Edinburgh and Melbourne." Sheldrake documents cases of this in his book *Morphic Resonance.*[470] We can witness the evolution of other species when they learn new behaviors that become "instinctive." Their morphic fields can evolve before our eyes.

---

[469] Rupert Sheldrake, "Morphic Resonance and Morphic Fields – An Introduction," *Rupert Sheldrake, sheldrake.org/research/morphic-resonance/introduction,* accessed July 1, 2024,
[470] Sheldrake, *Morphic Resonance.*

It appears at first glance that the Collective Unconscious of Jung and the Over-Soul of Emerson are set and unchanging, but they are not. They too are evolving. We just don't live long enough to notice the changes. The archetypes of Jung have been with us for centuries, but new archetypes can evolve as our lifestyles and environments change. The Over-Soul contains the experience of all people before us. Each of us continues to add to the content of the Over-Soul/Collective Unconscious.

The Over-Soul and History

I know, this entire essay seems to be a diversion from the earlier ones, but it all fits together. As I noted earlier, my thesis is not linear; it is too complicated a thesis to treat in linear fashion. Instead, it is more like a puzzle with each essay another puzzle piece. All the pieces fit together, to make a complete picture. I wish it could be simpler with linear thinking, but it just isn't.

You can murder a civilization, as we have seen in the prior essay. You can destroy or rewrite written history, but the true spirit of the past still lives on in a spiritual plane, the Over-Soul. It cannot be destroyed. It remains a part of all of us. That eternal Spirit always remains an intrinsic element of our collective human essence. It is a fundamental part of who we are.

And, we are more connected than we think. All people, all of us, are connected and animated by this Spirit. We all share the Over-Soul. And that is precisely the point. We share a world. We share a past. We share a consciousness. We are but parts of one creature, and that creature is God.

So how would the world be different if we all realized this fact, and if this self-knowledge became fundamental to our schemas? What would we live for? How would our societies change?

Wrapping It Up

- The Over-Soul, as conceived by Ralph Waldo Emerson, is a collective consciousness that connects all humans and stores all experiences, thoughts and emotions experienced by all humans living and dead.

- Emerson and the Transcendentalists believed that by cultivating self-reliance and intuition, individuals could tap into the Over-Soul and realize their unique potential.

- This concept of the Over-Soul challenges the notion of individuality, suggesting that we are all part of a greater spiritual whole.

- Carl Jung's concept of the Collective Unconscious has similarities to Emerson's Over-Soul, despite Jung not being directly influenced by Transcendentalist writings.

- Whereas Jung caught glimpses of the other world beyond the veil, Swedenborg visited it and communicated with spirits daily for decades and recorded what he learned.

- There are many other sources of pretty much the same idea: Ludwig Feuerbach's idea of a universal spirit that thinks through individuals; the ancient Roman thinker Varro's concept of the Soul of the World.

- Emanuel Swedenborg also spoke of the collective unconscious, calling it the psychic body. He wrote that people's consciousness resides not in the body but in the psychic body, one shared by all of us.

- Why is it that this idea of a collective unconscious recurs throughout history? There must be some inherent truth in these ideas that some of us are able to land upon.

- Rupert Sheldrake expanded on this concept, naming this Collective Unconscious, a morphic field. Memory is not stored solely in the brain, but extends beyond us. Our biological inheritance involves morphic resonance from past members of the species. This allows individuals to tap into a collective memory.

- Sheldrake drew analogies between morphic fields and other fields in nature, such as magnetic fields (extending beyond the surfaces of magnets), gravitational fields (extending beyond objects) and solar radiation fields (extending beyond the sun's surface).

- Morphic fields extend beyond our bodies through intention and attention. Using morphic fields, we knowingly or unknowingly use our thoughts and focus to influence the world around us.

- Different types of entities, such as species, even chemical combinations, contain their own morphic fields, drawing memories from previous systems of the same type. (When monkeys learn a trick in one lab, monkeys in other labs can easily learn it, too.)

- When a civilization is obliterated, not all is lost after all. It still remains in the Collective Unconscious.

- Our individual psychological short-sightedness and chronic focus on ourselves often prevent us from fully accessing the wisdom of the Over-Soul or Collective Unconscious.

- The Over-Soul is shared by all and is an integral part of our collective human essence. For this reason, we should embrace the history of humanity as a whole. It is our history.

Essay 12
Seeking Meaning in a Godless Age – From Idealism to Tyranny

Of all follies there is none greater than wanting to make the world a better place.
— MOLIERE

Toynbee and the Purpose of History

According to Toynbee, the true purpose of civilizations is to guide us towards a deeper appreciation for and adherence to what he called the "laws of God," or in other words, a universal or spiritual truth. It is not that the leaders of civilizations have any idea of that purpose and are consciously trying to push humanity in that direction. No. Instead, civilizations fulfill this role without their being aware of it. [471]

Our civilizations are like schools for humanity, but they bring us along so slowly we don't live long enough to see much change. Just as we go from our first-grade teacher to our second-grade teacher, so

---

[471] I hope by now you understand that by God, I do not mean some old heavenly dude with a white beard who judges people and determines their ultimate fate.

humanity progresses from civilization to civilization. It is a slow process, unfortunately, too slow for us to perceive. Toynbee wasn't the first to have this thought. And, of course, this sounds much like Hegel to me.

These lofty ideas are one thing, but just how has humanity been doing on the spiritual plane lately? Maybe not so well. Many throughout the centuries have lamented that humanity was progressing materially, but it was difficult to determine whether any progress was being made in a spiritual sense.

As Theodore Parker wrote in a sermon, his era, the ante-bellum era, was a time for rapid material advancement. Poverty would soon be eradicated from the English-speaking world. Once our material needs were taken care of, we would be ready for a spiritual leap. He felt that the next great leap was to break away from the Jesus myths of Christianity: God is not centered on a person, no,

> *the real historical incarnation of God is in mankind, not in one person, but in all, and human history is a continual transfiguration [towards God]…mankind is the true son of God that abideth ever, to whom the Father says continually, 'Come up higher.'*[472]

Coming to this realization is the next step that humanity will take, and is presently taking, as more and more people in the western world come to grasp this ultimate truth—God resides in us. God is us.

We are awakening to this reality, but very slowly. As noted, our advance as a whole is so slow that we cannot perceive it. Instead, we are distracted by the ceaseless clamor of our everyday lives, our favorite television shows and the senseless babel of the internet. We are blind to the actual longer-term trend that unfolds slowly over generations.

Parker believed that our deepening unity with God is the ultimate goal of history, much like Toynbee (one hundred years later) and Hegel (a few decades before him).

---

[472] Theodore Parker, "Of Conscious Religion and the Soul," *Ten Sermons of Religion*, 66–67.

Reaction to Toynbee

Although Toynbee's twelve-volume A *Study of History* was very popular among the general public, it was not popular among academics. Toynbee became one of the broadest and most popular targets in historical writing. Attacking him became a widespread intellectual pastime in the 1950s. Entire volumes were published consisting of collected criticisms of his ideas.

As I mentioned in an earlier essay, Toynbee injected religious ideas into his story of history, and professional academics hated that. According to Toynbee, injecting religion into history "signals the historical imagination at its greatest."[473] So why the fuss? Other historians have done this same thing—Augustine, Voltaire and Marx. And being in the company of Augustine, Voltaire and Marx is not such a bad thing. Nonetheless, like a pack of lions taking down large prey, hundreds of nameless academics set their claws into Toynbee and did their best to take him down. They dismissed him as a hack.

Historians are deadly serious about their craft and did not take kindly to Toynbee approaching history differently. Here is an example of the vitriol he experienced:

> *We have to take into account the still widespread conviction that Toynbee is one of the greatest frauds of our fraudulent age, a man almost constitutionally incapable of getting his facts straight, incredibly arrogant in his claims to omniscience, a dabbler in the spurious and dangerous field of 'meta-history' and not even a good metaphysician.*[474]

Anyone who challenges orthodoxy, I suppose, should expect the same. It is a tired old game that people continue to play, generation after generation. Tear down the individual who dares to write something

---

[473] Roland Stromberg, *Arnold J. Toynbee: Historian for an Age in Crisis*, (Southern Illinois University, 1972), xiii.

[474] Stromberg, xiii.

new. At least they didn't torture and kill him like they used to do in the Middle Ages.

Does History Have Meaning?

Academicians today still dismiss Toynbee for injecting religion into history, and they also dismiss the linear view that humanity is progressing towards some end. If history is not a progression towards something, then what do we have instead? Chaos? Endless cycles? Random, meaningless social movements, beliefs and systems that morph into other equally meaningless movements? If the cynicism of the academicians is the overarching truth, then collective history must not have any meaning. But history must have a meaning. Enough with the academics. I am siding with Toynbee. History is linear. We are going somewhere.

Today, most people base their actions on rational thought, rather than on divine guidance or religious doctrine. This preference for rationality and reasoning over faith-based approaches has been advancing in the West for hundreds of years, really gaining momentum since the Enlightenment. As I write this, it seems that the human race is moving backwards with respect to Augustine's, Hegel's and Toynbee's evolutionary path towards the Infinite. I think this retrograde movement is just more random fluctuation in the larger movement towards the ultimate end. The larger trajectory takes centuries. As our lives are so short, we likely cannot perceive it. We can only sense the fleeting ripples in the massive tide of progress.

Disaffection with Religion

I understand why people have left churches. Organized religion, well, especially the Catholic Church, through its history of hypocrisy, corruption and decadence has weakened the case for God. But Catholicism is not alone; other Christian sects have not been immune to the corrupting influence of power and wealth. Many of them have the same problems as the Catholic Church.

As noted in an earlier essay on groups, all groups tend towards totalitarianism. It is intrinsic in the nature of groups. The larger and more powerful the groups get, the more they need to control their members thoughts and actions and the more damage they tend to do to both outsiders and insiders.

The Catholic Church followed this predictable path. The Church has alienated generations through centuries of institutional sins, including torturing and executing heretics, using high church offices to generate wealth, selling of indulgences, massacres, wars, crusades, etc. It is right to be disappointed, if not disgusted, by the past sins of the Church. Certainly. And it is right to question whether an organization with such a tainted track record can ever be a force for good in the world.

It is likely that all large religions have power-hungry people in high positions who only care about their own personal power and gain. That is human nature. But that does not mean that there is no God. It only means that human organizations tend towards totalitarianism.

We must not conflate the existence of God with the inherent limitations of human organizations. As we discussed earlier in an essay on religion, they are different categories entirely. God is one thing, and organizations that are supposed to shepherd us to God are something entirely different. But many people do conflate the two and use this flawed reasoning to justify atheism. It is a poor argument, actually.

If the religious organizations are not to be trusted, then why should we trust them to define God or to lead us to God? Perhaps we shouldn't. But that doesn't mean there is no God. God is out there. It is just a matter of discovering God for yourself, like Krishnamurti said. Whether you want to believe or not, God is still out there.

God may not be what our religions would have us believe, and I am certainly not going to try to explain what God is. We are all different, we all perceive the world differently, which would mean, then, that we will all perceive God differently. My vision of God is not yours. Our paths to God are individual paths, like Krishnamurti said. Religions and gurus may guide us, but strict adherence to their paths will not necessarily lead anyone to God.

The problem is that most people don't have a clue how to find God for themselves and they need a path; hence, we have religions. What a conundrum! Religions are not to be trusted. But God exists. And most of us need guidance to find God so we turn to religion. Except, religion is not to be trusted. . .and I guess this continues in an endless spiral circling down the toilet. Meanwhile people continue to live and die with the imperfect solution religion offers, failing to strike out on their own to make or find their connection to God.

Relative Morality

Nietzsche famously wrote:

> *God is dead. God remains dead. And we have killed him. How shall we comfort ourselves, the murderers of all murderers?. . .Is not the greatness of this deed too great for us? Must we ourselves not become gods simply to appear worthy of it?*[475]

Many have different interpretations of what Nietzsche was writing about when he claimed God was dead. But it is commonly held that he was referring to the fact that God is no longer the bedrock upon which our schema is built.

If there is no God, on what foundation do we build our morality? If figures like Moses, Jesus or Mohammed never communed with the divine, then their teachings lose all divine authority. Then wouldn't Socrates's, Robespierre's or Vladimir Lenin's words be just as valid? Without God as our moral anchor, in what or whom should we trust? This absence leaves us with moral relativity, where essentially anything can be justified, even murder or genocide.

Theodore Parker preached about the crisis of religion in his time, the 1850s. He argued that when religion does not receive its fair share of

---

[475] Friedrich Nietzsche, "The Madman," *The Gay Science*, section 125.

public esteem, the human condition becomes sad and dreary. No great ideas excite the public mind. The priests become fat, the people become convinced that God is dead, and as a result corruption starts in high places and swiftly spreads to the rest of us. It is then that a new church is needed. We Americans must have been in this state for quite a while.

What Happens When God is Dead?

Before we go any further, I want to reiterate something. A religion, as I am writing this, means a set of beliefs, rituals and hierarchy associated with some denomination or cult. One can believe in God and not be religious. The way I see it, to be religious is to belong to a religion. To believe in God, the Absolute, the Universe, Allah, whatever it be, is independent of being religious. It just means you believe in God, the Absolute, the Universe or Allah. Okay, let's move on.

The anti-religious movement in the West really took form during the Enlightenment in the mid-eighteenth century. Voltaire and his French contemporaries mercilessly ridiculed the Church with rational and satirical arguments. This incessant questioning and ridicule ended up convincing enough people that soon after, the French expelled the Church from society. One of the first actions of the French Revolution was to seize Church lands in 1789. This was followed by banning the Church from educating the youth.

Up until that time, the Church was running the education system in the country. With the expulsion of the Church and resulting closure of the schools, local governments were tasked with taking over education; but for the most part, they didn't have the resources and results were spotty. In 1802, thirteen years later, Napoleon finally set up a state education system in France. In the meantime, a generation of French people lost out on several years of education. Many of those who were in secondary school in 1789, at the start of the revolution, never graduated. From 1793 to 1794, these youngsters formed part of the mob that fueled the infamous Reign of Terror. During that Reign of Terror, besides the beheadings of thousands of notable citizens, it is said that 30,000 Catholic clergy were exiled and hundred murdered, often after being tortured.

Some would claim that the Reign of Terror is a more extreme example of what can happen when you remove religion from a society. But the Soviets removed religion and then sent over 18 million to the Gulag camps. The German Nazis were replacing existing religions with state-controlled ideology, a fusing of Christian and pagan elements with Nazi elements.[476] They killed over 6 million Jews and 5 million non-Jews in extermination camps. But in all of these examples, the state sought to replace the old religion with their new state religion, be it French Republicanism, Marxist Leninism or Nazism. So a major cause of all this bloodshed is not lack of religion, it is state religion. Consider the crusades—another 2 to 3 million killed by state-sponsored religion. Lack of religion is a different story. That just leaves people empty inside.

What Else Did We Lose When We Abandoned Religion?

So what are we missing now that religion has been jettisoned to a peripheral role in society? What good have we lost when we threw out religion? There are many good things that the Church gave us, even if its doctrine and history may be questionable. Alain de Botton (1969–) gives a thoughtful treatment of this topic in his book, *Religion for Atheists*. I will address three of the losses de Botton discusses: Virtue, Role Models and Community.[477]

Virtue

Our society puts a lot of focus on really bad actions some of us perform, such as murder, robbery and the like. Our daily news is full of it. We

---

[476] Denominational schools were banned. Catholic youth organizations were banned. Thousands of clergymen were interned at Dachau and about 33% of those imprisoned died there. The Christian ideology did not tolerate racial theories. The Nazi's ultimate goal was to remove all religions from the Reich, but the war took top priority from 1939 on.

[477] The ideas from these sections on Virtue, Role Models and Community all come from Alain de Botton's book, *Religion for Atheists* (Vintage Books, 2012).

have created a criminal justice system to deal with it. Once someone has committed such actions, the police or child protective services gets involved and it is too late. Once you are a felon, it is difficult to get a job or be trusted by society again. Once people have crossed the line and committed crime, they have often ruined themselves for life.

Religions address crime before it happens. The last five of the Ten Commandments prevent crime. You shall not murder. You shall not commit adultery. You shall not steal. You shall not bear false witness against your neighbor. You shall not covet. The major religions addressed smaller failings as well. They realized that not just crime but selfishness, dishonesty, drunkenness and laziness can ruin a society as well. If we don't lie, we honor our parents, we don't covet other people's things, we work hard and we stay sober, then we are almost certain not to commit the greater crimes that can forever ruin our lives. We can avoid being smashed by the criminal justice system and scorned by the greater society.

During the medieval period, from the time of Pope Gregory the Great (in the sixth century) onwards, the concept of the seven deadly sins was key to Catholic teachings. These seven deadly sins are: pride, greed, lust, envy, gluttony (which includes drunkenness), anger and sloth. Each of these deadly sins can be overcome with one of the seven corresponding virtues, which are humility, charity, chastity, gratitude, temperance, patience and diligence. Back then the sins and the virtues could be found in paintings, on the backs of Bibles and prayer books, on walls of churches and public buildings. They served as a moral compass by which people could orient their lives in a virtuous direction. And the constant repetition of these concepts ingrained them into everyone's schema.[478] But that instruction has, for the most part, been lost, at least in today's secular society. How many of us today could recite the seven deadly sins or the seven cardinal virtues?

A list of today's social ills can be seen as a consequence of too many of us indulging in the seven deadly sins. Political and business leaders

---

[478] de Botton, 85–87.

who care more for their own enrichment than the general good are proud and greedy. Drug and alcohol problems are a widespread form of gluttony. Addiction to pornography is rooted in lust. Hatred of those who think differently from us stems from too much pride and anger. All of these social ills proceed from the seven deadly sins. Does any institution besides religion teach us to avoid these shortcomings?[479] Or to pursue the corresponding virtues? When is the last time you heard someone exhorting us to practice temperance? We are not allowed to teach these virtues in schools. So where are we supposed to learn them? Some families teach them to their children, but society does not reinforce them. Many of us don't learn and practice the virtues and as a result we have social problems.

Role Models

Of all the living people you know of, how many are good role models for children? How many living people do you think are worthy of emulating? My guess is that there are very few.

Everyone needs role models. And our major religions used to provide them. The saints, with their fantastical legends, provided us with great examples to emulate. Saint Francis, a rich youth, gave away all his wealth and wandered Italy preaching and helping others. He tamed the fierce Wolf of Gubbio that was terrorizing a town by making peace with him. This story demonstrated his love for all creatures and his ability to bring peace through compassion. Saint Margaret of Antioch survived many tortures, including being swallowed by a dragon, and emerged unharmed. She served as a model of endurance and faith under persecution. Other saints perhaps are not role models, but instead offer us comfort, such as Saint Jude, the saint of lost causes. We can commiserate with her and receive from her a gentle sense of comfort, without needing to find a solution.[480]

---

[479] The Freemasons, the old Boy Scouts, and Trail Life USA are three exceptions I can think of.

[480] de Botton, 91–92.

What do we have now? Tiger Woods? Warren Buffet? Oprah? They are just people like us. They may do great things, but they are imperfect humans who make mistakes. They cannot compare to the tall tales of the saints. Many of the saints were beautiful souls whose faults have been forgotten. It is these larger than life, seemingly impossible role models that truly stretch our behavior and inspire us to do great things. The veracity of the stories of the saints is not important here. What is important is that these were extraordinary role models to aspire to. We lost these inspiring role models when we lost religion.

Community

Religion also provided us with a sense of community. In a church, we are all equal before God. The billionaire and the poor person stand on an equal footing in the congregation. We are all merely individuals trying to live according to the doctrine as best we can with what we have. It isn't like that at cocktail parties, where we are judged by our level of success. In society, we remain within our groups, rarely interacting with strangers. But church is one of the few places we can go to meet people that we don't know. And it is one of the few places in which we are most likely to find things in common.

Christian sermons often highlight the importance of love. Loving your neighbor, your enemy, your children, your fellow man. Without religion, where else are we to receive this exhortation? A society that is ruled by love of our fellow man is a happy society. A society focused on selfishness (also known as self-love) will be full of liars and cheaters. Ultimately, it will be dysfunctional, dangerous and unhappy. So, all in all, church, as imperfect as it is, can be valuable for individuals and for society.

Atheism, the Surrogate Religion

In many cities in the Western world today, the influence of religion is minimal. Large parts of American and Western European societies have been secularized. While the majority believe in some form of God, the majority do not associate with any denomination. They do not attend services. This lack of religion leaves many of us with a sense of something missing, but we just don't know what we are missing. Often, we are so used to this missing element that we don't realize not everyone feels this void.

Without religion, who is going to comfort and guide us, week in and week out? How can we know we are going astray when we have no measuring stick to judge our actions by? The lack of a rule book, which I keep harping about, only applies to the non-religious. Religious people have a creed already. It is the non-churchgoers who are missing the spiritual and psychological benefits of a church. We just don't recognize it, as many of us have been in this desert for so long. So, I suppose an easy answer to my rule book problem is to just join a religion, any religion. It will not necessarily get you closer to God, but it may fulfill some deep human needs.

Alain de Botton addresses this issue in *Religion for Atheists*. He suggests that it is time to move beyond arguments about whether religious doctrines, including the existence of God, are real or not. Atheists can agree that religions are fabricated and agree that the religious will always think otherwise. Rehashing these stale arguments serves no purpose. Instead, atheists should just move on and recognize that religion does provide some important things that are sorely missing from our secular society today.

Religions realize that we are fundamentally just grown-up children, and so they treat us like children. And they are right to do so. We are spiritually and morally undeveloped. We need continual guidance so that we can aim our lives in positive directions. We need to be reminded to love our neighbor, not just ourselves. We need the occasional comfort that things are going to be okay. We need to escape our narrow preoccupation with our everyday problems and be exposed to the larger picture—the maturation of our souls. With this expanded perspective, we can see the issues that trouble us are really trivial after all. This is what organized religion provides us.

Recognizing this, some atheists are now forming "churches" to replace what they lost when they rejected religion. Overall, these atheistic churches are good for society and good for the individuals who participate in them, but they do not resolve the greater social problem that was alluded to by Nietzsche. These atheistic "religious" practices should be based on some authority, but what authority? Should they be based on the teachings of Jesus? Perhaps they should be based on the teaching of Tony Robbins, or why not Chairman Mao? How does one determine what are the good values that should be conveyed? And who has the authority to determine what teachings should be heard? Without social agreement on the nature of an Absolute, no values have any more credence than any other values. Without a unified set of beliefs that everyone agrees on, we will end up with a large number of organizations teaching various and conflicting values. And, this is pretty much where we are today.

But this is not a problem with atheistic religion in itself, it is a problem that accompanies "the death of God," which has created a vacuum in our collective souls. We have tried communism, Nazism and nationalism to fill this hole, but these ideologies have led to devastating waves of hatred, murder and war. The atheistic religion is merely a present-day attempt to address the emptiness and meaningless of our Godless world. But it is different in that it is likely to remain harmless, nothing like the movements that preceded it.

Positivism and the Religion of Humanity

About five decades after the demise of the Cult of Reason, another Frenchman, Auguste Comte,[481] introduced a religion that proved more successful than the previous revolutionary era attempts. Comte's Religion

---

[481] Comte is known as the founder of sociology and the coiner of the term "altruism." His emphasis on a scientific mathematical approach to decision-making has become the foundation for modern statistical analysis and business decision-making. He was well-known in intellectual circles and, it is said, greatly influenced John Stuart Mill, Karl Marx, Oswald Spengler and other thinkers.

of Humanity, like its unsuccessful forerunners, was not conceived in mystical revelation but rather was deliberately designed using rational thought. His aim was to foster social unity and advance human progress. This secular faith represented yet another attempt to apply logical thinking to the realm of spirituality and social organization.

Comte was born during the turmoil of the French revolution in Southern France. He was well acquainted with the excesses that had occurred in the name of "liberté, égalité, fraternité" during the revolutionary period. After years of rage, fear, hate, murder and war, French society was in need of stability. Comte developed a master philosophy that he hoped would achieve this, which he called Positivism. Comte's Religion of Humanity, described in his *Systeme de politique positive*, is an offshoot of his Positivist philosophy.

The basis of Positivism is that we do not and cannot know anything absolutely and what we know is relative, meaning we don't understand the essence of anything but only how some things relate to other things. The consistent relationships and sequences of events that we observe, we consider to be laws. But we don't know their essential nature or their ultimate cause and never will.[482] So there is no point in wasting mental energy on them. For example, he wrote that discussions of the existence or non-existence of God are a waste of time since we can never know for sure.

To Comte, the world's great religions might contain great humanitarian ideals and might serve a useful function in society, but they were not created by God. They were created by men, and their doctrines are based on imagination not facts. For this reason, they should be rejected. Questions addressed by religions, such as *where did the world come* from and *what happens after we die*, are of no importance, as we can only guess at answers and our answers would be most likely wrong.

Instead, imagine a world in which institutions were based on scientific truths; a world where rulers reject ideologies, greed and power, but work

---

[482] John Stuart Mill, *The Positive Philosophy of Auguste Comte* (Henry Hold, 1873), 11.

for the good of all people based on scientifically proven knowledge. This world would be without poverty, misery, war, starvation and other problems which are caused by the greed and stupidity of humanity. This is the world that Comte sought to bring into being.

You can say that Positivism is an engineer's religion. It is all so logical. All of our beliefs should be based on facts. By extension, Comte laid out that because human groups act in a predictable manner, sociology, the science of our social organizations, can be distilled into laws of social nature. Social organization should be based on these laws. Technocrat specialists should organize and run our societies based on these sociological laws.

Comte envisioned that scientists would run the schools, the governments and other institutions of society. These technocrats would use scientific sociology to control society so that there would be order and progress. He believed this Positivist vision could bring about this change.[483]

The Religion of Humanity was a natural outgrowth of Positivism. The religion was organized with a hierarchy and even a pope, the "High Priest of Humanity," sitting in Paris. The religion was designed to provide the social and emotional benefits of religion, while adhering to Positivist principles. Just as technocrats would run society in a Positivist paradise, in the Religion of Humanity, the priests would direct public opinion, arbitrate disputes and, of course, teach. Priests would be specially trained in a fourteen-year program to become experts in their craft. They would earn no money and could not hold any offices outside the priesthood. This would allow them to maintain a purely spiritual and moral authority.

In response to the scattering of Christian faiths, Comte idealized the unity of the Medieval Church. It is because of the historical unifying influence of the one Church that most people in the West still continue

---

[483] Sociology has matured and been perverted since then. Advertisers, governments, mass media and social media companies appear to be applying scientific sociology today, not for the common good of humanity but rather to brainwash us into purchasing their products or thinking their thoughts.

to share a common set of intellectual beliefs and values today. In his Religion of Humanity, Comte built on that Catholic foundation. He pretty much took the old Catholic prayers, songs and sacraments and revised them to worship "divine Humanity" rather than God. Instead of rejecting the devil, parents were asked to renounce "all sins of inordinate selfishness." According to Thomas Huxley, the religion was "Catholicism minus Christianity."[484] The sign of the cross, became the sign of Love, Order and Progress. The Lord's Prayer became

> *Holy Humanity,*
> *who are in all human time and space,*
> *Hallowed be thy Name,*
> *may thy recognition come to all men,*
> *and thy labors glorify the heavens and the earth.*
> *Grant us power to earn our daily bread,*
> *and deter us from erring as we strive to serve others aright,*
> *and teach us how to deliver each other from every evil,*
> *Amen.*[485]

In the religion, humanity itself was called "the Great Being" and was to be the object of worship, rather than Reason or Robespierre's Supreme Being. The Great Being included all those people who in the past, present and future, sought to improve humanity.

Comte's religion recognizes the basic truth I have been writing about. Humanity itself is an entity, we individuals are merely insignificant parts of it, and yet we all have an important part to play in helping humanity progress.

Love, not reason, is the underlying principle of the religion. Altruistic motherly love is key; and, therefore, the religion stresses the emotional and nurturing characteristics of women. The purpose of the religion is to get believers to act in the best interest of humanity as a whole. In fact,

---

[484] Rollin Chambliss, *Social Thought: From Hammurabi to Comte*, (Dryden, 1954), 424.

[485] Joseph Lonchampt, *Positivist Prayer*, trans. John G. Mills (Independent Republican Job Office, 1870), 29.

the Religion of Humanity provides the important qualities of religion that de Bottom pointed out. It encourages us to act unselfishly, to love and help others, all in the name of progressing the species.

The New York Positivist Society was established in New York City in the late 1860s and lasted for only a few years. Services were held every Sunday and during special Positivist holidays. Typically, about twenty people attended the Sunday services, and the special observances might have as many as forty attendees. The Springfield Republican commented on one such observance:

> *They seem to make of science a demi-god, and one at first feels repelled by the chilling character of their belief. Yet, on the other hand, they hold to and practically exhibit so high a faith in human nature, and such a conception of man's responsibility and duty, that their practice redeems their principles.*[486]

The Religion of Humanity spread throughout the world but was always a niche religion and never gained first-order status. While the religion has since faded from prominence[487] with only a small following remaining in Brazil, its core concept—the reverence for human potential and collective progress—continues to influence contemporary thought.

Oppression in the Service of Utopia

In some ways, Comte's vision of a society run by technocrats for the good of all seems similar to Plato's Kallipolis, which he described in *The Republic*, and to Karl Marx's dictatorship of the proletariat. In all three cases, there was, at least theoretically, an elite group that was uniquely qualified to run society for the good of society. These technocrats (or Plato's philosopher-kings or Marx's vanguard of the proletariat) all have the necessary superior knowledge and can steer society towards the best ends.

---

[486] "From New York," *Springfield Republican*, January 31, 1872, cited in Gillis Harp, *Positivist Republic*, 34–35.

[487] The religion's website was removed from the internet in the 2010s.

The recurring problem is, what do you do with people who just won't conform? These troublemakers get in the way and spoil everything. Comte and Plato would make sure that they were heard and that they would be involved in making decisions. But the cynic in me knows that many of us are just contrary people. We just want to do things our own way. Vladimir Lenin had a solution for these people: imprisonment, hard labor and death. After all, what is a little pain for a handful of individuals in comparison to the perfection of society. It seems to me, although it can never be proven, that if Plato or Comte were given the opportunity to organize and run a society, they would be forced into becoming ruthless authoritarians. Obstacles, that is, contrarian people, would have to be eliminated so that humanity could reach its utopian world.

Taking this into account, it appears to me that, ultimately, if the Religion of Humanity, for all of its attractive qualities, found itself the preeminent world religion, it would end up just as oppressive as the Marxists were in the Soviet Union.

Positivists and Marxists

Comte was not a socialist or a communist. His positivist ideology did not advocate for any economic or political system. While the Religion of Humanity may have had some socialist elements in it, he proposed a hierarchical order in which the technocrats, the greatest experts in the scientific theories of sociology, would hold the highest positions of power and would lead society forever. And they would lead it in a way that would benefit society most.

Karl Marx (1818–1883) advocated for a working-class revolution, which would replace the existing leaders with a "vanguard," that is, the well-educated, rightly-connected, elite revolutionaries, who were supposed to lead society until the people were ready to lead themselves, culminating in a dictatorship of the proletariat. But the same story keeps repeating itself in all these Marxist revolutions. An elite group replaces the vanquished evil rulers; but this "vanguard" never relinquishes control and they become as bad, or worse, than the original tyrants. Once people assume power, they use it to enrich themselves and become reluctant to give it up. This must be a law of human nature. In the end, Marxist revolutions in practice and Comte's positivist and Plato's Kallipolian societies in theory end the same: elite leaders hold power indefinitely.

Anarchists, most notably, Mikhail Alexandrovich Bakunin, were vehemently opposed to the idea that anyone should have authority and power over society. In his view, it is political authority itself that is the problem. The anarchists opposed the positivists and the Marxists for this reason.

Anarchy and Socialism

Anarchism is one of three variants of socialism. One group believed in gradual change through the political process. Two other variants, the Marxists and the anarchists, both wanted a violent revolution to tear down the state. The Marxists believed that post revolution, the vanguard would set up a revolutionary government along socialist principles for the benefit of the people. Marxists are not the enemy of the state; they are the enemy of existing governments because they want to take their place and become the state.

Bakunin and the anarchists were an existential threat to the Marxists. After a hypothetical revolution, rather than creating a new government, the anarchists believed that the state should be abolished completely. This was a problem for people who were fighting to create a comfortable position for themselves in a future government or who wanted to control the lives of other people. With no state, the organizers of the revolution would not be needed. Their time to be important would have passed.

We all know the tendency of good people entering politics: they change from being wide-eyed idealists into cunning political hypocrites. The same is true of governments themselves, no matter how well-intentioned the government begins. A revolutionary socialist government, meant to free and uplift the people, ends up oppressing them. We have seen it in Cuba, North Korea, Nicaragua, the Soviet Union, China and elsewhere.

The anarchists understand this, while the Marxists do not. The anarchists believe that all forms of government lead to oppression. Governments, whatever the original inspiration for them, end up being all about maintaining power or gaining more power over the people. According to Bakunin, Marxists believe

> *that only a dictatorship—their dictatorship, of course—can create the will of the people, while our answer to this is: No dictatorship can have any other aim but that of self-perpetuation, and it can beget only slavery in the people tolerating it.*[488]

This is the fundamental disagreement between the socialists and the anarchists. Both groups share the same goal, which is a free, egalitarian society, free of classes and repressive government. But their means of getting there are completely different. As Bakunin saw it, a fundamental tenant of Marxism is that "in order to free the masses, they have first to be enslaved" by the Marxist government. Marxists believed that since Marxist theory and the latest scientific discoveries in sociology reside in only a select few, the vanguard, those few should steward the people as long as needed. If there were no governing body, then the select few (Marx and his friends) would be swept away by the uneducated, neanderthal worker revolutionaries as they created their own free, but unsophisticated, institutions. The people still wouldn't be free though. They would just be ruled by the ruffians instead of the sophisticated Marxists.

The Marxist orientation was one of top-down thinking. They intended to create a state that imposed socialist ideology on the people. Anarchist thinking was completely different. Certainly, both the Marxists and the Anarchists believed in destroying the government and destroying all means of subordinating the worker to the will of the rich and

---

[488] Michael Bakunin, "Federalism, Socialism, Anti-Theologism," archive.org, accessed January 1, 2025.

powerful. But once the revolution took place, what did the anarchists propose?

According to Bakunin, associations are the answer. People naturally form associations when it is mutually beneficial. Agricultural cooperatives are an example. Farmers pool their money to purchase agricultural machinery that they could not have access to if they worked separately. Farmers use cooperatives to transport their produce. They pool their produce to get better prices from buyers. Farmers' credit unions are another example. Farmers often have to borrow to purchase fertilizer and seed, only to pay back after harvest. Large banks may not want to lend such small amounts and, if they do lend, they may charge high interest. So farmers band together in some countries and pool their capital in credit unions to provide the financing farmers need.

But this doesn't answer the question: What would the anarchists have done differently than the socialists? It is here that the anarchist message falls short, at least in my opinion. They don't have a lot of theory or guidelines on how to set up an anarchist system. It is supposed to just happen after the revolution. Meanwhile, as we wait for these magical associations to form, the most violent and oppressive of us will use force to put themselves in power, establishing systems to enslave the rest of us. We would probably end up in a dystopian, warlord-type feudalism.

I cannot think of any examples of successful anarchistic socialism. Sure, there are farm cooperatives in many countries; but how do you apply anarchistic theory to a nation of 350 million people? How do you put together and maintain a military and weapons that can defend the nation against enemies? Who is going to invest the money to develop the latest weaponry? It just cannot be done under anarchism. Structure is needed, which means we must have government, which means, to some extent, there must be oppression by the government of those people who do not obey. That is the nature of humanity in large numbers, the nature of large groups. I don't think there is any way around that. The question is, how much oppression will the people be willing to bear?

Top-down change, such as Marxism, is brutal, but it can be effective. Bottom-up change, advocated by anarchists, respects the individual's right to choose, but may take generations to amount to anything. And we have never seen anarchy evolve successfully in large nations. I cannot imagine that anarchy could ever mature before being hijacked.

The Top Down in Ayn Rand's Anthem

The idea of collectivism is that individuals should see the group as the entity of supreme importance, certainly much more important than an individual's life. That idea, in itself, is not evil. The problem is that when governments impose collectivism on peoples, freedom is lost, excellence is suppressed and populations become enslaved. As much as government tries, you cannot enforce equality. When governments get involved, the individual becomes subjugated to the group and, to varying degrees, sacrificed for the leaders' vision of the common good or, perhaps more realistically, sacrificed for the wealth, power and security of the leaders.

Leaders have often attempted to mold societies on a collectivist vision, especially in the twentieth century. Collectivism took hold in Europe after World War I, not only in the Soviet Union but also in Fascist Italy and Nazi Germany. It has since spread to China, North Vietnam, North Korea, Burma, Cuba, Nicaragua, Venezuela and many other places.

When she was twenty-six, Ayn Rand (1905–1982) escaped the Soviet Union. She wanted to be a writer but saw no possibility of publishing great writing under the Soviet system. Once in America, she penned powerful novels on the curse of collectivism. She wrote:

> *I have lived in the City of the Damned, and I know what horror men permitted to be brought upon them.*[489]

Her short dystopian novella, *Anthem*, is considered science fiction. But the thing is, there is no science in the novella. The most modern invention in the story is a candle, which in the story takes ten people to

---

[489] Ayn Rand, *Anthem* (The Caxton Printers, 1977), 103.

invent and fifty years to be approved by the appropriate committees. Rand was writing about the enforced equality she experienced in the Soviet Union.

In *Anthem* every aspect of life is dictated by the state. People are told what their occupations are to be, where to live, when to sleep, when to eat. People don't even have proper names. The government has reduced their names to numbers. It is a sin, a moral transgression, to have personal values or personal ideas—any sort of freedom. In fact, there is no word for "I," "me," or "mine." Instead, they use the words "we," "us," and "ours." The citizens are forced to recite national slogans, such as:

> *We are one in all and all in one.*
> *There are no men but only the great WE,*
> *One, indivisible and forever.*[490]

(Oh no! This sounds exactly what I have been suggesting in these essays!)

The children are forced to repeat before sleep:

> *We are nothing.*
> *Mankind is all.*
> *By the grace of our brothers are we allowed our lives.*
> *We exist through, by and for our brothers who are the State.*
> *Amen.*[491]

Ayn Rand's point in writing Anthem can be summed up in this paragraph:

> *At first, man was enslaved by the gods. But he broke their chains. Then he was enslaved by the kings. But he broke their chains. He was enslaved by his birth, by his kin, by his race. But he broke their chains...And he stood on the threshold of the freedom for which the blood of the centuries behind him had been spilled...But then he gave up all he had won...What brought it to pass? What disaster*

---

[490] Rand, 19.
[491] Rand, 21.

took their reason away from men? What whip lashed them to their knees in shame and submission? The worship of the word 'We. [492]

As she saw it, people became enslaved under these collectivist dictatorships because many people really do believe in collectivism as a moral good. It is the example of the early Christians, after all. And by believing in it, people contribute to their own enslavement. [493]

North Korea

Most people who read Anthem will probably think to themselves *this is too fantastic—something like this can never happen; Ayn Rand is taking it too far*. But for the most part, what Rand describes can happen. In fact, it is happening today. Many societies worldwide are gradually embracing collectivism, eroding personal liberties under the guise of promoting the common good. As I write this essay, the society that appears to be furthest along this path to hell is North Korea.

According to Yeonmi Park, who escaped from North Korea in 2007, just like in *Anthem*, the country had no words for "I", "me" or "mine." There were no words for "love of another person" either, as that was considered a selfish concept. Individual thinking of any kind was discouraged. You could be even criticized for wearing clothes that were different from other people's. [494]

In 1974 Kim Jong Il released a set of guidelines called the "Ten Principles for the Establishment of the Monolithic Ideological System." The Ten Principles were written to ensure that party members remained ideologically consistent with and loyal to the regime. No differing opinions would be tolerated. Absolute agreement would be required. The guidelines emphasized the absolute authority of the party leadership, the importance of maintaining unity and discipline within the party

---

[492] Rand, 101–102.

[493] aynrand.org/novels/anthem, accessed January 1, 2005.

[494] Yeonmi Park, *Joe Rogan Experience* #1691, August 3, 2021, youtube.com/watch?v=ZGJm4bjRaaE.

and the need to promote the personality cult of the leader. They also stressed the importance of ideological indoctrination of, and control over, all aspects of society. It sounds like it was copied from George Orwell's *1984*. This strict centralization of society and control over the minds of the people is still used to ensure compliance with the leadership of North Korea and their ideology.

The Ten Principles were incorporated into school curricula, propaganda materials and other forms of public communication. Citizens were encouraged to study and follow them. As a result, the principles became an important part of the North Korean schema, and adherence to them was seen as a measure of one's loyalty to the regime.

The people willingly accept economic hardships, believing their sufferings would contribute to the nation's future well-being. Dissenters and rule-breakers are informed on by their neighbors and families and many are sent to prison camps. Amnesty International reported that some of the prison camps house as many as 20,000 people.

Just like in Rand's Anthem, North Koreans are awash in propaganda. The government maintains complete control over the minds of the people. The government restricts radio and television station availability and controls broadcast content. Possessing internet, televisions or radios that can pick up foreign programming is punishable, as foreign media is a threat to state ideology. Even possession of overseas books or magazines is punishable. Political slogans in accordance with party doctrines are pasted on walls everywhere. People are forced to attend weekly political study sessions and are expected to memorize the political lectures they hear, and they do.[495]

So there you go. We start out with our ideals of equality, collectivism and contribution, and we end up in a nightmare.

---

[495] North Koreans have remarkable memories from continuous practice.

Enforcing Ideology is the Curse

How does this collectivist dream go so wrong, like in North Korea or Rand's *Anthem*? Rand and her ideological followers have placed the blame on the idea of equality. Equality is not necessarily bad. Not at all. But as Stephen D. Cox (1948–), the editor of *Liberty Magazine*, wrote:

> *If "equality" means equal obedience to a social plan, then. . .the plan has to be imposed by force. And certain people will have to enforce it. These people will constitute a separate class, superior to everyone else. Such a class will consist, not of the best, but of the worst elements of society—people who are willing to enslave, torture, and kill their "brothers" in order to maintain a lie.*[496]

If you have to impose equality on a people, or any ideology really, then you run into problems. The top-down method in most cases requires brutality.

This was the same approach taken by the medieval Church. It imposed its religious ideology on people and harshly punished those who deviated, much like the regimes in the Soviet Union, North Korea and Ayn Rand's Anthem.

This top-down method stifles innovation. Where were the great pioneers, inventers and discoverers of medieval period? They didn't exist unless they were aligned with the authorities and their ideology. Individuals were afraid to express alternative viewpoints. The great painters of the time painted religious scenes for the Church. It was when and where Church control started to crack that the great outpourings of innovation in the Renaissance and the Enlightenment periods happened in the arts, literature, science and technology. Collectivism and the Church were not the root of the problem. Lack of freedom was.[497]

---

[496] Stephen Cox, "Ayn Rand's Anthem: An Appreciation," *The Atlas Society*, July 7, 2010, atlassociety.org/post/ayn-rands-anthem-an-appreciation.

[497] Some may counter that the Soviet Union is a great example to the contrary. Party ideology was rigorously enforced and millions suffered loss, prison and death for not towing the party line. Yet, the Soviets produced worldclass athletes and invented a huge

And it is here that Bakunin is exactly right. Whoever is in charge will do what they need to do to maintain their power, including censorship, mind control and the punishment of dissidents. They will tell whatever story the collective wants to hear, but they will work to maintain their own position of authority at all costs.

Piecing it Together

So, what does it all mean? Here I have taken you from Toynbee to the Religion of Humanity to Bakunin to Ayn Rand and North Korea. It all seems to tie together, in a jigsaw puzzle sense, but it is not linear thinking at all. Let me try to piece it together.

In humanity's endless pursuit of societal and spiritual progress, we often encounter the paradox that the very institutions we create to foster our advancement end up hindering the very creativity and innovation they were meant to nurture.

From Toynbee's vision of civilizations evolving towards the divine to Comte's scientific utopia, even to Marx's utopia, each approach reflects humanity's yearning for a higher state of being. Yet, these utopian visions frequently clash with the reality of how governments really work. It is governments that create the environment for a people to flourish, and it is governments that crush those who are not in line with the prevailing ideology.

This suppression of freethinkers is not accidental but inherent to the nature of power. I wrote earlier that as groups grow, their need to control their members increases. You see it in businesses all the time. As a business takes on more employees, there arise stricter controls over expenses, behavior, dress and everything else. In the same way, as governments mature, they maintain order by increasingly controlling

---

number of things we take for granted now, such as blood transfusions, blood banks, microwave ovens, LED bulbs, a nuclear power plant. But were these geniuses free? No. Their energies were constrained to serve the state's ends. Hundreds of thousands of Soviet geniuses who did not toe the line were ground under the wheel of the Soviet system and were never allowed to develop their gifts.

behavior and thought. This increasing control comes at the expense of personal liberty and the overall creativity of the society. The problem is that the key to spiritual progress is the successive freeing of the human spirit, the very opposite of what our systems have been doing.

This recurring theme in humanity's history points to a fundamental flaw in how we structure our societies. The idea that a select few can dictate the journey of spiritual or moral evolution for the rest of us ignores the clear reality that revolutionary leaps forward in thought or spirituality come from disconnected individuals such as Rousseau, Thomas Paine, Ramakrishna, Christ or Mohammed—people who are not towing the line of social or political acceptability. The schema-changing progress that is ahead of us, ultimately, will come from the same types of free-thinkers. It always has.

Bakunin was onto this, although Bakunin was focused on class conflict. You cannot have a revolution to free the masses from the grip of the elite, only to have the revolutionary leaders become the new elite. So, it is the nature of human organizations that appears to be at the root of the problem. And it is our power-hungry, greedy, and corruptible human nature, when put into a position of authority, that is the weak link in our human organizations.

Bakunin advocated for anarchy—organizations that spontaneously emerge voluntarily to benefit people, rather than hierarchies. But even these, when they grow too large will slip into the same pattern, curbing the thoughts and doings of the free.

When you look at both the enforced collectivism (top-down) and voluntary community building (bottom-up), the real question comes to mind:

> *can true spiritual or moral progress come from an organization forcing its beliefs on people, or can it only arise from within each individual, free from the oppressive shadows of authority?*

History tells us, that the top-down coercive approach fails—and even voluntary structures, as they grow, can stifle us. True progress, then, must come from the individual, not from any external system.

Wrapping It Up

- Toynbee wrote that civilizations evolve towards a higher spiritual consciousness. This idea, while not unique, suggests that there is a purpose to historical progression beyond mere material and technological advancement.

- History is linear, progressing towards some end. In this we oppose the academic view that history might be chaotic or cyclical without intrinsic meaning.

- The hypocrisy and shortcomings of organized religion have led many to distrust religion. But religion is a creation of humans and is therefore predictably imperfect. Religion is merely our imperfect systemization of aligning with God. If religion is corrupt, it does not follow that God does not exist. It only means that human institutions are ultimately corrupted.

- As people have let religion slip from their lives, they are missing many good things that religion used to provide. This includes the constant exhortations to be virtuous, the role models of saintly people, and a community where all people are equal in the eyes of God. Some atheists have started a church in order to provide those benefits without the confounding religious doctrines or the corrupt legacy of historic religious institutions.

- Nietzsche's proclamation of "God is dead" questions how a society can operate without absolute moral standards, that is, moral standards based on God. If there is no external authority, such as a god, to set moral standards, society can devolve into social chaos, with different factions following different standards. Or, it can lead to an authoritative government that defines the new standard.

↝ Auguste Comte's attempted to establish a secular religion based on scientific principles and humanistic ideals. His Religion of Humanity worshiped the "Great We." It aimed at societal order and progress like the utopian visions of Plato or Marx.

↝ How would Comte, Plato or Marx, as individual people, have handled vocal dissidents or non-conformers if they had been involved in putting their theories into practice? It is likely in all cases, if they had become successful, they would have been authoritarian, oppressing freethinkers.

↝ Both anarchists and Marxists promoted overthrowing the government, but Marxists just wanted to replace the leaders with themselves. They promoted a model of top-down organization, where ideals were forced on the people from the top. In contrast, anarchists believe in a stateless society where individuals voluntarily associate and organize themselves, which would be considered a bottom-up model. Bottom-up governmental models take a long time to form and probably are not realistic for nations with millions of people.

↝ Ideologies, whether religious or political, when enforced by a government, inevitably end up totalitarian, where individual freedoms are sacrificed for the "collective good" as defined by those in power.

↝ Those free-thinking individuals that authoritarian governments would silence are the ones who would lead the world forward. We create governments to keep order and allow the human spirit to flourish; but in order for governments to maintain order, people who think for themselves must be squelched, marginalized or removed. That means however well-meaning their intentions, the very governments we create to promote the human race hold it back.

Essay 13
The False Postulate of Self and the Key to the Next Revolution

The more we understand the interconnectedness of
all life, the less we can afford to be selfish. The whole
notion of selfishness might be seen as a kind of myopia,
a failure to see the vast web of relationships that define
our existence.
— RUPERT SHELDRAKE

Progress and Patience

Leading by example is wonderful. But coercing others to go along with your plans? Well, that is another story. As we've noted in the last essay, the problem is that a lot of people who want to bring about change use government or some other organization to achieve their goals through coercion, either outright or subtly. Remember our discussion of Camus' book *The Rebel*, where he investigated the tendency for idealists to justify any action, even murder, to bring about their dream society—the society that is always so close, but somehow never seems to arrive. So our rulers turn to silencing and punishing critics. They are blind to the harm they inflict, stunting the very society they long to perfect. As a result, people become more cautious in what they think, write or say. Freedom becomes stifled. Innovation becomes stifled and the quality of life for all diminishes—all ironic outcomes when compared to the idealist's desired end.

Idealists are usually in a hurry. They want change. But if they let it happen naturally, they might die before seeing it. So they insist on trying to create change during their brief lifetimes.

They forget or don't want to accept that ultimately the world is not about the individual at all. It is about humanity. We are all replaceable. And individually, although we may hold important positions, we are still of little consequence. When we are dead, we are nothing.[498] The unceasing current of history continues without us. Still, in the end, it is humanity itself we are trying to change when we push social or political agendas, so why would we think we should change it on such an abbreviated timeline as our lifetimes? Liberalism, republican government, capitalism and the middle class developed organically from the bottom up over centuries and they are still here.

On the other hand, the Russian Revolution was a rapid, comprehensive makeover of society. People were forced into communism in the Soviet Union. Top-down change can be fast and powerful, but short-lasting. It took only sixty-nine years for the Russian communist system to collapse. It is here no more.

So, again, leading by example is wonderful. If you want change, be change. Demonstrate it, and let your example spread. Don't force it on others. This is bottom-up action. It can be so much more substantial and lasting than the soul crushing top-down coercion. The bottom-up works of countless individuals, such as Jesus, Beethoven, Lemkin and

---

[498] Though we may be replaceable and our individual legacies fleeting, each of us still does contribute to the entirety of human experience, the oversoul or collective consciousness. Our actions, thoughts, and creations remain a part of this enduring narrative, even after we die.

Schweitzer, continue to have an outsized effect on human civilization today. Successful religions emerge bottom-up, rather than top-down. In other words, people chose to believe in them voluntarily, rather than have the religions forced on them by authorities or threats of violence.

Many of the problems of the world can be slowly overcome through the work of generations of men and women. Scottish philosopher, John Stuart Mill (1806–1873) wrote:

> *All the grand sources. . .of human suffering are in a great degree, many of them almost entirely, conquerable by human care and effort; and though their removal is grievously slow—though a long succession of generations will perish in the breach before the conquest is completed.*[499]

Things take time to fix, and multitudes will suffer in the meantime. But remember, it is not about the individuals. It is about the whole, which has its own timeframe. It is unfortunate to us down here, but true. Humanity is like a glacier, moving slowly but surely. Whereas we, as individuals, are like sparks, bright but fleeting.

I introduced a previous essay with a famous quip by French playwright and actor, Molière (1622–1673):

> *Of all follies there is none greater than wanting to make the world a better place.*

I agree wholeheartedly with what he says. And I, in writing this series of essays, am engaging in precisely this folly, but that is a different point.

I would like to rephrase it here.

> *Of all follies there is none greater than expecting to see your actions make the world a better place. It takes more time than you have.*

---

[499] John Stuart Mill, *Utilitarianism*, ch. 2, https://tinyurl.com/2bnqnj3u.

The Religion to Come

Why do I even mention that change requires patience? Because a new religion is coming, and it is one that I hope recognizes the unity of humanity, just like the Religion of Humanity did. But to be successful, this new religion must stem from a prophet, not a thinker like Comte or a politician like Robespierre. The religion must be fresh. It must offer people a new perspective and give them hope. It cannot be one that is forced on people. That just doesn't work. And if it is to grow organically, bottom-up, that will take lifetimes.

Toynbee wrote all about the coming new religion. Remember, he wrote that Western Civilization was declining. According to the historian, the fact that a civilization is declining does not indicate that a generation or a people has failed. It is just a cycle that inevitably happens. It is during these civilizational declines that new higher religions are born. Toynbee claimed that the advancement of religion is the real purpose of civilizations in the first place. Or as Hegel would put it, our growing spiritual consciousness, which is partially elevated by advances in religion, carries the Spirit of History forward.

When a civilization is in decline, the old institutions break down and the old ways of seeing the world no longer serve us. We reject the old ways because they just don't seem to apply anymore. A revolutionary new framework of thought then becomes necessary to make sense of the world. This new framework validates us, reassuring us that we are not collectively heading towards the sewer and that individually we are not wasting our lives. This is why low points in secular history can lead to high points in spiritual history.

Toynbee gives examples of declining civilizations and the consequent births of religions. In the second century, Roman civilization had exhausted its creative energies. The leadership was in decline in the political and military spheres. The Empire was therefore unable to adapt to the changing circumstances and external threats. Rome became even more corrupt and decadent (I know, hard to imagine). The people lost faith in traditional Roman values and institutions. Citizens no longer believed in the old ideals of civic virtue and patriotism that had sustained them in previous centuries. Out of this arose a new orientation towards life, Christianity.

Over several decades in the late sixth to the early seventh centuries of the Common Era, the Middle East sustained a decades-long series of sieges, battles and political intrigue between two of the greatest powers of the world at that time, the Byzantines and the Persians. The conflicts exhausted the region. Many cities and towns were looted and destroyed. Large numbers of people were killed or displaced. Trade routes were disrupted. The remaining local economies were ruined as resources were diverted towards the military. It was during this low point, when everything was in a shambles, that Islam erupted onto the scene. Both the Byzantines and Persians were exhausted from continual war and could not stop the advancing Arab armies. According to Toynbee, the Prophet Mohammed and his followers offered a new way of life that provided a needed sense of order and meaning to people during this time of chaos. After the conquest, new systems of government were put into place based on new fundamental beliefs. Islamic law was introduced in many regions. Mosques were constructed. And the people gradually adopted the new religion. But the conversion did not place in a week. It took many decades for it to occur. Religion moves slowly.

Christianity and Islam emerged long ago. So, what's happening today?

As Western Civilization appeared to be in decline when he was writing his books (in the 1930s through the 1960s), Toynbee predicted that a new great religion should arise soon. Academics hated reading that assertion, especially since it came from a historian. This violated their totally artificially siloed conception of the academic world. Historians were not supposed to predict anything. But Toynbee did not just predict the emergence of a new major religion, he predicted its character. He compared seven major religions and found that, overall, they all had the same idea. Like Ramakrishna, he saw that all religions are but separate paths to the One True God.[500] He speculated that the four larger religions might merge.

Who knows? He may be right. We are still waiting for an answer to that. But with the widespread use of new technologies, societies around the world have already merged to a great extent. Most nations wear similar clothes now. They eat at similar fast-food restaurants, live and work in similar buildings and have access to the same technology (cell phones, televisions, cars and the internet). The same movies are watched all over the world (except in North Korea). Our lifestyles and aspirations are merging. As we are becoming homogeneous, Toynbee's prediction becomes more and more believable. The events of the world affect everyone now. In the early 2020s, we have had COVID, climate change, the war in Ukraine and the Israeli-Palestinian conflict. All the world has been and is being affected by these events.

Even though it seems more and more likely that Toynbee will be proven right, we must remember that nobody can predict the future accurately. History does not move along a linear path. Instead, history is periods of calm punctuated by unexpected radical and violent change. But what we can recognize is that, for the most part, among the urban centers in North America and Europe, Christianity has long since lost its grip on the lives of the people and their institutions. Christianity, upon which the Western World's schema was based, has been cast aside by large segments of the population; and the Western World is hungry for meaning. Something is coming. Just what will it be?

Of course, I cannot pretend to answer this question. Nobody can. But let's examine the question from a different angle.

Our Ship of Fools

As I have mentioned repeatedly, we human beings are clueless. It appears to be by design. Since the beginning of time, we have lived without an authoritative rule book. So throughout the centuries we did the best we

---

[500] Toynbee, *A Study of History*, vol. 7, (Oxford University, 1954), 440.

could and created our own rule books, which we then called religions. It is likely true that the rockstar founders of these religions could see well beyond the rest of us, much like the man who escaped Plato's cave. But those who followed these prophets and transformed their prophetic utterances into religions were men, and they unwittingly integrated their lack of understanding and their human limitations into the religions. And now, the religions, as we have them, are only so good. They are flawed and do not lead us to the pure understanding of our place in the world, the understanding that our prophets tried to communicate.

Many, pointing out the shortcomings of our religions, have rejected them altogether. They have looked instead to their intellects for direction. They have based their beliefs on rational thinking, which is limited and suspect. It seems, the more intelligent an individual is, the more they tend to rely on their intellect. But these intellectuals often pretend that their minds can resolve anything. They are wrong. This approach just cannot work. The Ultimate Reality out there cannot be grasped intellectually. Using rational arguments centuries ago, David Hume debunked rationality as irrational. The intellect is inadequate for comprehending what is really going on in the world.[501] The mind is great at mastering some things, but that doesn't make it great at everything.

---

[501] Our understanding is limited by the limitations of our five senses and by our faulty intellectual wiring. Here are some examples of what I mean:

- We are always trying to apply a beginning and ending to things. Who came up with that requirement? Isn't it possible that some things are not governed by time? The need to inject time into everything is a limitation of our minds.
- We understand difficult concepts only when delivered in stories. Jesus dumbed his truths down into stories that we might understand them. Our simplicity is comical, really.
- We make generalizations, and we call that learning. Our generalizations are always partially correct, but also always partially wrong. No matter how much we refine our generalizations, they are never completely right every time.
- We consciously or unconsciously ignore facts that do not align with our pre-conceived notions.

This is what I mean when I say our hard-wiring limits our understanding of the world. Our mental limitations preclude us from ever grasping the truth, whatever it may be.

On top of that, our thinking is shamefully stunted or deformed by the groups we belong to. We will utter preposterous things to belong, and we often do it unconsciously. Why is it that when a Democrat is president, Democrats are pro-war and Republicans are anti-war and when a Republican is president, they switch positions—and both look at you smugly as if nothing is awry?

We are hopelessly incapable of understanding anything important. So much for the intellect leading us to Truth.

Toynbee believed that the things we can see and sense aren't fully understandable on their own. Even our knowledge of basic objects is limited because they're just small pieces of a much larger puzzle— the vast universe—which stays mostly mysterious to us. The key to explaining the entire picture is hidden in the parts we can't see or grasp.[502]

It is easy to accept that truism in the abstract, but what do you do with it? If we cannot perceive the truth or understand it, then what is the point of even trying? It is much easier to let it go and copy other people whom we see as heroes or role models.

That seems like a good plan; but it is not, because these heroes are not gods. They are flawed individuals just like us. They may have achieved great things in some areas, but they are weak in others. That is part of being human.

Besides, as great as you think your heroes are, you can never be them. That is their job. You will always fall short of their example because you are you, and not them. You can only be great at being yourself. That is your job.

I think we have to go back to what Krishnamurti said when he dissolved his order.

> *You have the idea that only certain people hold the key to the Kingdom of Happiness. No one holds it. No one has the authority*

---

[502] Arnold J. Toynbee, *An Historian's Approach to Religion*, 274–275.

*to hold that key. That key is your own self, and in the development
and the purification and in the incorruptibility of that self alone
is the Kingdom of Eternity.*[503]

We cannot look to heroes, our intellects or our religions to answer our
most pressing questions. So still the problem remains. We live our lives
hopelessly without any certainty of what is most important, all of us
viewing life differently. And so, human society is chaos and always
has been. Billions of individuals run this way and that, all with false
perceptions of Truth, all trying to achieve different ends. We are just like
a kindergarten class run amok with no teacher in the room. That is us,
just older children. All of us are mistaken. None of us has a clue. The
knowledge we have now—we made it all up. Each of us chooses what
to believe, and every bit of what we choose is partially or completely
wrong. Some of us create great things. Some of us destroy great things
created by others. Some hurt and kill others in pursuit of ultimately
insignificant goals.

Sometimes we work together. We form groups, which themselves fight
other groups, but none of these groups truly address the ultimate truth.
Like individuals, groups usually pursue pointless ends that, given the
perspective of centuries, amount to nothing. Groups are merely composed of clueless individuals held together by their common mispercep-
tions. As a whole, our history, our present, and our future are utter chaos
and folly. To take oneself seriously is the mark of an unserious person.

Imagine a ship afloat on the ocean. It is full of people, all of whom are
mentally and emotionally impaired in different ways. But there is no
authoritative leader on board. Everyone is equal, and most think that
they are best suited to lead the ship, so there is conflict. There is little
agreement on anything, or any agreements made do not last long. There
is no official captain. There are no navigation instruments. They think
they can steer the ship using the wheel and rudder, but really these

---

[503] Krishnamurti's speech to the Order of the Star in the East, August 3, 1929. For complete
speech, visit kfoundation.org/dissolution-speech, last accessed January 1, 2025.

efforts are of little use because they do not know where they should go. They can't agree which direction the ship should sail. One pulls this way; another, that. Nevertheless, the ship will go where it will, and the individual wills of the passengers really cannot affect its overall course. This ship is human society. Our Earth is this ultimate ship of fools.

But, at the same time, the course of the ship is indeed directed by the passengers. They just don't realize how they are affecting the ship's motion. The ship of humanity is not steered by any individual. It is steered by the aggregate—all of us. It's like the will of us all combines in some mysterious way and that determines the direction we take as a whole. And that is the magic of it all. This unknown force of humanity, the collective will, to which we all contribute, guides us, much like the winds, the waves and tides steer our metaphorical ship.

No reason to feel bad about this. This is reality and it has always been this way throughout the centuries. You can fool yourself about your self-importance, but really, it is best to confront this reality and then decide on the best course of action for yourself.

Once you can release yourself from taking yourself seriously, you can relax and give things their proper perspective. Taxes? People have always paid taxes. Quit whining. Someone stole something of yours? They have been doing that for centuries. This is part of the human experience. Unhappy with your government? Governments have always created problems for the governed. This is all little stuff. And it is what people who are immersed in themselves are concerned about.

Moving Beyond Selfishness and Aligning with the Absolute

In order for humanity to move beyond where we are today, we individuals must move beyond our instinctive self-centeredness. This is very difficult because it is woven into our nature. We must take care of our needs in order to survive.

Toynbee pointed out that self-centeredness is an intellectual error because nobody is the center of the Universe, although many act as if they were. It is a moral error because no creature has the right to act as if it were the center of the Universe.[504] Self-centeredness, according to the Historian,[505] is the root of all evil. And he is not alone; many others have concluded the same.

Losing our self-centeredness is the hardest task we can undertake. But if we can do it, the reward is much greater than the struggle. Toynbee puts it this way:

> *In giving up self-centeredness he will have felt as if he were losing his life; but in achieving this act of self-sacrifice he will find that he has really saved his life, because he will have given his life a new centre, and this new centre will be the Absolute Reality that is the spiritual presence behind the phenomena.*[506]

I am calling this spiritual presence God.

Once we drop our intense focus on ourselves, we can be open to what is really true, we can experience God.[507] And God's will becomes our will.[508] Only then can we align ourselves with the spiritual order of the world. Toynbee wrote that this aligning should be our personal goal, bringing oneself "into harmony with this absolute spiritual reality."[509]

It is once you are in this communion, that's when you can achieve knowledge that you could not get otherwise. Remember the narratives of the mystical experiences we discussed earlier. Those peakers understood things that our rational brains just cannot grasp. It is through communion we can learn the underlying laws of the spiritual world,

---

[504] Arnold J. Toynbee, *An Historian's Approach to Religion*, 4-5.

[505] Allow me this, I like to call Toynbee "the Historian."

[506] Toynbee, *An Historian's Approach to Religion*, 275.

[507] They are not the only ones of course. There are countless people who have professed this. This topic is really deep, well beyond my experience. Alas, my ego remains intact. Two good guides on this are Krishnamurti and Alan Watts.

[508] Arnold J. Toynbee, *An Historian's Approach to Religion*, 277.

[509] Arnold J. Toynbee, *An Historian's Approach to Religion*, 274.

real knowledge, and then we can try live in accordance with them. This is the elusive rule book. It is extremely difficult to get your hands on.

You can achieve harmony through spiritual practice, a sustained deep prayer or meditation practice. But the thing is, you cannot force it. You cannot decide to commune with the Absolute, and then go and do it. Your determination and wits cannot make it happen. It is like you cannot force a butterfly in nature to land on your head. All you can do is create the circumstances in which the butterfly might choose to alight, and you wait. It either happens or it doesn't. It is the same with mysticism. It is inexplicable. Very few of us put ourselves in a position to reach this communion, and of those, only a few will be blessed with it.

If the butterfly indeed did land and you have caught some understanding, you may try to put it to words, so that you can remember it always; but the profundity often is lost in translation and over time it fades and is lost forever. Regardless of the fleetingness of these moments, they change us and as they change us, they change the collective consciousness of Humanity.

The Unwritten Laws

Many peakers have greatly influenced humanity and our collective mindsets, often in ways that we do not recognize. Almost all of the essays in this book actually coalesce around the mystical truths revealed to us from peakers. I have presented their ideas as rationally as I could, but at their core, they originated from the mystical insights of peakers.

Which leads us to the next topic, the unwritten laws.

I have collected some of the most important concepts from these essays into a series of unwritten laws. All of them have their origins in mysticism, they were not derived through rational thought. While reason can retroactively analyze or articulate these insights, their origins often lie in a non-rational, spiritual realm.

Even if you hadn't read these essays, some of these unwritten laws should be obvious in retrospect. They have been in plain view, but we continually overlook them. Once they are expressed, you will recognize that you already knew some of these unwritten laws to be true. But it is when we elevate these concepts and present them as laws that they take on more significance intellectually. I hope they make it to your conscious mind, residing there, becoming a part of your core beliefs.

When I say "laws," I am not talking about laws created by political bodies or scientists but rather "natural laws" that describe patterns that occur consistently under certain conditions without exception and can be used to reliably predict outcomes. If there were exceptions, then the law would have to be amended or abandoned.

One other thing: scientific laws such as the Law of Gravity, Newton's Laws of Motion, and the Law of Conservation of Energy do a great job explaining our world. But people got by with no problem before these laws were discovered and named. But once they were proclaimed as laws, our intellectual horizons expanded, and further discoveries were made.

Just as those patterns we now call laws existed before they were discovered and named; other patterns—unnamed laws—exist now, regardless of whether we have recognized and named them or not. They are just hiding in plain sight, like Newton's laws once did. Once most of us recognize these concepts as laws, our thinking will change. It will expand in a new direction, taking us further as a species towards our ultimate destiny.

I will try to list some of those laws here. I am certain to leave some out.[510]

> ❧ *The Law of History*: Augustine, Hegel, Toynbee and others recognized it—human history is pointed somewhere. History has

---

[510] There are other laws that I am not re-presenting here because they distract from the main point currently under discussion and were the focus of other essays:

- The Law of Groups: once a group is formed it lives a life of its own and self-preservation becomes of utmost importance.
- The Law of Large Groups: as groups grow, they develop stricter rules and enforce them increasingly or they will fall apart.
- The Law of Orthodoxy: groups need orthodoxy and will root out unorthodox thinkers.
- The Law of Power: once people attain great power in an organization, they use their position to enrich themselves and become reluctant to give it up.

meaning. We just may not know what it is. Countless individuals have suffered immeasurably through the ages. Still, Humanity is progressing in some great direction and we all contribute to it. We just won't live long enough to know quite where we are headed.

    ❧ *The Law of Unity*: All humans are connected. We are connected not only to those of us who are alive now, but to all of humanity that has ever lived, and ever will. This connection was described by Varro as the Soul of the World, by Emerson as the Over-Soul, by Jung as the Collective Unconscious and by Sheldrake as Morphic Resonance.

    ❧ *The Law of the Infinite*: Our lives may be short and seemingly insignificant, but we are a part of the great creature we call Humanity. The Human Spirit is immortal. It will live forever and we should all feel proud to play a part in it. We belong here. We each have unique gifts we can use to contribute to the Spirit of Humanity. We are all on the same team.

    ❧ *The Law of Loving*: Only loving others gives us fulfillment. Winning the lottery, or an academy award will bring momentary excitement, but sharing our lives with people we love and enjoy brings a more fulfilling and deeper satisfaction. And the more love we give, the more fulfillment we have.

    ❧ *The Law of Giving*: If you give to others freely without wanting anything in return, the Universe will take care of you. You will always have enough. As fast as you give your treasure away, it will be replenished so that a flow is established. By giving, you become an indispensable hand of God, carrying out the will of God. But not only that, it is in giving that we are happiest.

If you live your life in harmony with these laws, you will thrive. When we devote our time and energy to helping Humanity progress, be it through a political movement, a donation to a charity, a new invention, caring for others, or building a school in some remote village, our hearts feel full.

Our need for meaning is fulfilled. We are contributing to Humanity. And even if generations from now, our descendants laugh at our efforts because they appear silly or naive in retrospect, it doesn't matter. By giving to the Whole, we are fulfilling very important personal needs. But more importantly, we are helping Humanity progress.

On the other hand, you can say that these laws are too high-level. They don't explicitly say what you should be doing. Assuming these Laws are true, we still don't really have a rulebook. So what are we supposed to do? How do we live? What do we prioritize?

I think I can partially answer these questions, but before I do, I want to share with you a tradition that goes a long way towards an answer. Of all places, it is from the great center of racial hatred, South Africa. It is there that people have come closest to living this principle than anyone else in the recent past.[511] They call it Ubuntu.

Ubuntu when placed into action can be a powerful force for good. After apartheid ended in South Africa, Nelson Mandela (1918–2013) became the country's first black president, marking a new era of political equality. When the Blacks gained power, they did not seek retribution, as you would expect, for the decades of oppression and state-sponsored murder by the white government. Instead, they used Ubuntu as a guiding principle in the post-apartheid South African political system.[512] Rather than dividing and punishing, they sought forgiveness, reconciliation and unity.

---

[511] According to a friend of mine, South African politics has since degenerated into a cynical political morass of racial suspicions and hatreds. But it appears that it was beautiful for a brief period.

[512] Unfortunately, forces of modernization and urbanization have increased individualism in South Africa, and Ubuntu as a political philosophy has been mostly sidelined. Even though Ubuntu is still referenced in political discourse and has been integrated into the constitution and in legal decisions, the politics of South Africa have changed course once again away from idealism.

Ubuntu

I had never heard of the term until I read *The Book of Joy* by writer Douglas Carlton Abrams (1967–). The book documents a series of discussions between Archbishop Desmond Tutu (1931–2021) and the fourteenth Dalai Lama (1935–) on the topic of happiness and suffering. In this remarkable book, Tutu speaks quite a lot about the concept of Ubuntu.

Ubuntu stems from the traditional values of the Bantu-speaking communities in South Africa. The word, Ubuntu, is a Bantu term meaning "humanity" or a more literal translation would be "I am because we are." It refers to the universal bond that connects all of humanity.

Tutu said,

> *I could not speak as I am speaking without having learned it from other human beings. I could not walk as a human being. I could not think as a human being, except through learning it from other human beings. I learned to be a human being from other human beings. We belong in this delicate network. It is actually quite profound...*

We flourish only when we are in communion with others.

> *This God is community, fellowship. Being created by this God, we are created in order to flourish. And we flourish in community.*[513]

Happiness does not come from focusing on our own needs. We get happiness from helping other people.

> *If we think we want to get joy for ourselves, we realize that it's very shortsighted, short-lived. Joy is the reward, really, of seeking to give joy to others. When you show compassion, when you show caring,*

---

[513] Dalai Lama and Tutu with Abrams, 60, 62.

when you show love to others, do things for others, in a wonderful
way you have a deep joy that you can get in no other way.[514]

Ideally, we would all follow Tutu's guidance and focus on bringing joy to others. The more we help others, the more joy we experience; and this joy becomes contagious to those around us, further reinforcing the joy we feel.

On the other hand, if we focus on ourselves and making ourselves happy, it doesn't always turn out so well. Tutu continues,

> *You can't survive on your own. . .in next to no time the person who*
> *is totally selfish goes under. You need other people in order to be*
> *human. That's why when they want to punish you, they put you*
> *in solitary confinement. Because you can't flourish without other*
> *human beings. They give you things that you cannot give yourself,*
> *no matter how much money you have. And so, we speak of Ubuntu.*
> *A person is a person through other persons. And there must have*
> *been some people who said, "Ah, what a primitive way of thinking."*
> *It's the most fundamental law of our being. We flout that—we*
> *flout it at our peril.*[515]

But Ubuntu is only a concept, a philosophy. It is not a religion. It has no sacred texts, no ritual, no messenger of God, no authority structure. It is not the religion that Toynbee was expecting. What it is, is a true understanding of the nature of Humanity. Ubuntu is fundamentally true, and it embraces three of the laws I outlined above—the Laws of Loving, Giving and Unity.

Concluding Thoughts

I have already presented the idea more than once that we don't have a clue what the Truth is. We may accept some hand-me-down, preformulated ideology and choose to base our lives on that or we may adopt

---

[514] Dalai Lama and Tutu with Abrams, 293.

[515] Dalai Lama and Tutu with Abrams, 270.

some group's schema. And that is what most of us do. Most of us just go along with the rest of them. It is so much easier.

Most of us live life merely reacting to situations and never realizing that we get to make a choice. But we do. We *can* be choosers here. As there is no clear book of rules for life, we get to choose the truth we live by. Whether you recognize you are playing the game or not, you are still playing the game. Understand that. Once you recognize that you are an active player in the game of life, rather than a passive victim, you can make your moves, rather than let others make them for you.

Even with no fundamental understanding or rule book, we are not completely lost. We do know a few things: There is a God. We know that God is not a bearded old man in the sky, forever watching and judging us. No, not at all. All of us together comprise God. The soul of Humanity is God and we are all unique manifestations of God. Being unique, we all have unique paths in this life. Yet we are connected to one another as we are all part of one God.

We get to choose how we go about living. Because we get to choose our paths, our values and our goals, our job is to be ourselves as much as we can be. We must develop our talents and sensibilities. We must develop our intelligence and our character. So, why not strive for perfection and by doing so help Humanity along its way?

Knowing that Humanity is one, why not, as much as possible, play the game to help Humanity progress to the next level? Isn't that the point? Many of us aim to do this when we state our objective is making the world a better place. But I suggest that we reevaluate our methods.

If the goal is promoting Humanity towards perfection, whatever that is, then we have two responsibilities: We must develop our own talents in whatever field it is we can excel. Our second responsibility is to help others develop their talents. We all have different talents, and we must develop ours and support others in developing theirs. It benefits everyone.

As a thought experiment, imagine for an instant a world in which everyone on the planet has developed themselves fully. We would have millions of Nikola Teslas, Leonardo da Vincis, Albert Schweitzers and Nelson Mandelas striding the earth. Every one of those people improved the lot of the rest of us. What if we all could do that?

That should be the goal.

Our governments should develop systems that empower all of us to live unfettered lives. We should not tolerate any limitations on our freedom to excel—not by any institution.

Not much of what I have written is new. Others have embraced the Unity of Humanity idea to varying degrees and many have tried to lead the way in this respect—some using authoritarian means, and some not. The Church preached brotherhood at different times but it was hopelessly corrupt as an organization; and the salvation our major religions offer is all about the individual. In theory, Comte's Religion of Humanity could have been very effective, but it failed to gain traction. The communists tried to enforce brotherhood, and that failed. Besides a scattering of some enlightened local communities throughout the ages, the togetherness concept just hasn't caught on.

These failures demonstrate that unity must well up from within the community, not be forced on us top-down from an institution. People have tried, it seems, over and over, to bring about this Ubuntu type brotherhood, but we always seem to trip up over ourselves. Selfish people get into positions of leadership, forget or ignore their original values and exploit the system for their personal benefit. In this respect, history has repeated itself so far.

But I don't believe we will stumble at this point forever. I hope I have demonstrated that the history of Humanity has been one of evolution. We are progressing towards something, and I would like to believe we are progressing towards a better collective consciousness. As Hegel claimed, we are the consciousness of the world. The more of us who become aware, the greater the universal consciousness becomes.

Being only one person out of the billions, I humbly suggest that we have evolved as far as we are able with the central, outdated, limiting belief that we take for granted—that we are individuals. This one belief, more than any other, is irreconcilably linked to selfishness, which is the root of human evil. It is this one postulate upon which everything else that we think and believe is based. We must replace this tired assumption. It holds us back from taking meaningful steps towards the ultimate destiny of Humanity.

Bibliography

The sources listed here are those that I have either quoted or paraphrased. I left the Bible and the US Constitution out, since they are so easily found. I have separated my sources into three categories: Books, Articles and Other.

Books

Abrahamian, Andray. *Being in North Korea*. 2020.

Augustine. *City of God*. 1887. Accessed on January 1, 2025 at newadvent.org/fathers/1201.htm.

Augustine. *Confessions*. 1887. Accessed on January 1, 2025 at newadvent.org/fathers/1101.htm.

Bakunin, Michael. *Bakunin on Anarchy*. 1972.

Balashov, Yuri and Rosenberg, Alex. *Philosophy of Science, Contemporary Readings*. 2002.

Baudrillart, Alfred. *The Catholic Church, the Renaissance, and Protestantism, Lectures Given at the Catholic Institute of Paris. January to March 1904*. 1907.

Blavatsky, Helena. *Isis Unveiled*. 1919.

Bossuet, Jacques. *Discourse on Universal History*. 1681. Accessed on January 1, 2025 at archive.org/details/discourseonunive0000boss/page/n5/mode/2up.

Bradford, William. *Of Plymouth Plantation*. 1908. Accessed on January 1, /2025 at archive.org/details/bradfordshistor04bradgoog/page/n286/mode/2up.

Bryonis, Speros. *Byzantine and Europe*. 1967.

Burchard, Brendon. *High Performance Habits*. 2017.

Camus, Albert. *The Rebel*. 1956. Accessed on January 1, 2025 at cyberdandy.org/wp-content/uploads/2021/07/Albert-Camus-The-Rebel_-An-Essay-on-Man-in-Revolt-Vintage-International-1992.pdf

Carlyle, Thomas. *The French Revolution: A History*. 3 volumes. 1851.

Carroll, John. *The Wreck of Western Culture, Humanism Revisited*. 2008.

Cary, Earnest Ph.D. *Dio's Roman History* with an English Translation. vol 9. 1955.

Chambliss, Rollin. *Social Thought: From Hammurabi to Comte*. 1954.

Change, Jung and Halliday, Jon. *Mao: the Unknown Story*. 2005.

Colonna, Jerry. *Reboot: Leadership and the Art of Growing Up*. 2019.

De Botton, Alain. *Religion for Atheists*. 2012.

de Las Casas, Bartolomé. *A Short Account of the Destruction of the Indies*. 1992. Accessed on January 1, 2025 at https://tinyurl.com/27qsvv6b.

Descartes, Rene. *Principles of Philosophy*. 2017. Accessed on January 1, 2025 at earlymoderntexts.com/assets/pdfs/descartes1644part1.pdf.

Dostoevsky, Fyodor. *The Brothers Karamazov*. 1880.

Dray, William H. *Philosophy of History*. 1964.

Durant, Will & Ariel. *Age of Napoleon*. 1975.

Durant, Will. *Age of Rousseau*. 1967.

Durant, Will & Ariel. *Age of Voltaire*. 1965.

Durant, Will. *Caesar and Christ*. 1944.

Durant, Will. *The Age of Faith*. 1950.

Durant, Will. *The Reformation*. 1957.

Durant, Will. *The Story of Philosophy*. 1926.

Emerson, Ralph Waldo. *The Essential Writings of Ralph Waldo Emerson*. 2009.

Erickson, Irvin. *Raphael Lemkin and the Concept of Genocide*. 2017.

Fox, John. *Fox's Book of Martyrs*. 1583. Accessed on January 1, 2025 at archive. org/details/ACTESAndMonumentsByJohnFoxe1583/mode/2up.

Feuerbach, Ludvig, *Thoughts on Death and Immortality from the Papers of a Thinker,* trans. J.A. Massey. 198. Accessed at pdfcoffee.com/feuerbach-thoughts-on-death-and-immortality-pdf-free.html.

Gibbon, Edward. *The History of the Decline and Fall of the Roman Empire*. 1993.

Grant, Madison. *The Passing of the Great Race or the Racial Basis of European History*. 1916.

Guevara, Che. *Che Guevara Reader: Writings on Politics and Revolution*. 2003.

Harp, Gillis. *Positivist Republic*. 1994. Book is about Comte.

Hatten, Douglas. *The Recognitions of Clement*. 2008.

Helvetius. *Treatise on Man*. 1969.

Hodson, Geoffrey. *J. Krishnamurti and the Search for Light*. 1935. Accessed on January 1. 2025 at anandgholap.net/Krishnamurti_And_The_Search_For_Light-Geoffrey_Hodson.htm.

Homer, *The Iliad*. Richard Lattimore's translation. 1961. Accessed on January 1, 2025 at archive.org/details/the-iliad-homer-lattimore/page/65/mode/2up.

Hume, David. *Treatise of Human Nature*. 1739.

Irvin-Erikson, Douglas. *Raphael Lemkin and the Concept of Genocide*. 2017.

Isherwood, Christopher. *Ramakrishna and His Disciples*. 1965.

James, William. *Varieties of Religious Experience*. 1917.

January, Brendon. *Genocide: Modern Crimes Against Humanity*. 2007.

Kelly, Dean M, *Why Conservative Churches are Growing*, 1977.

Kennedy, Emmet. *A Cultural History of the French Revolution*. 1989.

Koehler, John. *Stasi: The Untold Story of the German Secret Police*. 1999.

Konnert, Mark. *Medieval to Modern: Early Modern Europe*. 2017.

Dalai Lama [The] and Tutu Desmond with Abrams, Douglas. *The Book of Joy*. 2017. Discussions between Dalai Lama and Archbishop Desmond Tutu.

Layton, Deborah. *Seductive Poison*. 1999. Book is about People's Temple, Jim Jones, and the Jonestown Massacre.

Lemkin, Raphael. *Axis Rule in Occupied Europe*. 1944.

Lemkin, Raphael. *Totally Unofficial: The Autobiography of Raphael Lemkin.* 2013.

Leshan, Lawrence. *The Medium, the Mystic and the Physicist. Toward a General Theory of the Paranormal.* 1974.

Lewis, C.S. *Mere Christianity.* 2001.

Luther, Martin. *Martin Luther's Complete Writings.* Vol. 15. 1899.

Luther, Martin. *Table Talk.* 1884.

Lutyens, Mary. *Krishnamurti: The Years of Awakening.* 1975.

Maillane, Durand. *Histoire de la Convention Nationale.* 1825. Accessed November 21, 2023. rodama1789.blogspot.com/2019/05/the-fete-de-la-raison-at-notre-dame.html.

Maslow, Abraham. *Religions, Values and Peak-Experiences.* 1994.

Midlarksy, Manus I. *The Killing Trap: Genocide in the Twentieth Century.* 2005.

Mill, John Stuart. *The Positive Philosophy of Auguste Comte.* 1873. Accessed January 1, 2025 at archive.org/details/cu31924029049322/page/n5/mode/2up.

Mill, John Stuart. *Utilitarianism.* 1863. Accessed on January 1, 2025 at archive.org/details/isbn_9781543003963/page/n1/mode/2up.

Newton, Isaac. *Quaestiones quaedam Philosophiae Certain Philosophical Questions.* Accessed January 1, 2025 at https://tinyurl.com/28ha9jua.

Nietzsche, Friedrich. *The Gay Science.* 1974. Accessed on January 1, 2025 at philoslugs.wordpress.com/wp-content/uploads/2016/12/the-gay-science-friedrich-nietzsche.pdf.

O'Brien, Paul. *Great Decisions, Perfect Timing: Cultivating Intuitive Intelligence.* 2015. Book about decision making using I-Ching.

Osho. *The Mustard Seed.* 1975.

Osho. *The Secret of Secrets.* 1982.

Parker, Theodore. *Ten Sermons of Religion.* 1853. Accessed on January 1, 2025 at archive.org/details/tensermonsofreli00inpark/page/n13/mode/2up.

Pascal. *Pensées.* 1670.

Peck, Mark Gregory. *A Most Holy War: The Albigensian Crusade and the Battle for Christendom.* 2008.

Pinkard, Terry. *Hegel: A Biography.* 2000.

Pinker, Steven. *Enlightenment Now: The Case for Reason, Science, Humanism and Progress* 2018.

Plato, *Apology*. Trans. Benjamin Jowett. 2008.

Rand, Ayn. *Anthem*. 1977.

Robbins, Tony. *Awaken the Giant Within*. 2007. Book about empowering yourself to do great things.

Roosevelt, Theodore. *Gouverneur Morris*. 1888. Accessed January 1, 2025 at archive.org/details/gouverneurmorris02roos/mode/2up.

Roosevelt, Theodore. *The Winning of the West*. Part 1. 1908. Accessed on January 1, 2025 at archive.org/details/winningofwestvol01roos/page/n7/mode/2up.

Routh, C. R. N. *They Saw It Happen in Europe 1450-1600*. 1965.

Russell, Bertrand. *History of Western Philosophy*. 1945.

Schopenhauer, *The World as Will and Idea*. 1883.

Schweitzer, Albert. *Out of my Life and Thought*. 1998.

Schweitzer, Albert. *Reverence for Life: Sermons 1900-1919*. 1973.

Schweitzer, Albert. *The Spiritual Life: Selected Writings of Albert Schweitzer*. 1996.

Sheldrake, Rupert. *The Science Delusion*. 2013.

Smuts, Jan. *Holism and Evolution*. 1999. Accessed on January 1, 2025 at archive.org/details/20191002holismandevolution.

Solzhenitsyn, Aleksandr. *The Gulag Archipelago*. Vols. I-II. 1974.

Sorley, William Ritchie. *Moral Values and the Idea of God*. 1919.

Spengler, Oswald. *The Decline of the West*. 1928.

Stromberg, Roland. *Arnold J. Toynbee: Historian for an Age in Crisis*. 1972.

Swedenborg, Emanuel. *Collected Minor Works*. Accessed on January 1, 2025 at swedenborg.com/wp-content/uploads/2013/03/swedenborg_foundation_minor_works.pdf.

Swedenborg, Emanuel. *Secrets of Heaven*. 2008.

Swindoll, C. *Living Above the Level of Mediocrity*. 1989.

Tolle, Eckhart. *The Power of Now*. 1999.

Tolstoy, Leo. *Essays and Letters*. 1903.

Tomkins, Calvin. *The World of Marcel Duchamp*. 1887-1968. 1966.

Toynbee, Arnold J. *A Study of History*. 12 Vols. 1934-1961.

Toynbee, Arnold J. *An Historian's Approach to Religion*. 1956.

Trobridge, George. *Swedenborg, Life and Teaching*. 1955.

Vernon, Roland. *Star in the East: Krishnamurti, the Invention of a Messiah*. 2002.

Waite, Judge C. B. *History of the Christian Religion to the Year Two Hundred*. 1881. Accessed on January 1, 2025 at https://tinyurl.com/29a9jj23.

Washington, Peter. *Madame Blavatsky's Baboon*. 1993.

Watts, Alan. *The Book on the Taboo Against Knowing Who You Are*. 1989.

Weber, Max. *The Sociology of Religion*. 1963. Accessed on January 1, 2025 at archive.org/details/sociologyofrelig0000unse_g3z2/page/n5/mode/2up.

Welles, James F. *The Story of Stupidity*. 1997.

Welles, James F. *Understanding Stupidity*. 1986.

Wilson, Colin. *Religion and the Rebel*. 1957.

Wilson, Colin. *The Occult*. 1971.

Xenophon, *The Persian Expedition*. 1949.

Articles

Anonymous. "Do the ends justify the means?" GotQuestions.org. Accessed November 17, 2023 at gotquestions.org/ends-justify-means.html.

Arab Weekly Staff. "3000 Year-old wall destroyed in Ninevah, Iraq." *The Arab Weekly*. March 4. 2021. https://tinyurl.com/22tnk4fa.

Arnold, Chris. "Former Wells Fargo Employees Describe Toxic Sales Culture. Even At HQ." *North County Public Radio*. October 4. 2016. https://tinyurl.com/28jja68y.

Blount Anna E., M.D. "Large Families and Human Waste." *Birth Control Review*. Vol. II. No. 9. September 1918.

Brickner, Darrell. "Bye. bye. baby? Birthrates are declining globally - here's why it matters." World Economic Forum. June 15. 2021. weforum.org/agenda/2021/06/birthrates-declining-globally-why-matters.

Cox. Stephen. "Ayn Rands Anthem: An Appreciation." *The Atlas Society*. July 7. 2010. atlassociety.org/post/ayn-rands-anthem-an-appreciation.

Daalder, Ivo H. "NATO in the 21st Century: What Purpose? What Missions?" Brookings Institution. April 1, 1999. https://tinyurl.com/ywznpter.

Diamandis, Peter H. "The World is Still Better Than You Think." October 10, 2017. diamandis.com/blog/the-world-is-still-better-than-you-think.

Donaldson, Zoe R. and Larry J. Young. "Oxytocin, Vasopressin, and the neurogenetics of sociality." *Science*. November 7, 2008. pubmed.ncbi.nlm.nih.gov/18988842.

Donnally, Grant E. and Michael Norton. "Even for the Very Rich, More Money Brings Happiness." *Wall Street Journal*. December 7, 2017. wsj.com/articles/even-for-the-very-rich-more-money-brings-happiness-1512662638.

Douglass, Frederick. *The North Star*. January 26. 1849. Accessed on January 1, 2025 as Document 6 at https://tinyurl.com/22vpbu4x.

East, Edward M. *Birth Control Review*. Vol. XIV. No. 4. April 1930.

Evans, Jonathan. "U.S. Adults are More Religious than Western Europeans." *Pew Research Center*. Sept 5, 2018. https://tinyurl.com/2xk8mkhj.

Freedman, J. and S. Fraser, "Compliance without pressure: The foot-in-the-door technique." *Journal of Personality and Social Psychology*. 1966. Issue 4.

Gino, F., S. Ayal and D. Ariely. "Self-serving altruism? The lure of unethical actions that benefit others." *Journal of Economic Behavior and Organization*. 2013. Vol. 93.

Geoghegan, Kev. "Utopia writer Dennis Kelly defends violent scenes." *BBC News*. June 17, 2014. bbc.com/news/entertainment-arts-27886003.

Hankins, Frank H., Ph.D. "Does America Have Too Many Children?" *Birth Control Review*. Vol. X. No. 2. February 1926.

Harris, Mark. "Inside the First Church of Artificial Intelligence." *Wired*. Nov 15. 2017. wired.com/story/anthony-levandowski-artificial-intelligence-religion.

Hewlett, Sylvia Ann. "Executive Women and the Myth of Having It All." *Harvard Business Review*. April 2002. https://tinyurl.com/y6oenwsl.

Hodson, Geoffrey. "Camp-Fire Gleams, An Account of the camp-fire meetings of the Order of the Star in August 1927." *The Herald of the Star*. Accessed on January 1, 2025 at alpheus.org/html/source_materials/krishnamurti/gleams.html#gleams.

Spielmann, Peter James. "U.N. Predicts Disaster if Global Warming Not Checked." *AP News*. June 29. 1989. https://tinyurl.com/y2tdhbyf.

James Leon. "A Comparison of Keywords in the Dynamic Psychology of Jung, Swedenborg and Freud." *Journal of Psychology and Clinical Psychiatry*. August 8, 2015. medcraveonline.com/JPCPY/a-comparison-of-keywords-in-the-dynamic-psychology-of-jung-swedenborg-and-freud.html.

Kahan, Daniel. "How Politics Makes Us Stupid." *Vox*. Jul 22. 2014. https://tinyurl.com/pwedrno.

Benjamin, Kathy. "Lottery Winners Who Were Murdered." *Grunge*. June 5. 2023. grunge.com/1301397/lottery-winners-murdered.

Keller, Jared. What Makes Americans So Optimistic?" *The Atlantic*. March 25. 2015. https://tinyurl.com/ybpa9v85.

Kranhold, Kathryn, Bryan Lee, and Mitchel Benson. "New Documents Show Enron Traders Manipulated California Energy Costs." *The Wall Street Journal*. May 7. 2002. wsj.com/articles/SB1020718637382274400.

Lyttle, Charles. "Deistic Piety in the Cults of the French Revolution." *Church History*. March 1933. Vol. 2. No. 1.

McLeod, Saul. PhD. "Solomon Asch Conformity Line Experiment Study." *SimplyPsychology*. Last updated October 24. 2023. simplypsychology.org/asch-conformity.html.

Miller, G. "The U.S. is the Most Overworked Developed Nation in the World." *20SomethingFinance*. Last updated January 13, 2020. 20somethingfinance.com/american-hours-worked-productivity-vacation.

Morano, Mark. "Green Guru James Lovelock on Climate Change: 'I don't think anybody really knows what's happening. They just guess' – Lovelock Reverses Himself on Global Warming." *Climate Depot*. April 3, 2014. https://tinyurl.com/2944lf6c.

NBC News Staff. "'Gaia' scientist James Lovelock: I was 'alarmist' about climate change." *NBC News*. April 23, 2012. https://tinyurl.com/2yvfklon.

Newsweek staff writer. "The Day of the Living Buddhas." *Newsweek*. March 5. 2000. newsweek.com/day-living-buddhas-156733.

Raskin, Sam. "Pope Francis calls declining birth rate in Italy a 'tragedy'." *New York Post*. December 26. 2021. https://tinyurl.com/y24ldlwt.

Roberts, Joel. "Enron Traders Caught on Tape." *CBS News*. June 1. 2004. cbsnews.com/news/enron-traders-caught-on-tape.

Ruse, Michael. "God is Dead. Long Live Morality." *The Guardian*. March 15. 2010. https://tinyurl.com/2ympzjnr

Sanger, Margaret. "Birth Control and Women's Health." *Birth Control Review*. Vol. 1. No. 12. December 1917.

Sanger, Margaret. "The Eugenic Value of Birth Control Propaganda." *Birth Control Review*, Vol. 5. No. 10, October 1921.

Schuller, Govert. "Krishnamurti and the World Teacher Project: Some Theosophical Perceptions." *Theosophical History Occasional Papers*. Vol. 5. 1997. Introduction by James Santucci. https://tinyurl.com/2d6fg4d4.

Schultz, Chris. "An interview with Dennis Kelly about Utopia, the show too bleak for TV." *New Zealand Herald*. April 20. 2017. https://tinyurl.com/2c4upff2.

Schweitzer, M. and C. Hsee. "Stretching the truth: elastic justification and motivated communication of uncertain information." *Journal of Risk and Uncertainty*. Vol. 25, 2002.

Sheldrake, Rupert. "Morphic Resonance and Morphic Fields - an Introduction." Sheldrake.org. Accessed on January 7, 2024 at sheldrake.org/research/morphic-resonance/introduction.

Smith, Gregory, et. al. "Decline in Christianity in the U.S. has Slowed, may have Leveled off." Pew Research Center, Accessed on June 1, 2025 at pewresearch.org/religion/2025/02/26/religious-landscape-study-executive-summary/

Smith, Warren. "Panchen Lama's 70,000 Character Petition." 1997. Accessed on January 1, 2024 at rfa.org/english/news/tibet/warrensmithbooks/Warren5A.pdf.

Sol, Mateo. "9 Signs You've Had a Mystical Experience." *LonerWolf*. Accessed on January 1, 2024 at lonerwolf.com/mystical-experience.

Taylor, Chris. "70% of Rich Families Lose Their Wealth by the Second Generation." *Money.com*. June 17. 2015. money.com/rich-families-lose-wealth.

The Independent Staff. "James Lovelock: The Earth is about to catch a morbid fever that may last as long at 100,000 years." *The Independent*. January 16, 2006. https://tinyurl.com/27y263um.

The Week staff writer. "Wells Fargo Phony-Account Scandal Explained." *The Week*. September 17, 2016. https://tinyurl.com/2bwfkgho.

Umphress, E. and J. Bingham and M. Mitchell. "Unethical behavior in the name of the company: the moderating effect of organizational identification and positive reciprocity beliefs on unethical pro-organizational behavior." *Journal of Applied Psychology*. 2010. Vol. 95. Issue 4. doi.org/10.1037/a0019214.

Vince, Gaia. "One last chance to save mankind." *New Scientist*. Accessed on January 1, 2025 at https://tinyurl.com/24l5u9bn.

Vollset et al. "Fertility, mortality, migration, and population scenarios for 195 countries and territories from 2017 to 2100: a forecasting analysis for the Global Burden of Disease Study." *The Lancet*. 2020. ol. 396. Issue 10258.

Hasse Walum, et al. "Genetic variation in the vasopressin receptor 1a gene AVPR1A associates with pair-bonding behavior in humans." *PNAS*. Accessed January 1, 2025 at https://doi.org/10.1073/pnas.0803081105.

Weir, Kristin. "The Pain of Social Rejection." *Monitor on Psychology*. April 2012.

Wells, H G. "H.G. Wells Speaks on Birth Control." *Birth Control Review*. Vol. 15. No. 11. November 1931. Accessed on January 1. 2025 lifedynamics.com/wp-content/uploads/2023/01/1931-11-November.pdf.

Wilson, Colin. "Maslow, Sheldrake and Peak Experience." *Critique: A Journal of Conspiracies and Metaphysics*. January 8, 2019. Accessible at medium.com/@simplysanj/maslow-sheldrake-and-the-peak-experience-651466deb2d4.

Wright, Todd. "Eckhart Tolle for Christians." *Todd WrightNow.com*. February 7. 2010. https://tinyurl.com/2xmtx5wf.

Yetwin, Neil B. "Thoreau, Jung, and the Collective Unconscious." *Thoreau Society Bulletin*. No. 265. Winter 2009.

Zhang, Yun and He Bin and Sun Xu. "The Contagion of Unethical Pro-organizational Behavior: From Leaders to Followers." *Frontiers in Psychology*. 2018. Vol. 9. Issue 1102. https://doi.org/10.3389/fpsyg.2018.01102

Zuber, Devin. "The Sage and His Mystic: Ralph Waldo Emerson and Emanuel Swedenborg." Accessed on January 1, 2025 at newchurchhistory.org/articles/dz2002.php.

Other: Encyclopedia Articles, Essays, Lawsuits, Letters, Podcasts, Speeches

Anonymous. "Ludwig Andreas Feuerbach." *Stanford Encyclopedia of Philosophy*. Last updated September 20, 2023. https://tinyurl.com/23myx427.

Anonymous. "Realism and Theory Change in Science. *Stanford Encyclopedia of Philosophy*. Last revised July 11, 2022. https://tinyurl.com/y7lehbce.

Anonymous. "Scientific Progress." *Stanford Encyclopedia of Philosophy*. Last updated January 22, 2024. https://tinyurl.com/28m586mw.

Bakunin, Michael. "Federalism, Socialism, Anti-Theologism." Accessed on January 1, 2025 at marxists.org/reference/archive/bakunin/works/various/reasons-of-state.htm.

Bakunin, Michael. "Rousseau's Theory of the State." Accessed on January 1, 2025 at marxists.org/reference/archive/bakunin/works/various/rousseau.htm.

Besant, Annie. Letter from the President. General Report of the Theosophical Society. 1929.

Brydone-Jack, Ashley *A Christian Philosophy of History: St. Augustine and The City of God*. Honors College Thesis. Accessed on January 1, 2024 at ir.library.oregonstate.edu/concern/honors_college_theses/mk61rj778.

Chamberlain, Neville. "Peace in Our Time" speech. September 20, 1938. Accessed on January 1, 2025 at https://tinyurl.com/2agscbm4.

Damore, James. Lawsuit against Google. Accessed on January 1, 2023 at scribd.com/document/368692388/James-Damore-Lawsuit.

Emerson, Ralph Waldo. "Every man is a divinity in disguise, a god playing the fool." Commencement Address to Harvard Divinity School. 1838. Accessed on January 1, 2025 at emersoncentral.com/texts/nature-addresses-lectures/addresses/divinity-school-address.

Federal Energy Regulatory Commission (FERC). "Final Report on Price Manipulation in Western Markets." March 2003. Accessed on May 1, 2025 at https://tinyurl.com/29qxhghz

Kaczynski, Theodore. "Industrial Society and Its Future." Accessed on January 1, 2025 at archive.nytimes.com/www.nytimes.com/library/national/unabom-manifesto-1.html.

Kennedy, Robert F. Jr. "Robert F. Kennedy Jr: CIA, Power, Corruption, War, Freedom, and Meaning." *Lex Fridman.* Podcast #388. Accessed on January 1, 2025 at lexfridman.com/robert-f-kennedy-jr-transcript.

Knabe, Hubertus. "The dark secrets of a surveillance state." TED Salon. Berlin. 2014. https://youtu.be/IWjzT2l5C34?si=FnvnAEykx50djJM9.

Krishnamurti, Jiddu. "Dissolution Speech" where he disbanded the Order of the Star in the East. August 13, 1929. Accessed January 1, 2025 at kfoundation.org/dissolution-speech.

Lonchampt, Joseph. Positivist Prayer. trans. John G. Mills. Republican Job Office. 1870.

Park, Yeonmi, *The Joe Rogan Experience* podcast #1691 with Yeonmi Park, August 3, 2021.

Robespierre, Maximilien. "On the Festival of the Supreme Being." 1794 Speech at the Festival of the Supreme Being. Accessed on January 21, 2025 at historyplace.com/speeches/robespierre.htm.

United Nations, Article II of the Convention of the Prevention and Punishment of the Crime of Genocide. Accessed on January 1, 2024 at un.org/en/genocideprevention/genocide.shtml.

Index

Skeptika Press
www.skeptikapress.com